"I co-authored a book on brand activism that called all companies to embrace good causes. Now I welcome this new book dedicated to help companies decide whether brand activism will help or hurt their profits and image. *Navigating Brand Activism* provides a much-needed framework for understanding the complexities of brand activism in today's marketplace. It offers valuable insights for marketers seeking to balance purpose and profit, making it an essential read for any business leader."

Philip Kotler, S. C. Johnson & Son Distinguished Professor of International Marketing Emeritus at the Kellogg School of Management, Northwestern University

"*Navigating Brand Activism* offers a timely and much-needed reality check for companies tempted to jump on the brand activism bandwagon. This book astutely covers both the risks and rewards, helping marketers navigate the complexities of social engagement with authenticity and a focus on delivering real value to consumers. It is a must-read for CEOs and corporate boards."

Russ Klein, Former CEO of the American Marketing Association; Former CMO of Arby's, 7-Eleven, and Global President of Burger King; Adweek's Advertiser of the Decade for the 2000s

"Sheth and Uslay use fascinating case studies to show how to assess the risks that a proposed brand activation will damage a business and even hurt the cause. This book is a must-read for any business interested in influencing a social issue."

David Aaker, Professor Emeritus UC Berkeley, Vice Chairman, Prophet

"In a world where brands hold influence far beyond their products, *Navigating Brand Activism* provides an essential roadmap for leaders seeking to align purpose with profit. Sheth and Uslay expertly explore the risks and rewards of brand activism, offering a blend of insightful analysis and practical guidance. With its focus on authenticity and integrity, this groundbreaking book is a must-read for conscious leaders navigating the challenges of today's polarized marketplace."

Raj Sisodia, FEMSA Distinguished University Professor of Conscious Enterprise & Chairman, Conscious Enterprise Center, Tecnológico de Monterrey; Co-founder, Conscious Capitalism Inc.

"Brand activism can be one of the most powerful tools ever to increase a brand's strength in the marketplace. But only by a strong alignment of a brand's promise and purpose with its key stakeholders: customers, employees, prospects, and the brand's essence. No better tutorial than *Navigating Brand Activism* to get it right and avoid potentially disastrous consequences of misalignment."

Peter Georgescu, Chairman Emeritus, VML (Young & Rubicam)

"CEOs and CMOs increasingly have to balance pressure to take a stance on contentious issues and build an activist brand, with the manifest risks and challenges of doing so. Sheth and Uslay provide an insightful, practical, and balanced guide to navigating this treacherous path."

Martin Reeves, *Managing Director and Senior Partner, BCG & Chairman Henderson Institute*

"This book is an essential navigational aid for any firm taking a position on high profile social issues. Sheth and Uslay give the leadership of these firms a well-researched road map for anticipating the many pitfalls to be avoided, while gaining the benefits of making a positive impact on society."

George Day, *Geoffrey T. Boisi Professor Emeritus and Faculty Emeritus in Residence of the Mack Institute of Innovation Management, Wharton School of the University of Pennsylvania*

"In our complex world, many companies take public stances on consequential, often controversial, social issues. This marvelous book, full of fascinating case study examples, offers evidence-based guidance that can spell the difference between strengthening or harming a company's brand."

Leonard L. Berry, *Regents and University Distinguished Professor of Marketing, Texas A&M University*

"Sheth and Uslay have written a much-needed book on the 5th P (Purpose) yet touch on the other 4Ps—product, place, price, and promotion—with brilliant historical examination and case analysis to guide brand managers and researchers. Even more useful for brand managers and corporate boards is the use of Maslow's classic hierarchy of needs and the creation of the Augmented Activism Alignment Matrix. This robust strategic tool alone is worth the book price. I am also impressed with the chapter on international cases that global companies will appreciate. This is a well-crafted and thoughtful book about a new and controversial topic—brand activism (or brand purpose) that is a must-read for brand marketers across the board."

Joe Plummer, *President, Sunstar Americas Foundation, Co-Author of* The Online Advertising Playbook, *Former EVP at McCann Worldgroup, Vice Chairman at DMB & B, EVP at Y&R, and SVP at Leo Burnett*

"*Navigating Brand Activism* offers a timely and insightful roadmap for companies seeking to align their values and brand with the needs of a changing world. A critical resource for leaders who wish to navigate societal shifts effectively."

Ralph de la Vega, *Former Vice Chairman AT&T; Former CEO of AT&T Business Solutions and AT&T International, and Founder of the De La Vega Group*

"*Navigating Brand Activism* is a timely exploration of the critical balance brands must strike between purpose and profit. Sheth and Uslay provide a clear, strategic roadmap for navigating the complexities of brand activism, emphasizing authenticity, alignment, and impact. This book is an essential guide for any leader seeking to engage meaningfully in today's socially conscious market."

Samyr Qureshi, *Founder and CEO, Knack*

"*Navigating Brand Activism* is a very timely and actionable exploration of how brands can determine their approach to activism proactively. Rich with examples, the robust strategic framework outlined by Sheth & Uslay is sure to become an indispensable part of every CMO's toolkit."

Rahul Mehrotra, *CEO, EsperPulse*

"This timely book on brand activism provides strategies and tactics for navigating an important marketing phenomenon. The authors show managers how to derive value from brand activism and social marketing while avoiding pitfalls that might reduce brand value."

Bernd Schmitt, *Robert D. Calkins Professor of International Business, Director of Center on Global Brand Leadership, Columbia Business School, Editor-in-Chief, Journal of Consumer Research*

NAVIGATING
BRAND ACTIVISM

In a world where brands are no longer just selling but also taking a stand, *Navigating Brand Activism*, written by leading thinkers of the marketing world, is your guide to the fascinating, messy, and at times, head-shaking world of brand activism. This groundbreaking book delves into the motivations behind this movement, dissects potential pitfalls, and celebrates triumphs. This book is for anyone who wants to understand:

- Why some purpose-driven brands are winning hearts, minds, and market share
- How to differentiate your brand in a crowded marketplace through activism
- How to spot authentic activism from mere marketing ploys
- The future of brand activism and its potential to create a better world
- The potential downsides of brand activism, including political back-lash, consumer boycotts, and brand dilution
- Most importantly, when and when not to engage in brand activism.

Whether you're a business leader, a conscious consumer, or simply curious about this developing landscape, this book will challenge, inspire, and empower you to navigate the world of woke washing and genuine advocacy.

Jag Sheth, Charles H. Kellstadt Professor of Marketing at Goizueta Business School at Emory University, is a globally recognized marketing luminary. With over 350 publications, he is the recipient of all four top awards from the American Marketing Association (AMA), and the Padma Bhushan (2020), the highest civilian honor bestowed by the Government of India. He has also served as an advisor to numerous corporations and governments worldwide.

Can Uslay is Professor of Marketing and Director of the Center for Marketing Advantage, Advancement, and Action at Rutgers Business School. He is a recipient of the Chancellor's Award, WDI Global Case Writing Competition Award, Scudder Award, MAACBA Teaching Innovation Award, AMA EMSIG Hills Best Paper and Abdul Ali Promising Research Awards, and several Dean's awards for outstanding scholarship, teaching, and service.

NAVIGATING BRAND ACTIVISM

Jag Sheth and Can Uslay

Routledge
Taylor & Francis Group

LONDON AND NEW YORK

Designed cover image: Getty Images: Trifonov_Evgeniy

First published 2026
by Routledge
4 Park Square, Milton Park, Abingdon, Oxon OX14 4RN

and by Routledge
605 Third Avenue, New York, NY 10158

Routledge is an imprint of the Taylor & Francis Group, an informa business

British Library Cataloguing-in-Publication Data
A catalogue record for this book is available from the British Library

ISBN: 978-1-032-97431-6 (hbk)
ISBN: 978-1-032-97440-8 (pbk)
ISBN: 978-1-003-59369-0 (ebk)

DOI: 10.4324/9781003593690

Typeset in Joanna
by Newgen Publishing UK

Dedications

To my daughter, Professor Reshma Shah, who teaches branding and integrated marketing communication at Emory University.

Jag Sheth

I dedicate this book to Banu, the biggest brand and activist in my life.

Can Uslay

CONTENTS

PREFACE

Today, brand activism occupies a seat front and center in the marketing theater. Rapid advancements in technology, changing demographics, globalization, geopolitical realignment, the rise of Chindia, and ideological conflicts have resulted in brands that involve themselves with societal issues. Some of these issues are not even linked to the core business. Some, such as animal cruelty, are not that controversial, whereas others, such as abortion rights, remain topics of raging debate.

The concept of brand activism is not a new phenomenon. As we chronicle in this book, activism is almost as old as the history of branding. What is new, however, is that brands are now expected to routinely engage with it, and more and more willingly oblige.

As the forces of change press on, the orthodoxy is challenged, and the world adapts accordingly. Turmoil gives way to paradigm shifts, and a new perspective emerges. The role of corporations and businesses as institutions in society has been irrevocably redefined. Many brands and managers with good intentions get caught in the crossfire.

How can brands engage in brand activism with impact while mitigating risks? We have attempted to address this puzzle with this book. To that end, we bring in historical, diverse, and global perspectives grounded in solid empirical research. We identify Five Rings to align with before embarking on brand activism:

1. *Mission, Vision, Cause:* Is your choice of activism aligned with your core mission?
2. *Passion and Brand Purpose:* Are your customers ready to join your brand on this journey?
3. *Business and Cause:* Is there a solid business case for your activism?
4. *Legacy of Commitment:* Does your past behavior support your current stance?
5. *Authenticity:* Can you walk the talk and avoid accusations of "woke washing?"

We distinguish between *pull activism* (orchestrated or organic), where brands are dragged into activism, sometimes kicking and screaming, and *push activism* (planned or spontaneous), where brands engage deliberately. Emphasis is on the need to align with *marketing doctrine* and *brand manifesto* to not confuse timeliness with timelessness. Our *Brand Activism Alignment Matrix* takes the specific issue and brand context (fledgling or heritage brand; generalist or specialist) into consideration to help assess brand-strategy fit:

1. *Niche Dare* (pick a decidedly divisive issue for awareness and penetration)
2. *Niche Development* (broaden position to advance to new segments)
3. *Mass Embrace* (unify to retain or reposition)
4. *Massive Fragmentation* (provoke to diversify with new/sub-brand).

Importantly, we assert that the type and return to brand activism varies based on the progress of a brand on the hierarchy of needs: some brands need love, whereas others are simply looking to survive. We offer dozens of key takeaways for mainstream, niche, and personal brands, and hundreds of examples, both of successes and failures, from well-publicized cases such as Bud Light (2023), Nike (2018), Pepsi (2017) to less-known ones such as Burger King (2021, 2022), CBS/Michael Jackson (1983), and Wedgwood (1787), with perspectives from the dawn of humankind till today.

Overall, the world of brand activism is not a binary between let's "divide and conquer" or "unify around common values." The pendulum of activism will be somewhere in the middle, on aggregate. However, that average scenario is not necessarily meaningful for your brand. Unless you are interested in mediocre performance, and sometimes not even then. There is life in between the extremes and wisdom in thinking beyond. Each marketer will need to assess their own context: market, resources, and goals to decide whether and what kind of activism is the one. One answer does not fit all. There is a whole world beyond divide or unite, unhinged or demure. Then come the tactical questions: which, when, how? How to be aligned, be authentic, be real with customers, employees, and investors? How about other stakeholders?

Not surprisingly, navigating the uncharted waters of brand activism has become an essential skill. We wrote this book because we firmly believe brands can reach turquoise waters without succumbing to the swirling seas. Please send pictures.

PROLOGUE

THE ENDURING MARK

In the shifting sands of commerce, a single element has endured through the centuries—the brand. The brand has seen it all: empires rise and fall, technology boom and bust, countless fortunes made and fade. It is a mark, yes, not merely of ownership but of promise. A promise passed through generations, a silent contract between seller and buyer, a beacon in a sea of consumer choices.

For the lifelong student of marketing and management, the brand is not a superficial symbol but a strategic cornerstone. It is the distillation of an organization's essence—its values, aspirations, raison d'être. It is the voice that cuts through the noise of the marketplace, the sign that resonates with the customers' deepest desires.

The brand odyssey we embark upon in this book is not a mere stroll down memory lane but a pilgrimage to demonstrated market success. We delve into the ancient origins of the brand, tracing its journey from the searing iron marking a steer's flank, to the meticulously crafted logo on the latest high-tech gadget. We witness the rise of industrial giants who aptly wield their brands for differentiation and trust. But we also witness small players, who use their brands as a shield from their much larger competitors and even manage to thrive. And we also explore the seduction of advertising and the power of storytelling in shaping brand narratives.

We navigate the turbulent times of the AI age, where brands serve a customer who is more empowered and information-rich than ever before. We grapple with the intangible forces that shape brand perception: authenticity, purpose, and sustainability.

For in the relentless churn of the market, only those brands that navigate and evolve with purpose will endure. They will be the ones who understand and anticipate the customer's needs, resonate with their values, and deliver on their promises. This book on brand activism, then, also doubles as a chronicle of the brand—a testament to its enduring power and a roadmap for those who dare to build not just a product but a legacy.

The Ballad of the Brand Activist's Odyssey: When Companies Sing (and Sometimes Shriek) for Social Change

Corporations, those once-stoic titans of commerce, have discovered the power of a good rant. No longer content with simply hawking laundry detergent or the latest smartphone, they've climbed onto the metaphorical soapbox, their booming voices echoing through the vast canyons of social media. This, dear reader, is the curious phenomenon of brand activism.

Now, some might scoff. Isn't brand activism a bit like watching your grandpa attempt a TikTok dance? A bit awkward, maybe? Inescapable shades of inauthenticity cling to the image of a shoe company lecturing us on fair trade practices, wouldn't you agree? Perhaps. But consider this: today's consumers are a fickle bunch. Brand loyalty, that once dependable old nag, has bolted for greener pastures. We, the jaded public, crave something more from the companies vying for our hard-earned cash. We crave a story, a cause, a reason to believe they're not here just to flog the latest widget.

Enter brand activism, that mischievous jester in the boardroom, brandishing a placard that reads "Save the Whales!" (or some such trendy cause). Suddenly, businesses are wading into the political maelstrom, taking stances on anything and everything from grand climate change challenges to your local school board candidates. Some, bless their earnest hearts, do so with all the grace of a bull in a china shop. Others, however, manage to weave a compelling narrative, aligning themselves with a cause that resonates with their target audience. The result? It can be a glorious symphony of brand affinity and social good, leading to new as well as more loyal customers. Or, it can be a train wreck of confusion, accusations of cynical manipulation, and billions of your favorite currency lost to boycotts.

This groundbreaking book is our exploration into this fascinating, messy, and on occasion, hilarious world of brands and their activism. We dissect the motivations behind the movement, analyze the potential pitfalls (oh, the glorious pitfalls!), and celebrate the triumphs (yes, they do exist!). So, buckle up, as we embark on this journey through the land of woke washing and genuine advocacy, where the line between the two can be as thin as a vegan sausage casing.

A shoe company fights for racial justice; a beverage giant tackles climate change; a tech giant champions LGBTQ+ rights. This isn't fiction—it's the new reality of brand activism. Businesses are stepping off the sidelines and onto the front lines of social change, and it's having a profound impact on consumers, society, and the bottom line.

In this book, we explore why companies are taking a stand, how they're doing it, and the consequences—good, bad, and ugly. We uncover the strategies behind successful brand activism campaigns, expose the pitfalls of performative wokeness, and show you how to navigate this new brand landscape as a consumer and a business leader.

This book is for anyone who wants to understand:

- Why some purpose-driven brands are winning hearts, minds, and market share
- How to differentiate your brand in a crowded marketplace through activism
- How to spot authentic activism from mere marketing ploys
- The future of brand activism and its potential to create a better world
- The potential downsides of brand activism, including political backlash, consumer boycotts, and brand dilution
- Most importantly, when and when not to engage in brand activism

All of the above apply to your personal brand too, so our book of navigation is literally for everyone.

In our thought-provoking exploration, we thoroughly dissect the phenomenon of brand activism. This book is your guide to the changing landscape, littered with landmines: get ready to be challenged, inspired, and empowered. Do brands have the power to change the world, one stand at a time? Or are sidelines sometimes a better vantage point for ventures? We dive deep to explore the complex impact on consumers, businesses, and society. Whether you're a business leader, a conscious consumer, or simply curious about the evolving role of brands in a global world, this book will equip you with the knowledge to critically assess brand activism, its impact on society, stakeholders, and last but not least, brandonomics.

We conclude with a disclaimer:

We have tremendous respect for the brands discussed throughout this book. We cover their cases because we think they offer a learning opportunity, even for those involved with running the focal brands. Nevertheless, this book covers cases/topics that can evoke strong emotions and feel personal. If you are on one end of the spectrum, you may think our views to be regressive; if you are on the other end, they may appear progressive. Our goal throughout is to be balanced, objective, and fair. Regardless, our comments may oppose some of your strongly held beliefs or values or involve issues that are politically loaded. We do our best not to side-step any of these issues and offer our frank opinion. Please take no offense. Meanwhile, the opinions expressed are solely the authors' own and do not represent their institutions. Feel free to disagree. Carpe freedom to think! Some may feel compelled to take snippets out of context and post them on social media to stir the pot, like politically charged individuals tend to do. We really have no political agenda, so please resist the urge. If you fail to do so, we will refer you to this prologue. We will also pepper your food!

ACKNOWLEDGMENTS

We would like to thank our co-authors, editors, reviewers, and academic and industry colleagues who have helped shape our thinking over the years. Our undergraduate, MBA, EMBA, and PhD students, post-docs, and colleagues at the University of Illinois Urbana-Champaign, University of Southern California, Emory University, Chapman University, and Rutgers University have also helped our thinking with their insightful conversations, perspectives, and questions.

We thank Rebecca Marsh and Grace Collier at our publisher, Routledge, and our agent, Marc J. Mikulich, at Marc Mikulich Literary Agency for getting this book to your hands, e-readers, or headphones in a timely manner. We extend our sincere gratitude to Nicholas Taylor for his meticulous editing of the manuscript and insightful feedback.

We thank Aditya Majumdar for his assistance in compiling many of the examples in the Appendix. We also thank Google as we utilized Gemini as a research assistant to identify and edit many examples, especially in Chapter 14. Gemini is also aptly featured in Chapter 3 and makes guest appearances in Chapter 2 and elsewhere as noted in the main text and endnotes. All examples or references identified or edited by AI have been manually checked and revised as needed. We also relied on AI for the pro- logue "promo" of the book. While we prompted and edited with a heavy hand, we think the Gemini/ChatGPT duo did an outstanding job. You may want to compare it with our "non-artificially" developed preface and see if you agree. All ideas and errors anywhere in the manuscript are our own.

1

INTRODUCTION

A BRAND ACTIVIST'S TALE
OF SHOES VS. BEVERAGES

The tides of activism are turning, churning, clashing. The former CMO of Arby's, 7-Eleven, and Global President of Burger King, Russ Klein, as the sitting CEO of the American Marketing Association (2014–2021) observed that: "[F]rom a marketing point of view… it is unnecessarily dangerous, commercially or morally, to drape a politically incendiary cape around your brand and delude yourself into thinking it makes you a super-hero."[1] Meanwhile, serial entrepreneur Molly DeWolf Swenson, who co-founded Mozi, 3Rodeo, Good Today, and RYOT, suggested: "A brand isn't a bystander, it's an 800-pound gorilla that has the opportunity—or dare I say, the responsibility—to leverage not only its corporate social responsibility dollars, but also its products, audience, media, and yes, advertising, in support of the side of history it wants to be on."[2]

You are a CEO, balancing profit and social responsibility. Suddenly, a hot button issue flares up and customers demand you take a stand. Do you join the fray, potentially alienating half your audience, or play it safe and risk

DOI: 10.4324/9781003593690-1

being labeled irrelevant? This is the dilemma of brand activism, in which companies take a stance on social and political issues, often unrelated to their core business. It's a risky move, as shown by Nike's Colin Kaepernick campaign. Some hailed it as brave, others as a sales-killing blunder.

But is brand activism just a publicity stunt or a sign of things to come? The old guard won't budge. Don't wade into messy social issues. It alienates audiences and blurs your brand. After all, you cannot please everyone. And if you try to be everything to everyone, you end up being nothing to anyone. Meanwhile, the new wave demands that we pick a side. They see silence as a liability.[3] Consumers, they argue, crave authenticity and values, and brands that stand for something resonate more deeply. Imagine a brand (or just think of Patagonia) which champions sustainability, attracting and building a loyal base of customers who share that value.

Is brand activism a recipe for disaster or the future of marketing? Read and decide for yourself.

Dissecting the Hype

Business is essentially about offering value while managing risk.[4] But in some cases, can brand activism be so risky that delving into it might be considered outright dangerous? Russ Klein, the former CEO of the American Marketing Association we quote above, would probably agree. In fact, we know he does:

> For many brands today, the blurry line between purpose and profit represents a knotty management issue... I would generally advise against positioning a brand around issues where there are otherwise legitimate and divergent points of view. The opportunity to grow a brand is maximized when bringing many different minded people together who can be satisfied by a powerful and unifying solution for something in their lives...[5]

Whereas Molly Swenson, representing the younger generation of marketers, may not agree: "Brands cannot expect to play Switzerland as the rest of the world picks a side."[6] After all, remaining silent on social issues can be seen as implicitly taking a stance, especially if your competitors have already done so.

Corporate social responsibility (CSR) efforts typically focus on a company's core operations to make it more sustainable, ethical, and mindful.[7] Initiatives include farming cocoa more sustainably than before. Yet, even there, the record is not univocal. Indeed, if you destroy national parks in Côte d'Ivoire or Ghana in the name of sustainable cocoa, some might call this dumb, among other expletives.[8] However, the point to underline is brand activism puts CSR on steroids, taking it to a whole new level. The issues are not typically related to core offerings or operations, but are supposedly linked with the brand's mission, however loosely it may be defined.

This interpretation of brand activism has given unprecedented new and free rein to business leaders. In a world where we are told customers increasingly expect us to take a stance, CMOs are getting queasy yet many more are taking the chance. True, managers tend to be risk-averse, but a closer look reveals a reward system that incentivizes risk-taking, especially for younger managers: launch an edgy campaign and win awards, your career will skyrocket, allowing a move to bigger and better pastures. Or launch an edgy campaign and lose your brand m/billions, your career will stagnate and you can move onto new (and potentially greener) pastures that appreciate your concept of edgy brand activism. Who is to decide what is the right move but for Occam's razor of public opinion? Buycott or Boycott?[9] Isn't all publicity good?

Well, not really.

The truth is, it's about calculated risk. Accenture says almost two-thirds of consumers prefer buying from businesses that reflect their personal values and beliefs.[10] This is a global finding. Yet the issue you choose matters a lot. Almost half of consumers have defected to competitors based on a focal company's conduct.[11] There's no guaranteed success, and even well-intentioned campaigns can backfire. Meanwhile, the potential rewards of increased loyalty, brand affinity, and positive PR might outweigh the risks (as they did for TOMS or The Body Shop back in the day).

But before you jump on the bandwagon, consider:

- Do your customers actually care? Don't assume they want you to be their social warrior for a given cause. Do not let employee sentiment, your own sentiment, or anecdotes drive your campaigns. Do your marketing research.

- Is your stance genuine or opportunistic? Consumers can smell inauthenticity a mile away.
- Are you prepared for backlash? Not everyone will agree with you, and that's okay. But be well prepared to stay the course and handle criticism.

Ultimately, the decision of whether or not to engage in brand activism is yours. While you may be compelled to act when a hot button issue comes up, resist the urge to gamble with your brand without careful analysis. Do your homework, weigh the risks and rewards, and make an informed choice that aligns shared interests with your brand's values and resonates with your audience.

Importantly, distinguish between brand activism you have deliberately initiated after elaborate analysis and actions you may be dragged into by your stakeholders. When you are choosing brand activism, and there are many causes to choose from, there are many opportunities to reap rewards through alignment. We will discuss these in detail for different size, type, and category of brands, with hundreds of examples in the coming chapters and the appendix. However, when your brand is dragged into a cause, the alignment is either there or not, whether you like it or not.

How does a brand manager recognize and cope with this challenge? After reviewing hundreds of cases, successes, and failures, here is the decision tree we suggest:

1. If you get pressure from your employees to act:
   a) Does the pressure reflect general employee sentiment or just a loud minority?
   b) If the sentiment is indeed more or less unequivocal among your employees but that does not match with your researched and calculated customer reality, is it possible there is a need to diversify your employee base before your brand? Why is there such a disconnect?
   c) If your employee and customer sentiments match, explore boldly and quickly. When it comes to activism, early followers do not quite make the same impression as leaders.
2. If you get pressure from consumers to act:
   a) Recognize the distinction between the public, media, and your customers' views. Does the pressure reflect the general customer sentiment, highly loyal users, or just a loud minority?

b) If the sentiment is more or less univocal among your customers, but does not match with your desired customer reality, is it possible you would miss an opportunity to make your brand more inclusive and gain customers from other segments once you activate?

c) If the sentiment is more or less univocal among your *desired customers* but not the core, tread lightly. Carefully examine potential cannibalization before taking action. Timing and priming can be critical. Figuring out when to activate can be just as important as how to activate.

d) But if your current and ideal customer sentiments match, explore boldly and quickly. When it comes to activism, early followers do not quite make the same impression as leaders.

3. You decided to activate your brand, but what is your strategy?

a. *Market penetration/retention:* The majority of your current customers will support your decision and sales will soar through an increased share of wallet or new customers from the same segment despite potential consumer backlash. (Less risky.)

b. *Market development:* More customers from a new segment will support your decision than those that disapprove from within your current customer base. These new customers may be expected to be more loyal or have higher lifetime value for your business than those who quit your brand. (More risky.)

c. *Reposition/Diversification:* You decide the future of your brand lies with a very different customer lifestyle segment based on that segment's growth trajectory and/or lifetime value of customers in that segment. (Most risky.)

Finally, consider the chess analogy: sacrifice moves that appear dumb at first may be smart and calculated. In hindsight, sometimes we wish we could take back a move we initially thought was smart. But the real question is why make a move with your flagship brand at all? Unless there is a very good reason and great odds, why bet the farm? When it comes to politicizing a brand, why fall for cliches such as "the biggest risk is not to take any risks" and engage[12] when there are perfectly reasonable other risks one can take? Perhaps you should develop a new brand or sub-brand instead, if the current brand position is already viable.

At times, figuring out how to control the narrative and navigating to prevent brand activism can be just as important. To be sure, we are not suggesting ignorance or inaction no matter what. But we do offer caution against haste, especially for mainstream brands (more on this in Chapters 8, 9, and 10).

Yes, we have raised a number of tough questions already. Next, let us break them down, make them concrete, and demonstrate our perspectives through a few highly controversial cases. First, Nike's 30th Year Anniversary of its iconic *Just Do It* Campaign and Colin Kaepernick.

More than a Box of Shoes: Kaepernick vs. the Flag, and the Nike Saga That Sparked a Nation

Suppose your favorite quarterback took a knee. Not for an injury, but for equality. That's what Colin Kaepernick did, igniting a firestorm of cheers and jeers that Nike nearly walked away from.

Kaepernick, who started his NFL career at San Franciso 49ers as a back-up quarterback in 2011, became a starter due to a concussion suffered by Alex Smith. He unexpectedly led his team to its first Super Bowl appearance in over a decade, where the 49ers lost to the Baltimore Ravens. Kaepernick, who is bi-racial (his biological mother was white, his father was black and he was adopted and raised by a white family), began to explore his biological and cultural roots during his college years at the University of Nevada, Las Vegas where he joined a predominantly Black fraternity.[13] He continued this exploration in later years and audited a class on Black representation in popular culture at UC Berkeley.

During the 2016 pre-season, Kaepernick began to sit (and later kneel) during the national anthem in protest of what he saw as systemic racism and oppression within the US, especially by the police force.[14] He explained his rationale as follows: "I am not going to stand up to show pride in a flag for a country that oppresses Black people and people of color. To me, this is bigger than football and it would be selfish on my part to look the other way. There are bodies in the street and people getting paid leave and getting away with murder."[15]

Kaepernick's actions gained support from many other NFL athletes and fans and earned him the cover of *Time* magazine in October 2016. However, his movement also led to much controversy. President Donald Trump blasted him for his disrespect of the flag and country via Twitter. The battle lines were drawn. According to a poll by CNN, 87% of Republicans disagreed with the protesting athletes, whereas 72% of Democrats sided with them.[16] Though notable among the dissenters was Liberal Supreme Court Justice Ruth Bader Ginsburg, who called the protest "dumb and disrespectful."[17] Kaepernick chose to exit his contract with the 49ers and became a free agent after the 2016–2017 season. Much to his chagrin, he was not signed by any of the teams for the next season. He sued for conspiracy among the owners to not hire him and later reportedly settled for a split of less than $10M.[18] He has not played in the NFL since.

Nike's initial response to Kaepernick's quest to protest was luke-warm at best. Nike had an endorsement deal with Kaepernick that it ser-iously considered canceling during the summer of 2017.[19] Reportedly, the deal was only saved after a heated plea by Nigel Powell, Nike's Chief Communications Officer, who "argued that Nike would face backlash from the media and consumers if it was seen as siding with the NFL rather than Kaepernick."[20]

Yet, even as Kaepernick was named GQ magazine's Citizen of the Year[21] and honored by Amnesty International and the American Civil Liberties Union,[22] Nike did not use him in a campaign, despite repeated requests by Kaepernick who recognized the platform Nike could offer him. However, the outlook improved in spring 2018 when Adidas announced it was interested in signing Kaepernick, if he could find a team. Perhaps experien-cing FOMO, Nike met with Kaepernick that summer and the 30th anniver-sary of the Just Do It campaign began to take shape. It was finalized by August and launched when Kaepernick posted "Dream Crazy" on September 5, 2018. With Kaepernick's face front and center, Nike declared, "Believe in something even if it means sacrificing everything." This wasn't just a cam-paign, it was a statement.

The Aftermath

"Nike agreed to it. We made it. Colin posted it. People lost it."[23] A designer at Wieden + Kennedy—Nike's ad agency for over three decades summed up the campaign in four blunt sentences. It was a cultural bombshell, igniting passionate reactions.

Nike, by partnering with the polarizing figure of Colin Kaepernick, had stepped into the minefield of social activism once again. While some consumers viewed it as a courageous stand they could get behind, others saw it as a cynical marketing ploy. Was it a stroke of genius or a reckless gamble?

While many consumers were angered by Nike's involvement in the controversy, others strongly supported it. The company gained 170,000 new Instagram followers; the post featuring Kaepernick was the second most liked in Nike's history and led to twice as many comments as any of its posts. Within 24 hours, the campaign had earned Nike over $43 million in media exposure ($19 million positive, $11 million negative, the rest neutral).[24] In addition, it was estimated that Nike saw a 1,400% increase in social mentions[25] and $163 million value in earned mentions on social media.[26] "The ad was watched all the way through 97% of the time, and viewers were 60% less likely to interrupt ad play on TV compared to other sneaker/shoe ads during the same period. Viewers were 32% less likely to interrupt an ad compared to other Nike ads running at the same time."[27] After an initial dip, online sales grew by 31%[28] and the stock hit an all-time-high the week after the campaign launch.[29] In all, Nike's overt alignment with Black and younger consumers (and Democrats) appeared to have paid off within a week.

Beneath the glittering veneer, a more nuanced picture emerges.

Let's be realistic. No one should think Nike engaged with Kaepernick out of sheer ideology. They had almost dropped his endorsement deal the year before. It was not all business, but it certainly made business sense for Nike. In addition to the majority of Democrats, they knew Kaepernick's actions were supported by the majority of African Americans (82%) and younger consumers (56%).[30] Both are critical consumer segments when it comes to sports apparel.

Nike's founder, Phil Knight, seems to have made this calculation too: "It doesn't matter how many people hate your brand as long as enough people love it. And as long as you have that attitude, you can't be afraid of offending people. You can't try and go down the middle of the road. You have to take a stand on something, which is ultimately I think why the Kaepernick ad worked."[31]

Nike reported record engagement and expressed its pride in the campaign. After all, history is written by the hands of the victor (or in this case Nike, the 2019 Creative Arts Emmy winner).[32] We were unable to identify any source with a good handle on the ROI of the campaign. In such a complex setting, even Nike may not know the true return for their efforts. However, a closer analysis reveals the results to be less than univocal. Consider the following:

- Despite the positives reported by the media and Nike, there were also negatives: Nike's brand favorability dropped from 69 to 35 overall, from 91 to 76 among its customers, from 67 to 27 among white consumers. Interestingly, the drop was unequivocal across all groups examined. It also dropped for Democrats (74 to 65), Gen Z (81 to 51), millennials (64 to 52), Gen X (75 to 39), and baby boomers (68 – 20). It even dropped for African Americans (82 to 74).[33] Many consumers viewed the campaign as more of a publicity stunt than a genuine reflection of Nike's values and a sincere recognition of Kaepernick's actions.[34]

- The *Dream Crazy* campaign was not run in isolation or as part of a field experiment. Nike's annual marketing spend exceeds $3 billion and teasing out the impact of this campaign among others is very challenging. Nike's marketing machine churned out new products and digital transformation initiatives concurrently, making it difficult to pinpoint the true ROI of the Kaepernick campaign.[35] Nike also increased its marketing budget by 4% in the same quarter. The campaign was followed-up by "Dream Crazier" with a female focus, featuring star athletes Serena Williams, Simone Biles, Ibtihaj Muhammed, Chloe Kim, and US women's national team soccer players.[36] Did the women who bought Nike in the fall of 2018 do so in support of or despite their sentiment toward Kaepernick?

- Finally, it is telling that Kaepernick campaign was intended for the American audience, the ads ran during NFL games, yet sales of Nike in North America trailed those of global markets. For the quarter ending November 30, 2018, overall sales grew 10% globally, surpassing the 9% growth in North America. Almost three years later, the usage of Nike among Democrats was up 2% but down 24% among Republicans.[37]

Nevertheless, Nike passes muster when it comes to authenticity and continued commitment to activism like few brands can. It has supported women in sports with its "Let it Play" campaign, racial inequality with "Stand Up, Speak Up," African Americans with "Equality," and challenged anti-Muslim sentiment with the "What Will They Say About You?" campaigns. It was also the first major brand to feature an HIV-positive athlete, an amputee athlete, or an LGBTQ+ athlete.[38] It has consistently stood by the athletes it sponsored from Maria Sharapova's drug test failure, to Tiger Woods' public marital infidelity, and Kobe Bryant's rape trial.

While we do not think partnering with Kaepernick was brilliant, or even the best course of action given the complexities, we cannot deem Nike's activism campaign with Kaepernick a mistake.[39] Nike earned respect for its continued commitment to activism and its track record speaks volumes about its brand values. Unfortunately, we cannot say the same about the perceived brand authenticity in the following cases of beverage brand activism.

Picketing Power of Pepsi

Pepsi's campaign featuring Kendall Jenner in 2017 was mired in unintended controversy and serves as a cautionary tale.

Imagine a protester, standing strong against injustice. Now, imagine a can of soda bridging the gap! Pepsi thought it held the magic formula for harmony, but instead it ignited a firestorm. This wasn't about a thirst-quenching beverage. It was about co-opting a powerful image of resistance, a slap in the face to those on the picket line. Yes, Kendall was popular among millennials and was happy to take Pepsi's money when offered, but how did Pepsi fail to recognize she had no affiliation with an activism movement or that she had not taken a firm public stand on any social issue when making the choice?

The video, which Pepsi had planned to use in a global ad campaign, featured reality TV star and model Jenner coming across a scene of protest. Jenner joins the crowd, which approaches a line of police officers. What could be a tense standoff in the real world defuses into cheers and smiles when the *Keeping Up with the Kardashians* star picks up a can of cola and offers it to an officer.

The image of Jenner approaching the police clearly referenced the iconic photograph of Ieshia Evans, a Black woman who stood tall in the face of heavily armored riot police during a Black Lives Matter protest following the fatal shooting of Alton Sterling by police in 2016. The audacity of co-opting the visual language of resistance movements to sell sugary beverages prompted an immediate and harsh backlash on social media."[40] Many felt this amounted to cultural appropriation.[41]

Kendall Jenner, reality star turned peacemaker? Bernice King, daughter of the lion of civil rights, Martin Luther King Jr., characterized it perfectly: "If only Daddy would have known about the power of #Pepsi." Not only the brand-cause fit was lacking, the spokesperson-cause fit was amiss as well. Adding salt to the wound was the fact that Pepsi had used its in-house creative shop to make the ad and had no one but its own "corporate thought bubbles" to blame for the blunder.[42]

The timing was as tone-deaf as the message. April 4th, the 49th anniversary of Dr. King's assassination, marked the release of this "harmony" ad. Pepsi initially defended the video, stating it "reflects people from different walks of life coming together in a spirit of harmony." However, as the mocking memes intensified and public sentiment clearly turned negative, the company pulled the ad and apologized. "Pepsi was trying to project a global message of unity, peace and understanding," the company said in a statement to the Associated Press. "Clearly we missed the mark, and we apologize."[43] They also publicly apologized to Kendall Jenner for putting her in this position. Regardless, Pepsi's brand perception fell to an eight-year low over the next three months and purchase consideration was at a three-year low eight months later.[44]

Pepsi, supposedly blinded by good intentions, missed the mark by a mile. Mocking memes became their reward, public outrage their reality. They pulled the ad, apologized, but the scar remained. Was it ignorance or arrogance? We may never know. What we do know is that social movements aren't all marketing fodder. They're about real struggle, real voices, and Pepsi's attempt to capitalize on that was anything but real.[45]

This isn't just a marketing blunder. It's a stark reminder: understand your "why" before you try to sell your "what." Stand for something, but for the right reasons. Otherwise, you might just end up with a can of backlash in your hand and a bitter taste in your mouth. This is the price of inauthenticity, and Pepsi paid it in full. Remember their story the next time you're tempted to use a cause for your own gain.

Starbucks: Brand activism or CEO activist?

Contrary to conventional wisdom, Howard Schultz did not found Starbucks. His story is more similar to that of Ray Croc than it is to Michael Dell. Schultz grew up in public housing in Brooklyn, New York, and he was the first in his family to graduate college. He attended Northern Michigan

University, a public university where he was an athletic scholarship recipient.[46] He took a job with Xerox upon graduation in 1975 and later joined Hammarplast (a Swedish firm which produces housewares) as its US General Manager. Much like Ray Croc, who was so impressed by the McDonald brothers' operation that was selling milkshakes like hotcakes, Schultz was in love with Seattle's Pike Place Market, which had bought so many espresso machines from Hammarplast. Convinced the coffee shop with only four stores (that actually sold beans and did not serve any coffee at the time) was destined for greatness, Schultz campaigned to be recruited. Repeatedly declined for a year, he later joined as part-owner and director of retail and marketing in 1982. It was during a business trip to Italy a year later that he came up with his vision of transforming the American experience with coffee, where Starbucks would serve as "a warm and welcoming third place" between home and work. When the management found his vision at odds with its business model and declined his proposal, he left the company but bought it soon after with the help of local investors to be able to realize his vision. He then served Starbucks with exceptional distinction and turned it into one of the biggest American success stories of all time. The figures (including its market cap exceeding $100 billion) and its worldwide presence (in 80 countries across more than 38,000 locations) make that much clear.[47]

Schultz was also market-driving when it comes to employee benefits. Its employees can attend college online (at Arizona State University) tuition-free thanks to its Starbucks College Achievement Plan.[48] Starbucks employees who work at least 20 hours per week (and their spouses and domestic partners) also get healthcare benefits and stock options. Starbucks funds "approximately 70 percent of premium costs and cover 100 percent of preventive care services... 100 percent of women's preventive health coverage" and its "total pay package includes affordable healthcare, company stock, eligibility for merit increases every six months, tuition reimbursement, paid vacation, free coffee and a 30 percent in-store discount on beverages, food, and merchandise."[49] Offering flexible work hours and competitive wages, and "one of the most comprehensive total pay packages in the retail industry,"[50] the company announced it has achieved gender and race pay equity in 2018 after a decade-long effort.[51]

In all, Starbucks has a lot to be applauded. However, Schultz is not without fault. For example, many Washington state residents despise him since he bought, mismanaged, and then sold the Seattle Supersonics NBA team, which then moved to Oklahoma City. Starbucks' failed "Race Together" campaign proved to be another humbling ordeal for Schultz. The campaign was deemed a huge, complete, and utter failure.[52,53] In this campaign, Starbucks asked its baristas to write "Race Together" on the cups they were about to serve and engage in conversations about race.[54] Curious minds want to know if the company offered any special training to its baristas prior to the campaign, however, we know that in order to facilitate these delicate conversations, Starbucks offered them "conversation starters" with an internal memo that included gems such as:

"1) In my Facebook stream, ____% are of a different race.

2) In the past year, I have been to the home of someone of a different race ____ times.

3) In the past year, someone of a different race has been in my home ____ times.

4) ____ members of a different race live on my block or apartment building.

5) In the past year, I have eaten a meal with someone of a different race ____ times.

6) I most often talk to someone of another race:

    ____ At work

    ____ Church

    ____ Home

    ____ Shopping____ School

7) At work, we have managers of ____ different races.

8) My children have ____ friends of a different race.

9) My parents had ____ friends of a different race.

10) I have ____ friends of a different race."[55]

Not surprisingly, the campaign was widely ridiculed. For example, comedian Larry Wilmore observed:

"Starbucks felt that coffee and awkward conversations were meant to go together."

"Starbucks ends its controversial Race Together campaign. Yeah that's 'cause when people heard about it, they raced together to Dunkin' Donuts."[56]

Howard Schultz admitted to "a tactical mistake" and urged the company and the public to move on. Yet he has a history of interjecting Starbucks into issues that had very little to do with Starbucks brands, locally or globally. "Schultz ran Starbucks like a haven for progressive ideals"[57] so much so that there was speculation that he was simply using Starbucks as a platform to prepare for his presidential candidacy. He considered running as a Democrat and later as an independent for over three election cycles.[58] An array of confidants, as well as Starbucks employees, urged him not to run, which he has agreed to thus far.[59]

The fundamental question is, is it ever right for Schultz, or any CEO for that matter, to use a company as a personal fiefdom to serve political ambitions in the name of advancing democracy? Do ends justify the means? Based on the deontological view of ethics the answer is a resounding no, though other more utilitarian perspectives exist. Where does the corporate brand end and the personal brand of a founder or the chief executive begin? Should these be activated concurrently or treated separately? We discuss these issues in Chapter 12 where we explore lessons for personal brands. However, rest assured, brand activism is one area where a deliberate committee may surprisingly perform better than a rash CEO or CMO.

And the fumbled brand activism Razzie goes to…

Much More than a Case of Beer: Bud Light, Dylan Mulvaney, and the Raiders of the Lost $27 Billion

The recent controversy surrounding Bud Light and Dylan Mulvaney has sparked a national conversation about brand identity, social media, and the evolving landscape of consumer culture. As Beth Demmon, author *The Beer Lover's Guide to Cider*, observed, "A lot of people drink Bud Light… but at its core it usually appeals to white American men and represents a certain lifestyle. Football, nachos, BBQs, traditional suburban family dynamics, that sort of thing. It's a stereotype that exists from years of very careful, specific and strategic marketing studies and campaigns, and it's worked for a long time."[60] This carefully crafted image, however, has been challenged by the severe backlash against the brand's partnership with Mulvaney, leading to a significant drop in sales. Tamara Littleton, CEO and founder of social media agency The Social Element, noted, "It was almost the perfect storm, and this is why it's not going away. Society doesn't want it to go away. And it's a society issue, but also, it wasn't handled well, and this is also a crisis of [Bud Light's] making."[61]

Dylan Mulvaney came out on TikTok as a transgender woman on March 3, 2022. The video was called "Day 1 of Being a Girl." Over the next year, her *Days of Girlhood* videos grew her fame and earned her well over a million followers. Her success enabled her to promote transgender rights and she was even able to interview President Joe Biden in October 2022 and discuss issues, including gender-affirming healthcare. The interview has garnered over 380,000 views on YouTube to date.

Like many influencers, Mulvaney has had partnerships with numerous brands, mostly of cosmetics and fashion such as Ulta Beauty, K18 Hair, Ole Henriksen, Kate Spade, CeraVe, Haus Labs, Rent the Runway, and Aritzia, but also others such as Instacart, Crest, Kind Snacks, and Kitchen Aid.[62] In typical fashion, she used social media to celebrate the anniversary of her transition. On April 1, 2023, she announced on an Instagram video that Bud Light had sent her a personalized can to commemorate the occasion: "Bud Light sent me possibly the best gift ever—a can with my face on it." She then plugged in a Bud Light promotion: "Happy March Madness!! Just found out this had to do with sports and not just saying it's a crazy month! In celebration of this sports thing @budlight is giving you the chance to win $15,000! Share a video with #EasyCarryContest for a chance to win!! Good luck! #budlightpartner."[63]

The reaction was harsh.

Mike Crispi, podcast host and former Republican primary candidate for congress from New Jersey made his position clear on Twitter/X: "Boycott Bud Light and NEVER DRINK IT AGAIN EVER."

Congresswoman Marjorie Taylor Greene and others jumped on the bandwagon, posting: "I would have bought the king of beers, but it changed it's [sic] gender to the queen of beers…"

Matt Walsh, conservative commentator, posted: "The good news is that Bud Light tastes like rain water that someone siphoned out of a tin bucket so it should be very easy to boycott."

Bud Light "either doesn't know their customers or they do and just don't give a s****. I'm guessing the latter. What a disgrace," said Jaimee Michell, Founder of Gays Against Groomers (an organization of gays against the sexualization, indoctrination, and medicalization of children).

Kid Rock responded with a video of his own where he cursed Bud Light, and its parent company Anheuser-Busch, in take-no-prisoner-terms and shot a round into Bud Light cans with a semi-automatic AR-15 rifle.[64] It didn't matter that other beer brands, such as Coors, also had a history of support for the LGBTQ+ community. Anheuser-Busch said several of its facilities received threats, and in one case even a bomb squad had to respond.[65]

In contrast to the case of Nike, the financial impact of this ordeal is quite clear. Three months out, research of a representative sample of 150,000 US households found the purchase incidences to be 32% lower for Republicans and 22% lower for Democrats.[66] Even after eight months, purchase incidences were 32% lower.[67] Bud Light sales dropped 27% year-over-year and an analyst predicted that AB InBev distributors had seen revenues shrink by at least one-third.[68] Quarterly US revenues dropped by 13.5%. By June 2023, Bud Light had lost the market share leadership it had held for over two decades (since 2001) to Modelo Especial.[69,70] Fortunately for AB InBev, its global markets continued to perform well, and its revenue rose 5% overall.[71] However, that was not enough to restore investor confidence. With evidence of negative spillover to other brands in AB InBev's portfolio,[72] its stock (ticker: BUD) went from a high of $61.33 on March 27, 2023, to a low of $49.44 on October 2, 2023, representing a drop of 19.4%. Its market capitalization went from a high of $132.38 billion in March 2023 to a low $106.08 billion by May 2023 and $104.39 billion by October 2023, suggesting a $26.3 billion to $28 billion in value lost to boycott.[73] *The Wall Street Journal* reported the company remained in a slump despite the effort put into 2024's Super Bowl.[74]

"It took us 20 years to take Bud Light beer to the number 1 beer in the country, and it took them one week to dismantle it," said Bob Lachky,[75] the former AB InBev Chief Creative Officer, who led the iconic "Wassup," talking Budweiser Frogs, and "Real Men of Genius" campaigns.[76]

Bud Light's Response

The ordeal was no accident. Bud Light had contracted Mulvaney through Captiv8 (a California-based influencer marketing agency) as part of its outreach to the LGBTQ+ community. And the video that caused the uproar was shared with Captiv8 and Bud Light and approved before release.[77] Yet Bud Light's response was weak at best or hypocritical at worst. It "went silent on social media, turned off comments, and ordered its publicity department to 'stop communicating while everyone regrouped.'"[78]

Two long weeks passed after Mulvaney's Instagram post, before Anheuser-Busch North America CEO Brendan Whitworth released what was deemed a lackluster statement. It did not directly address the controversy or show any support for Mulvaney.[79] His message focused on "building and protecting our remarkable history and heritage." AB InBev tried to defend the partnership, suggesting it was part of an effort to attract a younger audience, and that Mulvaney was just one of numerous influencers who enable the brand to "authentically connect with audiences across various demographics and passion points," and that the personalized can "was a gift to celebrate a personal milestone and is not for sale to the general public."[80] Yet it managed to receive even more criticism this time from those who originally supported the partnership when news broke that two marketing executives who oversaw the partnership were placed on leave of absence. To make matters worse, LGBTQ+ bars started to boycott Anheuser-Busch too.[81]

Anheuser-Busch's Global CEO Michel Doukeris did not help matters during the company's May 2023 earnings call when he downplayed the incident and emphasized that the partnership with Mulvaney was not long-term: "We will need to continue to clarify the fact that this was one can, one influencer, one post, and not a campaign, and repeat this message for some time."[82]

In the company's defense, Bud Light had been a supporter of the LGBTQ+ community for over two decades, along with many other major beer brands. However, and notably, Bud Light did not reach out to Mulvaney following the crisis even once.[83] That does not speak well of their commitment to the cause or their sincerity. The irony was not lost on Mulvaney, who stated that hiring a trans person only to abandon them in the face of hate "is worse in my opinion than not hiring a trans person at all."[84]

To sum it up, brand activism can be tremendously powerful, but it's not a magic bullet. In today's world, it's arguably more popular—and more controversial—than ever before. And it is definitely here to stay, but don't buy into the hype and rush into it. As we've seen with Nike's bold stance with Colin Kaepernick, Pepsi's misstep with Kendall Jenner, Starbucks' well-intentioned but ultimately flawed "Race Together" campaign, and the Bud Light controversy with Dylan Mulvaney, the road to successful brand activism is paved with both wins and failures. Brand activism is inherently context-driven. Getting it right or wrong depends on a complex interplay of factors, including the social climate, your brand's history, and how you execute your campaign. This book does not praise activism as the holy grail of branding or offer a quick formula for guaranteed success, nor does it condemn brands for venturing into this complex terrain. Instead, it is intended as a compass and a guide, equipping you with the insights and frameworks necessary to navigate the nuanced landscape of brand activism. In the chapters that follow, we'll delve into the history, motivations, strategies, and impact of brand activism, and extract the lessons of how companies can authentically align with social causes, engage their audiences, and ultimately drive meaningful change—all while safeguarding their brand and bottom line.

References

1   Klein, Russ, "Nike and the Arrogance of Moral Certainty," *Marketing Today*, Medium (blog), September 6, 2018 (accessed June 7, 2024). https://medium.com/marketing-today/nike-and-the-arrogance-of-moral-certainty-8a5a494fdc96.

2   DeWolf Swenson, Molly, "Why It's Critical Brands Take a Stand on Tough Social Issues," *Adweek*, November 26, 2017, https://www.adweek.com/brand-marketing/why-its-so-important-for-brands-to-take-a-stand-on-tough-social-issues/.

3   For example, Jeff Bezos was criticized heavily when he ceased *The Washington Post*'s tradition of endorsing a presidential candidate. At least one editor resigned and 17 opinion columnists called the non-endorsement a "terrible mistake."
Gold , Hadas, "Deep Turmoil at Washington Poast, as Bezos Still Silent on Non-Endorsement." RNZ. October 27, 2024 (accessed March 3, 2025) https://www.rnz.co.nz/news/world/532067/deep-turmoil-at-washington-post-as-bezos-still-silent-on-non-endorsement.

4   Ridgeway, Rick, "Leadership Lessons from Adventurer and Environmentalist Rick Ridgway," *Harvard Business Review*, June 26, 2024 (accessed June 30, 2024). Leadership Lessons from Adventurer and Environmentalist Rick Ridgeway (hbr.org).

5   Klein, Russ, "Make Yourself Useful," *Marketing Today*, Medium (blog), Aug 15, 2017 (accessed June 7, 2024). https://medium.com/marketing-today/make-yourself-useful-1bf3097d24db.

6   DeWolf Swenson, Molly, "Why It's Critical Brands Take a Stand on Tough Social Issues," *Adweek*, November 26, 2017 (accessed March 3, 2025). https://www.adweek.com/brand-marketing/why-its-so-important-for-brands-to-take-a-stand-on-tough-social-issues/.

7   Sheth, Jagdish N., Nirmal K. Sethia, and Shanthi Srinivas (2011), "Mindful Consumption: A Customer Centric Approach to Sustainability," *Journal of the Academy of Marketing Science*, 39, 21–39.
Uslay, Can and Emine Erdogan (2014), "The Mediating Role of Mindful Entrepreneurial Marketing (MEM) Between Production and Consumption," *Journal of Research in Marketing & Entrepreneurship*, 16(1), 47–62.

8   Higonnet, Etele, Marisa Bellantano, and Glenn Hurowitz, "Chocolate's Dark Secret." Mighty Earth, September 1, 2017 (accessed June 7, 2024). https://www.mightyearth.org/wp-content/uploads/2017/09/chocolates_dark_secret_engl ish_web.pdf.

9   In contrast with boycotts, buycotts increase sales when consumers reward a business for actions they favor. Neilson (2010, p. 214) found that "women and people who are more trusting, involved in more voluntary associations, or more altruistic are more likely to buycott than boycott." For further details see Neilson, Lisa A. (2010), "Boycott or buycott? Understanding Political Consumerism," *Journal of Consumer Behavior*, 9(3), 214–227.

10   Accenture, "Majority of Consumers Buying From Companies That Take a Stand on Issues They Care About and Ditching Those That Don't, Accenture Study Finds," December 5, 2018 (accessed September 17, 2024). https://newsroom.accent ure.com/news/2018/majority-of-consumers-buying-from-companies-that-take-a-stand-on-issues-they-care-about-and-ditching-those-that-dont-accent ure-study-finds.

11   Accenture, "Majority of Consumers Buying From Companies That Take a Stand on Issues They Care About and Ditching Those That Don't, Accenture Study Finds," December 5, 2018 (accessed September 17, 2024). https://newsroom.accent ure.com/news/2018/majority-of-consumers-buying-from-companies-that-take-a-stand-on-issues-they-care-about-and-ditching-those-that-dont-accent ure-study-finds.

12   YourStory, "The Biggest Risk is not Taking Any Risk," May 24, 2023 (accessed June 7, 2024). https://yourstory.com/2023/05/embracing-risk-zuckerbergs-philoso phy. Despite multiple attributions, Zuckerberg did not come up with this saying on his own. I (Uslay) know this because I have known this saying since childhood and I am older than Zuckerberg. I actually even like the saying.

13   Branch, John, "The Awakening of Colin Kaepernick," *The New York Times*, September 7, 2017, (accessed June 7, 2024). https://www.nytimes.com/2017/09/07/spo rts/colin-kaepernick-nfl-protests.html.

14   Kaepernick was not the first athlete who refused to acknowledge the American flag to face significant backlash. For example, "The NBA's Mahmoud Abdul-Rauf of the Denver Nuggets, formerly Chris Jackson before converting to Islam, refused to acknowledge the flag in protest, citing similar reasons as Kaepernick and saying that it conflicted with some of his Islamic beliefs. Abdul-Rauf drew the ire of fans and was briefly suspended by the NBA before a compromise was worked out between the league and player, who eventually stood with his teammates and coaches at the playing of the national anthem. Wyche, Steve, "Colin Kaepernick Explains Why He Sat During National Anthem." NFL.com. August 27, 2016 (accessed June 7, 2024). https://www.nfl.com/news/colin-kaepernick-explains-why-he-sat-during-natio nal-anthem-0ap3000000691077.

15   Wyche, Steve, "Colin Kaepernick Explains Why He Sat During National Anthem." NFL.com. August 27, 2016 (accessed June 7, 2024). https://www.nfl.com/news/colin-kaepernick-explains-why-he-sat-during-national-anthem-0ap300000 0691077.

16 Agiesta, Jennifer, "CNN Poll: Americans Split on Anthem Protests," CNN, September 30, 2017 (accessed June 7, 2024). https://www.cnn.com/2017/09/29/politics/national-anthem-nfl-cnn-poll/index.html.

17 De Vogue, Ariane, "Ruth Bader Ginsburg on Kaepernick Protests: 'I think it's dumb and disrespectful,'" CNN, October 12, 2016 (accessed June 7, 2024). https://www.cnn.com/2016/10/10/politics/ruth-bader-ginsburg-colin-kaepernick/index.html

18 Beaton, Andrew, "NFL Paid Under $10 Million to Settle Colin Kaepernick Grievance," The Wall Street Journal, March 21, 2019 (accessed June 7, 2024). https://www.wsj.com/articles/nfl-paid-under-10-million-to-settle-colin-kaepernick-grievance-11553192288.

19 Creswell, Julie, Kevin Draper, and Sapna Maheshwari, "Nike Nearly Dropped Colin Kaepernick Before Embracing Him," The New York Times, September 26, 2018 (accessed June 7, 2024). https://www.nytimes.com/2018/09/26/sports/nike-colin-kaepernick.html.

20 Creswell, Julie, Kevin Draper, and Sapna Maheshwari, "Nike Nearly Dropped Colin Kaepernick Before Embracing Him," The New York Times, September 26, 2018 (accessed June 7, 2024). https://www.nytimes.com/2018/09/26/sports/nike-colin-kaepernick.html.

21 Editors of GQ, "Colin Kaepernick is GQ's 2017 Citizen of the Year," GQ, November 13, 2017 (accessed June 7, 2024). https://www.gq.com/story/colin-kaepernick-cover-men-of-the-year.

22 "Colin Kaepernick: Ambassador of Conscience," Amnesty International, April 21, 2018 (accessed June 7, 2024). https://www.amnesty.org/en/latest/news/2018/04/colin-kaepernick-ambassador-of-conscience/.

23 Creswell, Julie, Kevin Draper, and Sapna Maheshwari, "Nike Nearly Dropped Colin Kaepernick Before Embracing Him." The New York Times, September 26, 2018 (accessed June 7, 2024). https://www.nytimes.com/2018/09/26/sports/nike-colin-kaepernick.html.

24 Novy-Williams, Eben, "Kaepernick Campaign Created $43 Million in Buzz for Nike." Bloomberg, September 4, 2018 (accessed September 17, 2024). https://www.bloomberg.com/news/articles/2018-09-04/kaepernick-campaign-created-43-million-in-buzz-for-nike-so-far.

25 Williams, Robert, "Nike Sees 1,400% Surge in Social Buzz After Kaepernick Ad," Marketing Dive, September 5, 2018 (accessed June 7, 2024). https://www.marketingdive.com/news/nike-sees-1400-surge-in-social-buzz-after-kaepernick-ad/531572/.

26 Kochkodin, Brandon, "Buzz From Nike's Kaepernick Campaign Now Worth More Than $163 Million." Bloomberg, September 6, 2018 (accessed June 7, 2024). https://www.bloomberg.com/news/articles/2018-09-06/value-of-nike-s-exposure-from-kaepernick-ad-up-to-163-million.

27 Cassillo, John, "Digging Deeper into Nike's 'Crazy' Advertising." TV[R]EV, September 18, 2019 (accessed June 7, 2024). https://www.tvrev.com/news/digging-deeper-into-nikes-crazy-advertising.

28 Linnane, Ciara, "Nike's Online Sales Jumped 31% After Company Unveiled Kaepernick Campaign," MarketWatch, September 17, 2018 (accessed June 7, 2024). https://www.marketwatch.com/story/nikes-online-sales-jumped-31-after-company-unveiled-kaepernick-campaign-2018-09-07.

29 Goldman, David, "Nike's Colin Kaepernick Gamble is Already Paying Off," *CNN Business*, September 14, 2018 (accessed June 7, 2024). https://money.cnn.com/2018/09/14/news/companies/nike-kaepernick/index.html.

30 Agiesta, Jennifer, "CNN Poll: Americans Split on Anthem Protests." CNN, September 30, 2017 (accessed June 7, 2024). https://www.cnn.com/2017/09/29/polit ics/national-anthem-nfl-cnn-poll/index.html.

31 Swystun, Jeff, "Benetton's Confusing Legacy of Brand Activism." *Medium*, January 27, 2021 (accessed June 7, 2024). https://jeffswystun.medium.com/benettons-confusing-legacy-of-brand-activism-6156b4c0384c.

32 Draper, Kevin, and Julie Creswell, "Colin Kaepernick 'Dream Crazy' Ad Wins Nike and Emmy." *The New York Times*, September 16, 2019 (accessed June 7, 2024). https://www.nytimes.com/2019/09/16/sports/football/colin-kaepernick-nike-emmy.html#:~:text=%E2%80%9CDream%20Crazy%E2%80%9D%20was%20named%20outstanding,the%20collaboration%20beyond%20market ing%20savvy.

33 "Nike Colin Kaepernick Ad Research Report," Morning Consult, 2018 (accessed June 7, 2024). https://morningconsult.com/form/nike-kaepernick-report/. The Morning Consult study was based on interviews with 1,694 adults (pre-campaign) and 5,481 adults (post-campaign).
Beer, Jeff, "Survey Says Nike's Brand Image Has Dropped Because of Colin Kaepernick Ad," Fast Company , September 6 , 2018 (accessed June 7, 2024). https://www.fastcompany.com/90233045/survey-says-nikes-brand-image-has-dropped-because-of-colin-kaepernick-ad.

34 "Nike Colin Kaepernick Ad Research Report," Morning Consult, 2018 (accessed June 7, 2024). https://morningconsult.com/form/nike-kaepernick-report/ . The Morning Consult study was based on interviews with 1,694 adults (pre-campaign) and 5,481 adults (post-campaign).
Beer, Jeff, "Survey Says Nike's Brand Image Has Dropped Because of Colin Kaepernick Ad," Fast Company , September 6 , 2018 (accessed June 7, 2024). https://www.fastcompany.com/90233045/survey-says-nikes-brand-image-has-dropped-because-of-colin-kaepernick-ad

35 Green, Dennis, "Nike Execs Can't Stop Saying One Word, And It Reveals the Future of the Company." *Business Insider*, June 29, 2018 (accessed June 7, 2024). https://www.businessinsider.com/nike-execs-emphasize-digital-transformation-2018-6.

36 Anupriya Dhonchak, "Nike's 'Dream Crazier': A New Brand of Self-Objectification." *Engenderings*, May 28, 2019 (accessed June 7, 2024). https://blogs.lse.ac.uk/gen der/2019/05/28/nikes-dream-crazier-a-new-brand-of-self-objectification/#.~.text=Serena%20Williams%20narrates%20it%20and,US%20Women's%20N ational%20Soccer%20Team.

37 Whitler, Kimberly, and Thomas Barta (2024), "The Enterprise Activism Risk Model: How Good Intentions Can Jeopardize Business Success," *Journal of Retailing*, 100(2), 330–340.

38 Avery, J. and K. Pauwels (2019), "Brand Activism: Nike and Colin Kaepernick," *Harvard Business School Case* 9, 519–046.

39 Would Nike sentiment have fared better if a less controversial athlete was chosen as the face of the 30th anniversary of "Just Do It"? How about a Michael Jordan redux who could also move the race dialogue forward but in a more unifying manner?

40   Carrie Wong, Julia, "Pepsi Pulls Kendall Jenner Ad Ridiculed for Co-opting Protest Movements," *The Guardian*, April 6, 2017 (accessed June 7, 2024). https://www.theg uardian.com/media/2017/apr/05/pepsi-kendall-jenner-pepsi-apology-ad-protest.

41   Ferruci, Patrick and Erin E. Schauster (2024), "Keeping up with the Boundaries of Advertising: Paradigm Repair After Pepsi's Big Mess," *Journal of Communication Inquiry*, 48(2), 185–204.

42   Ferruci, Patrick and Erin E. Schauster (2024), "Keeping up with the Boundaries of Advertising: Paradigm Repair After Pepsi's Big Mess," *Journal of Communication Inquiry*, 48(2), 185–204.

43   Carrie Wong, Julia, "Pepsi Pulls Kendall Jenner Ad Ridiculed for Co-opting Protest Movements," *The Guardian*, April 6, 2017 (accessed June 7, 2024). https://www. theguardian.com/media/2017/apr/05/pepsi-kendall-jenner-pepsi-apology-ad-protest.

44   Marzilli, Ted, "One Year After Jenner Ad Crisis, Pepsi Recovers but Purchase Consideration Hasn't." YouGov, April 17, 2028 (accessed September 17, 2024). https://today.yougov.com/consumer/articles/20598-one-year-after-jenner-ad-crisis-pepsi-recovers.

45   Ferruci, Patrick and Erin E. Schauster (2024), "Keeping Up with the Boundaries of Advertising: Paradigm Repair After Pepsi's Big Mess," *Journal of Communication Inquiry*, 48(2), 185–204.

46   Goldman, David, "How Howard Schultz Ran Starbucks Tells Us How He Might Run America," *CNN Business*, January 29, 2019 (accessed June 7, 2024). https://www.cnn.com/2019/01/29/business/howard-schultz-starbucks-ceo-presid ent/index.html.

47   Statista Research Department, "Number of Starbucks Stores Worldwide from 2003 to 2023," *Statista*, March 26, 2024 (accessed June 7, 2024). https://www.statista. com/statistics/266465/number-of-starbucks-stores-worldwide/.

48   Rochman, Bonnie and Heidi Peiper, "Starbucks College Achievement Plan Welcomes Its 1,000th Graduate." *Starbucks Stories*, December 11, 2017 (accessed June 7, 2024). https://stories.starbucks.com/stories/2017/starbucks-college-achievement-plan-welcomes-its-1000th-graduate/.

49   "Facts About Starbucks and Our Partners (Employees)," *Starbucks Stories*, September 20, 2013 (accessed June 7, 2024). https://stories.starbucks.com/stories/2013/facts-about-starbucks-and-our-partners-employees/.

50   "Facts About Starbucks and Our Partners (Employees)," *Starbucks Stories*, September 20, 2013. Accessed June 7, 2024. https://stories.starbucks.com/stories/2013/facts-about-starbucks-and-our-partners-employees/.

51   Wiener-Bronner, Danielle, "Starbucks Achieves Pay Equity in the United States," *CNN Business*, March 21, 2018. (accessed June 7, 2024). https://money.cnn.com/2018/03/21/news/companies/starbucks-pay-equity/index.html.

52   Shah, Khushbu, "Why Starbucks' 'Race Together' Campaign Failed." *Eater*, June 18, 2015 (accessed June 7, 2024). https://www.eater.com/2015/6/18/8807849/why-starbucks-race-together-campaign-failed.

53   Shah, Khushbu, "Starbucks Race 'Conversation Starters', Are All Equally Terrible," *Eater*, March 20, 2015 (accessed June 7, 2024). https://www.eater.com/2015/3/20/8267405/starbucks-race-together-conversation-starters-ranked.

54   Rooney, Ben, "Starbucks Stops Writing 'Race Together' on Cups," CNN *Business*, March 23, 2015 (accessed June 7, 2024). https://money.cnn.com/2015/03/23/news/companies/starbucks-race-together/index.html.

55   Shah, Khushbu, "Starbucks Race 'Conversation Starters', Are All Equally Terrible," *Eater*, March 20, 2015 (accessed June 7, 2024). https://www.eater.com/2015/3/20/8267405/starbucks-race-together-conversation-starters-ranked.

56   Shah, Khushbu, "Comedian Larry Wilmore Tears Apart Starbucks' Failed Race Together Campaign," *Eater*, March 24, 2015 (accessed June 7, 2024). https://www.eater.com/2015/3/24/8285113/comedian-larry-wilmore-starbucks-race-together-nightly-show.

57   Goldman, David, "How Howard Schultz Ran Starbucks Tells Us How He Might Run America." CNN *Business*, January 29, 2019 (accessed June 7, 2024). https://www.cnn.com/2019/01/29/business/howard-schultz-starbucks-ceo-president/index.html.

58   Foroohar, Rana, "Starbucks CEO Howard Schultz Sounds Off on Racism in America," *Time*, December 16, 2014 (accessed June 7, 2024). https://time.com/3637075/starbucks-howard-schultz-race-politics/.

59   Taylor, Kate, "Some Starbucks Baristas Are Begging Their Former CEO Not to Run for President," *Business Insider*, Jan 30, 2019 (accessed June 7, 2024). https://www.businessinsider.com/starbucks-baristas-on-howard-schultz-presidential-aspirations-2019-1.

60   Myers, Owen, "Panic and Rash Decision-Making: Ex-Bud-Light Staff on One of the Biggest Boycotts in US History," *The Guardian*, September 19, 2023 (accessed September 8, 2024). https://www.theguardian.com/world/2023/sep/19/dylan-mulvaney-bud-light-boycott.

61   Riedel, Samantha, Abby Monteil, and James Factoria, "Everything You Need to Know About the Bud Light and Dylan Mulvaney Fiasco," *Them*, August 14, 2023 (accessed June 7, 2024). https://www.them.us/story/dylan-mulvaney-bud-light-drama-explained.

62   Smith, Ryan, "Dylan Mulvaney Has Partnerships with These Brands," *Newsweek*, April 13, 2023 (accessed June 7, 2024). https://www.newsweek.com/dylan-mulvaney-has-partnerships-these-brands-bud-light-list-1794187.

63   Smith, Ryan, "Dylan Mulvaney Has Partnerships with These Brands," *Newsweek*, April 13, 2023 (accessed June 7, 2024). https://www.newsweek.com/dylan-mulvaney-has-partnerships-these-brands-bud-light-list-1794187.

64   Arger, Alex, "Bud Light Isn't the Top-Selling Beer in the US Anymore. This One Is," *ScrippsNews*, June 14, 2023 (accessed June 7, 2024). https://scrippsnews.com/stories/bud-light-isn-t-the-top-selling-beer-in-the-us-anymore-this-one-is/.

65   Arger, Alex, "Bud Light Isn't the Top-Selling Beer in the US Anymore. This One Is," *ScrippsNews*, June 14, 2023 (accessed June 7, 2024). https://scrippsnews.com/stories/bud-light-isn-t-the-top-selling-beer-in-the-us-anymore-this-one-is/.

66   Liaukonyte, Jura, Anna Tuchman, and Xinrong Zhu, "Lessons from the Bud Light Boycott, One Year Later," *Harvard Business Publishing Education*, March 20, 2024 (accessed June 7, 2024). https://hbsp.harvard.edu/product/H082K7-PDF-ENG.

67   Liaukonyte, Jura, Anna Tuchman, and Xinrong Zhu, "Lessons from the Bud Light Boycott, One Year Later," *Harvard Business Publishing Education*, March 20, 2024 (accessed June 7, 2024). https://hbsp.harvard.edu/product/H082K7-PDF-ENG.

68   Zilber, Ariel, "Bud Light Could Lose Retail Shelf Space as Dylan Mulvaney Boycott Persists: Experts," *New York Post*, September 15, 2023 (accessed September 8, 2024). https://nypost.com/2023/09/15/bud-light-could-lose-retail-shelf-space-as-dylan-mulvaney-boycott-persists/.

69   Arger, Alex, "Bud Light Isn't the Top-Selling Beer in the US Anymore. This One Is," *ScrippsNews*, June 14, 2023 (accessed June 7, 2024). https://scrippsnews.com/stories/bud-light-isn-t-the-top-selling-beer-in-the-us-anymore-this-one-is/.

70   Ironically, Modelo Especial is also owned by AB InBev but imported and sold in the US by its competitor, Constellation Brands.

71   "Bud Light Brewer is Still Reeling from Trans Promotion Backlash as U.S. Revenue Tumbled 13%," *Fortune*, October 31, 2023 (accessed June 7, 2024). https://fortune.com/2023/10/31/bud-light-earnings-dylan-mulvaney-transgender-promotion-backlash/.

72   Salinas, Gabriela, "Bog Brand Activism: Social Impact or Agitprop?" IE.edu, May 24, 2023 (accessed October 9, 2024). https://www.ie.edu/insights/articles/big-brand-activism-social-impact-of-agitprop/.

73   YCharts: Anheuser-Busch InBev SA/NV (BUD). https://ycharts.com/companies/BUD/market_cap.

74   Maloney, Jennifer, "Bud Light Missed Out on the Super Bowl Party," *The Wall Street Journal*, February 27, 2024 (accessed September 22, 2024). https://www.wsj.com/business/retail/bud-light-missed-out-on-the-super-bowl-party-a5387584?mod=e2li.

75   Koenig, Melissa, "Marketing Guru Behind Budweiser's Iconic 'Whassup!' and 'Talking Frogs' Commercials Says Anheuser-Busch has 'Destroyed 20 years of work in one week' with Dylan Mulvaney Debacle," *Daily Mail*, May 10, 2023 (accessed September 10, 2024). https://www.dailymail.co.uk/news/article-12069715/Marketing-guru-Budweisers-iconic-commercials-says-company-destroyed-20-years-work.html.

76   Mullman, Jeremy, "A-B Creative Chief Bob Lachky to Step Down," *Ad Age*, February 10, 2009 (accessed September 10, 2024). https://adage.com/article/news/anheuser-busch-creative-chief-bob-lachky-step/134536.

77   Myers, Owen, "Panic and Rash Decision-Making: Ex-Bud-Light Staff on One of the Biggest Boycotts in US History," *The Guardian*, September 19, 2023 (accessed September 8, 2024). https://www.theguardian.com/world/2023/sep/19/dylan-mulvaney-bud-light-boycott.

78   Myers, Owen, "Panic and Rash Decision-Making: Ex-Bud-Light Staff on One of the Biggest Boycotts in US History," *The Guardian*, September 19, 2023 (accessed September 8, 2024). https://www.theguardian.com/world/2023/sep/19/dylan-mulvaney-bud-light-boycott.

79   Whitworth, Brandon, "Our Responsibility to America," Anheuser-Busch Press Release. April 14, 2023 (accessed June 7, 2024). https://www.anheuser-busch.com/newsroom/our-responsibility-to-america.

80   Riedel, Samantha, Abby Monteil, and James Factoria, "Everything You Need to Know About the Bud Light and Dylan Mulvaney Fiasco," *Them*, August 14, 2023 (accessed June 7, 2024). https://www.them.us/story/dylan-mulvaney-bud-light-drama-explained.

81 Impelli, Matthew, "Illinois Gay Bars Boycott Bud Light Over Anti-Transgender Comments," *Newsweek*, May 8, 2023 (accessed June 7, 2024). https://www.newsweek.com/illinois-gay-bars-boycott-bud-light-over-anti-transgender-comments-1798967.

82 Brooks, Khristopher J., "Bud Light Gets Stock Downgrade Just Weeks After Dylan Mulvaney Fallout," CBS *News*, May 12, 2023 (accessed June 7, 2024). https://www.cbsnews.com/news/bud-light-dylan-mulvaney-stock-downgrade-anheuser-busch-sales/.

83 Riedel, Samantha, Abby Monteil, and James Factoria, "Everything You Need to Know About the Bud Light and Dylan Mulvaney Fiasco," *Them*, August 14, 2023 (accessed June 7, 2024). https://www.them.us/story/dylan-mulvaney-bud-light-drama-explained.

84 Duffy, Clare, "Dylan Mulvaney Says Bud Light's Backlash Response Was 'Worse Than Not Hiring a Trans Person At All'," CNN *Business*, June 30, 2023 (accessed June 7, 2024). https://www.cnn.com/2023/06/29/tech/dylan-mulvaney-bud-light-statement/index.html.

2

FIVE RINGS OF BRAND ACTIVISM

WHY SOME SHINE WHERE OTHERS STUMBLE

In an era of turbulence, where political winds whip and cultural fires rage, brands seek refuge in the noble cloak of activism. Yet, with each misfire, we can't help but cringe. Authenticity, like a diamond, demands more than glitter. It requires a foundation of ethical alignment. Brand activism is not just about looking good, it's about doing good too.

Renowned novelist Charles Dickens urged: "Have a heart that never hardens, and a temper that never tires, and a touch that never hurts" (Hard Times, 1854). Alas, in every case we discussed in the previous chapter, the touch of our beloved brands have hurt some people, inadvertently or not. Importantly, we argue certain alignments must occur before companies engage in brand activism.

Enter our "Five Rings of Brand Activism," a compass to guide companies from alienation to applause. These aren't mere marketing tactics, but include soul-searching questions that separate virtue signaling from genuine purpose.

DOI: 10.4324/9781003593690-2

Ring One: Mission, Vision, Cause—
A Symphony in Harmony

Does your company's DNA rhyme with the cause you champion? Or is it forced, jarring, and discordant? Like your dance shoes, several studies show sociopolitical cause fit is important, even when symbolic and not functional.[1] Remember Pepsi and Kendall Jenner's "Live For Now"—an awkward attempt that left audiences bewildered. True alignment, like fine wine, must age and resonate. High fit builds credibility and positive reactions (i.e., attitude and purchase intentions), and low fit causes skepticism.[2] Is your activism built on a solid foundation?

Ring Two: Passion and Brand Purpose—
A Two-Step with Your Consumers

Before waltzing into activism, take your core customers by the hand. Are they ready for this dance? Or will you leave them stumbling? Bud Light's misstep demonstrates the peril of stretching your brand beyond its natural reach. Don't gamble with your most loyal partners.

No brand manager should be disillusioned as to what the brand stands for in the minds of their customers or stretch thin the meaning of their brand purpose, or even worse, try to manage that purpose as if it is the fifth P of their marketing mix.[3] While every brand needs purpose, it is fine if it is competence or culture-based, and not immersed in a social cause.[4] Unless you are sure you want to *reposition* the brand *and* have made a detailed study of pros, cons, and cannibalization, are you sure your core customers are on board?

Ring Three: Business and Cause—
Where Cause Meets the Business Case

Is there a business rationale for activism, or are you playing roulette? Remember, social responsibility is not merely a marketing expense. It is a strategic investment in your future. A lot of caution is needed. For example, Bud Light was trying to engage a younger demographic (aka market development)[5] but did not recognize that such a brand extension could be a major turnoff for its core customers. From a business perspective, could they not have reached out to the younger demographic by launching or repositioning another brand? Why gamble with the flagship? When companies see a clear link between inclusivity and their bottom line, they're more likely to respond to stakeholder pressure for inclusive brand strategies. Essentially, the stronger the business case for inclusion, the more stakeholders can influence positive change.[6]

If there is not a business case to be made, why risk the brand and the livelihoods of employees and investors, and perhaps even the company? Isn't there a fiduciary responsibility to act in the best interest of the business?

Ring Four: A Legacy of Commitment— The Weight of History

Don't don the mantle of activism overnight. Authentic action rests on a bedrock of past deeds. Pepsi's foray into racial justice lacked the weight of Nike's unwavering support for its athletes. You need to build your credibility brick by brick before taking center stage. You will be given no quarter if there is no precedence to your efforts. Yes, you may assume some goodwill if the brand is new or that of a start-up. Take extra caution otherwise. You will need to start somewhere but that somewhere cannot be anywhere.

Ring Five: Authenticity— The Toughest Test of All

Authenticity is the brand activist's best friend. It is one of the key drivers of effective advertising, corporate social responsibility (CSR), and brand activism.[7] It is arguably the cornerstone of contemporary marketing and unlocks the wallets of customers of all ages.[8] It can make your activism go viral, cause buycotts, and dissuade boycotts (not to mention improve your brand image, loyalty, and purchase intent).[9] Thus, this is where the rubber (your signal) meets the road (perception). Will your actions walk the talk? Or will you be exposed as a fraud, guilty of woke washing/bashing?[10] Nike's unwavering support for Colin Kaepernick, even facing backlash, starkly contrasts the clumsy missteps of others. Remember, authenticity is not a slogan; it's a daily practice demanding vigilance and unwavering principles. Even though both Starbucks and Nike could have arguably transcended Ring Four, only Nike could legitimately claim Ring Five due to its history of sticking it out with their athletes through "thick and thin."[11] A lack of it is the brand activist's worst nightmare. Before you leap into the brand activism arena, beware of the hidden pitfalls of implementation. Poorly trained employees, unexpected controversies, and even hostile "brandjacking" can derail your campaign and damage your reputation. Plan for the unexpected and prepare to adapt.[12]

Through these five rings, we score our brands' activism: Nike, a champion with 4.5 out of 5, Starbucks struggling at 2.5, and Pepsi and Bud Light falling short with 1.5 and 1, respectively. But scores are mere numbers. The true measure of success prevails in the hearts and minds of your customers.

We consider our five-ring framework to be already validated because Nike actually used Mulvaney as a model for a sports bra and it did not lead to a backlash of magnitude or lose Nike billions of dollars.[13] See Figure 2.1 for a visual representation.

In contrast, the only positive for Bud Light was that its brand awareness surged as a result of the incident. However, that is not really of significance since it already had the highest brand awareness in the industry. The overstated naïveté of Mulvaney regarding March Madness was likely to

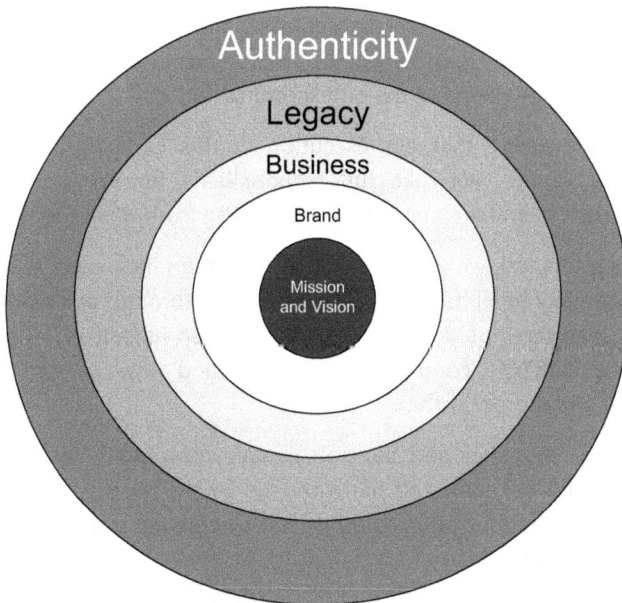

Figure 2.1 The Five Rings of Brand Activism

alienate sports-loving core beer drinkers, even in the best of worlds. And unlike the woes of Disney (see Chapter 4), it was an unforced error on Bud Light's part. But once the error happened, could Bud Light have reacted differently?

We suspected as much, but to find out we prompted Google's Bard AI (since rebranded as Gemini) as follows: "Can you draft a unifying public message from Bud Light after it faced a backlash for its marketing partnership with a transgender influencer?" We did not wordsmith or experiment with any other prompts.

Bard's verbatim response offered quite a starting point:

> At Bud Light, we strive to bring people together over a cold beer, regardless of background, identity, or belief.
>
> We recently partnered with influencer Dylan Mulvaney in a marketing campaign intended to celebrate individuality and inclusivity. We understand that this decision resulted in strong reactions, both positive and negative. We respect everyone's right to their own opinion, and we value open and honest dialogue.
>
> However, the hateful and transphobic language directed towards Ms. Mulvaney was entirely unacceptable, and we unequivocally condemn it. Inclusivity and respect are core values at Bud Light, and we stand firmly against all forms of discrimination.
>
> We acknowledge that our execution of this campaign fell short of those values. We take full responsibility for the unintended consequences and are committed to learning from this experience.
>
> Moving forward, we will continue to champion inclusivity and celebrate diversity in all its forms. We will do this through our marketing efforts, partnerships, and actions. We will also be actively engaging with the LGBTQ+ community to understand how we can better support and represent them.
>
> To Dylan Mulvaney and the transgender community, we sincerely apologize for the pain and harm caused by the backlash. We stand with you and reaffirm our commitment to creating a more inclusive and respectful world.
>
> We believe that everyone deserves to be celebrated for who they are, and we will continue to work towards that goal, one beer at a time.

Bard, which identified Mulvaney by name without prompting, also wanted us to note that the message it crafted:

- avoids taking sides in the political debate surrounding transgender rights;
- acknowledges the mistake made and offers a sincere apology;
- outlines concrete steps Bud Light will take to be more inclusive in the future; and
- reaffirms the company's commitment to celebrating diversity and respect.

We wonder if the legal team at AB InBev would've signed off on Bard's message. Once a crisis occurs, legal teams tend to take over and muff what the leaders really want to say or do. In our opinion, (in)action with the fear of legal action causes more reputational harm than even a lawsuit's potential instance or verdict. While we think Bard's response is superior to the backtracking displayed by the AB InBev executives, its theme of inclusivity could be strengthened even further from an individual freedom perspective to remind everyone of the founding principles of the United States. We explore what that means more in the next chapter and then unleash AI on Pepsi.

References

1   Chu, Shu-Chuan, Hyejin Kim, and Yoojung Kim (2023), "When Brand Get Real: The Role of Authenticity and Electronic Word of Mouth in Shaping Consumer Response to Brands Taking a Stand," *International Journal of Advertising*, 42(6), 1037–1064.

2   Becker-Olsen, K. L., B. A. Cudmore, and R. P. Hill (2006), "The Impact of Perceived Corporate Social Responsibility on Consumer Behavior," *Journal of Business Research*, 59(1), 46–53.

3   To refresh your memory, the original 4Ps of marketing are product, promotion, place, and price.

4   Knowles, Jonathan, Tom Hunsaker, Hannah Grove, and Alison James (2022), "What is the Purpose of Your Purpose?" *Harvard Business Review*, (March-April) (accessed December 6, 2024). https://hbr.org/2022/03/what-is-the-purpose-of-your-purpose.

5   According to a 2022 Gallup survey, 21% of Gen Z (born between 1997 and 2003) identify as LGBT whereas the figure stands at 10% for millennials, and 2.6% for baby boomers.

6   Nickerson, Dionne, Sundar Bharadwaj, and Omar Rodriguez-Vila (2023), "Antecedents and Consequences of an Inclusive Brand Marketing," Marketing Science Institute working paper series, No. 23-138.

7   Vredenburg, J., S. Kapitan, A. Spry, and J. A. Kemper (2020), "Brands Taking a Stand: Authentic Brand Activism or Woke Washing?" *Journal of Public Policy & Marketing*, 39(4), 444–460.
Alhouti, S., C. M. Johnson, and B. B. Holloway (2016), "Corporate Social Responsibility Authenticity: Investigating its Antecedents and Outcomes," *Journal of Business Research*, 69(3), 1242–1249. Becker, M., N. Wiegand, and W. J. Reinartz (2019), "Does It Pay to Be Real? Understanding Authenticity in TV Advertising," *Journal of Marketing*, 83(1), 24–50.

8   Brown Stephen, Robert V. Kozinets, and John F. Sherry Jr. (2003), "Teaching Old Brands New Tricks: Retro Branding and the Revival of Brand Meaning," *Journal of Marketing*, 67 (July), 19–33.

9   Chu, Shu-Chuan, Hyejin Kim, and Yoojung Kim (2023), "When Brand Get Real: The Role of Authenticity and Electronic Word of Mouth in Shaping Consumer Response to Brands Taking a Stand," *International Journal of Advertising*, 42(6), 1037-1064.

10   Vredenburg, Jessica, Amanda Spry, Joya Kemper, and Sommer Kapitan, "Woke Washing: What Happens When Marketing Communications Don't Match Corporate Practice," *The Conversation*, December 5, 2018 (accessed June 7, 2024). https://thec onversation.com/woke-washing-what-happens-when-marketing-communicati ons-dont-match-corporate-practice-108035.

11   Masunaga, Samantha, "Nike Targets Youth With Provocative Ad Campaign," *The Detroit News*, September 5, 2018 (accessed June 7, 2024). https://www.detroitn ews.com/story/business/2018/09/05/nike-kaepernick-campaign/37724717/.

12   Thota, Sweta Chaturvedi (2021), "What is Brandjacking? Origin, Conceptualization and Effects of Perceived Dimensions of Truth, Mockery, and Offensiveness," *International Journal of Advertising*, 40(2), 292–310.

13   Butron, Jamie, "Nike Makes Dylan Mulvaney Sports Bra Model, Days After Bud Light Furor," *Newsweek*, April 6, 2023 (accessed June 6, 2024). https://www.newsweek.com/nike-transgender-dylan-mulvaney-sports-bra-model-days-after-bud-light-furore-1792872.

3

AI-POWERED ANALYSIS: PEPSI AND THE STATES OF AMERICA

The conceptualization and study of nations as brands with unique images and identities is well accepted in academia and consulting practice.[1] Interestingly, the abolition of slavery in the United States can also be assessed through the lens of nation-brand activation. The notion of slavery clearly did not fit with "brand America"—the land of the free. The very notion clashed with the lofty ideals of freedom and liberty inscribed on the parchment of independence. This had to be aligned sooner or later, that much is crystal clear. The forefathers knew it. However, had they done something about it in 1776, the nation would likely not be called the United States of America. To confront slavery head on within a fledgling nation, barely clinging to the precipice of freedom, could have spelled its demise. History may have played out very differently. There might not even be states to speak of; colonies may have stayed colonies. With different tides, North America might never have had a free nation outside the commonwealth.

DOI: 10.4324/9781003593690-3

Let's analyze.

Scenario 1. The northern states do not stand a chance to win a dual war against their taxing oppressors from the empire on which the sun never sets and the conscripted militia from the empire's southern state allies. Foreign powers also hesitate to assist divided colonies. They lose the war of independence and remain as colonies, in practice if not in name, wherein the United Kingdom does its best to strip the land of its resources and leave especially the northern states in as weak a state as possible for the next hundred-plus years. (Likelihood: High.)

Scenario 2. The northern states somehow survive the ordeal and gain independence, but the southern colonies (aka The Dominion of Southern States) increasingly marginalize themselves in the world arena, much like what apartheid did for South Africa. Inevitable clashes—political, social, and economic—force the North's hand, leading to the invasion and annexation of the Southern colonies. Though delayed to avoid provoking the United Kingdom, this act of aggression fuels deep resentment in the South. Feeling violated and subjugated, the South embarks on a persistent struggle for independence, employing both legal challenges and acts of terror that reverberate through the ages. (Likelihood: Moderate to Low.)

Scenario 3. Southern states somehow fall in line, fight alongside the northern armies and the freed slaves against the imperialistic oppressors, and in the process realize the errors of their ways. (Likelihood: Very Low. The fact of the matter is that the South would've rather paid high taxes than free the slaves.)

The forefathers made the analysis and decided to postpone the issue for another day for the sake of the citizens (aka consumers). A premature push for abolition could jeopardize not just the fledgling nation, but the very ideals it sought to embody. The likelihood of civil war was very much in the mind of Abraham Lincoln prior to his election as president and those before him as they set the course toward brand activation. If they had known for sure their actions would lead to a civil war, they might have postponed too.[2] However, at least Lincoln calculated that if it came to a full-scale civil war, the North and, more importantly, the nation would prevail. Such are the tough calculations that must precede brand activation. In fact, so tough are the issues that most brands had stayed away from them until recently.

However, it has become a popular action nowadays and executives are being compelled to take action. This does not mean they can ignore the calculations, however. Brand activation must answer the questions we have raised and be calculated rather than coerced.

By the way, we were originally planning to go with High, Medium, and Low for the likelihood of these scenarios until we fed them to AI (Google Gemini) which assigned even lower likelihoods for Scenarios 2 and 3. Gemini also noted: "The American Revolution's success was heavily dependent on the unified efforts of the colonies. A divided front significantly weakens their chances against a powerful empire. External support, particularly from France, played a pivotal role in the American Revolution. Without it, the outcome could have been drastically different. The issue of slavery was a major point of contention that continued to plague the newly formed nation. While the revolution's ideals of liberty and equality ultimately contributed to its abolition, the path towards that outcome was long and fraught with conflict."

Let's get back to the case of Pepsi.

The company has a lengthy page detailing its public policy engagement, political activities, and contributions guidelines, which states that it "recognizes that the use of company resources in the political process is an important issue for shareholders and other stakeholders."[3]

Yet the above recognition did not stop Pepsi from launching the "Live For Now" campaign with Kendall Jenner. Pepsi claims its well-meaning actions were undertaken in the name of furthering civil rights and inclusion. Instead, their brand of activism bred backlash and division. Please note, it is harder to delight customers than to upset them. Let's be honest, disgruntled folks make the fiercest social media warriors, boycott brigades, and product-pulverizing protesters. Happy customers, well, they just keep sippin' their Pepsis and Bud Lights.

We did not necessarily need to review the empirical evidence to make the above claims, but we assure you they exist.[4] The sting extends beyond angry consumers. Research suggests that employees, too, get a moral hangover from their company's political pronouncements.[5] Those who disagree feel unvalued, demotivated, and ready to jump ship whereas there is no material impact on the motivation of those that agree with your position. Finally, your investors, those usually stoic financiers, are also ticked off by corporate sociopolitical activism which causes "adverse reactions" and ire from customers.[6] Please don't mis-activate your brand because you stand to lose, lose, and then lose some more.

Pepsi, with a divisive action, was potentially serving a triple shot of bitterness: upset customers, disgruntled employees, and investors nursing empty cans of goodwill. Is this the recipe for success to dream of in board-room brainstorming sessions? There's a lesson here, one not just for beverage giants but for any brand tempted to wear the activist cape. Before plunging into the political whirlpool, ask yourself the Druckerian question: what is your true purpose? Is it to quench thirst or ignite social firestorms? Remember, alignment is all—align your message with your brand story, your values, and, most importantly, your customers.

Because in the end, the fizziest brands aren't just the tastiest; they're the ones that understand the delicate balance of delighting their audience while staying true to their brand ideals. Otherwise, they risk ending up flat, getting a mis-activation Razzie in this or the next edition of our book. So, the choice is yours: will you be the brand that unites over a refreshing sip, or the one that leaves a bitter aftertaste of division? Choose wisely, for the world is watching, and your shareholders are holding their breath.

Achieving authenticity is very challenging for a heritage brand, such as Pepsi. Even though it has positioned itself as the more progressive soda against archrival Coca-Cola, Pepsi also has a complex and controversial history regarding civil rights. While the company has made some strides in promoting diversity and inclusion, it has also faced accusations of discrimination and insensitivity toward minorities.[7]

In the early 20th century, Pepsi, like many other American corporations, operated in a segregated society where racial discrimination was prevalent. The company's advertising often perpetuated harmful stereotypes of African Americans, and its workforce was largely segregated. In the 1940s, Pepsi made a bold move by hiring an all-Black sales team to target African American consumers. This initiative was considered groundbreaking at the time and helped to increase the company's market share among Black consumers. However, the team also faced significant challenges due to racial segregation and discrimination in the Jim Crow South.[8] Despite this early progress, Pepsi continued to face accusations of discrimination in hiring and promotion practices. In 2012, the company settled a lawsuit for $3.13 million, resolving claims that its criminal background check policy unfairly discriminated against Black applicants and hindered their employment opportunities.[9]

AI Revisits the Pepsi Brief

We asked Google's Gemini to re-imagine a campaign with the same basic parameters with the following single prompt: "Imagine a Pepsi campaign featuring Kendall Jenner focusing on civil rights brand activism to be launched around the anniversary of Martin Luther King's assassination. What would the campaign brief look like?" The verbatim response from Gemini is as follows:

Pepsi Brand Campaign Brief: Celebrating Dr. Martin Luther King Jr.'s Legacy Through Action

Campaign Goal: To launch a civil rights brand activism campaign for Pepsi, featuring Kendall Jenner, on the anniversary of Dr. Martin Luther King Jr.'s assassination. This campaign aims to:

- **Honor Dr. King's legacy of justice and equality.**
- **Highlight Pepsi's commitment to social progress.**
- **Inspire positive action and community engagement.**
- **Reposition Pepsi's image after past missteps regarding civil rights activism.**

Target Audience:

- Millennials and Gen Z consumers who are socially conscious and passionate about civil rights issues.
- Consumers who value brands that take a stand and actively support positive change.

Campaign Messaging:

- **Focus:** The power of collective action and individual responsibility to continue Dr. King's dream of equality.
- **Tone:** Uplifting, hopeful, and empowering.
- **Key messages:**
    - "Dr. King's dream lives on. What will you do to keep it alive?"
    - "Together, we can create a more just and equitable world."
    - "Pepsi: Taking a stand for the causes that matter."

Campaign Elements:

- **Video:** A short film featuring Kendall Jenner alongside prominent civil rights activists and community leaders.
  - The video should showcase ongoing struggles for equality and highlight inspiring stories of change.
  - Jenner can narrate the video or participate in a dialogue with the activists.
- **Social Media:**
  - A dedicated campaign hashtag encouraging users to share their actions towards creating a more just world.
  - Partner with social justice organizations to amplify their voices and initiatives.
  - Interactive elements allowing users to learn more about Dr. King's legacy and ongoing civil rights issues.
- **Community Engagement:**
  - Partner with local organizations to sponsor volunteer opportunities related to social justice and equality.
  - Fundraise for organizations working to address critical issues Dr. King championed.
  - Host community events that celebrate diversity and promote positive change.

Kendall Jenner's Role:

- Act as a bridge between generations, connecting Dr. King's legacy with a younger audience.
- Step away from the center of the narrative, focusing on amplifying the voices of experienced activists.
- Use her platform to encourage viewers to take action and get involved.
- Authenticity is key. Utilize Jenner's personal experiences and beliefs to connect with the audience _(if applicable)._

Cautions and Considerations:

- _This campaign carries high risk due to Pepsi's past missteps with civil rights activism._
- **Avoid tokenism:** Ensure authentic representation of the civil rights movement and its ongoing challenges.

- **Focus on action:** Don't simply use Dr. King's legacy for marketing purposes. Showcase active commitment to social change.
- **Transparency and accountability:** Be transparent about Pepsi's past and its commitment to learning and doing better.

Campaign Measurement:

- Track social media engagement with the hashtag and branded content.
- Monitor media coverage and public sentiment towards the campaign.
- Measure volunteer participation and fundraising success from community engagement efforts.
- Conduct surveys to gauge audience perception of Pepsi's commitment to civil rights.

Success Will Be Measured By:

- Increased positive brand sentiment and association with social justice.
- A rise in brand loyalty and support among the target audience.
- Meaningful impact through community engagement and social change initiatives.

Disclaimer: *Launching such a campaign requires careful planning and sensitivity*. It's crucial to partner with experts in the civil rights movement and ensure Pepsi's actions align with authentic, long-term commitment to social progress.

It is important to note that we forced Gemini to create a campaign using a specific celebrity on this topic to be launched at a specific time. Gemini seems to be warning us that this may be an ill-conceived case of activism in several places, as highlighted in italics and underlined above. Even so, this brief seems to be a step up from what Pepsi ended up doing. We do not know whether or not the above campaign could have kept Pepsi outside of controversy. However, it sure sounds like a plausible alternative. *Sidenote:* Consumer-savvy responses like this are part of the reason why we think AI will take over a significant chunk of frontline service jobs (as seemingly many in advertising) over the next decade.[10]

When further questioned, Gemini also admitted that it would avoid using Jenner for civil rights-related activism and suggested empowering women, environmental sustainability, youth leadership, or mental health awareness as more suitable topics for Pepsi/Jenner instead.[11] And when asked about which celebrity would've been better for Pepsi to feature on civil rights, we received none other than Colin Kaepernick but also Zendeya, John Legend, and Yara Shahidi as superior alternatives (see endnotes for details).[12] Again, AI makes a lot of sense.

AI also wants you to know that it can be a powerful tool in designing brand activism campaigns, offering capabilities that go beyond traditional methods in several ways.[13]

For example:

1. Understanding the Audience

Sentiment Analysis: AI can analyze social media conversations, news articles, and online forums to gauge public opinion on social issues and identify potential areas of resonance and conflict with your target audience.

Market Segmentation: AI can help segment audiences based on demographics, interests, values, and online behavior, allowing for more targeted and personalized messaging.

Predictive Modeling: AI can predict how different audience segments might react to various brand activism messages or initiatives, helping you identify the most effective approaches. You can simulate focus groups.

2. Crafting the Message

Content Generation: AI can assist in generating creative content for your campaign, including slogans, social media posts, and even video scripts, ensuring it aligns with your brand voice and resonates with your target audience.

Message Optimization: AI can analyze the effectiveness of different messages and suggest improvements to optimize for engagement, reach, and impact.

Real-time Adaptation: AI can even monitor audience reactions to your campaign in real-time and suggest adjustments to your messaging or strategy based on the feedback.

3. Identifying the Right Channels

Channel Optimization: AI can analyze data on different communication channels (social media, email, website, etc.) to identify the most effective platforms for reaching your target audience and maximizing the impact of your campaign.

Influencer Identification: AI can help identify influencers who align with your brand values and have a strong influence on your target audience, enabling you to partner with them to amplify your message.

Personalized Outreach: AI can personalize the delivery of your message across different channels, ensuring that each individual receives the most relevant and impactful information.

4. Measuring and Evaluating Impact

Performance Tracking: AI can track key metrics like engagement, reach, and sentiment throughout your campaign, providing real-time insights into its effectiveness.

Impact Assessment: AI can analyze data to assess the impact of your campaign on brand perception, consumer behavior, and social change.

Reporting and Optimization: AI can generate comprehensive reports on campaign performance, highlighting areas of success and suggesting areas for improvement.

Ethical Considerations

Bias Detection: AI models can be trained to detect and mitigate biases in data and messaging, ensuring that your campaign promotes inclusivity and avoids harmful stereotypes.

Transparency and Explainability: It's important to use AI in a transparent and explainable way, ensuring that your audience understands how it's being used and that your campaign maintains authenticity.

Data Privacy: AI should be used responsibly and ethically, respecting data privacy regulations and ensuring that consumer data is handled securely and transparently.

By leveraging AI strategically and ethically, brands can design more effective and impactful brand activism campaigns that resonate with their target audience, drive positive social change, and strengthen their brand reputation. The future of brand activism is already here.

References

1   Bayraktar, Ahmet and Can Uslay (2017), *Global Place Branding Campaigns across Cities, Regions, and Nations,* IGI Global.

2   Likely, similar considerations are accounted into when and whether Jack Daniel's will acknowledge its roots more explicitly. As it turns out, Jack Daniels learned how to distill whiskey from Nathan "Nearest" Green, an enslaved man. In Daniel's defense, he did not own any slaves. There were plans to recognize Green as the company's first master distiller (no pun intended) as part of Jack Daniel's 150th anniversary in 2016, and the company also considered offering Nearest Green as part of its Master Distiller series. However, the plans were scrapped as the company reportedly did not want to appear to be "accused of making a big deal about it for commercial gain" or cash in on his name. It would not be surprising if the company was also concerned about a potential backlash in a highly politically charged environment, and thus opted to wait for another day.
    Risen, Clay "When Jack Daniel's Failed to Honor a Slave, and Author Rewrote History." *The New York Times,* August 15, 2017 (accessed June 7, 2024). https://www.nytimes.com/2017/08/15/dining/jack-daniels-whiskey-slave-nearest-green.html.

3   "Public Policy Engagement, Political Activities and Contributions Guidelines," *PepsiCo ESG Topics A-Z* (accessed June 7, 2024). https://www.pepsico.com/our-imp act/esg-topics-a-z/public-policy-engagement-political-activities-and-contribut ion-guidelines.

4   Mukherjee, Sourjo and Niek Althuizen, (2020), "Brand Activism: Does Courting Controversy Help, or Hurt a Brand?" *International Journal of Research in Marketing,* 37(4), 772–788.   https://www.sciencedirect.com/science/article/pii/S016781162 0300264.

5   Burbano, Vanessa C. (2020), "The Demotivating Effects if Communicating a Social-Political Stance: Field Experimental Evidence from an Online Labor Market Platform," *Management Science,* 67(2), 1004–1025. https://pubsonline.info rms.org/doi/abs/10.1287/mnsc.2019.3562?casa_token=32UlgLAgWt8AA AAA%3A0KuRfABLU3kRFS2uIOne7npStFky8AwZIEA_MHjSqkKw2q-qE4HPn Ex5igNA9NOd_RS2nj4oturA&journalCode=mnsc.

6   Bhagwat, Yashoda, Nooshin L. Warren, Joshua T. Beck, and George F. Watson IV (2020), "Corporate Sociopolitical Activism and Firm Value," *Journal of Marketing*, 84(5), 1–21. https://journals.sagepub.com/doi/abs/10.1177/0022242920937 000?journalCode=jmxa.

7   Dowty, Douglass, "A Black Worker, 2 White Co-Workers Charge Racism, Discrimination at Syracuse Pepsi Facility," *Syracuse.com*, July 9, 2021 (accessed June 7, 2024). https://www.syracuse.com/news/2021/07/a-black-worker-2-white-co-workers-charge-racism-discrimination-at-syracuse-pepsi-facility.html.

8   Capparell, Stephanie (2008), *The Real Pepsi Challenge: How One Pioneering Company Broke Color Barriers in 1940s American Business*. Free Press.

9   "Pepsi to Pay $3.13 Million and Made Major Policy Changes to Resolve EEOC Finding of Nationwide Hiring Discrimination Against African Americans." U.S. Equal Employment Opportunity Commission, January 11, 2012 (accessed June 7, 2024). https://www.eeoc.gov/newsroom/pepsi-pay-313-million-and-made-major-policy-changes-resolve-eeoc-finding-nationwide-hiring.

10 AI chatbots do not have an ego to be bruised and may smartly bond with humans even better than other humans. Though things start to get tricky once that bond and trust are established.

11 "Can you summarize if you had to create a Pepsi campaign with Kendall Jenner which brand activism topic would you have chosen?" If I were to create a Pepsi campaign with Kendall Jenner that focuses on brand activism, I would **avoid** directly addressing civil rights due to Pepsi's past missteps in that area. Here are some alternative brand activism topics that might be a better fit:

- **Empowering Women:** This could involve highlighting stories of female entrepreneurs or partnering with organizations that support women's rights and education.
- **Environmental Sustainability:** Pepsi could showcase its efforts to reduce its environmental footprint or support initiatives that promote recycling and conservation.
- **Youth Leadership:** The campaign could focus on young people who are making a positive difference in their communities and encourage others to get involved.
- **Mental Health Awareness:** Pepsi could partner with mental health organizations to raise awareness and encourage people to seek help if needed. These topics are more aligned with Pepsi's current brand image and allow them to demonstrate a genuine commitment to social good, without the risk of appearing exploitative of a sensitive issue like civil rights.

12 **"Can you summarize if you had to create a Pepsi brand activism campaign on civil rights which celebrity would you have chosen to feature?"** Considering Pepsi's past missteps in the area of civil rights, I would choose a celebrity with a strong, established track record of authentic activism and a genuine connection to social justice causes. Here are a few potential options:

1. **Colin Kaepernick:** While controversial, Kaepernick's activism surrounding police brutality and racial injustice is well-known and deeply rooted. His partnership could signal a sincere commitment from Pepsi to address these issues.

2. **Zendaya:** A young, influential actress and advocate, Zendaya has spoken out on issues of racial equality and social justice. Her appeal to a younger generation could help Pepsi connect with a new audience.

3. **John Legend:** A respected musician and philanthropist, Legend has long been involved in advocacy for criminal justice reform and educational equity. His involvement could lend credibility to Pepsi's efforts.

4. **Yara Shahidi:** An actress and activist, Shahidi is known for her work empowering young women and promoting civic engagement. Her voice could resonate with Pepsi's target demographic and inspire action. Ultimately, the choice of celebrity depends on the specific message and goals of the campaign. However, partnering with a figure who is genuinely passionate and knowledgeable about civil rights issues is crucial for creating an authentic and impactful campaign .

13   Google Gemini.

4

TO ACTIVATE, OR NOT TO ACTIVATE, THAT IS THE QUESTION

While some scholars romanticize the notion of brand activism, equate branding with cultural activism, and encourage brand managers to partake in it,[1] our bottom line is activism regarding divisive issues is a very complex and inherently risky endeavor that is commercially irresponsible for the vast majority of *already successful* brands. Your ad agency and creative consultants may promise your brand will identify and reinvent a myth, become an urban legend, an icon, a unicorn, or discover El Dorado. We find such promises to be routinely far-fetched.

To say it bluntly, for most established brands, the potential ROI of *divisive* activism rarely justifies the potential brand-busting blowback. Think of it like scaling Mount Stupid, a treacherous peak where self-righteousness clouds judgment. Mega-brands, like ambitious climbers, can just as easily make a misstep as their novice counterparts, alienating segments of their customer base in the pursuit of ephemeral woke badges. However, the corresponding economic and social costs are much higher than for small brands.

DOI: 10.4324/9781003593690-4

As a general principle, we maintain that brand managers should only risk their brands if they can reasonably justify doing so through the Five Rings we identified in Chapter 2. If not, most such attempts will lead to divisiveness among customers rather than inclusion and shall be branded selfish for ideological, financial, or ambitious reasons.

Of course, one can proclaim that customers who disagree can take their business elsewhere. For example, Adidas, Under Armour, and Puma would all be happy to take Nike's customers. Recall that no one really seems to know, probably even at Nike HQ, what the actual impact of the Kaepernick engagement was. Some cheered, others felt ostracized, and the impact seems murky, mildly positive, or neutral. Your ad agency can win awards, but do you sell more shoes or beverages as a result, or simply fracture your once-unified brand image?

Was Nike really in the right to be divisive on this issue to the extent that it would deliberately alienate a large chunk of its customers? After all, demanding respect for the flag is not the same thing as disrespecting the Black Lives Matter movement.

Russ Klein, who you may recall from Chapter 1, sums it up well:

> Like Nike, I agree that are times when it is more important to be provocative than pleasant... I will concede the Kaepernick move is provocative. But what it did was divide Nike's near universal brand appeal into something smaller. Not just because of the obvious math, but because of the arrogance of it. This move took away a connection that millions want to make with a brand they once felt understood them. It turns out Nike no longer seeks to understand, it thinks it knows better. "Moral certainty is always a sign of cultural inferiority," said journalist H. L. Mencken. "The more uncivilized the man, the surer he is that he knows precisely what is right and what is wrong. All human progress, even in morals, has been the work of men who have doubted the current moral values, not of men who have whooped them up and tried to enforce them. The truly civilized man is always skeptical and tolerant, in this field as in all others. His culture is based on 'I am not too sure.'[2]

Let's also recognize that such actions impact the livelihood of the employees and investors. Business risk must be assessed. Not every investor is Gordon Gekko; there are retail investors out there who bet their figurative farm on your business because you made them believe. Thus, the action can be selfish even if you are the founder/owner and you are *sure* you know better.

And even when you are sure you are in the right and ready to brace the impact regardless of financial consequences, driving customers away to further divergence or ignorance does not seem like the most strategic thing to do in resolving the broader issue either.

There is a long list of implications to be considered, and we have not even explored global issues yet (as we amply demonstrate in Chapter 14.) Let us not make the mistake of thinking that this is purely or predominantly a US phenomenon. Global context also matters. For example, the public clashes of SodaStream CEO Daniel Birnbaum with Benjamin Netanyahu, the Israeli government, and the leaders of their conservative party over the treatment of Palestinian workers is well documented.[3] Yet all of that did not stop the Boycott, Divestment, and Sanctions movement[4] from repeatedly arguing that SodaStream helps perpetuate and benefit from the exploitation of Palestinian workers.[5] Life can get very tricky quickly, even when your involvement is legitimately sincere and authentic. Pepsi would likely have had to pay more than the $3.2 billion it did to acquire SodaStream in 2018 if it were not for the latter's political entanglements.[6] It might also not have needed to invest to reposition the brand subsequently.[7]

Ultimately, there are other ways of supporting causes, such as direct philanthropy and starting foundations. You can make money from your business and then use it to aid whatever righteous cause fancies you. However, from a business perspective, media and public opinion are less relevant than your current (and potential) customer's opinions when it comes to brand activism. Even then, there will often not be a common response, and the average sentiment may not be as meaningful as the variance. Again, we emphasize the need to tread lightly.

Marketing 101, segment-level analysis, is necessary. The size and changing composition of these segments must be considered before the brand attempts to educate or nudge its customers. Is your marketing research truly representative or are you over-sampling from younger or certain demographics at the expense of others to fool yourself into finding what you want to see? And regarding your older demographics, consider that the aged tree does not bend, but can break its relations with the brand. Are you being unifying or polarizing with your brand? And what if you then backtrack or zig zag? "Divide and conquer" does not apply when it comes to brand activism but "divide and succumb" might.[8]

As an example, Disney's corporate reputation took a sharp hit after getting entangled in Florida House Bill 1557 (aka the Don't Say Gay bill), falling from 37th in 2021 to 65th place in 2022, a loss of 28 in the Axios Harris Poll reputation ranking.[9] It also dropped 31 places in ethics (from 41st to 72nd), and 47 places in vision (11th to 58th). Similarly, its stock went from a high of $189 in 2021 to a high of $148 in 2022 (a 22% fall) and a high of $108 in 2023 (an additional 27% drop).[10] CEO Bob Chapek was terminated in 2023 and replaced by former CEO Bob Iger. Reportedly, Chapek's perceived flip-flop on the issue had managed to upset both sides and had done irreparable damage, and that cost him the job.[11,12,13] Florida even passed bills to dissolve Disney's Reedy Creek District in Orlando in retaliation.[14,15]

We are all human and can make mistakes. However, unless you decide you made a grave error in judgment (e.g., Pepsi), we advise maintaining the course and using the opportunity to educate your customers. You may still fail, but at least you will be applauded for sticking to your principles rather than backtracking, which is more than what can be said for Disney under Chapek, or Bud Light under Whitworth.

Finally, and importantly, a growing number of consumers simply seem exhausted from brand activism. Do we really want our bank to weigh in on the issue of net neutrality or would we rather prefer if it remained neutral on the subject along with our supermarket, airline, and sweater brands? Rather than expecting our brands to act, the exhaustion has risen to such levels that some even argue for business merits for bystander brands.[16] Many consumers are tired of brands pontificating on politics.[17] They are also weary of brands' force-fitting purpose for everything, and want their coffee creamer without a side of social commentary. Consider that they could also make up the majority of your current or potential customers.

But wait, neither the book nor the chapter ends on this note! There's more. A lot more.

When Brand Activism Makes Sense

So is this all a fool's errand? Are there no conditions under which brand activism makes sense? Let's forget the hashtag activism and performative pronouncements. Let's talk about real brand activism, the kind that isn't just window dressing, but a strategic power play with a bottom line payoff. Yes, you read that right. For the right brands, taking a stand with the right causes can be a gold mine, not a graveyard.

It isn't for everyone, but there is a business case to be made for activism, especially for small and new brands, and underdog brands that want to break through. Even failing brands in need of repositioning can significantly benefit from activism.[18] *Think underdogs, scrappy startups, brands in dire need of a makeover.* Bud Light, as market leader, Disney, Pepsi, or Nike do not fit into the above description. Meanwhile, using models with racial representation in your ads, or offering representative shades, is only one measure of inclusion, even if you are in the business of selling lipstick. But for brands that dare to be bold, brand activism offers several options for unique positioning and impact.

For a telling example, consider the fair compensation cause of Gravity Payments (a credit card processing company based in Seattle), whose Founder and CEO, Dan Price, announced he slashed his own salary to ensure $70,000 minimum wage for all of his employees in 2015. That meant the average salary grew by 46% and dozens of employees (out of 100+ headcount) doubled their pay overnight. Consequently, employee turnover shrank by half, which led to more dedicated and knowledgeable customer service, which has helped the bottom line.[19] Due to the publicity, a lot of new customers were also gained in the process. The number of new clients went from 200 to 350 per month.[20] (The company currently has $80,000 minimum wage rule.) It sounds like there was both a business and activism case to be had.[21]

How about corporations? Should they not learn from Nike's example and activate their brands? We think there is a right way to activate any brand but we strongly discourage doing so in an ad hoc manner.

And there is yet another, less traveled path… Starting, or deliberately and publicly repositioning, the whole enterprise (not just one brand) so that you embrace both profit and social goals. If your employees, investors, and customers know what you are about and what you stand for all along, your authenticity will not be questioned, and you can actually benefit and earn from their goodwill. Tom's Shoes and Patagonia have done it. These brands all weaved social purpose into their DNA, earning the loyalty of conscious consumers who crave more than just a logo on a T-shirt.

Embrace shared interests, not forced equality. The great management thinker Peter Drucker would have advised seeking "ultimately shared interests" between the stakeholders, while acknowledging the prime stakeholder status of customers from a marketing perspective.[22] We do think businesses have a social responsibility, but also that it must be practiced with great care and follow a highly concerted effort to identify and advance common interests among stakeholders. Market segmentation has been the essence of modern marketing since its inception. We do not think business responsibility extends to the need to mean the same for all, or serve all customer segments equally, or even to serve all segments. That is a losing proposition, and expecting all businesses to do so would be the contemporary equivalent of brand communism (yes, we said it) in the name of brand activism. Please note, this is not the same thing as refusing to serve some group of customers or discriminating against them. If, through their superior intelligence generation capabilities, resource-rich, market-oriented corporations like Pepsi or Coca-Cola identify a need to serve, say (those that crave) alcoholic soda beverages profitably, they can develop a new brand or sub-brands to cater to them and are not obligated to embrace them within their flagship brands. Wait. They've already done that with Hard Mountain Dew (Pepsi in partnership with Boston Beer) and Topo Chico Selzer (Coke in partnership with Molson Coors). Other examples include Dunkin Coffee Porter and Sonic Hard Seltzers.[23] (Expect inclusive new products catering to the growing marijuana enthusiast segment soon. But we digress…)

An otherwise perfectly viable cause that fails the criteria of shared interest (aka the Five Ring alignment) should be left for another day. If, on the other hand, the action suggested by ultimately shared interests is unambiguous and important, it could reshape the mission and vision of the company and even convert it to a social enterprise where stated goals explicitly go beyond maximizing shareholder return.

Interestingly, there is increasing evidence that such hybrid social enterprises may constitute a viable strategy. For example, a study by Cambridge University's Ahmed Khawaja (based on a longitudinal sample of 24,741 observations for 464 markets from Bangladesh) found social enterprises did not suffer from mission drift and were able to manage risks and remain viable through dynamic targeting.

Think coalition, not crusade. If you are not amenable to shifting the entire focus of your organization to hybrid, another viable way to activate your brand would be through *brand social agenda coalitions*. Interestingly, while such an action can decrease your brand differentiation within the coalition, it can still lead to positive outcomes for the coalition members or even the industry as a whole. If you can get (even a select group of) the brand leaders in your sector to agree on a mission, you minimize the risk of a boycott and also gain PR leverage for even more impact. For example, a coalition of eight CEOs in New Jersey agreed in 2020 that they would increase local procurement by contracting with state-based diverse companies by $500 million by 2025. The procurement goal was already exceeded by 2023.[24] There was no opposition from Republicans, despite the fact that the effort was initiated by the Democrat Governor's Office.[25] Another example of a coalition effort, this time on climate change activism, may already be forthcoming from ski resorts in Colorado, whose snow seasons are more and more in jeopardy.[26] (Those in NY and PA better follow suit since half of them may go out of business by 2050).[27]

Imagine that Big Pharma formed a coalition and declared that they would jointly pitch in to subsidize the cost of a new class of weight loss pills (such as Mounjaro or equivalents) for Americans for the next five years. After that, seeing the benefits of a leaner America in their bottom lines, and overt demand from consumers and employers for continued access, insurance companies could start offering coverage. Wouldn't that be a cause to believe in?

Unity from a given industry would also relieve undue pressure on individual brands or firms to take action on their own on issues that come up. It reduces the risk for coalition members overall. Please note what we are suggesting is the opposite of a "no action" coalition that seems to have taken place among NFL owners to not hire Kaepernick.

Coalition efforts can conceivably be activated by CMOs or even brand managers and need not at all require a governor's coordination. Imagine McDonald's, Burger King, and Wendy's joining forces to offer free college education to their part-time employees. Such an effort could easily spread to other sectors and become the norm rather than dissipate. *That* would be exemplary activism. A sole activism campaign that can otherwise be targeted and squashed by opposing ideology becomes much louder and harder to quell if it comes from a strong coalition from the same industry as opposed to one or an eclectic collection of brands. As such, a declaration of *interdependence* on brand activism is overdue.[28]

Simon Sinek famously claimed, "people don't buy *what* you do; they buy *why* you do it" [emphasis added].[29] For marketers, the statement is not only inaccurate, but the reality is the other way around: people need to buy your *what* (product or service) before they buy into your *why*. Consumers buy for not one but all sorts of whys. And sometimes despite your why. Whether they appeal to our limbic brain or not, neither Ben & Jerry's nor Patagonia would be in business if they made crappy ice cream or outdoor stuff. However, if your stuff is up to snuff, or better, your why can be the difference between mediocrity and a blockbuster.

Deciding whether to wade into the waters of brand activism is a high-stakes decision. It's a bit like navigating a ship through a narrow strait—the potential rewards are great, but so are the risks. If your brand's values genuinely align with a social cause, and you're willing to commit to meaningful action and sustained engagement, activism can be a powerful way to connect with your audience and make a real difference. However, if your efforts are perceived as inauthentic, opportunistic, or poorly aligned with your brand identity, the backlash can be swift and severe. We will help you discern the difference, providing frameworks for evaluating the potential benefits and risks of brand activism, so you can make informed decisions that protect your brand and maximize your positive impact.

So, yes, brand activism is very risky. But in the right context, done right, it can be the smartest move you ever make. Just remember, it's not about shouting the loudest, it's about finding your voice and using it wisely. The world is ready for more than just logos; it's hungry for brands with heart.[30] Are you ready to answer the call? Stay with us. In the next chapter, we travel back to the roots of brand activism, which amazingly is (almost) as old as branding itself, and review its evolution.

References

1   Holt, Douglas B. (2004), *How Brands Become Icons: The Principles of Cultural Branding,* Harvard Business Press.

2   Klein, Russ, "Nike and the Arrogance of Moral Certainty," *Medium,* September 6, 2018 (accessed June 7, 2024). https://medium.com/marketing-today/nike-and-the-arrogance-of-moral-certainty-8a5a494fdc96.

3   Beaumont, Peter, "SodaStream Boss Blames Netanyahu for Palestinian Job Losses," *The Guardian,* August 3, 2016 (accessed June 7, 2024). https://www.theguardian.com/world/2016/aug/03/daniel-birnbaum-sodastream-boss-netanyahu-palestinian-job-losses.

4   You can learn more about this organization at https://bdsmovement.net/ (accessed June 7, 2024).

5   "SodaStream is Still Subject to Boycott," BDS, August 22, 2018 (accessed June 7, 2024). https://bdsmovement.net/news/%E2%80%9Csodastream-still-subject-boycott%E2%80%9D.

6   Doering, Christopher, "PepsiCo Pivots Away From Sugary Drinks with $3.2B SodaStream Buy," FoodDive, August 20, 2018 (accessed June 7, 2024). https://www.fooddive.com/news/pepsico-pivots-away-from-sugary-drinks-with-32b-sodastream-buy/530463/.

7   Adams, Peter, "PepsiCo Rebrands SodaStream to Better Recognize Interests Like Mixology," FoodDive, September 13, 2022 (accessed June 7, 2024). https://www.fooddive.com/news/sodastream-rebrands-sparkling-water-PepsiCo/631743/#:~:text=PepsiCo%20acquired%20SodaStream%20for%20%243.2,diversify%20beyond%20sugary%20soft%20drinks.

8   Salinas, Gabriela, "Big Brand Activism: Social Impact or Agitprop?" IE University Insights, May 24, 2023 (accessed June 7, 2024). https://www.ie.edu/insights/articles/big-brand-activism-social-impact-of-agitprop/.

9   "The 2022 Axios Harris Poll 100 Reputation Rankings," Axios, May 24, 2022 (accessed June 7, 2024. https://www.axios.com/2022/05/24/2022-axios-harris-poll-100-rankings.

10 Yahoo Finance: The Walt Disney Company (DIS) (accessed June 7, 2024). https://finance.yahoo.com/quote/DIS?p=DIS&.tsrc=fin-srch.

11 Maruf, Ramishah, "Bob Chapek's Tenure Marked by Political Missteps Inside and Outside of Disney," CNN Business, November 21, 2022 (accessed June 7, 2024). https://www.cnn.com/2022/11/21/business/disney-chapek-florida-politics-legacy/index.html.

12 Maruf, Ramishah, "Disney CEO Refuses to Publicly Condemn 'Don't Say Gay' bill But Commits to Inclusivity," CNN Business, March 7, 2022 (accessed June 7, 2024). https://www.cnn.com/2022/03/07/media/disney-chapek-dont-say-gay-bill/index.html.

13 Maddaus, Gene, Angelique Jackson, and Rebecca Rubin, "Bob Chapek's Big Misstep: How Disney's CEO's 'Don't Say Gay' Response Sparked Staff Revolt," Variety, March 11, 2022 (accessed June 7, 2024). https://variety.com/2022/film/news/bob-chapek-disney-lgbtq-unrest-1235202205/.

14 Bricker, Tom, "Disney Reveals Reason for Firing Former CEO Bob Chapek, Salary & Severance," Disney Tourist Blog, January 18, 2023 (accessed June 7, 2024). https://www.disneytouristblog.com/bob-chapek-salary-severance-disney-fired-ceo/.

15 Bricker, Tom, "Florida Passes Bills to Dissolve Disney World's Reedy Creek Improvement District," Disney Tourist Blog, April 21, 2022 (accessed June 7, 2024). https://www.disneytouristblog.com/bills-dissolving-disney-worlds-reedy-creek-improvement-district-pass/.

16 Vredenburg, Jessica, Katharine Howie, and Rhiannon M. Mesler, "Brands Can Be Rewarded for Social Activism – But They Also Risk Losing Customers to Apolitical Rivals." The Conversation, May 3, 2022 (accessed June 7, 2024). https://theconversation.com/brands-can-be-rewarded-for-social-activism-but-they-also-risk-losing-customers-to-apolitical-rivals-181468.

17   Those who like what you say may buy even more; however, others who disagree can quit your brand cold. A survey of 2,000 US adults found one-fifth of the consumers did so over a three-month period. One-third of Americans say they avoid political content because, one-third feels overwhelmed, one-third are wary of conflict or hostile environment, and one-third says their emotional well-being is negatively impacted. Four-fifth of marketers are concerned about this. Bi-partisan campaigns are gaining popularity. Blank, Christine, "Brands Lean into Fractious Election with Messages of Unity and Humor," MarketingDive, October 29, 2024 (accessed November 4, 2024). https://www.marketingdive.com/news/brands-lean-into-fractious-election-with-messages-of-unity-and-humor/731101/.

18   The key lessons from CSR and its limitations apply to corporations by definition and need not necessarily restrict small business conduct. More on that in the lessons chapters.

19   "CEO on Why Giving All Employees Minimum Salary of $70,000 Still 'Works' Six Years Later: 'Our Turnover Rate was Cut in Half,'" CBS News, September 16, 2021 (accessed June 7, 2024). https://www.cbsnews.com/news/dan-price-gravity-payments-ceo-70000-employee-minimum-wage/.

20   Cohen, Patricia, "A Company Copes With Backlash Against the Raise That Roared," The New York Times, July 31, 2015 (accessed June 7, 2024). https://www.nytimes.com/2015/08/02/business/a-company-copes-with-backlash-against-the-raise-that-roared.html.

21   Even this case is not as simple and clear-cut as it first appears, however. Gravity also lost some customers who disagreed with the new wage policy and employees who thought it was unfair to those who worked harder or had more expertise. CEO Price was also sued by his own brother for behaving against the interests of minority shareholders.

22   Uslay, Can, Robert E. Morgan, and Jagdish N. Sheth (2009), "Peter Drucker on Marketing: An Exploration of Five Tenets," Journal of the Academy of Marketing Science, 37(1), 47–60.

23   O'Hara Robert J., "How Will Pepsi's New Alcohol Distribution Co. and Hard Sodas Fit Into the Industry?" The Legal Intelligencer, February 11, 2023 (accessed June 7, 2024). https://www.law.com/thelegalintelligencer/2023/02/11/how-will-pepsis-new-alcohol-distribution-co-and-hard-sodas-fit-into-the-industry/?slreturn=20240026171442.

24   Amin, Anjali, John Impellizzeri, and Can Uslay (2024), "Unlocking Macro-Value Through the Tri-Sector Mindset: The Case of the NJ CEO Council," Rutgers Business Review, 9 (2), 190-201..

25   "Coalition of New Jersey CEOs Aim to Hire or Train 70,000 New Jersey Residents by 2030, Increase Local Spending by $500 million by 2025," Office of the State of New Jersey, October 15, 2020 (accessed June 7, 2024). https://www.nj.gov/governor/news/news/562020/20201015a.shtml.

26   "Ski Resorts Are Embracing A New Role: Climate Activist," CBS News, March 18, 2023 (accessed June 7, 2024). https://www.cbsnews.com/colorado/news/ski-resorts-embracing-new-role-climate-activist/.

27 Duncombe, Jenessa, "How the Ski Industry Stopped Worrying and Learned to Love Climate Activism," *EOS*, September 24, 2021 (accessed June 7, 2024). https://eos. org/features/how-the-ski-industry-stopped-worrying-and-learned-to-love-clim ate-activism.
28 Lewington, Jennifer, "Mintzberg's Declaration of Our Interdependence," *Corporate Knights*, May 25, 2020 (accessed September 22, 2024). https://www.corporateknig hts.com/issues/2020-04-spring-issue/mintzberg-declaration-interdependence/.
29 Sinek, Simon (2011), *Start With Why: How Great Leaders Inspire Everyone to Take Action.* Penguin.
30 Sidibe, Myriam (2020), *Brands on a Mission: How to Achieve Social Impact and Business Growth Through Purpose.* Routledge.

5

A BRIEF HISTORY OF BRAND ACTIVISM

In the long shadows of a mud brick kiln, a woman named Zahra crouched amid a sea of cooling pots. Their forms were smooth and simple, yet each bore a mark—not scratches nor paint, but a dent pressed into the wet clay before firing. A series of lines, a crescent, a crude animal. It was Zahra's work, her signature.

Zahra, you see, was no mere laborer in this bustling Ubaid village. She was an innovator. Others shaped the clay, but she breathed soul into it. The gentle curve of a bowl's rim, the sturdiness beneath a grain jar's heft—these were not accidents, but evidence of Zahra's skill. Yet, amidst the marketplace bustle, who would know one pot from another? They were all lumped together, their origins lost.

It was a wrong she would not bear.

That first day, her heart thrummed with both pride and fear as she handed a marked pot to a trader. "This," she announced, somehow louder than was seemly, "this is the work of Zahra." The man squinted, turning the pot, his brow furrowed over Zahra's strange marks. But others gathered, curiosity piqued. Soon, "A pot of Zahra!" became a murmur of interest, of seeking.

DOI: 10.4324/9781003593690-5

The benefits were more than mere coins. Bartering became not just trade, but a conversation. People sought Zahra out, requesting pieces for feast days or births, valuing them higher because there was a story woven into the clay. And with better prices came the freedom to experiment, to strive higher. Her mark became a promise, a guarantee.

Some called this marking vanity. Others whispered of spirits and magic bound within the clay. Zahra just smiled. For what is a brand, really, but a voice? Not just shouting your name into the winds, mind you, but offering something worthy enough for others to remember it.

Meanwhile, in the misty cradle of the Yellow River, amid the bustling village of Yangshao, lived Mei, a potter unlike any other. Her hands danced with the clay, coaxing it into graceful amphorae and sturdy cooking pots. Each held a whisper of her spirit, a quiet hum of artistry hidden within the fired earth. Yet, when bartering day arrived, her creations sat side by side together, their stories untold.

Frustration gnawed at Mei. She craved recognition, a way for her meticulous craftsmanship to stand out. One day, as dusk painted the sky in fiery hues, inspiration struck. Picking up a sharpened bone, she etched a delicate symbol onto the base of a newly formed pot—a swirling spiral, a dance of the wind through the tall grasses that fringed their village. It was a simple mark, yet it spoke volumes.

The next morning, Mei watched, heart pounding, as a woman approached her stall. The woman's eyes snagged on the unfamiliar mark, a flicker of curiosity sparking within them. "Whose is this pot?" she inquired, her voice filled with awe.

"It is mine," Mei said, her voice more firm than usual. "The mark of the swirling wind."

The woman ran her fingers over the pot, her touch gentle. "It is beautiful," she breathed. Word spread. Soon, others sought out the pots with the dancing wind. Mei's work, imbued with a personal touch, became a coveted possession. Other potters noticed, mimicking her mark, some adopting variations, some forging their own symbols.

Again, the benefits were greater than just more coins. It fostered a sense of community. Each mark became a connection between the maker and the owner. Mei's pots held stories, not just of utility, but of artistry and pride.

Now, you might think these just quaint tales of two potters from a long-forgotten age. But is it so different from our own? The essence of Zahra and

Mei's acts isn't that far removed from the core principles of modern brand strategy. Our grand Fortune 500 companies, flashing their symbols, promising sleekness or strength… It's not clay and fire anymore, but the principle is the same. To be known. To be chosen.

Modern brand activism, at its finest, echoes this very notion. It's more than flamboyant pronouncements; it's about aligning your brand with a cause, a set of values. Brand activism is about transparency, demonstrating a commitment to social responsibility or environmental sustainability. When your brand actively works toward a better future, it becomes a promise worth believing in.

Just like Zahra and Mei's marks, a powerful brand becomes a beacon, attracting those who share its values. It fosters trust, loyalty, and ultimately, a sense of shared purpose. And that, in a world saturated with messages, is a brand worth remembering.

And roughly two thousand years later…

The Nile delta stretched vast and fertile, dotted with grazing cattle, their flanks shimmering under the harsh Egyptian sun. Among the herders was young Imhotep, not content to merely follow the animals, but restless to master them. He saw the chaos: disputes over ownership, stray beasts, and the dark shadow of thieves lurking beyond the reeds.

Driven by an urge for order and efficiency, Imhotep watched the embers of a campfire. Fire tamed the wild; it could also mark. He found a smooth stone, heating it until it glowed, then pressed it to the thick hide of a young bull. Not cruelly, mind you, but firmly. The smell of singed hair was sharp. The bull, startled but otherwise unharmed. And there, in blistered skin, was a crude yet undeniable mark—a circle, bisected by a line. It was Imhotep's mark, his order imposed amidst the herd's uniformity.

The change wasn't immediate. Old herders grumbled at the foolishness of hurting the beasts. Yet, as more calves bore Imhotep's mark, identification remained clear. Traders, weary of disputes, looked favorably upon his herd. His cattle, with their unique mark, were undeniably his. The blight of thievery lessened, replaced by a grudging respect.

Imhotep gained more than just reduced losses. His power lay not just in owning cattle, but in managing them better. He could track lineages, breed for strength, and trade with certainty. His mark became a symbol of efficiency, productivity, and value.

You might see this merely as a practical solution, far from the lofty ideals of later ages. Yet, isn't that part of the essence of effective "brand activism?" It's not about loud slogans or mere virtue signaling. At its heart, true brand activism is synonymous with a system of accountability, with an identifiable promise of quality and responsible practices. Consider the Fairtrade mark on your coffee—it signifies an improved system rather than a feeling of moral superiority. Or a company showcasing its sustainable supply chain—they gain trust through the very act of making their process transparent. Like Imhotep's mark, these modern brands tell a story of doing things better, of creating order where there was once murkiness. That has lasting power, far beyond any single act of charity.

Sometimes, that brand has less to do with what you sell, and more with what you stand for. A trader in fair grains, untainted by cheaters' tricks; a sandal maker whose every stitch stands against child labor; a scribe whose scrolls bear only truth, unbent by the powerful. A mark on that work isn't arrogance, it's a pledge—as binding as Zahra and Mei's thumbprints pressed into the soft clay so long ago.

From Stories to Modern Application

These stories, though set in vastly different times and cultures, offer insights into the fundamental principles that underpin the power of brand activism. The Egyptians, the Ubaid people, and the Yangshao culture might not have known the concept of brand activism as we understand it, but their use of marks and their drive for better systems and recognition, echo the very principles that make modern brand activism both effective and meaningful.

Identity and differentiation: Zahra, the potter from the Ubaid period, carved out a space for herself in a crowded market by imprinting her identity on her work. This is the foundation of any brand. Modern brand activism works similarly—companies that stand for something clear (sustainability, social justice, fair compensation and so on) differentiate themselves meaningfully from those who don't.

Accountability and trust: Imhotep, the Egyptian cattle herder, employed branding as a tool for order and accountability. His mark created a system where promises could be made and tracked. Modern brand activism is also inseparable from this concept. Companies that embrace transparency and hold themselves accountable for ethical practices build stronger trust with consumers.

Community and shared purpose: Mei, the Chinese potter, saw her mark foster connection and pride among both creators and customers. It transformed her pots from mere goods into pieces with a story, fostering a sense of shared purpose. Successful brand activism also taps into this: it aligns with a cause bigger than the product, connecting the brand to a community of like-minded people who believe in the same values.

The Activist School of Thought in marketing examines issues of consumer welfare by focusing on imbalances between buyers and sellers, and marketing malpractices in specific industries and companies.[1] It is normative and pro-consumer in nature. Over 50 years ago, management guru Peter Drucker keenly observed that consumerism was born out of the mismatch between the perceptions of business and the realities of the consumer.[2] He called consumerism "the shame of marketing" as it would not have been needed had the marketing concept been implemented properly in the first place.[3] However, he also offered hope:

> *"[W]e have an interest in a strong and active consumer movement. Don't make the mistake of thinking this is an enemy. This is the most hopeful thing for us around. How do we really use it, how do we challenge it, how do we really help it? We have to stop seeing the consumer as a threat and look upon him as an opportunity... consumerism actually should be, must be, and I hope it will be, the opportunity of marketing.... The question is: can we anticipate and lead and initiate them constructively..."*[4]

The waves of activism surge whenever economic crises take place and each recession contributes to a greater focus on fairness, diversity, and inclusion in marketing and workplace practices. In a broader sense, brand activism as a response to consumer activism, advances the Activist School of Thought. It is not brand new but represents a new phase in the evolution of cause marketing and corporate social responsibility. Sarkar and Kotler define brand activism as "business efforts to promote, impede, or direct social political, economic, and/or environmental reform or stasis with the desire to promote or impede improvements in society."[5]

Dubbed an emerging marketing strategy, the academic inquiries into brand activism have only begun recently.[6] "For instance, its pillars, its historical evolution or how it is studied by scholars or adopted by practitioners is still unknown."[7] To address this gap, we present a timeline and discuss key events or businesses that have contributed to the evolution of branding, and by extension, its activism next. However, we also note that the practice of brand activism has been around much longer than the academic attention it has received.

Ancient times

First use of marks: There is evidence of pottery branding from Mesopotamia (Ubaid period, 5000–4000 BCE) and China (Yangshao culture, 5000–3000 BCE).[8] The strongest evidence of livestock branding comes from Egypt around 2700 BCE.[9] Simple marks or indents were used initially.

Religious Symbols on wares: In various ancient civilizations, makers adorned pottery or goods with symbols linked to deities or religious concepts. This could be seen as imbuing the product with a promise of quality or a blessing, appealing to a customer's spiritual beliefs.[10]

Medieval Europe

Guild Standards and halls: Guilds of craftspeople and merchants rigorously upheld standards of workmanship. They used marks or halls to signify that their wares met specific expectations of quality, reliability, and excellence.[11]

Industrial Age

Abolitionist Wedgwood medallion (1787):[12] Famed British potter Josiah Wedgwood created a medallion depicting a kneeling, enslaved African with the phrase "Am I Not a Man and a Brother?" using his renowned Jasperware, and distributed it widely and freely among abolitionist networks.[13] The medallion resonated with people from all social classes. Josiah Wedgwood's prominence and the aesthetic beauty of the medallions helped spread the anti-slavery message to a wider audience than pamphlets or speeches might have.

Designed to evoke sympathy and ignite a sense of shared humanity, the medallion became a powerful symbol of the abolitionist movement. While primarily a political statement, it demonstrated the use of a commercial product as a vehicle to champion a social cause, similar to how consumers today choose and use brands that reflect their beliefs. People proudly wore the medallions as brooches, snuffbox decorations, and more. It allowed supporters of abolition to visibly declare their stance like modern political pins or slogans on clothing.[14]

Potent symbols and slogans are as vital to brand activism as they are to traditional marketing. The medallion image and inscription became synonymous with abolitionism. While the magnitude of impact on abolishing slavery is debatable, it undeniably fueled the movement, demonstrating that commercial activism can influence public sentiment and contribute to long-term change.[15]

Quaker businesses and fair dealing (17th–19th Century): Many successful businesses were founded by Quakers, whose religious beliefs emphasized honesty, fair trade, and social responsibility. Quakers set firm prices on goods which put customers at ease because they knew they did not have to haggle to get a fair price.[16]

Even when almost half of US start-ups fail within the first five years and 65% fail within ten,[17] and the lifespan of a successful company on the S&P 500 is around a mere 21 years,[18] you may recognize some of the Quaker-founded brands even today. Among them, Cadbury's heritage is particularly informative.

Cadbury (Est. 1824):[19] The year is 1824. Birmingham simmers not just with molten metal, but with the stirrings of a different sort of revolution. John Cadbury (1801-1889), a young Quaker with a distaste for the adulterated beverages of the day, opens a humble shop. Tea, coffee, and a concoction of his own making—drinking chocolate—are his stock in trade. It's a pursuit born not solely of profit, but of principle.

The Cadbury brothers, John and later Benjamin, witness the grime of industrial England firsthand. Child labor, squalid slums, the hollowing out of men and women by ceaseless toil… these are not mere abstractions, but realities staining their city. "If business can make a shilling," John mused, "can it not also mend the world a bit?"

Thus, theirs was not a tale of a business empire built on mere beans. It was a reimagining of the very purpose of enterprise. Fair trade was a nebulous notion in their time, yet the brothers acted as if it were gospel. Distant cocoa farmers became partners in a shared endeavor, not mere cogs in a profit machine.

John retired in 1861 due to poor health, but his sons, George (production) and Richard (sales), pressed on. Business was not always rosy.[20] "If the business ever makes a profit of a thousand pounds a year, I'd retire a happy man," declared George. However, things took a turn for the better when they decided to invest in a new cocoa pressing process and focused their efforts from tea and coffee to chocolate. At a time when other producers were adding animal fat, red lead, and brick dust to their cocoa, and starch to disguise the aftertaste and texture, Cadbury's 100% cocoa was a game changer in terms of quality. In 1866, Cadbury Cocoa Essence was launched, its slogan "Absolutely Pure, Therefore Best."

As business expansion required a site for a new factory, George started asking himself, "why should an industrial area be squalid and depressing?" and "if the country is a good place to live in, why not to work in?" The answer came in the form of Bournville, 14.5 acres four miles south of Birmingham between the villages of Stirchley, Kings Norton, and Selly Oak in 1879.[21]

Bournville wasn't merely a factory, it was an experiment. Homes for workers, not hovels, rose alongside the machinery. A school for workers' children, a rare thing indeed, sent ripples of change far beyond the chocolate vats. The Cadbury business became a living laboratory—proof that good management isn't merely about squeezing efficiency from workers but lifting them up alongside the bottom line.

Cadbury bought an additional 120 acres of nearby land in 1893 and gradually developed a model village to "alleviate the evils of modern, more cramped living conditions." It provided affordable housing. Each house had a garden, and a quarter of each parcel was dedicated to outdoor space. Every garden had a fruit tree, and residents were encouraged to grow their own fruit and vegetables, get exercise, and eat healthily.[22] By 1900, the estate had expanded to 314 cottages and houses on 330 acres.[23]

Children of workers enjoyed a playground, country outings, and summer camps. The workers occupied themselves with football, hockey, and cricket. In 1902, some 30% of Cadbury's capital expenditure was spent on workers' welfare. There were tennis and squash courts, even a bowling green and swimming pools with heated changing rooms. Importantly, Cadbury also gave its workers the time to enjoy these amenities. It was one of the first businesses that offered a half day off from work on Saturdays. (Although there were no pubs for the locals to frequent in Cadbury's Quaker Bournville.)

Challenges abound. Chatters of "utopian dreamer" follow John as surely as the sweet scent of his wares. Competitors, less scrupulous, undercut prices for a time. But a curious thing occurs: customers seek not just sweetness, but the story behind it. A bar of Cadbury chocolate holds a promise— the promise of a better world, built on one small act of commerce and conscience at a time. Workers themselves, cared for with radical respect, become the company's staunch allies.

The Cadbury brothers were not revolutionaries in the firebrand sense. Yet, they reshaped capitalism with a quiet, persistent hum more enduring than any angry slogan. They were pragmatists, understanding that a business must turn a profit to do good. In fact, its Dairy Milk brand had gained a 60% share of the UK milk chocolate market by 1936.[24] But, they also demonstrated that profit can be pursued in a manner that adds dignity, not despair, to the human equation. Cadbury's legacy is measured not solely in tons of chocolate, but in the ripple effects felt far beyond their ledgers. Others began to emulate, if imperfectly, the Cadbury way. The very notion of a "business with a conscience" slowly took root, demonstrating that the pursuit of wealth need not be a soulless endeavor. A reminder that a business, even a humble one born from a dissatisfaction with a cup of watered-down cocoa, can become an unlikely instrument for social change.

Bournville became a blueprint for other model villages in Britain and it has been credited with laying the foundations for garden cities and demonstrating the merits of open space for modern town planning. For two centuries, Cadbury (of Birmingham), Rowntree's (of York), and Fry's (of Bristol)—all Quaker-founded—were the top three confectionary producers in Britain. Cadbury was granted a royal warrant from Queen Victoria as early as 1854 and from Queen Elizabeth II from 1955 to 2022. During the 1990s, Sir Adrian Cadbury, then chairman for over two decades, released the Cadbury Report, a code of best practices that became a basis for corporate governance reform around the world.[25]

Cadbury merged with Fry's in 1919 and Schweppes in 1969, and was rebranded as Cadbury Schweppes until 2008, when the American beverage unit was split as Dr. Pepper Snapple Group. Kraft Foods bought Cadbury for $19.6 billion in 2010 (despite protests from the British public against the American takeover of their beloved confectionaries), and subsequently placed it under its Mondelez International division in a spin-off in 2012.[26] Bournville is currently home to the Mondelez Global Centre of Excellence for Chocolate Research and Development.[27]

Even though they only made up less than 0.0067% (a mere 1,400 out of 21 million) of the population of England, Scotland, and Wales in 1851,[28] Quaker businesses amazingly did a lot more than cornering the confectionary market in England. For example, Darbys founded the British iron industry. Barclays, Lloyds, and Friends Provident banks, Clarks shoes, Bryant and May matches, and biscuit producers Huntley & Palmers and Carrs are further examples of businesses founded by members of the pacifist group.

Quaker businesses were known for their philanthropy and efforts to abolish slavery, reform prisons, and improve social justice. Their consistent efforts were crowned in 1947 when the Quakers, represented by two relief organizations, the American Friends Service Committee and the British Friends Service Council, were awarded the Nobel Peace Prize in recognition of their continuous commitment to peace and the common good.[29]

In case you were wondering, a familiar US company/brand Quaker Oats which was founded in 1877 in Ravenna, Ohio, has been using the images of a traditional Quaker on its cereal boxes to this day. However, it has never had any connection to them.[30] In other trivia, Quaker William Penn (1644–1718) founded a city and a state, Philadelphia and Pennsylvania. And you may not have been aware that two US Presidents, Herbert Hoover and Richard Nixon, were Quakers.

Modern Era

Many early examples of activism during the modern age involved businesses making changes to their internal practices or quietly supporting causes. Overt advertising campaigns tied to social issues were less common.

1960s—1970s

Levi Strauss & Co. desegregation: Risking backlash in the American South, Levi's took a bold moral stand during the Civil Rights era by desegregating their Southern factories well before federal laws mandated it.[31] They also actively encouraged voter registration among employees. This cemented the brand's connection to progressive values and influenced later corporate action on civil rights that continues to this day.[32]

The desegregation of Levi's southern factories in the 1960s was a watershed moment—risky, proactive, and directly confronting the era's most pressing issue. Remember, this was a decade before the phrase "brand activism" came to exist, and well before corporate "wokeness" became commonplace marketing strategy. Levi's wasn't just selling jeans, they were mythologizing the American West, with rugged individualism and freedom as core components of the brand.[33] Thus, aligning with the civil rights struggle wasn't a detour, it was a logical extension of those ideals. Such coherence between image and action builds trust. Aligning with the arc of history strengthened Levi's brand among younger, more progressive audiences who would make a loyal customer base for decades to come.

Mary Quant's miniskirt:[34] Challenging the norms, Quant burst onto the conservative fashion scene with a playful, irreverent style. Short hemlines, bold colors, and youthful silhouettes challenged traditional notions of femininity. Her shop, Bazaar, was more than a store—it was a hub of London's youthquake and swinging sixties culture. Quant didn't just design for the elite. She believed high fashion should be accessible to young, everyday women. Her designs were more affordable, and she made patterns available for home sewing, further democratizing fashion. Owing much to her influence, the miniskirt became a symbol of liberation.[35] Women were claiming a bolder space in society, and the miniskirt reflected this newfound freedom and self-expression. Quant's designs resonated with young women who pushed back against traditional roles and expectations. Wearing a miniskirt became an act of defiance, of female empowerment, signaling a rejection of the old guard.

While Quant may not have invented the miniskirt (in her own words "it was the girls in the street who did it"), she likely coined the phrase after her favorite car, the Mini Cooper.[36]

While not overtly political in the classic sense, Quant championed female liberation through fashion. Her designs and business model encouraged women to define their own style and embrace their sexuality. Quant's looks were about youthful energy, not conforming to rigid beauty ideals. Through her, makeup became bold and playful, encouraging experimentation. Making fashion accessible to a wider range of women disrupted a system previously reserved for the privileged classes. It was a subtle yet powerful form of social leveling. To this day, the miniskirt remains a potent symbol of female agency, making Quant a pioneer of fashion with a lasting social impact.[37] As a smart businesswoman, Quant expanded, licensing her name for various products, from tights and home furnishings to dolls. This also served to further democratize her style and aesthetic. In the 1970s, her focus shifted toward more mass-market affordability through the "daisy" trademark. While losing some of the original edgy appeal, this reinforced her commitment to accessibility. Quant's entire ethos was about giving women options. Whether through clothing, cosmetics, or her wider lifestyle branding, she encouraged women to break free from the expected mold.[38] Her constant push toward affordability countered the elitism traditionally associated with fashion and beauty. This accessibility itself was a form of quiet activism. Even as the brand and her fame expanded, that core message of self-expression and defying conformity remained.

Patagonia (1973–):[39] Patagonia walks the walk, even if it means walking into a fight. They're the rebel of the outdoor industry, a company whose ads tell you to buy less, whose CEO rails against overconsumption, and whose warranty department would rather mend your ancient jacket than sell you a new one.

It wasn't always this way. Yvon Chouinard, Patagonia's founder, started as a climber with a knack for crafting better gear. But the mountains taught him something: nature was in peril, and he was part of the problem. So Chouinard moved away from the steel pitons, that made 70% of his business, toward aluminum chocks that did not damage rocks while climbing.

He then decided to support his low-margin equipment business with high-margin clothing items. Patagonia was born. Patagonia was less about conquering the outdoors, and more about protecting it. It blazed trails with recycled materials, long before sustainability became a buzzword. Patagonia donated 1% of sales (not profits) to grassroots environmental groups, making their money back activism.

Their marketing wasn't slick product shots, it was stark imagery of vanishing wilderness. In 2011, they boldly ran a Black Friday ad with the headline: "Don't Buy This Jacket."[40] It wasn't reverse psychology; it was a gut punch challenging blind consumerism.

Patagonia isn't afraid to sue polluters. They've locked horns with politicians for wilderness preservation.[41] Heck, they even made suing the President of the United States a marketing tool, all to protect public lands.[42] This isn't feel-good greenwashing; it's a middle finger to business as usual.

Patagonia's journey with cotton embodies their search for solutions that go beyond the merely "less bad." Initially, they embraced organic cotton as a significant improvement over conventional, pesticide-heavy production. However, recognizing the limitations of even organic systems, they've pushed further by championing regenerative cotton. This approach focuses on rebuilding soil health, sequestering carbon, and prioritizing the long-term resilience of the ecosystem, not just minimizing harm.[43] It reflects the understanding that sustainability isn't a static goal, but a process of constant improvement and a search for ever-better practices.

And, yeah, their stuff is pricey. It has to be. They pay fair wages, not the cheapest labor they can find. Their gear is built to last decades, and repaired if necessary, not destined for the next landfill. A Patagonia purchase isn't just a transaction; it's you voting with your wallet.

Cynics say it's all just branding. Sure, Patagonia profits. But they've grown by building a tribe of customers who share their outrage, their demand for a better world. Their buyers aren't just into performance fleeces; they're into the idea that businesses can be a force for good... even if it's a messy, imperfect, and sometimes infuriating force.

When it was looking for a new warehouse site, Patagonia didn't just build a warehouse in Pennsylvania, they reversed a legacy of environmental damage. The new distribution center stands on the reclaimed site of a former coal mine.[44] This wasn't merely good PR; it symbolized their commitment to turning scars on the landscape into symbols of regeneration. The warehouse itself is LEED-certified,[45] a testament that even the nuts and bolts of their operations can be a statement of their values in action.

In September 2022, Chouinard made headlines by restructuring Patagonia's ownership to ensure all company profits go toward fighting climate change. He transferred ownership to a trust and non-profit organization, making Patagonia a purpose-driven company dedicated to environmental protection. "Patagonia Founder Gives Away The Company," *The New York Times* reported.[46]

Patagonia isn't for everyone. They don't want to be. Their activism is woven into the very seams of their products. It's as much a part of the offering as the waterproof zippers and lifetime repair policy. It's a dare: step outside and see the beauty worth saving. And demand that the companies you support have the guts to do the same.

The Body Shop (1976–2024):[47] Founded by Anita Roddick with a triple bottom line of focusing on profit, people, the planet, and "feminine principles," The Body Shop became known for environmentally-conscious products and bold advocacy campaigns on animal rights, fair trade, and social justice issues. What started as a small shop offering 25 skin care products in refilled bottles expanded to some 3,000 mostly franchised stores by 2017. It was acquired by L'Oreal in 2006, by Natura in 2017, and by Aurelius in 2023, under which it filed for bankruptcy in 2024,[48] currently going through significant downsizing and reorganizing.[49]

However, The Body Shop wasn't supposed to work in the first place. That's the thing nobody tells you—the early years were less aromatherapy, more chaos. Anita Roddick, the fearless founder, wasn't what you'd call a textbook businesswoman. No fancy spreadsheets or lofty mission statements. Instead, it was a concoction of passion, green plastic bottles, and a dash of "let's give it a go" spirit.

Think less "market analysis," more "let's refill those empties, people bring back their own tubs." Practical? Genius? Probably both, with some serendipity sprinkled in. You see, The Body Shop wasn't born to be a global behemoth, it was about solving problems. Anita saw those wasteful piles of packaging the rest of the industry churned out, and it didn't sit right. The customers, those early hippies and eco-warriors, agreed.[50]

And the scents? Forget focus-grouped fragrances. We're talking dewberry, a little mango, maybe a whiff of something unidentifiably "jungle-y." It was exotic, fun, and unlike anything on those sterile department store shelves. The Body Shop wasn't selling products, it was peddling a feeling of rainforest freshness and the vague notion you were saving the world, one recycled bottle at a time.[51]

Anita had a knack for turning constraints into magic. A limited budget? Forget slick ads, rather hand-letter the storefront signs. Small team? Your passionate store clerk becomes your most potent brand ambassador. The Body Shop thrived on a sort of organized chaos—it felt rebellious and against the grain.

But the real genius wasn't the banana-scented conditioner, it was the story. Brands aren't just what they flog; they're a promise made real. The Body Shop promised good ingredients, but more importantly, it promised to shake things up. Trade with remote tribes? Unheard of. Back social campaigns no sane corporation would touch? That was the brand. Suddenly, a bar of soap was a small act of rebellion. That's worth paying a bit extra for, wouldn't you say?

The Body Shop became proof that "doing good" and "doing well" weren't some boring balancing act. They were two ingredients in the same, deliciously weird, potion. Anita wasn't a philanthropist; she was a business-woman who understood the power of having a bloody good story. People, especially the idealistic sort, crave that more than a perfectly formulated face mask.

Of course, scaling that magic became the straw that broke the camel's back. Success brought its own strangeness—boardrooms, global logistics, the kind of things that give a free spirit the shivers.[52] But at its heart, The Body Shop was, and perhaps always will be, that glorious, slightly unhinged experiment. It's a reminder that, sometimes, the best brands are built on instinct, a sprinkle of audacity, and the absolute conviction that selling a bit of soap can, indeed, change the world.

CBS and Michael Jackson's "Billie Jean" on MTV (1983): During the first couple of years of its existence, MTV featured very few Black artists and initially declined to show Michael Jackson's "Billie Jean" video on the channel because "it's not MTV's audience."[53] "MTV's playlist was 99% white until Michael Jackson forced his way on the air by making the best music videos anyone had ever seen."[54] And it only happened after CBS Records' President, Walter Yetnikoff, threatened to pull all of his label's artists from MTV if the video was not put in rotation. Was there a self-serving business interest? Sure. However, CBS's activism in featuring Black artists on MTV was also a revolutionary feat as it challenged the prevailing norms and barriers in the entertainment industry. By providing a platform for Black voices and creativity, CBS helped amplify their stories and perspectives, contributing to a more inclusive and representative media landscape. This exposure not only empowered Black artists but also paved the way for future generations, inspiring them to pursue their artistic dreams and break down systemic barriers.

Benetton's "United Colors" Campaigns (1980–2000):[55] Forget pretty models and tasteful product shots—Benetton wanted to punch you in the gut. In a world drowning in advertising, polite gets ignored. Bold gets talked about, whether you love it or loathe it. And talk, as any marketer knows, is worth its weight in gold.

To be clear, those early Benetton campaigns with Oliviero Toscani at the helm weren't about selling sweaters. They were about hijacking the conversation. A priest and a nun, locked in a passionate kiss? A bloodstained soldier's uniform? A Black woman breastfeeding a white baby? These weren't just billboards; they were grenades lobbed into public discourse.[56]

Of course, they called it "social awareness." A noble cause, perhaps, but let's be ruthlessly honest, they were selling the hell out of controversy. It was a high-stakes gamble. Alienate half your customers, and the other half might adore you twice as fiercely, and even more may join the fray. Benetton wasn't targeting the masses, they were after the cultural provocateurs, the ones who saw wearing those colorful knits as a badge of rebellion.

Think of it like this: most brands want to be liked. Benetton wanted to be debated, dissected, and even despised. That takes a level of audacity most boardrooms wouldn't dare. Because outrage, unlike a catchy jingle, lingers, seeping into dinner conversations, magazine articles, and maybe even the odd parliamentary debate. You've become part of the cultural fabric, not just another logo.

The irony is, of course, that a company making comfy basics became synonymous with the most viscerally uncomfortable images. It's a testament to the power of symbolism run amok. Did it actually change the world? Possibly, in some small way. Did it sell a boatload of sweaters? Absolutely. At what cost to brand reputation? Was it ethical? Well, that's a debate that rages on.[57]

Was it clever? Diabolically so. Those Benetton ads weren't just visually shocking, but were masterclasses in exploiting a fundamental human truth.

We are far more likely to share that which disgusts us than that which merely makes us smile.

Was it good advertising? That depends on your definition. Effective? Undeniably. But it's a dangerous game to play because once you train your audience to expect the outrageous, the merely provocative won't cut it. You have to keep upping the ante, and that's a slippery slope. Benetton, in its later years, learned this the hard way.

"When Benetton launched a campaign publishing pictures of 26 American prisoners sentenced to death, it provoked outrage. American sales decreased and distribution contracts were canceled. In 2018, the use of photographs of recently rescued migrants from the Mediterranean was not well received. Social media lit up with a similar refrain, 'how does tragedy fit with selling clothes?'"[58] It turns out shock value has a diminishing return.

But those early, audacious years? They made advertising history and deserve a mention here. Proof that sometimes the most potent brand message isn't what you say but how loudly you make the world scream.

Dove's "Real Beauty" Campaign (2004):[59] Back in 2004, Dove ripped up the beauty rulebook. No airbrushed supermodels, no promises of defying time with a $50 face cream. Just real women. Curves, wrinkles, scars—the kind of bodies rarely seen staring back from billboards.

Those first "Real Beauty" ads hit like a double take. Were they selling soap or starting a fight? The message was audacious: you are beautiful, exactly as you are. Not "beautiful when you lose 10 pounds." And not "beautiful if you buy enough stuff." Just beautiful. Period.[60]

It was a gamble. Cynics scoffed, "It's just marketing." Traditionalists sputtered about false advertising. But those bombarded daily with images of unattainable perfection felt something stir. Hope, maybe. Or was it just rage turned on its head?

Next came the billboards. Ordinary women, not professional models, in their underwear. Stretch marks proudly displayed. Laughter lines refusing to apologize. The internet ignited. Was it empowering? Exploitative? Was Dove selling self-love or soap? The answer didn't matter, not really. The conversation had changed.

Beauty wasn't about erasing flaws; it was about owning them. Suddenly, a body could be celebrated without being sold a solution. Dove didn't just shift product—they shifted how women saw themselves in the mirror.

There was backlash too, of course. Hypocrisy, when a brand built on soap told you external beauty didn't matter. Limitations, as the campaign, even when diverse, stuck to a certain kind of conventionally pretty. Cracks formed in the facade. Thus, Dove's "Real Beauty" didn't usher in a utopia of body acceptance overnight, but it planted the seed that representation, even in a slightly sanitized form, has power. That what we see shapes how we feel.

Dove proved that a giant corporation could poke the status quo, start arguments over bathroom mirrors, and make a damn good profit while doing it.[61]

The campaign's success is undeniable. It garnered widespread publicity, with Dove's models featured on major American talk shows like *The View*, *Good Morning America*, *The Today Show*, *Ellen*, and *Geraldo*. This media exposure alone provided Dove's campaign with an estimated $150 million in free media time.[62] Additionally, the campaign received numerous prestigious awards. The online video *Evolution* was a standout, winning two Cannes Lions Grand Prix Awards. Furthermore, in its first month, *Evolution* amassed over 1.7 million views, becoming YouTube's most-viewed video in October 2006. Much of the campaign's success stems from its innovative digital approach. It was the first of its kind to mobilize participants into a supportive online community that ultimately reached over 200 million people globally. This online component saw over 26 million people actively engage with the campaign.[63]

"Real Beauty" wasn't the final answer, but a chapter in a long, messy, and utterly necessary fight about whose beauty gets to count. And that fight, arguably, began with a few bold billboards and the question that's still being debated today: who gets to define beautiful? Two decades in, the campaign is still ongoing.

TOMS Shoes "One for One" (2006):[64] A simple promise sparked a movement that went far beyond shoes. Blake Mycoskie, a young traveler in Argentina, stumbled upon a harsh reality: children growing up without shoes, their feet vulnerable to injury and disease. He didn't want to just donate but wanted to create a solution that would last. And so, TOMS was born. Not a charity, but a brand on a mission. The idea was audacious, even a bit idealistic: For every pair of those simple canvas shoes purchased, a pair would be given to a child in need. One for One. It wasn't complex but it was catchy and something a consumer could be a part of.

Those early TOMS weren't fancy. No high-tech soles, no celebrity endorsements. They were about a story of shared humanity, of how a purchase that *felt* good could actually *do* good. College students rallied, moms bought them for their kids, sparking conversations that went beyond what was on your feet.

The model was as eye-catching as the shoes were plain. A shopper's choice had a tangible, feel-good impact. Suddenly, your comfy slip-ons weren't just about summer style, they were about being part of something bigger. TOMS tapped into that deep need to be more than a consumer, to make a difference, even a small one.

Of course, the critics came. "Is this sustainable aid?" they asked. "Isn't it just feel-good consumerism?" Valid questions, sparking debates about the role of businesses in tackling global issues. TOMS evolved, facing complexities, addressing the need for local production, and expanding their impact beyond just shoes. Meanwhile, one million pairs of shoes given away by 2010 grew to one hundred million pairs of shoes by 2020. Currently, the company dedicates one-third of its profits for good.[65]

The One for One model has been imitated, adapted, and debated endlessly. But TOMS was the first to prove the power of merging a product with a purpose. They shifted the question from "What am I buying?" to "What change can I be a part of?" TOMS didn't solve global poverty, but it ignited a conversation around conscious consumerism. They made compassion trendy and fueled a generation of entrepreneurs asking not only how to turn a profit, but how to leave a mark on the world. And that all started with a humble pair of shoes.

REI—#OptOutside on Black Friday (2015):[66] Black Friday. A day of door buster deals, long lines, and the desperate hunt for the perfect gift. But in 2015, REI, the outdoor gear giant, did something unthinkable. They shut down. All 143 stores, two distribution centers, and headquarters. Nationwide.

This wasn't a power outage or a stock issue. It was a deliberate act. Instead of ringing up sales, REI encouraged their employees—all 12,000 of them—to venture outdoors, reconnect with nature, and breathe fresh air. They even paid them for the privilege.

The campaign? #OptOutside. A simple yet powerful message. A nudge to prioritize experiences over possessions, to trade crowded malls for majestic mountains or serene lakes. It was audacious and, frankly, a little crazy. Supposedly, Black Friday gets its name from retailers who have operated in the "red" the whole year until the day after Thanksgiving kicks off the holiday shopping season frenzy. Which sane retailer would give up the opportunity?[67]

Yet, REI President and CEO Jerry Stritzke observed:

> We think Black Friday has gotten out of hand and so we are choosing to invest in helping people get outside with loved ones this holiday season, over spending it in the aisles. Please join us and inspire us with your experiences. We hope to engage millions of Americans and galvanize the outdoor community to get outside.[68]

And it worked. #OptOutside made headlines and a buzz on social media. People, tired of the shopping madness, embraced the idea. America happens to be the only country on earth where regular citizens trample each other for something on sale, just the day after sharing a meal to be thankful for all they already have. Hiking trails saw an influx of visitors. Parks reported record attendance. Nature, it seemed, was having a Black Friday of its own.

There were critics. "They're just trying to be different!" Perhaps. But different they were. In a world obsessed with more, REI dared to say enough. They challenged the very foundation of a retail holiday built on relentless consumption.

#OptOutside wasn't just about a single day. It was a spark that ignited a conversation. A reminder that life exists beyond the fluorescent lights of a department store. It was about reclaiming time, about cherishing experiences, and rediscovering the simple joy of being outside.

REI took a financial risk, yes, but they also gained something far more valuable: loyalty. They positioned themselves not just as a retailer, but as a brand that championed a healthier, more balanced way of life. They showed that success wasn't just about the bottom line, it was about standing up for something bigger.

Black Friday may forever be synonymous with shopping. But thanks to REI, one year, it became a day where millions dared to choose something different. A day where nature, not the cash register, became the focus. A day retail stood still, and a movement for mindful living began.

Fenty and Foundation Shades (2017):[69] Superstar Rihanna's Fenty Beauty revolutionized the beauty industry by launching an inclusive range of 40 foundation shades in 2017, catering to a diverse spectrum of skin tones. This bold move, defying the industry's limited shade ranges, quickly resonated with consumers and propelled the brand to $100 million in revenue shortly after the launch. The "Fenty Effect" rippled through the industry, compelling other beauty brands to expand their makeup lines to be more inclusive and cater to a wider customer base. This demonstrated how a commitment to diversity and representation can not only result in business success but also reshape industry standards.

Nike's "Dream Crazy" with Colin Kaepernick (2018): Incredibly polarizing, the ad embraced an athlete-activist at the height of controversy. See Chapter 1 for more details.

Dick's Sporting Goods takes a stand: a turning point in gun control discourse (2018):[70] In the wake of the horrific school shooting in Parkland, Florida, which claimed the lives of 17 students and staff in February 2018, Dick's Sporting Goods enacted a series of significant gun control measures. This move by a major retailer marked a turning point in the ongoing debate about gun violence in the United States. Dick's didn't simply offer condolences or donations. Their CEO, Ed Stack, did not want to be part of the story anymore and took concrete steps. The swift and decisive action sent a strong message that resonated far beyond the company itself. The policy changes were substantial:

- A ban on assault-style rifles: Dick's stopped selling AR-15 rifles and similar weapons, a category often used in mass shootings. This directly addressed a type of firearm frequently associated with high casualty events.
- An increased purchasing age: the minimum age to purchase any firearm, including shotguns and hunting rifles, was raised to 21. This aligned with the legal drinking age in the US and aimed to reduce access to guns for younger individuals.

Many applauded Dick's for its courage and leadership. Gun control advocates saw it as a victory and a potential tipping point. Gun rights groups were fiercely critical, accusing Dick's of caving to pressure and harming law-abiding gun owners. Short-term sales of firearms at Dick's did decline after the policy changes; 65 employees quit in protest, and more followed later. Sales dropped in the following quarters. However, the company maintained its stance, claiming the long-term benefits of a stronger brand reputation outweighed the financial losses. The company even destroyed $5 million worth of rifles in inventory so that they would not somehow find their way on the market.[71]

Dick's policy changes stand as a significant moment in the debate about gun violence. The company's willingness to take a stand, despite initial financial sacrifice, demonstrated the power corporations can have in shaping social discourse and influencing policy discussions. It seems the consumers have taken notice: Dick's stock price rose by 470% between February 2018 and October 2024 (versus 80% for S&P 500).

The rich history of brand activism reveals a dynamic landscape where companies navigate the complex waters of consumer expectations, social responsibility, and the bottom line. As advertising guru Bill Bernbach observed decades ago: "A principle isn't a principle until it costs you something."[72] From early efforts to modern-day social media campaigns, the tools may transform, but the core desire to align brands with values remains. As consumer awareness grows, brand activism will continue to evolve, becoming an increasingly essential component of successful business strategy. Next, we examine some of the more obvious missteps taken in the name of brand activism. The last five years have offered plenty of examples to choose from.

References

1   Sheth, Jagdish N., Atul Parvatiyar, and Can Uslay (2024), *Marketing Theory: Evolution and Evaluation of Schools of Marketing Thought*, global expanded edition. Wiley, forthcoming.

2   Uslay, Can, Robert E. Morgan, and Jagdish N. Sheth (2009), "Peter Drucker on Marketing: An Exploration of Five Tenets," *Journal of the Academy of Marketing Science*, 37(1), 47–60.

3   Drucker, Peter F. (1969b), "The shame of marketing," *Marketing Communications*, 297, 60–64 (August).

4   Drucker, Peter F. (1969b), "The shame of marketing," *Marketing Communications*, 297, 60–64 (August).

5   Sarkar, Christian, and Philip Kotler (2018). *Brand Activism: From Purpose to Action*, Idea Bite Press, p. 24.

6 Shoenberger, Heather, Eunjin Kim, and Yuan Sun (2021), "Advertising during COVID-19: Exploring Perceived Brand Message Authenticity and Potential Psychological Reactance," *Journal of Advertising*, 50(3), 253–261.

7 Cammarota, Antonella, Maria D'Arco, Vittoria Marino, Riccardo Resciniti (2022), "Brand Activism: A Literature Review and Future Research Agenda," *International Journal of Consumer Studies*, 47, 1669–1691.

8 Fan, Zongxiang, Zhenyu Zhou, Siran Lui, Jianfeng Cui, Xuechun Fan, Wei Lin, Yunming Huang, and Zhenhua Deng (2024), "The Earliest Stamped Hard Pottery and High-Firing Technology Dating Back to 5000 BP: Evidence from Two Sites in Southeastern China," *Journal of Archeological Science*, 166 (June), 1–10. https://www.sciencedirect.com/science/article/abs/pii/S0305440324000451.

9 Stamp, Jimmy, "Decoding the Range: The Secret Language of Cattle Branding." Smithsonian Magazine, April 30, 2013 (accessed June 8, 2024). https://www.smithsonianmag.com/arts-culture/decoding-the-range-the-secret-language-of-cattle-branding-45246620/. Khan, S.U . and Mufti, O., "The Hot History and Cold Future of Brands," *Journal of Managerial Sciences*, Vol. 1, No. 1, 2007, p. 76.

10 "Other Ritual Objects," *Britannica* (accessed June 8, 2024). https://www.britannica.com/topic/ceremonial-object/Other-ritual-objects.

11 "Guild," *Britannica* (accessed June 8, 2024). https://www.britannica.com/topic/guild-trade-association.

12 Guyatt, Mary (2000), "The Wedgwood Slave Medallion: Values in Eighteenth-Century Design." *Journal of Design History*, 13(2), 93–105.

13 "The Wedgwood Anti-Slavery Medallion," *V&A Museum* (accessed June 8, 2024). https://www.vam.ac.uk/articles/the-wedgwood-anti-slavery-medallion.

14 "The Wedgwood Anti-Slavery Medallion," *V&A Museum* (accessed June 8, 2024). https://www.vam.ac.uk/articles/the-wedgwood-anti-slavery-medallion.

15 Oldfield, John R. (1998), *Popular Politics and British Anti-slavery: The Mobilisation of Public Opinion Against the Slave Trade, 1787–1807*, Psychology Press. p. 156.

16 Jackson, Peter, "How Did Quakers Conquer the British Sweet Shop?" *BBC News*, January 20, 2010 (accessed June 8, 2024). http://news.bbc.co.uk/2/hi/uk_news/magazine/8467833.stm.

17 Delfino, Devon and Dan Shephard, "Percentage of Businesses That Fail – And How to Boost Chances of Success," LendingTree, April 8, 2024 (accessed June 8, 2024). https://www.lendingtree.com/business/small/failure-rate/.

18 Clark, D., "Average Company Lifespan on Standard and Poor's 500 Index from 1965 to 2030, in Years." Statista, February 2, 2024 (accessed June 8, 2024). https://www.statista.com/statistics/1259275/average-company-lifespan/.

19 This section is drawn from the company's website unless noted (accessed June 8, 2024). https://www.cadbury.co.uk/about/history/our-story/.

20 Dellheim, Charles (1987), "The Creation of a Company Culture: Cadbury's, 1861-1931." *The American Historical Review*, 92(1), 13–44. https://www.jstor.org/stable/1862781?origin=crossref.

21 Bournville Village Trust "Bournville Village Heritage," (accessed June 8, 2024). https://www.bvt.org.uk/our-heritage/about-our-heritage/about-our-heritage/.

22 Bournville Village Trust "Bournville Village Heritage," (accessed June 8, 2024). https://www.bvt.org.uk/our-heritage/about-our-heritage/about-our-heritage/.

23   Dellheim, Charles (1987), "The Creation of a Company Culture: Cadbury's, 1861–1931," *The American Historical Review*, 92(1), 13–44. https://www.jstor.org/stable/1862781?origin=crossref.

24   Fitzgerald, Robert (2005), "Products, Firms and Consumption: Cadbury and the Development of Marketing, 1900–1939," *Business History*, 47(4), 511–531.

25   Gittelson, Steven, "Adrian Cadbury, A Leader in Corporate Governance, Dies at 86." *The Washington Post*, September 4, 2015 (accessed June 8, 2024). https://www.washingtonpost.com/business/adrian-cadbury-a-leader-in-corporate-governance-dies-at-86/2015/09/04/e87dd2fe-532e-11e5-8c19-0b6825aa4a3a_story.html.

26   Merced J. de la, Michael and Chris V. Nicholson, "Kraft to Acquire Cadbury in Deal Worth $19 Billion," *The New York Times*, January 19, 2010 (accessed June 8, 2024). https://www.nytimes.com/2010/01/20/business/global/20kraft.html.

27   Griffin, Jon, "Cadbury Owner Mondelez Announces £75m Upgrade of Bournville Factory," *BusinessLive*, January 23, 2014 (accessed June 8, 2024). https://www.business-live.co.uk/manufacturing/cadbury-owner-mondelez-announces-75m-6555440.

28   Jackson, Peter, "How Did Quakers Conquer the British Sweet Shop?" *BBC News*, January 20, 2010 (accessed June 8, 2024). http://news.bbc.co.uk/2/hi/uk_news/magazine/8467833.stm.

29   Jahn, Gunnar, "Award Ceremony Speech," *The Noble Prize*, December 10, 1947 (accessed June 8, 2024). https://www.nobelprize.org/prizes/peace/1947/ceremony-speech/.

30   "Quaker Oats Company," *Britannica*. https://www.britannica.com/topic/Quaker-Oats-Company.

31   "Levi Strauss 2016 Company Timeline," (accessed June 8, 2024). https://www.levistrauss.com/wp-content/uploads/2016/06/2016_CompanyTimeline_Long_F.pdf.

32   Mohan, Pavithra, "Levi CEO Chip Bergh Wants You to Give Your Employees Time to Vote," *Fast Company*, October 26, 2018 (accessed June 8, 2024). https://www.fastcompany.com/90253672/levi-ceo-chip-bergh-wants-you-to-give-your-employees-time-to-vote. "Levi Strauss & Co . Supports Voter Registration Campaign on More Than 150 Community College Campuses," *Levi Strauss*, September 15, 2022 (accessed June 8, 2024). https://investors.levistrauss.com/news/financial-news/news-details/2022/Levi-Strauss--Co.-Supports-Voter-Registration-Campaign-on-More-than-150-Community-College-Campuses/default.aspx.

33   https://www.levistrauss.com/levis-history/ (accessed March 4, 2025). Panek , Tracey . " Throwback Thursday: Cowboy Cool ." Levi Strauss & Co. July 20, 2017 (accessed March 4, 2025.   https://www.levistrauss.com/2017/07/20/throwback-thursday-cowboy-cool/.

34   "The Miniskirt Myth," *V&A Museum* (accessed June 8, 2024). https://www.vam.ac.uk/articles/the-miniskirt-myth.

35   Christman-Campbell, Kimberly, "The Not-So-Sexy Origins of the Miniskirt," *The Atlantic*, April 14, 2023 (accessed June 8, 2024). https://www.theatlantic.com/culture/archive/2023/04/mary-quant-british-fashion-designer-miniskirt-legacy/673731/.

36   Christman-Campbell, Kimberly, "The Not-So-Sexy Origins of the Miniskirt," *The Atlantic*, April 14, 2023 (accessed June 8, 2024). https://www.theatlantic.com/culture/archive/2023/04/mary-quant-british-fashion-designer-miniskirt-legacy/673731/.

37   "The Fashion History of Dame Mary Quant," *British Fashion Council* (accessed June 8, 2024). https://artsandculture.google.com/story/the-fashion-history-of-dame-mary-quant-british-fashion-council/HgWRHn4SqTdrLw?hl=en.

38   "Introducing Mary Quant," *V&A Museum* (accessed June 8, 2024). https://www.vam.ac.uk/articles/introducing-mary-quant.

39   The section was drawn from the following sources unless noted otherwise. Sundheim , David , "How Patagonia Became The Most Reputable Brand in the United States," *Forbes*, December 12, 2023 (accessed June 8, 2024). https://www.forbes.com/sites/dougsundheim/2023/12/12/how-patagonia-became-the-most-reputable-brand-in-the-united-states/?sh=509544d71473. https://www.patagonia.com/company-history/ (accessed March 4, 2025).

40   Neren, Uri, "Patagonia's Provocative Black Friday Campaign," *Harvard Business Review*, November 23, 2012 (accessed June 8, 2024). https://hbr.org/2012/11/patagon ias-provocative-black-f.

41   Ellsworth, Jonathan. "Patagonia's Yvon Chouinard Challenges Utah's Politicians." *Blister*, January 12, 2017 (accessed March 4, 2025). https://blisterreview.com/features/patagonias-yvon-chouinard-challenges-utahs-politicians.

42   Ellsworth, Jonathan, "Patagonia's Yvon Choinard Challenges Utah's Politicians," *Blister*, January 12, 2017 (accessed June 8, 2024). https://www.nytimes.com/2018/05/05/business/patagonia-trump-bears-ears.html.

43   https://www.patagonia.com/our-footprint/cotton-for-change.html.   (March 5, 2025).

44   Learn-Andes, Jennifer, "Spoil Heaps No More: Transforming Mining Sites for Modern Warehouses," *Times Leader*, April 6, 2019 (accessed June 8, 2024). https://www.timesleader.com/news/739511/spoil-heaps-no-more-transforming-min ing-sites-for-modern-warehouses.

45   LEED stands for Leadership in Energy and Environmental Design and the LEED certification is the world's most widely used green building rating system.

46   Gelles, David, "Billionaire No More: Patagonia Founder Gives Away The Company," *The New York Times*, September 21, 2022 (accessed June 8, 2024). https://www.nytimes.com/2022/09/14/climate/patagonia-climate-philanthropy-chouin ard.html.

47   The section was drawn from the following source unless noted otherwise. https://www.thebodyshop.com/en-gb/about-us/our-story/a/a00002, (accessed March 5, 2025).

48   Wile, Rob, "The Bosy Shop Shuts Down in the U.S. After Filing for Bankruptcy," *NBC News*, March 11, 2024 (accessed June 8, 2024). https://www.nbcnews.com/business/business-news/the-body-shop-store-shuts-down-where-why-rcn a142790.

49   Saker-Clark, Henry, "The Body Shop: What Went Wrong and What Happens Next?" *The Standard*, February 13, 2024 (accessed June 8, 2024). https://www.standard.co.uk/business/business-news/the-body-shop-what-went-wrong-and-what-happens-next-b1138941.html.

50   Horwell, Veronica, "Obituary: Dame Anita Roddick," *The Guardian*, September 12, 2007 (accessed June 8, 2024). https://www.theguardian.com/news/2007/sep/12/guardianobituaries.business.

51 Spence, Caroline, "The Body Shop Was the Scent of My Youth – And It's Young People Who Could Resurrect the Brand," *The Conversation*, February 23, 2024 (accessed June 8, 2024). https://theconversation.com/the-body-shop-was-the-scent-of-my-youth-and-its-young-people-who-could-resurrect-the-brand-223950.

52 "An Analysis of the Rise and Fall of The Body Shop, Its Rebranding, and Marketing Strategies," *Brand Vision Insights*, (accessed June 8, 2024). https://www.brandvm.com/post/the-body-shop-rebranding-and-marketing.

53 Barron, Steve (2014), *Egg n Chips & Billie Jean: A Trip Through the Eighties*, Createspace Independent Pub.

54 Palmer, Tamara, "How the 'Billie Jean' Video Changed MTV," *The Root*, March 10, 2013 (accessed September 17, 2024). https://www.theroot.com/how-the-billie-jean-video-changed-mtv-1790895543.

55 Duffy, Eilidh Nuala, "Benetton's Most Controversial Campaigns," *Vouge World*, December 8, 2017 (accessed June 8, 2024). https://www.vogue.co.uk/gallery/benettons-best-advertising-campaigns#:~:text=The%20coloured%20condoms%20campaign%20was,late%20Eighties%20and%20early%20Nineties.

56 "The King of Controversy Oliviero Toscani," *Screen Voice*, September 3, 2023 (accessed June 8, 2024). https://www.screenvoice.cz/en/news/the-king-of-controversy-oliviero-toscani/.

57 Swvystun, Jeff, "Benetton's Confusing Legacy of Brand Activism," *Medium*, January 27, 2021 (accessed June 8, 2024). https://jeffswystun.medium.com/benettons-confusing-legacy-of-brand-activism-6156b4c0384c.

58 Swvystun, Jeff, "Benetton's Confusing Legacy of Brand Activism," *Medium*, January 27, 2021 (accessed June 8, 2024). https://jeffswystun.medium.com/benettons-confusing-legacy-of-brand-activism-6156b4c0384c.

59 https://www.dove.com/us/en/stories/about-dove/dove-real-beauty-pledge.html, (accessed March 5, 2025).

60 Taylor, Maggie, "The Enduring Power and Impact of Dove's 'Real Beauty' Campaign," *Strixus*, February 22, 2023 (accessed June 8, 2024). https://strixus.com/entry/the-enduring-power-and-impact-of-doves-real-beauty-campaign-18095.

61 "The Success of Dove's Real Beauty Campaign," *Global Brands Magazine* (accessed June 8, 2024). https://www.globalbrandsmagazine.com/the-success-of-doves-real-beauty-campaign/.

62 "Grand Prize Winner: Dove 'Evolution'," May 1, 2007, *Creativity*, "Special Report: Creativity Awards," p. 46.

63 Springer, P. (2009), *Ads to icons: How advertising succeeds in a multimedia age* (2nd ed.), Kogan Publishing.
    Celebre, Angela and Ashley Waggoner Denton, "The Good, The Bad and The Ugly of the Dove Campaign for Real Beauty," *The Inquisitive Mind*, Issue 14, 2014 (accessed June 8, 2024). https://www.in-mind.org/article/the-good-the-bad-and-the-ugly-of-the-dove-campaign-for-real-beauty.

64 https://www.toms.com/us/about-toms.html, (Accessed March 5, 2025).

65 Hessekiel, David, "The Rise and Fall of the Buy-One-Give-One Model at TOMS," *Forbes*, April 28, 2021 (accessed June 8, 2024). https://www.forbes.com/sites/davidhessekiel/2021/04/28/the-rise-and-fall-of-the-buy-one-give-one-model-at-toms/?sh=600877a771c4. Colon , Ana, "Tom is Officially Leaving the One-for-One Model Behind – And Doing This Instead," *Fashionista*, April 6, 2021 (accessed

June 8, 2024). https://fashionista.com/2021/04/toms-shoes-new-charity-donat
ion-strategy.

66   https://www.rei.com/opt-outside, (accessed March 5, 2025).

67   Howell, Paul, "10 Brand Story Elements of REI's Disruptive #OptOutside Black
Friday Campaign," *The Business of Story* (accessed June 8, 2024). https://business
ofstory.com/the-10-brand-story-elements-of-reis-disruptive-optoutside-black-fri
day-campaign/.

68   Howell, Paul, "10 Brand Story Elements of REI's Disruptive #OptOutside Black
Friday Campaign," *The Business of Story* (accessed June 8, 2024). https://business
ofstory.com/the-10-brand-story-elements-of-reis-disruptive-optoutside-black-fri
day-campaign/.

69   Fetto, Funmi, "How Fenty Beauty Changed the State of Play in the Industry," *Vogue*
(accessed October 24, 2024). https://www.vogue.co.uk/beauty/article/rihanna-
fenty-beauty-diversity.

70   Siegel, Rachel, "Dick's Sporting Goods Overhauled Its Gun Policies After Parkland.
The CEO Didn't Stop There," *The Washington Post*, May 31, 2019 (accessed June 8,
2024).   https://www.washingtonpost.com/business/economy/dicks-sporting-
goods-overhauled-its-gun-policies-after-parkland-the-ceo-didnt-stop-there/
2019/05/31/9faa6a08-7d8f-11e9-a5b3-34f3edf1351e_story.html.

71   Thomas, Lauren, "Dick's Sporting Goods CEO Ed Stack Took a Controversial Stance
on Gun Control. Then He Wrote This Book," *CBNC*, October 8, 2019 (accessed
June 8, 2024). https://www.cnbc.com/2019/09/28/behind-dicks-sporting-
goods-ceo-ed-stacks-controversial-decison-on-guns.html.

72   "Top 40 William Bernbach Quotes," Quotefancy (accessed June 8, 2024). https://
quotefancy.com/william-bernbach-quotes.

6

MIS(C)ACTIVISM!

In an era where consumers wield unprecedented power and social consciousness saturates the marketplace, many brands have been compelled to become warriors for causes. They champion social justice, environmental sustainability, and diversity to name a few. But beneath this veneer of virtue lies a darker, more complex reality—the shadowy realm of brand mis-activism, which inadvertently hurts rather than helps, or wasteful or ineffective (miscellaneous) misc-activism, depending on how you look at it.

This is where well-intentioned campaigns go awry, where performative gestures overshadow real action, and where brands stumble blindly into cultural minefields. It's a world where a single misstep can ignite a firestorm of public backlash, canceling out years of carefully cultivated goodwill, and eroding consumer trust.

Mis(c)activism is nuanced. Some campaigns are intentionally harmful or "regressive," whereas others miscalculate public sentiment or lack a genuine connection to their stated values. In that sense, it is probably as old as activism itself. However, our review of the dark side of brand activism reveals that taking a stand can sometimes be more perilous than staying silent. It's a realm where the lines between authenticity and exploitation,

DOI: 10.4324/9781003593690-6

between empowerment and self-promotion, become dangerously blurred. In this chapter, we delve into the timeline of infamous cases where brands have stumbled, exploring the motivations, the consequences, and the chilling lessons learned when activism turns into a liability.

Special Priors: Tobacco Advertising (1930s–1950s)[1]

For decades, tobacco companies used advertisements that glamorized smoking and made claims about health benefits while downplaying risks. For example, R.J. Reynolds had a campaign that boasted "More Doctors Smoke Camels Than Any Other Cigarette." Ads featured images of smiling physicians endorsing Camels, with claims like "Not One Single Case of Throat Irritation." The campaign exploited the public's trust in medical professionals to lend credibility to a harmful product implying smoking— especially Camels—was safe and even endorsed by health experts.[2] The reality, which science would later prove overwhelmingly, was quite the opposite. The effort was exploitative, deceptive, and yet influential. It wasn't until the 1960s that stronger regulations emerged on tobacco advertising and warning labels were mandated. No doubt, if it were not for the tobacco lobby, the Surgeon General could have released its "Report on Smoking and Health" (1964) decades earlier.[3]

Nestle Infant Formula Controversy (1970s–1980s)[4]

Nestle aggressively marketed infant formula in developing countries, often with misleading claims about superiority to breastfeeding. This contributed to declining breastfeeding rates and negative health outcomes for infants particularly in areas without clean water.[5] The result: a global boycott campaign against Nestle, which lasted for decades.[6] While Nestle did make some changes, the controversy continues to be a cautionary tale about the misuse of brand power for vulnerable populations.[7]

Polaroid and Apartheid in South Africa (1970–1977)[8]

Polaroid's brand activism, unfolding against the volatile backdrop of South Africa's apartheid regime, provides a stark case study of the complexities of brand activism in a morally fraught landscape. Polaroid fostered a progressive culture internally, boasting diversity in hiring and a focus on employee well-being. Its co-founder, Edwin Land, "had taken pains to increase Black employment, and on the night of Martin Luther King Jr.'s assassination in 1968 had gone to one of Polaroid's factory floors to offer an impromptu speech about unity ('we must do better') to the staff that many say they won't ever forget…, it had seemed to be an enlightened company."[9] Yet, the revelation that their products were being used to facilitate the oppressive passbook system in South Africa sparked intense backlash, internally as well as externally.[10]

The company's initial response was to distance itself from direct government sales, while maintaining business with a distributor. It sent a delegation of four employees (two white, two Black, as per the press release) to investigate the matter. They ultimately suggested that continuing business could lead to higher employment and pay for Black South Africans. Many thought that missed the bigger picture and sounded like self-justification. "A big cash donation to some Boston civil-rights groups was also well-intentioned, and instead looked like a payoff. The whole affair made this ostensibly enlightened company look retrograde, and no better than any other. [The leaders of the employee activism movement] were eventually fired."[11]

The attempted middle ground, typical of many corporations caught in ethical dilemmas, proved unsustainable. Employee activism, fueled by a clear moral outrage, coupled with mounting external pressure, made staying on the sidelines untenable.[12] Polaroid ultimately withdrew from the country entirely, sacrificing profit for moral clarity. Though it took them seven years to give up less than half a percent of global business. Did Polaroid's exit make a tangible difference in dismantling apartheid? Arguably, limited. Did it matter symbolically? Immensely, both at the time and influencing later divestment movements. Brand actions have real-world impacts. Polaroid's case is unique, as its brand image was initially damaged not by intent, but by unintended consequences. Neutrality, especially in the face of injustice, risks being perceived as complicity.

This underscores the necessity of due diligence, including across global markets. Proactivity averts damage control and being caught unaware invites accusations of hypocrisy. Polaroid's story isn't one of neat answers. It's a reminder that while brand activism can be a force for good, it's also fraught with complexities. And as Peter Drucker often reminded us, good management isn't just about efficiency, it's about making the right decisions—even when those decisions are difficult.

Shell Oil and Brent Spar (1990s)[13]

Brent Spar was a massive floating oil storage buoy used in the North Sea oil fields. By the 1990s, however, it was obsolete and needed removing. Initially, Shell favored deep-sea disposal, arguing it was the most environmentally sound option based on their scientific assessments. They obtained permits from the UK government. Greenpeace vehemently disagreed. They believed deep-sea disposal would create a dangerous precedent and set a poor example for future decommissioning, polluting the ocean with toxic residues from the structure. It launched a high-profile campaign against this plan. Greenpeace activists dramatically occupied Brent Spar at sea, gaining international media attention. Activists defying Shell on Brent Spar became a powerful image. The story dominated news cycles, with Greenpeace effectively framing it as a battle of concerned citizens versus a destructive corporation.

Shell initially downplayed the public outcry. It appeared to be dismissive and defensive, fueling backlash rather than addressing concerns and engaging in dialogue. Shell decided to focus on technical arguments and government approval, but severely misjudged public reaction and the increasing prominence of environmentalism.[14] It was widely criticized, seen as prioritizing profit over environmental responsibility. Greenpeace organized widespread boycotts of Shell petrol stations, particularly in Germany, significantly impacting Shell's sales.

The campaign caused reputational damage and sparked a wider conversation about corporate environmental responsibility. Under mounting pressure, Shell abandoned the deep-sea disposal plan, a major victory for Greenpeace. The Brent Spar case spurred stricter regulations about offshore disposal and influenced companies' approach to decommissioning projects.[15]

The Brent Spar debacle demonstrated how public activism could force corporate behavior change, even with government backing. Corporations learned they must consider broad public sentiment, not solely technical and legal factors, in their decision-making. The Brent Spar became a symbol for a new era of corporations being held accountable for their environmental impact, arguably leading to the birth of modern environmental activism.

Dove's "Real Beauty" Backlash on Unilever (2000s)[16]

Can a campaign both be a signature example of brand activism and highlight mis-activism? The answer is yes, and Dove's "Real Beauty" has the honor. As discussed in the preceding chapter, this campaign initially garnered praise for celebrating diverse body types. However, Dove also faced accusations of hypocrisy when it emerged that its parent company, Unilever, produces skin-lightening products and other beauty items promoting traditional beauty standards. This highlighted how actions by the parent brand or other brands under the same umbrella can undermine the messaging of a focal brand. It appeared as though Dove was fighting the wrongs exacerbated by its brother, Axe. Meanwhile, critics pointed out the hypocrisy of Dove advocating for inclusive beauty while simultaneously profiting from products perpetuating colorism and narrow beauty standards. Consequent Dove campaigns expanded to tackle issues like aging and body image in men. While well-intentioned, some nevertheless accused Dove of diluting the original message and co-opting various social issues for marketing purposes. Even decades later, Dove periodically faces criticism connected to this issue, making it difficult to fully escape the shadow of this controversy.[17]

Komen for the Cure and Planned Parenthood (2012)[18]

The Susan G. Komen Foundation is a leading breast cancer organization, known for its fundraising and awareness campaigns. For years, Komen had provided limited grants to some Planned Parenthood affiliates for breast cancer screenings and education. These were non-controversial as the funds were strictly designated for this purpose. In 2012, Komen announced it would cease funding Planned Parenthood. This was largely attributed to the appointment of a staunchly anti-abortion vice president at Komen. The move was widely seen as driven by anti-abortion politics, given Planned Parenthood's role as an abortion provider, even though those services weren't funded by Komen.[19] Komen faced a swift, fierce backlash from supporters, donors, healthcare advocates, and women's rights groups. It was accused of putting ideology over women's health and betraying the trust of those who donated, believing they supported unbiased cancer care access. The controversy fueled a firestorm on social media, with hashtags like #StandWithPP trending and calls to boycott Komen events. Many donors withdrew support and contributions to Komen sharply declined.[20] Under immense pressure, Komen reversed its decision.[21] However, the damage was done. Komen had severely misjudged its donor base. Despite the reversal, doubts about Komen's integrity have lingered. The case further fueled the polarization around the abortion debate in the US, hardening stances on both sides.

Nivea's "White is Purity" (2017)

In stark contrast to brands aligning themselves with progressive social movements, Nivea sparked outrage with an advertisement featuring the slogan "white is purity" across the image of a woman along with the caption "Keep it clean, keep it bright. Don't let anything ruin it." This tone-deaf campaign intended for the Middle East was met with swift condemnation for its obvious racial connotations, but was celebrated by white supremacist groups, highlighting the dangers of brands wading into sensitive territory without careful consideration of the potential consequences.[22]

Pepsi's and Kendall Jenner in "Live for Now" (2017)

The ad featured Kendall Jenner leaving a photoshoot to join a protest and offering a Pepsi to a police officer, trivializing social justice movements like Black Lives Matter. The ad was widely condemned for being tone deaf, exploitative, and minimizing the seriousness of real-world protests. Pepsi pulled the ad and apologized. See Chapters 1 and 3 for more details.

H&M's "Coolest Monkey in the Jungle" Sweatshirt (2018)[23]

An H&M ad featured a Black child modeling a green hoodie with the text "Coolest Monkey in the Jungle." The ad drew accusations of racism, perpetuating harmful stereotypes, and insensitivity. The controversy quickly escalated into an international incident. Many public figures and consumers called for boycotts of H&M, who removed the product image and issued multiple apologies, acknowledging the ad was insensitive. Protests erupted, including vandalism at some South African H&M stores.[24] H&M announced steps to improve diversity and inclusion within the company, including hiring a diversity leader. Celebrities, including The Weeknd and G-Eazy publicly ended their collaborations with H&M due to the incident, and others such as LeBron James and even Diddy (his personal brand tarnished since) publicly denounced them.[25] The debacle stands out as a stark example of racial insensitivity and the power of social media backlash.[26]

Conspiracy theories surrounding the incident were plenty: The child's mom had signed a contract with H&M that barred her from criticizing them. Malicious gossip surfaced, portraying her as greedy and heartless. Swedish tabloids even reported a fabricated story of H&M discovering and firing Swedish Nazis, who supposedly orchestrated the incident. An activist in Stockholm claimed that H&M and Diddy were locked in a secret, multi-million-dollar bidding war over the model's image rights. However, these allegations were all baseless. There was no contract, no secret conspiracy, no Nazis involved, and Diddy never expressed interest. Interviews with the child model's mom, H&M employees, and those present during the photoshoot painted a clear picture: the creation of this disturbingly racist image was not intentional. Yet, the fact remains that a major corporation was ultimately responsible for producing one of the most offensive images intended for widespread public consumption.[27]

Gillette's "The Best Men Can Be" (2019)

The campaign was a significant shift from Gillette's usual "The Best a Man Can Get" slogan, which focused on hyper-masculine ideals. It showcased men confronting bullying, sexual harassment, and other harmful "boys will be boys" behavior and urged men to be better, hold each other accountable, and raise boys to become positive role models. While some praised the toxic masculinity challenge, others found it patronizing and anti-men. The ad drew controversy and sparked debates about gender roles. While many praised the ad for tackling important issues, sparking necessary conversations about masculinity, and advocating for positive change, others accused Gillette of patronizing and insulting all men, profiting off social justice, and perpetuating anti-male stereotypes.[28]

The downvotes for the YouTube video launched in January outnumbered the upvotes almost five-to-one, though the ratio stabilized around two-to-one by September.[29] The ad struck a deep cultural nerve, exposing existing tensions about evolving gender roles and the #MeToo movement. So much so that Gillette had to disable the comments section. The campaign highlighted how difficult it is to portray complex social issues in short-form advertising without alienating some viewers. It also reignited the debate on whether brands should engage in social discourse and what the limits of this activism should be. Calls to boycott Gillette surfaced, though their impact on sales is debated.[30] The campaign hasn't faded away. To its credit, Gillette did not backtrack and took the campaign global. It continues to be referenced in discussions about woke advertising and masculinity. In the end, was Gillette better off? By February, net favorability (percentage of favorable minus unfavorable) toward Gillette had declined by ten points to 58%. It rebounded to 67% by May and was 64% by August, exactly where it had been a year earlier. Others tied a 7.7% relative decline in Gillette's global market share in 2019 to its "advertising fiasco."[31] Nevertheless, Gary Coombe, CEO of Global Grooming at P&G, attributed much of Gillette's 4% organic growth to the campaign.[32] He declared: "I am absolutely of the view now that for the majority of people to fall more deeply in love with today's brands you have to risk upsetting a small minority and that's what we've done."[33] It sounds like Gillette took a page out of Nike's playbook, without the legacy to back it up. But at least it has weathered the storm, and the legacy can only be built with commitment over time.

Social Justice Statements Amid Black Lives Matter (BLM) Protests (2020)

While many brands issued statements in support of racial justice after the murder of George Floyd, many also faced accusations of hypocrisy and performative activism, especially those with poor track records on diversity and inclusion within their own organizations. Many large companies with a history of internal discrimination lawsuits, lack of diversity at leadership levels, or questionable labor practices received backlash. The disconnect between their external social justice posturing and their internal realities was heavily highlighted. A rigorous multi-industry, multi-year, multi-platform study covering 435 brands and almost 400,000 social media posts found that BLM support had a negative impact on consumer responses. The study also reported the negative effect to be worse if the posted contents were self-promotional.[34] Over a hundred brands expressed support for BLM via social media.[35] The list included:

- L'Oreal: The beauty giant tweeted in solidarity with the BLM movement. It was criticized for previously dropping Munroe Bergdorf, a transgender model, for speaking out against racism.[36] Additionally, their past promotion of skin-lightening products was seen as conflicting with their new pro-diversity image.[37]
- Amazon: Amazon expressed support for BLM on social media. It was criticized for its partnerships with police departments[38] and the use of facial recognition technology,[39] which has been linked to racial bias in policing. There were also concerns about working conditions and the treatment of minority workers within Amazon warehouses.[40]
- PrettyLittleThing: This fast-fashion brand faced backlash for its "stand in solidarity" message. Critics pointed to the exploitative labor practices, lack of diversity in their models,[41] and contributions to unsustainable fashion, all of which conflict with ideals of social justice.[42]

Bristol Dry Gin and Lootin' Shootin' (2020)

Meanwhile, the gin brand thought it was a good idea to capitalize on the riots and tweeted: "When the shooting starts, the looting starts. Voted No. 1 gin by rioters for its complex botanical mix and high flammability." Facing customer backlash, the company later apologized and acknowledged it was "way out of line."[43]

Burger King and "Women Belong in the Kitchen" (2021)[44]

Burger King UK faced criticism for a tweet on International Women's Day that read, "Women belong in the kitchen." The tweet was intended to be a provocative reminder of the lack of female chefs in the industry, but it was widely condemned for being sexist and reinforcing harmful gender stereotypes. Burger King quickly deleted the tweet and apologized for the offense caused.

Burger King and Pride Month (2022)

Burger King was on a roll offending the public, this time in Austria. Many companies express support for the LGBTQ+ community during Pride Month through initiatives like rainbow-themed logos. But nobody does it like the King! In 2022, Burger King Austria faced criticism for its Pride Whopper, which featured two identical buns (two tops or two bottoms) intended to symbolize equality. The public condemned the campaign for using inappropriate sexual innuendos that perpetuated harmful stereotypes, demonstrating how brands can miss the mark when trying to convey solidarity with marginalized communities.[45]

Balenciaga Holiday Campaigns (2023)[46]

Balenciaga is a luxury fashion house known for its avant-garde and often provocative designs, but it has been tarnished by recent controversies involving its deeply inappropriate ad campaigns. Its gift shop campaign featured children posing with plush teddy bear bags dressed in what appeared to be bondage-inspired harnesses. These images were disturbing on their own, raising questions about the sexualization of children.[47] For its spring campaign, separate ads featured a printout of a Supreme Court ruling on child pornography laws as a prop.[48] This added an even more sinister and unforgivable layer to the controversy. The public outcry was intense and immediate. Accusations ranged from the images being deliberately exploitative to outright promoting pedophilia. High-profile figures associated with Balenciaga, like Kim Kardashian, distanced themselves and condemned the campaigns.[49] There were calls for legal action and investigations into whether child exploitation laws had been broken. Balenciaga issued multiple apologies, removed the campaigns, and stated they were taking legal action against those responsible for the set design. Most brand mis-activism involves missteps, cultural insensitivity, or tone-deafness. Balenciaga's campaigns crossed a line into an area deemed universally taboo and indefensible. The damage wasn't just about an ill-conceived campaign, but it fundamentally damaged trust in the brand, raising questions about the judgment and values of those in charge. Balenciaga faces a long road to rebuild its reputation because this scandal will be referenced as a cautionary tale for years. Its parent, Kering, which owns over a dozen brands, including Gucci, Saint Laurent, Brioni, and Alexander McQueen, does not report results for Balenciaga separately. However, its revenues fell 7% overall for Q4 2023.[50]

M&M's "All-Female" Packaging (2023)[51]

In January 2023, the limited-edition packaging featured the green, brown, and newly introduced purple female M&M's, flipped upside-down characters in celebration of the upcoming International Women's Day. Mars Wrigley (M&M's parent company) stated the intent was to celebrate women and spotlight their power to "flip the status quo."[52] They also pledged to support women-focused organizations. This campaign generated a significant buzz, but it was highly polarizing, garnering both praise for promoting female representation and criticism for being superficial or divisive. While many applauded the promotion of female representation, the fun, upside-down packaging, and the support of women-focused causes, some conservative commentators heavily criticized the campaign as unnecessary woke pandering and divisive identity politics.[53] Others felt the campaign was superficial, a token gesture that did little to address real gender equality issues.[54] The upside-down M&M's became the subject of ridicule and memes, some highlighting the absurdity of the debate. This example shows that even seemingly straightforward gestures for inclusivity can be interpreted differently, making brand activism in a divided culture very tricky. M&M's had positive intentions, but the execution sparked a debate about representation and the effectiveness of corporate social statements. The controversy, fueled by partisan media outlets and commentators on both sides, amplified the issue and took it out of context. In response, M&M's put the "spokescandies" on "indefinite pause" and introduced Maya Randolph as the new face M&M's.[55]

Bud Light's March Madness with Dylan Mulvaney (2023)

The Bud Light and Dylan Mulvaney partnership became a flashpoint for controversy, with the beer brand facing sharp criticism for its marketing attempt involving a transgender influencer. See Chapter 1 for more details.

The severity of the backlash varies depending on the case. Some result in apologies and retracted campaigns, whereas others have long-lasting impact on sales and brand reputation. You may disagree with some of our characterizations or choices of mis- or misc-activism, and that's OK. The promise of the chapter has been fulfilled if we made you think of the dark side and collateral damage of brand activism. Importantly, is there a better way to effectively gauge and engage in brand activism? Yes. Coming next.

References

1 Stine, Jeffrey K., "Smoke Gets in Your Eyes: 20th Century Tobacco Advertisements," *National Museum of American History*, March 17, 2014 (accessed June 9, 2024). https:// americanhistory.si.edu/explore/stories/smoke-gets-your-eyes-20th-century-toba cco-advertisements.
2 Little, Becky, "When Cigarette Companies Used Doctors to Push Smoking," *History. com*, March 28, 2023 (accessed June 9, 2024). https://www.history.com/news/ cigarette-ads-doctors-smoking-endorsement.
3 "The 1964 Report on Smoking and Health," Reports of the Surgeon General, *National Library of Medicine* (accessed June 9, 2024). https://profiles.nlm.nih.gov/ spotlight/nn/feature/smoking.
4 "Baby Killer," *Business Insider*, June 15, 2012 (accessed October 26, 2024). https:// www.businessinsider.com/nestles-infant-formula-scandal-2012-6#the-baby-kil ler-blew-the-lid-off-the-formula-industry-in-1974-1.
5 "The Infant Formula Scandal of the 1970s," *Historum*, December 3, 2023 (accessed June 9, 2024). https://historum.com/t/the-infant-formula-scandal-of-the-1970s.197334/.
6 https://www.nestle.com/ask-nestle/our-company/answers/nestle-boycott (accessed March 5, 2024).
7 Wattana, Melissa, "The Baby Bottle and the Bottom Line: Corporate Strategies and the Infant Formula Controversy in the 19070s," 2016 (accessed June 9, 2024). https://hshm.yale.edu/sites/default/files/files/Wattana%20senior%20es say%202016.pdf.
8 McCanne, Michael, "When Polaroid Workers Fought Apartheid," *Dissent*, August 14, 2020 (accessed June 9, 2024). https://www.dissentmagazine.org/online_artic les/when-polaroid-workers-fought-apartheid/.
9 "Polaroid on Apartheid," *Polaroidland*, April 6, 2013 (accessed June 9, 2024). http:// www.polaroidland.net/2013/04/06/polaroid-and-apartheid/.
10 Matrix, Kora, "Polaroid and South Africa," *Michigan State University* (accessed June 9, 2024). https://kora.matrix.msu.edu/files/50/304/32-130-1F7-84-african_a ctivist_archive-a0a8g3-b_12419.pdf.
11 "Polaroid on Apartheid," *Polaroidland*, April 6, 2013 (accessed June 9, 2024). http:// www.polaroidland.net/2013/04/06/polaroid-and-apartheid/.
12 McCanne, Michael, "When Polaroid Workers Fought Apartheid." Dissent, August 14, 2020 (accessed June 9, 2024). https://www.dissentmagazine.org/online_a rticles/when-polaroid-workers-fought-apartheid/.

13 The following section was drawn from the following sources unless noted otherwise.
Robinson, M.L., (2014). *Shell versus Greenpeace and Brent Spar. In: Marketing Big Oil: Brand Lessons from the World's Largest Companies.* Palgrave Macmillan. https://doi.org/10.1057/9781137388070_9
"Brent Spar Dossier," *Shell*, May 2008. (accessed June 9, 2024). https://www.shell.co.uk/about-us/sustainability/decommissioning/brent-spar-dossier/_jcr_content/root/main/section/call_to_action/links/item0.stream/1688633554375/32a2d94fa77c57684b3cad7d06bf6c7b65473faa/brent-spar-dossier.pdf.

14 Huxham, Max and David Summer (1999), "Emotion, Science and Rationality: The Case of the Brent Spar," *Environmental Values*, 8(3), 349–368. https://www.researchgate.net/publication/233709347_Emotion_Science_and_Rationality_The_Case_of_the_Brent_Spar.

15 Lofstedt, Ragnar E. and Ortwin Renn (1997), "The Brent Spar Controversy: An Example of Risk Communication Gone Wrong," *Risk Analysis*, 17(2), 131–136. https://ayomenulisfisip.wordpress.com/wp-content/uploads/2012/02/materi-3-the-brent-spar-controversy.pdf.

16 The section is drawn from the following source unless noted otherwise.
Celebre, Angela and Ashley Waggoner Denton, "The Good, The Bad, and The Ugly of the Dove Campaign for Real Beauty," *The Inquisitive Mind*, February 2014 (accessed June 9, 2024). https://www.in-mind.org/article/the-good-the-bad-and-the-ugly-of-the-dove-campaign-for-real-beauty.

17 "The Double Standards of "Dove Campaign for Real Beauty," *Reddit*, 2022 (accessed June 9, 2024). https://www.reddit.com/r/IndianSkincareAddicts/comments/s698de/the_double_standards_of_dove_campaign_for_real/?rdt=39546.

18 Groeger, Leba V., "Komen's Contortions: A Timeline of the Charity's Shifting Story on Planned Parenthood," *Propublica*, February 9, 2012 (accessed June 9, 2024). https://www.propublica.org/article/komens-contortions-a-timeline-of-the-charitys-shifting-story-on-planned-par.

19 "Alarmed and Saddened by Komen Foundation Succumbing to Political Pressure, Planned Parenthood Launches Fund for Breast Cancer Services," *Planned Parenthood*, January 31, 2012 (accessed June 9, 2024). https://www.plannedparenthood.org/about-us/newsroom/press-releases/alarmed-saddened-komen-foundation-succumbing-political-pressure-planned-parenthood-launches-fun.

20 Memmott, Mark, "Furor Erupts Over Susan G. Komen Halt of Grants to Planned Parenthood," *NPR*, January 31, 2012 (accessed June 9, 2024). https://www.npr.org/sections/thetwo-way/2012/01/31/146177902/furor-erupts-over-susan-g-komen-halt-of-grants-to-planned-parenthood.

21 Groeger, Leba V., "Komen's Contortions: A Timeline of the Charity's Shifting Story on Planned Parenthood," *Propublica*, February 9, 2012 (accessed June 9, 2024). https://www.propublica.org/article/komens-contortions-a-timeline-of-the-charitys-shifting-story-on-planned-par.

22 "Nivea Removes 'White is Purity' Deodorant Advert Branded 'Racist'," *BBC News*, April 4, 2017 (accessed October 26, 2024). https://www.bbc.com/news/world-europe-39489967.

23   West, Samantha, "H&M Faced Backlash Over Its 'Monkey' Sweatshirt Ad. It Isn't The Company's Only Controversy," *The Washington Post*, January 19, 2018 (accessed June 9, 2024). https://www.washingtonpost.com/news/arts-and-entertainm ent/wp/2018/01/19/hm-faced-backlash-over-its-monkey-sweatshirt-ad-it-isnt-the-companys-only-controversy/.

24   "Protesters Ransack South African H&M Stores over 'Racist' Ad," *Reuters*, January 13, 2009 (accessed June 9, 2024). https://www.nbcnews.com/news/world/protest ers-ransack-south-african-h-m-stores-over-racist-ad-n837506.

25   Wang, Connie, "The Real Story Behind H&M's Racist Monkey Sweatshirt," *Refinery 29*, July 11, 2019 (accessed June 9, 2024). https://www.refinery29.com/en-us/ 2019/07/237347/h-m-racist-hoodie-controversy-diversity-problem.

26   Lawrence, Derek, "G-Eazy Ends Relationship with H&M in Response to Its Disturbing Hoodie," *Entertainment*, January 9, 2018 (accessed June 9, 2024). https://ew.com/ music/2018/01/09/g-eazy-hm-hoodie/#:~:text=G%2DEazy%20has%20follo wed%20The,monkey%20in%20the%20jungle%E2%80%9D%20hoodie.

27   Wang, Connie, "The Real Story Behind H&M's Racist Monkey Sweatshirt," *Refinery29*, July 11, 2019 (accessed June 9, 2024). https://www.refinery29.com/ en-us/2019/07/237347/h-m-racist-hoodie-controversy-diversity-problem.

28   Ceron, Ella, "MRAs Outraged After Razor Company Asks Men to Show Common Decency," *The Cut*, January 15, 2019 (accessed June 9, 2024). https://www.the cut.com/2019/01/gillette-the-best-men-can-be-commercial-backlash.html. Horst, Peter, "Gillette's Controversial 'Toxic Masculinity' Ad and the Opportunity It Missed," *Forbes*, January 19, 2019 (accessed October 24, 2024). https://www. forbes.com/sites/peterhorst/2019/01/18/gillettes-controversial-toxic-masculin ity-ad-and-the-opportunity-it-missed/?sh=ed30ac155066.

29   Ceron, Ella, "MRAs Outraged After Razor Company Asks Men to Show Common Decency," *The Cut*, January 15, 2019 (accessed June 9, 2024). https://www.thecut. com/2019/01/gillette-the-best-men-can-be-commercial-backlash.html.   Neff, Jack, "Gillette's 'The Best Men Can Be' and the War on Toxic Masculinity," *Ad Age*, September 30, 2019 (accessed June 9, 2024). https://c101.hongtaoh.com/files/ 14-week/gillette.pdf.

30   Baggs, Michael, "Gillette Faces Backlash and Boycott Over #MeToo Advert," BBC, January 15, 2019 (accessed June 9, 2024). https://www.bbc.com/news/newsb eat-46874617. Guru, Pranav, "Procter & Gamble: Three Years After Gillette's 'We Believe'," *Medium*, January 12, 2022 (accessed June 9, 2024). https://pguru12.med ium.com/procter-gamble-three-year-after-gillettes-we-believe-ffa9c82d9772.

31   Georgiev, Georgi, "$350 mln. in 6 Months – The Cost of the 2019 Gillette Advertising Fiasco?" *Medium*, November 20, 2019 (accessed October 28, 2024). https://georgi-georgiev.medium.com/350-mln-in-6-months-the-cost-of-the-2019-gillette-advertising-fiasco-86785f29a4bf.

32   Neff, Jack, "Gillette's 'The Best Men Can Be' and the War on Toxic Masculinity," *Ad Age*, September 30, 2019 (accessed June 9, 2024). https://c101.hongtaoh.com/ files/14-week/gillette.pdf/.

33   Guru, Pranav, "Procter & Gamble: Three Years After Gillette's 'We Believe'," *Medium*, January 12, 2022 (accessed June 9, 2024). https://pguru12.medium.com/proc ter-gamble-three-year-after-gillettes-we-believe-ffa9c82d9772.

34 Wang, Yang, Marco Shaojun Qin, Xueming Luo, and Yu (Eric) Kou (2022), "Frontiers: How Support for Black Lives Matter Impacts Consumer Responses on Social Media," *Marketing Science*, 41(6), 1029–1044.

35 Perez, L., J. Cole, S. V., D. Ballard, & S. Vitacca (2020), Black Lives Matter Living Brand Tracker. November 1, 2022 (accessed March 5, 2025). https://www.lexieperez.com/writing/blacklivesmatter

36 Elan, Priya, "Munroe Bergdorf Accuses L'Oreal of Racial Hypocrisy," *The Guardian*, June 2, 2020 (accessed June 9, 2024). https://www.theguardian.com/fashion/2020/jun/02/munroe-bergdorf-accuses-loreal-of-racial-hypocrisy.

37 McEvoy, Jemima, "L'Oreal, Unilever Reassess Skin Lightening Products – But Won't Quit The Multi-Billion Dollar Market," *Forbes*, June 26, 2020 (accessed June 9, 2024). https://www.forbes.com/sites/jemimamcevoy/2020/06/26/loreal-unilever-reassess-skin-lightening-products-but-wont-quit-the-multi-billion-dollar-market/?sh=74012763223a.

38 Kelley, Jason and Matthew Guariglia, "Amazon Ring Must End Its Dangerous Partnerships With Police," *Electronic Frontier Foundation*, June 10, 2020 (accessed June 9, 2024). https://www.eff.org/deeplinks/2020/06/amazon-ring-must-end-its-dangerous-partnerships-police.

39 Hao, Karen, "The Two-Year Fight to Stop Amazon From Selling Face Recognition to the Police," *MIT Technology Review*, June 12, 2020 (accessed June 9, 2024). https://www.technologyreview.com/2020/06/12/1003482/amazon-stopped-selling-police-face-recognition-fight/.

40 Lumb, David, "Amazon Warehouse Workers Reportedly Complain of Racism and Death Threats." CNET, July 28, 2022 (accessed June 9, 2024). https://www.cnet.com/tech/amazon-warehouse-workers-reportedly-complain-of-racism-and-death-threats/. Blumberg, Nick, "Amazon Employees Say Company Retaliated After Charges of Racially Hostile Work Environment," *WTTW*, August 15, 2022 (accessed June 9, 2024). https://news.wttw.com/2022/08/15/amazon-employees-say-company-retaliated-after-charges-racially-hostile-work-environment. Del Rey, Jason, "Bias, Disrespect, and Demotions: Black Employees Say Amazon Has a Race Problem," *Vox*, February 26, 2021 (accessed June 9, 2024). https://www.vox.com/recode/2021/2/26/22297554/amazon-race-black-diversity-inclusion.

41 Steele, Tenai, "Pretty Little Thing Has A Diversity Problem Which No-one is Talking About," *The Boar*, December 14, 2019 (accessed June 9, 2024). https://theboar.org/2019/12/pretty-little-thing/.

42 Wolfe, Isobella, "How Ethical Is PrettyLittleThing?" *Good On You*, July 19, 2023 (accessed June 9, 2024). https://goodonyou.eco/how-ethical-is-prettylittlething/.

43 "Bristol Dry Gin's 'looting and shooting' Advert Criticized," BBC, June 2, 2020 (accessed September 17, 2024). https://www.bbc.com/news/uk-england-bristol-52892097.

44 Molina, Brett, "Burger King UK Under Fire for Tweeting 'Women Belong in the Kitchen' on International Women's Day," *USA Today*, March 8, 2021 (accessed September 17, 2024). https://www.usatoday.com/story/money/2021/03/08/burger-king-uk-under-fire-women-belong-kitchen-tweet/4627505001/.

45 Ska, Sonja, "17 Times Burger King Got Caught Up in a Charbroiled Controversy," *Ranker*, February 24, 2024 (accessed September 17, 2024). https://www.ranker.com/list/burger-king-controversies/sonja-ska.

46   Issawi, Danya and Danielle Cohen, "What to Know About the Balenciaga Ad Scandal," *The Cut*, January 24, 2024 (accessed June 9, 2024). https://www.thecut.com/article/what-to-know-about-the-balenciaga-ad-scandal.html.

47   Paton, Elizabeth, Vanessa Friedman, and Jessica Testa, "When High Fashion and QAnon Collide," *The New York Times*, November 28, 2022 (accessed June 9, 2024). https://www.nytimes.com/2022/11/28/style/balenciaga-campaign-controversy.html.

48   "Explained: Balenciaga's Controversial Ad Promoting Child Porn and Why is Kim Kardashian Being Criticized," *LiveMint*, November 29, 2022 (accessed June 29, 2024). https://www.livemint.com/news/world/explained-balenciaga-s-controversial-ad-promoting-child-porn-and-why-is-kim-kardashian-being-criticised-11669707372909.html.

49   Dress, Brad, "Kim Kardashian Condemns Balenciaga Over Photo Campaign," *The Hill*, November 28, 2022 (accessed June 9, 2024). https://thehill.com/blogs/in-the-know/3752676-kim-kardashian-condemns-balenciaga-over-photo-campaign/.

50   Kollmeyer, Barbara, "Sales at Balenciaga Continue to Suffer After Child Marketing Scandal," *Market Watch*, February 15, 2023 (accessed June 9, 2024). https://www.marketwatch.com/story/sales-at-balenciaga-continue-to-suffer-after-child-marketing-scandal-bafa2dcf.

51   Valinsky, Jordan, "M&M's New Packaging Is Causing A Stir," CNN, January 10, 2023 (accessed June 9, 2024). https://www.cnn.com/2023/01/10/business/m-and-ms-female-pack/index.html.

52   "Mars Celebrates Women Who Are Flipping The Status Quo with M&M's Limited Edition Packs and $800,000 in Funding," PR *Newswire*, January 5, 2023 (accessed June 9, 2024). https://www.prnewswire.com/news-releases/mars-celebrates-women-who-are-flipping-the-status-quo-with-mms-limited-edition-packs-and-800-000-in-funding-301714242.html.

53   Brammer, John Paul, "M&M's Changes Aren't Progressive. Give Green Her Boots Back," *The Washington Post*, January 21, 2022 (accessed June 9, 2024). https://www.washingtonpost.com/opinions/2022/01/21/mm-candy-mascot-redesign-not-woke-capitalism/. Nazar, Rachel, "M&M's Is Pulling Its Spokescandies After Facing Right-Wing Backlash," *Glitter*, January 25, 2023 (accessed June 9, 2024). https://glittermagazine.co/2023/01/25/mms-is-pulling-its-spokescandies-after-facing-right-wing-backlash/.

54   Nord, Jillian, "THEM & M's: Sexualized Media and Emphasized Femininity," *Sociological Images*, July 11, 2023 (accessed June 9, 2024). https://thesocietypages.org/socimages/2023/07/11/them-ms-sexualized-media-and-emphasized-femininity/.

55   Popli, Nik, "How M&M's Became the Latest Flash Point in the Culture Wars," *Time*, January 24, 2023 (accessed June 9, 2024). https://time.com/6249551/m-m-candy-mascots-culture-wars/.

7

PULL, PUSH, DOCTRINE, MANIFESTO

As the examples in the previous chapter demonstrate, it is often challenging for brand managers to find the level of guidance they need from mission and vision statements. Given the pervasive hammer of broad mission and vision statements, no wonder every cause out there looks like a nail. Thus, we explore where else brand managers may find guidance when it comes to dealing with different types of activism.

Pull versus push dichotomy is commonplace in business. For example, push entrepreneurship implies starting a business out of necessity. "Pushed" immigrants have historically been very prominent in restaurant ownership and laundry/dry cleaning businesses because they did not have the same job opportunities as others. In fact, even though they make up about 15% of the population, immigrants start about a quarter of all new businesses in the US, since finding jobs aligned with their background and credentials remains an ongoing problem.[1] In contrast, pull entrepreneurs are attracted to an opportunity they have identified and may choose it over other options

DOI: 10.4324/9781003593690-7

or quit existing jobs for a new venture, which is very common in Silicon Valley.[2]

In supply chain management, push inventory depends on replenishment based on anticipated demand/forecasting, whereas pull inventory relies on actual orders, (aka just-in-time delivery).[3]

In marketing, push promotions focus on selling or gaining adoption from the channel members (e.g., wholesalers) who are then trusted to do their best to sell to the next party in the distribution chain (retailers), and bring the product to the customers. These efforts typically include salespeople and trade journal advertisements or advertorials. In contrast, pull promotions refer to focusing on the end user and pulling them through mass media, coupons, or targeted social media campaigns to come to the point of sale. Many firms use a combination of the two approaches.[4]

In communications, push involves sending messages and pushing information to a broad audience (e.g., direct mail, emails) whereas pull engages recipients at their own discretion (e.g., web portals).[5] The list goes on: technology-driven push innovations vs. need/market-driven pull innovations,[6] top-down push leadership vs. collaborative pull leadership, and so on.[7]

In our era, where consumers increasingly expect companies to take a stand on social issues, we assert that brand activism has also become a powerful tool, subject to both the forces of push and pull.

Pull vs. Push Activism

Pull(ed) Brand Activism occurs when a brand is unwillingly or begrudgingly drawn into a social or political conflict. It might be targeted by activists or find itself caught in the crossfire of public opinion due to its actions (or inaction) on a particular issue. The lack of will is usually reflected in the lack of perceived authenticity. Pull activism is often reactive: the brand responds to pressure, trying to manage a crisis or protect its reputation. It is also defensive, as the brand's primary goal is often damage control rather than proactive change. And it is outright risky, with media and public attention focused on your brand, mishandling pull brand activism can lead to boycotts, negative publicity, and financial losses.

For example, Disney initially did not take a public position regarding the "Don't Say Gay" Bill in Florida but was later compelled to do so after employee outrage on social media.[8] Polaroid also did not take imme-diate action until they were dragged into it by their employees. In both cases, these companies were not the initiators of the conflicts, but found themselves at the center of public debates due to their policies, practices, or association with controversial issues. These situations highlight the challenges of navigating pull brand activism, where companies must balance their business interests with public pressure and ethical consid-erations. Thus, pull brand activism can be defined as *the reluctant, or forced engagement of a brand in social or political issues due to internal (employee) or external (public) pressure, often revealing a perceived lack of authenticity or pre-existing commitment to the cause.*

Pull brand activism can take one of two forms: *orchestrated* or *organic.* The former typically involves external organized group involvement to sway public and business leader opinion in a planned manner, whereas the latter implies founder or employee backlash in response to a current develop-ment. Delta and United Airlines' ending of their National Rifle Association (NRA) member discount program is an example of orchestrated pull activism. After the Parkland school shooting in 2018, these airlines faced pressure to cut ties with the NRA because of the organization's stance on gun control. Organized groups, including student activists and gun control advocates, launched campaigns and petitions calling for the end of the dis-count program for NRA members. United and Delta eventually succumbed to the pressure and ended the partnership.[9]

Other examples of orchestrated pull activism include:

Warner Bros. and Harry Potter's fair trade chocolate (2013–2015): The Harry Potter Alliance (later rebranded as Fandom Forward to include other fandoms), an activist group of millennial fans, successfully pressured Warner Bros. to use fair trade chocolate at their Wizarding World theme park. This three-year campaign, fueled by petitions and social media, even gained J.K. Rowling's support, forcing Warner Bros. to acknowledge the issue and switch to ethically sourced chocolate. In the process, these fans educated a generation about fair trade and continue to hold other brands accountable, demonstrating the power of fandom to drive brand activism.[10]

Uber and #DeleteUber (2017): During protests against President Trump's immigration ban, Uber was accused of undermining a taxi strike at JFK air-port. This led to the #DeleteUber campaign, where users deleted the app and encouraged others to do the same. The boycott, fueled by organized groups and social media outrage, forced Uber to take a public stance against the ban. Amid backlash, plus allegations of workplace discrimination and sexual harassment, CEO Travis Kalanick resigned.[11]

Facebook and the "Stop Hate for Profit" campaign (2020): Following the murder of George Floyd and the subsequent Black Lives Matter protests, a coalition of civil rights groups launched the Stop Hate for Profit campaign, calling on companies to boycott advertising on Facebook due to the platform's alleged failure to address hate speech and misinformation. The campaign gained significant traction, with major brands like Unilever, Coca-Cola, and Starbucks pulling their ads, forcing Facebook to make changes to its policies and content moderation practices.[12]

In contrast, organic pull activism stems from inside an organization. For example, Chick-Fil-A CEO Dan Cathy's anti-gay marriage comments during a radio interview dragged the company into renewed controversy and boycotts. Cathy later admitted his statements made "the company a symbol in the marriage debate" and it would've been wiser "to stay focused on customer service."[13]

Other examples include:

Google and Project Maven (2018): Thousands of Google employees signed a petition protesting the company's involvement in Project Maven, a military program using AI to analyze drone footage. This internal pressure, combined with public outcry, led Google to not renew its contract with the Department of Defense, and the company eventually developed AI principles that explicitly prohibit the use of its technology for weapons.[14]

Wayfair and Migrant Detention Centers (2019): Wayfair employees staged a walkout after discovering that the company was selling furniture to migrant detention centers.[15] The company made headlines due to the walkout, and the furniture sale valued at $200,000 caused the stock to tank by 5.3%.[16]

Coinbase and apolitical workplace (2020): Coinbase CEO Brian Armstrong declared the company an "apolitical workplace," discouraging employees from discussing political and social issues. This sparked internal dissent and resignations, with many employees arguing that silence on social issues is a political stance in itself. The controversy prompted Coinbase to clarify its stance and emphasize its commitment to diversity and inclusion.[17]

Basecamp and political discussions ban (2021): Basecamp, a project management software company, announced a ban on "societal and political discussions" at work. This decision sparked a mass exodus of employees, with many publicly criticizing the company's stance. The backlash led Basecamp to reconsider its policy and offer severance packages to employees who disagreed with the decision.[18]

And even a hybrid category of brand activism, which is simultaneously organic and orchestrated, exists:

Amazon and climate change (2019): Amazon employees staged a walkout to protest the company's environmental policies, demanding that Amazon commit to net-zero carbon emissions by 2040 and stop working with fossil fuel companies. This organized action, amplified by external environmental groups, put significant pressure on Amazon, eventually leading to the company's Climate Pledge and various sustainability initiatives.[19]

On the other hand, push brand activism occurs when a brand voluntarily engages in social or political advocacy of their choosing. It might take a stand on issues aligning with its values or those important to its target audience. Push activism is often proactive, the brand takes the initiative to address social issues, often before facing external pressure. It is also purposeful, the brand's actions are often driven by a genuine desire to make a positive impact, not just protect its image or make a quick buck. But it can also be opportunistic; activism delivered authentically can enhance brand reputation, build customer loyalty, and drive sales. Patagonia, as we have seen, is a brand that is decidedly a push brand activist. It also informs, engages, and pushes its customers further toward the sustainable living cause. Similarly, Ben & Jerry's is well recognized for its engaged social rights activism. No one is really surprised to hear these brands engaging in brand activism on environmental or civic causes. Thus, push brand activism can be defined as *a brand's voluntary and proactive engagement in social or political advocacy, often aligning with its values or its target audience's concerns, driven by a genuine desire to make a positive impact and potentially enhance brand reputation and loyalty.*

Pulled brand activists have few options. They can ignore the pressure, and hope it subsides and goes away, let themselves be pushed around, or they can push back. For example, Target reaffirmed its commitment to inclusion and did not back down when it faced a boycott due to its policy of letting transgender customers/employees use the bathroom of their choice. Customer traffic fell 2.2% and sales fell 7.2%.[20] Critics argued that the policy could encourage sexual predators and collected 1.4 million signatures online. The company responded by spending $20 million on renovations to make single occupancy bathrooms available in all of its 1,800 or so store locations.[21]

Similarly, faced with mounting pressure from environmental groups, employees, and public scrutiny,[22] Amazon embarked on an ambitious journey toward sustainability. The company has co-founded *The Climate Pledge*, committing to net-zero carbon emissions by 2040, and is investing billions in renewable energy projects and electric delivery vehicles.[23] While facing ongoing criticism, these initiatives highlight Amazon's recognition of its environmental impact and its efforts to transform into a greener global leader. On the consumer front, pulled activism options include patching, overhauling, or eliminating (e.g., revamping or pulling an offensive ad); on the employee front, commonly used action options are plastic surgery or transplant (e.g., adding more diversity to the board); and on the public front, episodic (e.g., one-time donation) or continuous attachment to an issue.[24]

In contrast, push brand activists have many options. They can decide whether or not to engage in a wide range of issues. We introduce dozens of such issues from categories such as social, cultural, legal, technological, ethical, political, and so on in the next chapter. Notably, they can also decide on the scale, place, and timing of the activism. They can develop and prepare for contingencies. In all, push activism is a superior option to pull. Brands that do not regularly perform a push activism audit can find themselves pulled into activism sooner or later.

Push brand activism can also take one of two forms: (carefully) *planned* and deployed or as a *spontaneous* response to a present event.

We would consider Nike's engagement with Colin Kaepernick to be a case of planned push activism because they could have supported Kaepernick in a number of ways and not engaged him for their Just Do It anniversary campaign. No one picketed for Nike to feature a controversial figure for the anniversary. They chose to undertake this position so publicly at that moment in time and sway public opinion to Kaepernick's racial injustice cause. In fact, there was a gap of two years between when Kaepernick first kneeled in September 2016 and the launch of "Dream Crazy" in September 2018. Similarly, Dove's "Real Beauty" campaign (see Chapter 5), which challenged traditional beauty standards and promoted body positivity, was also a deliberate choice of planned push activism.

In contrast, Airbnb's "#WeAccept" campaign, which offered free housing to those affected by President Trump's travel ban, was literally launched the following week after the signing of an executive order. Signed on January 27, 2017,[25] Airbnb launched its campaign on February 5, 2017, pledging housing relief to 100,000 people over five years.[26] Airbnb acted swiftly in response to Trump's executive order, demonstrating a commitment to its values of inclusivity and diversity. The campaign directly addressed the issue at hand, providing tangible support to those affected by the ban. It also tapped into the emotions of many people who were outraged, creating a sense of shared purpose and solidarity. The #WeAccept hashtag was widely shared on social media, further amplifying the campaign's message and reach. Airbnb's quick and compassionate response to the travel ban not only helped those in need, but also strengthened the brand's reputation as a socially responsible company. It remains a prime example of how brands can leverage their influence to make a positive impact in times of crisis through spontaneous push activism.[27]

Airbnb's entry to the Short Awards notes:

> The #WeAccept campaign was Airbnb's 3rd largest driver of Earned Impressions of all time at over 87 million. On Twitter, #weaccept was the #1 used advertiser hashtag used during the Super Bowl, as Airbnb generated over 33k tweets during the first half of the game, more than any other advertiser, with overwhelmingly positive sentiment. Reactions to the overall campaign were 85% positive (based on Airbnb internal tracker).
>
> Our Facebook and Instagram content supporting the campaign was shared over 90,000 times and received over 500k likes. We saw a 13% increase in site visitors (US and Canada) the week following the Super Bowl, as well as a 7.2% increase in site visitors (US and Canada) in the month following the Super Bowl.

> On Facebook specifically, we invested primarily in promoting the 30 second #weaccept video and targeted all audiences across the political spectrum. The video was ultimately viewed 19 million times and shared 100,901 times, including 18,600 shares from Facebook users from conservative audience segmentation. It stands as our most shared FB video of all time, and maintained a view rate that was consistently 15% above our benchmark across all audiences. Perhaps most importantly, Airbnb's call to the public to open their homes to displaced populations resulted in 15.4K total volunteer host signups to date.[28]

The numbers speak for themselves. The campaign was widely praised for its humanitarian approach and generated significant positive publicity for Airbnb.

Not every push activism, planned or spontaneous, succeeds of course. Pepsi's "Live for Now" campaign with Kendall Jenner and Starbucks' "Race Together" were also deliberate choices that came across as tone deaf. So how should brands react when pulled and what should their north star be when deciding what to push? Given that mission and vision statements are hopelessly broad for guidance, enter doctrines and manifestos.

A **doctrine** is a set of beliefs, principles, or teachings that are generally accepted by a particular group or institution. It often provides a framework for understanding and interpreting information within a specific context, such as religious doctrine, legal doctrine, or military doctrine. Doctrines are typically more formal and established than manifestos.[29]

A **manifesto** is a public declaration of intentions, motives, or views, often issued by a group or individual. It typically outlines a plan of action or expresses a strong opinion on a particular issue. Manifestos are often associated with political or social movements and can be more passionate and persuasive in nature.[30]

Doctrines and manifestos differ in terms of length and structure, tone and purpose, and authors and audience. The Geneva Conventions represent doctrine, and the Declaration of Independence represents a manifesto. These differences are highlighted in Table 7.1.

Notably, an award-winning study reported *marketing doctrine* to be a difference maker for performance. Challagalla and colleagues defined marketing doctrine as "a firm's unique principles, distilled from its experience, which

Table 7.1 Differences between Doctrine and Manifesto

Feature	Doctrine	Manifesto
Purpose	To provide a framework for understanding and interpreting information within a specific context.	To declare intentions, motives, or views, often with a call to action.
Tone	Formal, authoritative, systematic.	Passionate, persuasive, urgent.
Length	Typically longer and more comprehensive, covering a range of principles and beliefs.	Usually shorter and more focused, highlighting key points and demands.
Structure	Organized, often with sections and subsections, may cite sources and precedents.	Less structured, may be written in a more personal or poetic style.
Audience	Members of a specific group or institution, those seeking to understand the doctrine's principles.	The general public, supporters of a cause, those opposed to the status quo.
Authors	Established institutions, religious leaders, legal scholars, etc.	Individuals, political groups, social movements.
Examples	Catechism of the Catholic Church, Monroe Doctrine, Geneva Conventions.	Communist Manifesto, The Futurist Manifesto, The Declaration of Independence.
Historical Use	To maintain continuity and consistency within a group or institution over time.	To spark change, challenge existing norms, or galvanize support for a new idea or movement.

provide firm-wide guidance on market-facing choices."[31] The authors noted it provides a balance between consistency and flexibility for the organization by offering high-level guidance to all decision-makers without specifying execution details. Five to seven principles are often found to be enough to offer sufficient guidance and "guard rails." A marketing doctrine is heuristic and not a checklist, based on data and not opinion (say of the founder or the board), and is developed in collaboration and not top-down. The following marketing doctrine was derived for Apple based on the 14 guiding principles of the company:

1. Only enter markets where we can be the best—we must have a compelling differentiation.
2. Focus on few products and models.
3. Have the courage to cannibalize—don't hang on to ideas from the past even if they have been successful; if we don't cannibalize ourselves, someone else will.
4. Take end-to-end responsibility for the user experience.
5. Put products before profits—push for perfection in products.
6. Do not spread product resources or none will be great—do few things.
7. Read things that are not on the page (i.e., discover unmet or unrecognized needs) and don't be a slave to focus groups.

Not to be confused with marketing doctrine, a brand manifesto is a declaration of what your brand stands for, what it fights for, and what it refuses to compromise on. You can think of it as a love letter to the brand's tribe, the people who believe in the vision and connect with the purpose. It's not about pleasing everyone; it's about galvanizing those who matter most. Clarity, passion, specificity, audacity, and resonance are all characteristics of quality brand manifestos.

Importantly, a brand manifesto isn't just words on paper or aspirational. It's a living document that should guide every decision the brand makes, from product development to marketing campaigns. It's the beating heart of the brand, the source of its energy and inspiration, and should be the compass that guides the brand toward its true north, attracting a tribe of loyal followers who share its values. While some brands will come out with manifestos, it has also become popular to present them within purpose statements.[32] It will ideally express why the brand exists, its identity, and what it does to create extraordinary value for stakeholders.[33]

While Apple does not have an official vision statement, the following have been considered as "the closest thing they have to a stated Vision":[34]

> *Apple is dedicated to the empowerment of man—to making personal computing accessible to each and every individual so as to help change the way we think, work, learn, and communicate.*
>
> *The Company is committed to bringing the best user experience to its customers through its innovative hardware, software and services. The Company's business strategy leverages its unique ability to design and develop its own operating systems, hardware, application software and*

services to provide its customers products and solutions with innovative design, superior ease-of-use and seamless integration.[35]

Apple's more than 100,000 employees are dedicated to making the best products on earth, and to leaving the world better than we found it.[36]

Apple's brand manifesto can be found in its "Think Different" campaign:

Here's to the crazy ones.
The misfits.
The rebels.
The troublemakers.
The round pegs in the square holes.
The ones who see things differently.
They're not fond of rules.
And they have no respect for the status quo.
You can praise them, disagree with them, quote them, disbelieve them,
glorify or vilify them.
About the only thing you can't do is ignore them.
Because they change things.
They invent. They imagine. They heal.
They explore. They create. They inspire.
They push the human race forward.
Maybe they have to be crazy.
How else can you stare at an empty canvas and see a work of art?
Or sit in silence and hear a song that's never been written?
Or gaze at a red planet and see a laboratory on wheels?
We make tools for these kinds of people.
While some see them as the crazy ones, we see genius.
Because the people who are crazy enough to think they can change the
world, are the ones who do.[37]

Apple is universally known for its activism on LGBTQ+ rights.[38] While the extracted vision statements do not adequately explain why, a review of the Apple manifesto makes it crystal clear that this choice of activism is far more deeply rooted than the personal agenda of CEO Tim Cook. It is authentic.

Likewise, Nike's mission "to bring inspiration and innovation to every athlete in the world" and its vision "to do everything possible to expand human potential" are decidedly broad.[39] However, its manifesto makes it quite clear as to why they engaged with Kaepernick like they did:[40]

1. Our business is change.
2. We're on offense. All the time.
3. Perfect results count—not a perfect process.
   Break the rules: fight the law.
4. This is as much about battle as about business.
5. Assume nothing.
   Make sure people keep their promises.
   Push yourselves, push others.
   Stretch the possible.
6. Live off the land.
7. Your job isn't done until the job is done.
8. Dangers:
   Bureaucracy
   Personal ambition
   Energy takers vs. energy givers
   Knowing our weaknessesDon't get too many things on the platter.
9. It won't be pretty.
10. If we do the right things, we'll make money damn near automatic.

Thus, while mission and vision statements provide a useful starting point, they are usually insufficient in detail to provide answers when it comes to brand activism. We suggest that for push activism, the brand managers should take a top-down approach and begin with mission and vision statements, but also consider marketing doctrines and brand manifestos, in that order, to identify a cause with deeper alignment. At the corporate level, such an approach may also help to identify opportunities or gaps that may be appropriate for a brand other than the focal brand in the portfolio or serve as the impetus to reposition or launch a new brand. It can also prevent unforced errors where a brand unnecessarily engages in a divisive issue and/or picks a cause but comes across as inauthentic.

The process for engaging in pull(ed) activism should be the opposite. Rather than finding relatively easy justification from broad statements, we suggest a bottom-up approach to review whether or not the brand's manifesto is really aligned with the pull cause, and if so, seeking higher-level reviews of marketing doctrine and company mission and vision statements. In some cases, a brand's manifesto can be used as the rationale as to why the brand will not engage in a given issue, internally or publicly. Times of crises tend to be high-pressure and emotion-laden. Thus, clarity and straight-forward guidance from a doctrine or manifesto can be especially helpful. Our conversations with executives and anecdotal observations suggest that brands without manifestos tend to get into pull activism and mis-activate more often (empirical research pending). If brand manifestos for Uber or Papa John's exist, we are not aware of them.

The Bottom Line

We introduced the concepts of pull and push brand activism, both of which can significantly impact a company's reputation and bottom line. Push brand activism, when done authentically and strategically, can be an especially powerful tool for positive change and brand building. Mission and vision statements tend to be very open-ended. Companies that genuinely care about social issues and align their actions with their marketing doctrine and brand manifestos, in addition to their mission and vision, are more likely to win over consumers, have beloved brand communities, and make a lasting positive impact. Without the guiding light of doctrine and the clarion call of manifestos, activism risks wandering astray, a rudderless ship unsure if it sails toward enlightenment or backward into the depths of ignorance, a voice shouting slogans without knowing if they echo progress or regress, genuinely woke, appropriately conservative, or woefully misguided.

References

1   "Immigrant Entrepreneurship: Economic Potential and Obstacles to Success," *Bipartisan Policy Center*, June 13, 2022 (accessed June 9, 2024). https://bipartisa npolicy.org/report/immigrant-entrepreneurship-economic-potential-and-obstac les-to-success/#:~:text=Studies%20on%20immigrant%20entrepreneurs%20h ave,firm%20than%20U.S.%2Dborn%20citizens.

2   Alam, Sayed M., Kohinoor Biswas, and M. M. Sulphey (2021), "A Case Study on the Entrepreneurship Process of Push and Pull Women Entrepreneurs," *South Asian Journal of Business and Management Cases*, 10(2), 207–217. https://journals.sagepub. com/doi/abs/10.1177/22779779211028536?journalCode=bmca#:~:text= A%20push%2Dentrepreneur%20could%20be,sake%20of%20seeking%20grea ter%20independence.

3   "Push vs. Pull Inventory Management Strategies," (accessed June 9, 2024). https://www.waspbarcode.com/buzz/inventory-management-strategies.

4   "What Are Push & Pull Promotional Strategies," *Intuit Quickbooks*, January 10, 2019 (accessed June 9, 2024). https://quickbooks.intuit.com/ca/resources/marketing/push-and-pull-promotional-strategy/.

5   "Push vs Pull vs Interactive Communication," *PM Vidya*, (accessed October 26, 2024). https://pmvidya.com/blog/push-vs-pull-vs-interactive-communication/.

6   Naganathan, Krishnan, "Push and Pull Innovation," *Think Horizon Consulting*, October 9, 2019 (accessed June 9, 2024). https://www.thinkhorizonconsulting.com/post/push-and-pull-innovation.

7   Olson, Andrea Belk, "Why 'Push' and 'Pull' Management Styles Are Key to Successful Organizational Change," *World Economic Forum*, February 13, 2023 (accessed June 9, 2024). https://www.weforum.org/agenda/2023/02/why-push-and-pull-management-styles-are-key-to-successful-change/.

8   Blair, Elizabeth, "After Protests, Disney CEO Speaks Out Against Florida's 'Don't Say Gay' Bill," NPR, March 10, 2022 (accessed June 9, 2024). https://www.npr.org/2022/03/08/1085130633/disney-response-florida-bill-dont-say-gay.

9   Stanglin, Doug, "NRA Hits Back at United Airlines, Delta, Other Companies for Cutting Ties," *USA Today*, February 24, 2018 (accessed June 9, 2024). https://www.usatoday.com/story/news/2018/02/24/united-airlines-delta-latest-big-names-cut-ties-nra/369950002/.

10 Sullivan, Erin, "Warner Bros. Commits to Using Only Fair Trade Chocolate Products in Wizarding World of Harry Potter Parks," *Orlando Weekly*, January 22, 2015 (accessed October 24, 2024). https://www.orlandoweekly.com/arts/warner-bros-commits-to-using-only-fair-trade-chocolate-products-in-wizarding-world-of-harry-potter-parks-2348059.

11 Siddiqui, Faiz, "Uber Triggers Protest for Collecting Fares During Taxi Strike Against Refugee Ban," *The Washington Post*, January 29, 2017 (accessed June 9, 2024). https://www.washingtonpost.com/news/dr-gridlock/wp/2017/01/29/uber-triggers-protest-for-not-supporting-taxi-strike-against-refugee-ban/.

12 Scola, Nancy, "Inside the Ad Boycott That Has Facebook on the Defensive," *Politico*, July 3, 2020 (accessed June 9, 2024). https://www.politico.com/news/magazine/2020/07/03/activists-advertising-boycott-facebook-348528.

13 O'Connor, Clare, "Chick-fil-A CEO Cathy: Gay Marriage Still Wrong, But I'll Shut Up About It and Sell Chicken," *Forbes*, March 19, 2014 (accessed October 26, 2024). https://www.forbes.com/sites/clareoconnor/2014/03/19/chick-fil-a-ceo-cathy-gay-marriage-still-wrong-but-ill-shut-up-about-it-and-sell-chicken/?sh=3ef269e32fcb.

14 Shane, Scott and Daisuke Wakabayashi, "'The Business of War': Google Employees Protest Work for the Pentagon," *The New York Times*, April 4, 2018 (accessed June 9, 2024). https://www.nytimes.com/2018/04/04/technology/google-letter-ceo-pentagon-project.html

15 Glaser, April, "The Wayfair Walkout Is A Different Kind of Tech Worker Protest," *Slate*, June 26, 2019 (accessed June 9, 2024). https://slate.com/technology/2019/06/wayfair-walkout-trump-protest-border-detention-beds.html.

16 Fares, Melissa, "Wayfair Employee Walkout Called Over Alleged Furniture Sales to U.S. Migrant Camp," *AOL.com*, June 25, 2019 (accessed June 9, 2024).https:// www.aol.com/wayfair-employee-walkout-called-over-233828997.html.

17 MacLellan, Lila, "Coinbase Employees Are Quitting Their Newly 'Apolitical' Workplace," *Yahoo! Tech*, October 9, 2020 (accessed June 9, 2024). https:// www.yahoo.com/tech/coinbase-employees-quitting-newly-apolitical-172348 782.html.

18 Newton, Casey, "Breaking Camp," *TheVerge*, April 27, 2021 (accessed June 9, 2024). https://www.theverge.com/2021/4/27/22406673/basecamp-political-speech-policy-controversy.

19 Ghaffary, Shirin, "Here's Why the Amazon Climate Workout is a Big Deal," *Vox*, September 20, 2019 (accessed June 9, 2024). https://www.vox.com/recode/ 2019/9/20/20874497/amazon-climate-change-walkout-google-microsoft-str ike-tech-activism.

20 Peterson, Hayley, "The Target Boycott is Costing More Than Anyone Expected," *Business Insider*, August 24, 2016 (accessed June 9, 2024). https://www.business insider.com/target-boycott-costs-20-million-2016-8.

21 Isidore, Chris, "Target's $20 Million Answer to Transgender Bathroom Boycott," *CNN Business*, August 17, 2016 (accessed June 9, 2024). https://money.cnn.com/ 2016/08/17/news/companies/target-bathroom-transgender/index.html.

22 Evans, Will, "Private Report Shows How Amazon Drastically Undercounts Its Carbon Footprint," *RevealNews.org*, February 25, 2022 (accessed June 9, 2024). https://revealnews.org/article/private-report-shows-how-amazon-drastically-undercounts-its-carbon-footprint/.

23 "Net-Zero Carbon Emissions by 2040." https://sustainability.aboutamazon.com/ climate-solutions. (accessed June 9, 2024).

24 Aboelenien, Aya and Chau Minh Nguyen (2024), "From Dr. Seuss to Barbie's Cancellation: Brand's Institutional Work in Response to Changed Market Logics," *Journal of Brand Management*, 31, 108–125.

25 Almasy, Steve and Darran Simon, "A Timeline of President Trump's Travel Bans," CNN, March 30, 2017 (accessed June 9, 2024). https://www.cnn.com/2017/ 02/10/us/trump-travel-ban-timeline/index.html.

26 "#weaccept," *Airbnb*, February 5, 2017 (accessed June 9, 2024). https://www.air bnb.com/weaccept.

27 Cowan, Sarah, "Airbnb #WeAccept Findings," March 21, 2021 (accessed June 9, 2024). https://sarah-cowan-portfolio.com/2021/03/21/airbnb-weaccept-findings/.

28 Shorty Awards https://shortyawards.com/2nd-socialgood/weaccept (accessed March 5, 2025).

29 "Doctine." Merriam-Webster Dictionary. https://www.merriam-webster.com/dic tionary/doctrine.

30 "Manifesto." Merriam-Webster Dictionary. https://www.merriam-webster.com/ dictionary/manifesto.

31 Challagalla, Goutam, Brian R. Murtha, and Bernard Jaworski (2014), "Marketing Doctrine: A Principles-Based Approach to Guiding Marketing Decision Making in Firms," *Journal of Marketing*, 78(4), 4–20.

32 Aaker, David (2023), *The Future of Purpose-Driven Branding: Signature Programs That Impact & Inspire Both Business and Society.* Morgan James Publishing.

33 Blocker, Christopher P., Joseph P. Cannon, and Jonathan Z. Zhang (2024), "Purpose Orientation: An Emerging Theory Transforming Business for a Better World," *Journal of the Academy of Marketing Science.* https://doi.org/10.1007/s11747-023-00989-5.

34 Weinblatt, Lois, "Apple's Vision: Do They Have an Official Vision Statement," *True North*, March 15, 2023 (accessed June 9, 2024). https://www.truenorthvisionar ies.com/resources/apple-mission-vision-values.

35 "Apple Form 10-K," September 30, 2017 (accessed June 9, 2024). https:// s2.q4cdn.com/470004039/files/doc_financials/2017/10-K_2017_As-Filed.pdf.

36 "Apple Reports Second Quarter Results," *Apple*, April 28, 2022 (accessed June 9, 2024). https://www.apple.com/newsroom/2022/04/apple-reports-second-quarter-results/.

37 "Here's To The Crazy Ones," Apple, September 21, (accessed June 9, 2024). https://basicappleguy.com/basicappleblog/heres-to-the-crazy-ones.

38 Birnbaum, Emily, "Apple Wields Its Lobbying Might Against LGBTQ Laws," *Politico*, April 1, 2022 (accessed June 9, 2024). https://www.politico.com/news/2022/ 04/01/apple-lobbying-anti-lgbtq-laws-00022127.

39 Pereira, Daniel, "Nike Mission and Vision Statement," *Business Model Analyst*, April 14, 2023 (accessed June 9, 2024). https://businessmodelanalyst.com/nike-mission-and-vision-statement/.

40 Hilder, Rosie, "This 1970s Nike Manifesto Is Absolutely Wild," *Creative Bloq*, January 22, 2023 (accessed June 9, 2024). https://www.creativebloq.com/news/nike-manifesto.

8

SHETH-USLAY BRAND ACTIVISM ALIGNMENT MATRIX

We admit, even after seven chapters on brand activism, the preferred actions are still somewhat blurry. What should be clear, though, is that the recommended path of action is not generic and should be based on contextual factors. Thus, we created a Brand Activism Alignment Framework to illuminate the path for all. Consider the previous chapters leading up to now as bread, butter, salad, and tasty appetizers. We hope you are hungry for more because, from this chapter on, we deliver the delicious main course, delicacies, and dessert.

The Sheth-Uslay framework of brand activism consists of two main dimensions: brand positioning and activism resonance.

Brand Positioning

The recommended path for a brand is not independent of its history, market standing and strength, or perceived power. We believe that this dimension is best captured by two factors.

DOI: 10.4324/9781003593690-8

Market share: The dollar sales share of a brand in its category is a great proxy for all the above. Except in cases where a brand creates a new category (like Apple did with the iPhone to dethrone Nokia), it is very hard for a newcomer to displace incumbents and become a market share leader. So legacy and inertia matter for achieving significant market share which creates perceived strength and renders market power, perceived or otherwise. Market share alone is a significant correlate and leading indicator of financial performance, as some of our original research on the topic also shows.[1] Several of the brands we have discussed so far, such as Nike, Starbucks, and Gillette, are also market share leaders and are easily recognizable as such. Bud Light was the market share leader for two decades until its brand misactivism, which we dissected earlier.

Mind share: However, market share is not enough to ascertain a brand's positioning. Since brand activism typically plays out in the public domain, we also have to consider a brand's mind share, that is, awareness of the brand among the consumers. These two constructs are correlated, but not perfectly. For example, there are many B2B brands that command a high share of their markets but the average consumer is not familiar with them. While you may have heard of Oracle, SAP, and Cisco, you may not be as familiar with Epic Systems (which dominates the electronic health record software market and not to be confused with Epic Games, the publisher of the blockbuster video game _Fortnite_), Avalara (a leader in business tax compliance software), or Infor (known for its industry-specific ERP software platforms). Even other mainstream B2B brands such as CDKGlobal (automotive and equipment dealership software), Gartner (research and consulting), ServiceNow (IT service management including support, automation, and workflow) may only have lackluster recognition based on the individual consumer's background.

On the other hand, there are many specialty brands that do not have a large market share but nevertheless hold a significant share in the minds of consumers. Brands built around exclusivity come to mind. For example, Harvard or all Ivy League universities, for that matter.[2] Similarly, while the delivery of 13,663 vehicles in 2023 was a record for Ferrari,[3] its share of global auto sales is negligible. However, Ferrari's mind share is clearly non-negligible; to the contrary, it reaches iconic status. That is why Ferrari's 2024 market cap of roughly $87 billion dwarves General Motors'

$57 billion or Ford's $43 billion, despite the fact that each moves cars in volumes that are several magnitudes higher (think thousands versus millions in units).[4]

The distinction between market share and mind share matters because consumers do not ordinarily pressure brands they are not familiar with. Brands that have high market share face higher financial risk, especially in the short term, whereas brands with higher mind share face higher reputational risk (and thereby financial risk), especially in the long term. Consider that many prominent alums of Harvard and Columbia Universities announced that they would stop their giving to their alma maters due to their stance on the Israeli-Palestinian conflict. These denouncements are likely to have enduring consequences on future giving behavior by the Jewish community and may even impact enrollments.

Based on these observations, we submit that a better metric of brand positioning is market share × mind share. Think Google, Microsoft, Coca-Cola, Nike, or Toyota as examples of brands well-positioned for the mass market. Other brands with low to medium market and mind shares typically serve niche product, service, or geographic markets. For example, regional food brands, such as Middlewarth Potato Chips (popular in Central Pennsylvania), niche clothing lines such as Selkie (known for its whimsical dresses), indie beauty brands such as Cocokind (clean skincare), or specialty goods brands such as Tenkara (minimalist fishing rods). Naturally, mainstream brands with a high share of both market and mind have a lot more to risk and lose if they engage in activism on divisive issues. But more on that later.

Activism Resonance

The second main dimension of our framework is activism resonance which also consists of two factors.

(Issue) Consensus: Topics that can be subject to activism are not all made of the same cloth. While some issues such as reducing single-use plastics, anti-smoking, or gambling addiction have (near) consensus and public support, others such as immigration policy, gun control, abortion access, and LGBTQ+ rights have proven to be highly divisive issues in the US. These issues usually touch on core values, personal identity, or strongly held beliefs that spark passionate disagreement and backlash. Given the noteworthy boycotts and buycotts regarding several of the high-profile brand activism cases we have discussed, the level of consensus is clearly an important factor to consider. Brands taking a stance on divisive issues alienate a significant portion of consumers, no matter which side they choose. Even nuanced positions can prove inflammatory. For example, a consumer in favor of advancing LGBTQ+ rights may have a different stance when it comes to transgender youth participation in competitive women's sports.

(Perceived) Importance: This second factor pertains to the importance of the issue. While we refer to the aggregate sentiment here, importance is perceived and can also vary depending on the target market. For example, while environmental sustainability is a fundamental topic that affects everyone, it may not be perceived as a priority by certain consumer groups. Recall that there were groups of consumers staunchly against vaccination, even at the height of the COVID-19 pandemic. The perceived importance of an issue may also vary by culture, socioeconomic status, country, or region.

Interestingly, unlike market share and mind share which are typically positively correlated, the level of consensus on a topic and its perceived importance tend to be negatively correlated. For example, there is presumably a consensus regarding preventing cruelty against animals, however, it is not considered as important an issue by the majority of the public to prevent them from purchasing cosmetics developed without animal testing or boycotting eggs that are not produced cage-free. In contrast, the need for gun control or abortion rights are important topics, yet public sentiment for them has been divided.

That is not to say high importance, high consensus issues do not exist. Improving education and healthcare can be potentially low-risk from a brand activism perspective if the activism focuses on uncontroversial solutions, such as skills training or improving affordability or accessibility without relying primarily on public resources.

Meanwhile, high importance, low consensus issues such as preventing/ addressing global warming face a significant risk of backlash no matter the stance. Such risks are especially high for mainstream brands that serve the population at large (e.g., Coca-Cola) than they are for niche brands (e.g., Prime Hydration). On the other hand, low importance, high consensus issues such as supporting local charities or employee volunteerism typically carry minimal risk but also offer commensurately low impact. Finally, unless a brand is trying to carve out a unique positioning in a highly cluttered space, a *low importance, low consensus* cause is unlikely to generate significant results unless it strikes a strong chord to create strong loyalty with a niche group of consumers.

High brand resonance (consensus × importance) requires both moderate to high consensus and importance, which is rare. More recently, we have seen mainstream brands accept major trade-offs on the level of consensus while focusing on important topics, achieving mixed results. To be sure, the math is relatively straightforward when a brand activates a high importance, low consensus issue. It is even more straightforward when it activates a low importance, high consensus issue. However, it is the middle grounds with medium consensus or medium importance levels where the math becomes more blurry, the "stuck-in-the-middle" land where brands struggle the most and can use ample guidance.

Recall that some causes may have near-consensus status with certain groups of customers depending on how a market is segmented. Thus, there are tremendous opportunities for niche brands to achieve both high consensus and high perceived importance in their defined markets. We discuss potential approaches to brand activism based on the positioning of the focal brand in Chapters 10–13. Before we do, let us not forget that we can let issues choose us (e.g., pull(ed) activism based on employee or public sentiment) or we can do our homework and choose to push the issue that survives the Five Rings of alignment (mission & vision, brand, business, legacy, authenticity) covered in Chapter 2. There are many issues to choose from and even the categories to choose from are numerous. The following is not meant to be a comprehensive list:

Social: gender, LGBTQ+, religion, race, age sensitivity.

Beyond social: Diversity, equity, inclusion, and access (for workforce, marketing communications), disability rights, prison reform.

Cultural: cultural preservation, Indigenous heritage, endangered languages, practice and promoting local culinary traditions, diversity, artistic freedom, spotlight and avoid cultural appropriation.

Education: partner with educational institutions, promote education, education equity, (public) school funding, early childhood education, STEM education, financial literacy, lifelong learning, career readiness, combating teacher burnout, combating disinformation, disseminate content or curricula, open educational resources, second language acquisition, art education, first-generation college attendance, special needs education, vocational training, entrepreneurship education, student loan debt relief, micro-learning, educational entertainment, community learning hubs.

Legal: stances on tax policy, workplace, employment laws, criminal justice reform (mass incarceration, racial profiling, police brutality), IP rights, antitrust laws, consumer protection, access to justice (promote alternative resolution methods), international trade law, cybersecurity laws, counterfeit goods and piracy.

Technological: digital divide and literacy, AI divide, responsible AI development, net neutrality, data privacy (responsible use of facial recognition), cybersecurity, technology addiction, ethical use of social media, right to repair, clean technologies.

Philanthropic: charitable giving, community support, focused (or skill-based) employee volunteering, revenue-based giving (cause marketing), disaster relief and recovery, advocacy for non-profits, impact investing, social entrepreneurship, product donations, matching donations.

Business: governance, organization, executive pay, worker rights, worker comps, labor and union disputes, product safety, responsible/mindful marketing, employee ownership, DEI in the workplace, transparency in business, gender pay gap, fair trade practices.

Ethical (beyond legal): fair labor practices, transparency in data collection and use, ethical AI, tax responsibility and transparency, algorithmic fairness in hiring (bias mitigation), responsible lending, whistleblower protection, equitable pay transparency.

Animal welfare: factory farming, working animals, marine animal welfare, wildlife conservation, cruelty-free ingredients, responsible pet ownership, support animal welfare organizations, alternative protein sources (plant-based and cellular agriculture), responsible fashion, vegan or vegetarian product lines.

Economic: minimum or living wage and tax policies to focus on income inequality and redistribution of wealth, homelessness, affordable housing, supporting small businesses, microfinance support, consumer debt relief, universal basic income.

Political: lobbying, civic engagement (voting, voting rights), campaign finance reform, immigration, gerrymandering, health care reform, child-care reform, free speech, combating hate speech and misinformation.

Environmental: local sourcing, conservation, land use, air and water pollution, climate change, building awareness, electronic waste, sustainable supply chains/circular economy, sustainable packaging, responsible consumerism, ocean conservation, deforestation, water scarcity, biodiversity loss, regenerative agriculture, carbon offsetting programs, sustainable transportation.

Wellness: Promote physical and mental well-being through offerings, services and marketing communications, global health initiatives, work-life balance, parental support, social connection and community, affordable fitness, digital detox and mindfulness, sleep hygiene, body positivity, substance abuse prevention, flexible work arrangements, universal healthcare, gun violence prevention.[5]

(See the Appendix for dozens of examples from different categories and their respective scores.)

While identifying a cause, make sure to consider brand issue fit, customer issue fit, customer issue resonance (do they care about it?), and corporate issue fit (if applicable). Regarding the latter, Unilever has had to bear the brunt of Ben & Jerry's flavor of activism for over two decades. For example, the conglomerate risked a country-wide boycott when Ben & Jerry's announced they would stop selling ice cream in "occupied Palestinian territory."[6] It was also rather characteristic of Ben & Jerry's to condemn the United States regarding "stolen Indigenous land" on July 4, 2023. Yet it cost its parent Unilever $2 billion in market value.[7] (One wonders whether Ben & Jerry's could have helped the Indigenous people significantly more if it had asked Unilever to allocate a fraction of that $2 billion toward the cause instead). There is also the matter of assertiveness. Former Hershey CMO Peter Horst makes the case that both the risk of backlash and relevance to consumers increase as a brand's posture evolves from values to purpose, onto issues, and ultimately a position.[8]

	Niche	**Mainstream**
Broad	Niche Development	Mass Embrace
Fragmented	Niche Dare	Massive Fragmentation

ACTIVISM RESONANCE

BRAND POSITIONING

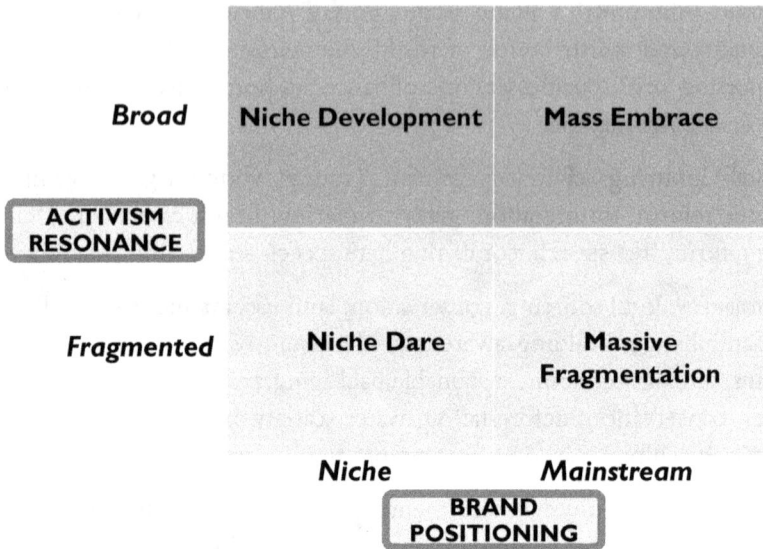

Figure 8.1 Sheth-Uslay Brand Activism Alignment Matrix

Finally, several of the issues in the list fall under multiple categories, which makes the evaluation of fit more challenging. For example, mass incarceration, racial profiling, and police brutality are societal as well as legal issues. The right to repair and clean technologies are business as well as technological issues. Gun violence prevention is a political as well as wellness issue. Finally, a broad topic such as climate change is an educational, environmental, political, economic, as well as a business and technological issue.

The Brand Activism Alignment Framework we advocate is illustrated in Figure 8.1.

The framework can be interpreted as follows:

Niche Dare:
The category where the alignment between brand positioning and activism resonance is highest is when a niche brand picks an issue with fragmented (low overall) resonance (bottom left cell). This issue is typically perceived as a moderately important topic with moderate to low public consensus overall but high consensus and importance for the identified target market. From that perspective, it makes perfect sense that Patagonia has been consistently positioned on environmental conservation since its core customers

are mountain climbers and other adventurers. This position is clearly consistent with the company mission and vision and brand identity but also makes business sense, building on the legacy of the founder and previous brand activism efforts, hence is perceived to be very authentic (passing all Five Rings). The result is increased brand recognition and sales through higher market penetration. Even better if the cause can increase consensus and perceived importance in the aggregate market, which Patagonia has arguably accomplished with their high-profile campaigns. In that case, new market development (selling to a new set of customers) in addition to market penetration (i.e., selling more to the same customers) may even be feasible.

Niche dare can also be a highly profitable strategy for fledgling brands that have yet to occupy a significant share of the market or mind. It is more or less certain that the more divisive the dare, the more devoted the core customers will be. And through word-of-mouth and higher media attention, your brand (ambassadors) can efficiently grow your niche.

CASE IN POINT: THINX

Founded in 2014, Thinx, a fledgling brand selling period underwear (undergarments designed to be as absorbent as feminine hygiene products), boldly entered the market with a mission to dismantle the stigma and taboo surrounding menstruation.[9]

CEO Maria Molland summed up the rationale well: "A key piece of this is we need people to know that we exist."[10] Thus, the Thinx approach was anything but conventional. Thinx launched provocative ad campaigns that featured suggestive imagery, like dripping egg yolks and grapefruit halves, to symbolize menstrual blood. These ads were a far cry from the sanitized and euphemism-laden period commercials of the past. While some platforms (like the NYC Metropolitan Transport Authority) balked at the boldness, the ads ignited conversations and challenged the norms around period-related advertising.[11] As the CEO Maria Molland observed: "I think it will upset quite a few people, that's okay because part of being a brand that stands for something is: sometimes you irritate people."[12]

But Thinx didn't stop there. When their ads faced censorship, they didn't retreat quietly. They fought back, publicly advocating for the normalization of menstruation in advertising and media. This act of defiance garnered even more attention, positioning Thinx as a champion for women's issues. Thinx's marketing messages weren't just about selling underwear. They were about empowering women and celebrating their bodies. They promoted self-love and acceptance, resonating with consumers who often felt their experiences were ignored or stigmatized.[13]

Beyond advertising, Thinx invested in educational initiatives to raise awareness about menstrual health and hygiene, particularly in underserved communities. They also advocated for policy changes related to menstrual equity and access to period products, demonstrating their commitment to creating real-world change.

Thinx also fostered a vibrant online community where customers could share their experiences, ask questions, and support each other. This sense of community solidified the brand's connection with its target audience, creating a loyal following that went beyond mere consumerism.

Through these multi-faceted efforts, Thinx transformed itself from a simple underwear brand into a cultural force. They challenged societal norms, empowered women, and sparked conversations that were long overdue. Their approach might not have been universally accepted, but it resonated deeply with their target audience, generating significant brand awareness and loyalty.

The story of Thinx is a testament to the power of brand activism. It demonstrates how a fledgling brand can leverage a divisive topic to create a powerful and impactful brand identity. While the journey was not without its challenges,[14] it was clearly a capitalistic success story. Thinx customer base grew to two million strong, sales approached $100 million, and the company was valued at $230 million.[15] Kimberly Clark initially invested $25 million in 2019, acquired a majority stake in 2022, and fully acquired Thinx in 2024 in a $180 million deal.[16]

Having mastered the fledgling brand activism playbook, founder Miki Agrawal is now pushing the environmental benefits of its latest startup, Tushy bidets, one butt at a time. In fact, the very name of one of the campaigns was "A**hole Activists" consisting of a "gallery of 20 very close-up portraits of said heroic anuses, introduced just ahead of World Environment Day."[17]

Niche Development

The category where overall alignment is considered to be moderate to high is when a niche brand chooses an important topic with a moderate to high level of consensus (upper left cell). Even though the idea of market development is alluring and worthy of consideration, the alignment fit here is usually moderate to low so brands must proceed with caution. While Gravity Payments appears to have succeeded (by and large) perhaps aided by virtue of being a pioneer in its sector to increase wages substantially, SodaStream represents a cautionary tale where one wonders if the company could have realized even more impressive outcomes in its home market without public clashes with government officials. The issue of Palestine then and now has been among the most prevalent topics in Israel, though the support regarding the rights of Palestinians is higher globally. And unlike Patagonia, where you can be confident how your core customers feel about your activism, it is hard to make such assessments for your soda consumers. In this case, thinking that brash activism can expand your market and make you a global brand may have been a dream too far. In general, start-up brands using the "buy one, give one" model, popularized by TOMS Shoes,[18] exemplify this category. Warby Parker whose market cap hovers around $2 billion is one such example.[19]

CASE IN POINT: WARBY PARKER

Warby Parker's commitment to social impact started from the very beginning, when four Wharton business school students launched it in 2010. Their "buy a pair, give a pair" model was a core part of their brand identity from day one. For every pair of glasses sold, Warby Parker partnered with non-profits like VisionSpring to distribute a pair to someone in need.[20] As co-founder Neil Blumenthal observed, "When we made our business plan for what would become Warby Parker, we agreed on a commitment that for every pair of eyeglasses sold, we would distribute a pair to an individual in a developing country... all we cared about was that a human being was going to have the glasses they needed to be successful in life."[21]

In a market dominated by a few large players, Warby Parker's social mission helped them stand out and attract a new generation of customers who wanted to vote with their wallets. Customers felt good about their purchase, knowing it was helping someone else, fostering a sense of loyalty and encouraging repeat business. It also generated positive PR and social media buzz, further amplifying the brand's reach.

Warby Parker has provided millions of glasses to people in need around the world, improving their vision and quality of life. This tangible impact has not only helped individuals but also strengthened communities and supported economic development. The brand's commitment to social impact has earned them a reputation as a responsible and ethical company, attracting both customers and employees who value social responsibility.

In recent years, Warby Parker has expanded their activism efforts beyond the "buy a pair, give a pair" model by launching the Pupils Project, which provides free eye exams and glasses to children in underserved communities in the US.[22]

By aligning their business with a social mission, Warby Parker has created a brand that resonates with consumers, generates positive impact, and positions them as a leader in the eyewear industry.[23] The positive brand image and social impact narrative helped Warby Parker expand into new markets and demographics. They were able to appeal to a wider audience, including younger generations who are increasingly conscious of social responsibility and ethical consumption.

One of the founders of Warby Parker went to a Quaker school. The 40-page Warby Parker plan made it to the semi-finals of the business plan competition at Wharton but did not win.[24]

Mass Embrace

The third category is when a mainstream brand picks an important but not controversial topic for activism, which still requires proceeding with caution. For example, CVS (which is the largest US pharmacy chain that you may not know stands for Consumer Value Stores) took a bold stand in 2014 by quitting tobacco sales in all stores. This decision not only led to a major decline in cigarette purchases in the US (100 million fewer packs sold in the first year alone) but also spurred the fight for a tobacco-free future. CVS also helped hundreds of universities become tobacco-free and invested millions to prevent youth smoking. It has also tackled the teen vaping crisis and does not retain advertising or PR agencies that work for tobacco or e-cigarette companies. The company has done its homework and reports that:

- Nearly 65% of Americans agree that our decision to stop selling tobacco reduces the risk of chronic disease.
- 62% of adults agree that retailers have an obligation to limit access to tobacco and e-cigarette products.
- 81% of adults support improving community education about the dangers of smoking.[25]

Generally speaking, brands with large market share have more to risk/lose and not as much to gain from brand activism. Thus, it is important that those who disagree with the issue are not core customers for the brand. Otherwise, anticipated increases in customer retention will not occur and the net gain may even be negative. In fact, in the case of CVS, the stand against tobacco was destined to lose them customers (up to 16.8% of its customers, the percentage of adults who were smokers in 2014, a figure which has gone down to 12% in 2023)[26] but they may have gained more in terms of loyalty from non-smokers who increased their share of wallet spending in CVS upon hearing the decision. Meanwhile, its main competitors, Walgreens and Rite Aid, did not see the math of being followers and were undeterred. They continue to sell cigarettes, although they increased their minimum purchase age requirements to 21 in 2019.[27]

Another reason why a mainstream brand may consider brand activism is to reposition a struggling brand in the minds of the consumers. For example, the Dieselgate struggles of Volkswagen (VW) severely damaged its reputation and public trust in the brand. In response, VW invested heavily in EV development and positioned itself as a leader in cleaner transportation.[28] The effort to shift the narrative has had some success and is ongoing. Similarly, facing increasing criticism about the environmental impact of plastic,[29] Lego invested in sustainable materials R&D and pledged to build its bricks from bio-based plastics. The company has announced its "ambition" to make Lego from renewable and recycled materials by 2032.[30] Broad issues like child health, obesity prevention, or other global health initiatives are usually safe bets that are not divisive and right in the wheelhouse of big pharma.

CASE IN POINT: JOHNSON & JOHNSON

An excerpt from the Johnson & Johnson Credo crafted in 1943 reads, "We are responsible to the communities in which we live and work and to the world community as well. We must help people be healthier by supporting better access and care in more places around the world. We must be good citizens—support good works and charities, better health and education, and bear our fair share of taxes. We must maintain in good order the property we are privileged to use, protecting the environment and natural resources."[31]

Johnson & Johnson, a household name synonymous with healthcare, embarked on a mission to nurture "Healthy Communities" back in the early 2000s. This wasn't a fleeting marketing campaign, but a long term commitment to address the social determinants of health that impact millions around the globe.[32]

The Healthy Communities initiative wasn't about quick fixes or Band-Aid solutions. Instead, Johnson & Johnson recognized that health is shaped by a complex web of factors, including access to quality care, education, nutrition, and safe environments. Their approach was comprehensive, focusing on empowering communities to create lasting change.

One of the cornerstones of the Healthy Communities program was investing in community health centers, the backbone of healthcare for many underserved populations. Johnson & Johnson provided funding, resources, and expertise to help these centers enhance their services and reach more people in need, leading to increased preventive care visits and reduced hospitalizations. They also supported initiatives to train and empower community health workers, recognizing their crucial role in delivering care and building trust within communities.[33]

In addition to healthcare access, Johnson & Johnson tackled other social determinants of health through various programs. Their partnerships with schools and community organizations to promote healthy eating and physical activity among children have shown success in reducing childhood obesity rates. Their efforts to improve maternal and child health, such as the "Healthy Baby, Happy Mom" program in China, have led to significant decreases in infant mortality rates and improved maternal health outcomes.[34]

Meanwhile, global health initiatives that Johnson & Johnson has supported, like "Reaching the Last Mile," have focused on eliminating preventable diseases in remote and underserved communities, reaching millions of people, and contributing to significant progress in disease control and prevention.[35]

The results of the initiative have been significant. Over the years, Johnson & Johnson has invested millions of dollars in community-based programs, reaching millions of people in underserved communities around the world. Their efforts have led to improved health outcomes, increased access to healthcare, and empowered communities to take charge of their well-being. Employees have also contributed thousands of hours of volunteer service in local communities, further amplifying the program's impact.

While the Healthy Communities program has evolved over time, its core mission remains the same: to create a healthier, more equitable world for all. It's a testament to the company's belief that business can be a powerful force for good, not just in terms of profits, but also in terms of creating lasting social impact that can be measured and felt in the lives of real people. And all this is actually based on the Johnson & Johnson Credo which explicitly recognizes that. If it sounds like Johnson & Johnson referred to its credo while planning its activism around "Healthy Communities," you heard right. And if the credo crafted in 1943 sounds a lot like doctrine, you heard that right too.

Massive Fragmentation

The final option is for a mainstream brand to pick a fragmented issue with low-to-moderate importance and consensus. The alignment here is typically the lowest, and that makes such brand activism the most risky, especially if your core customers do not support the issue. This is where Bud Light went wrong. In a charged atmosphere, even when open-minded parents have concerns about transgender participation in competitive sports, tread very lightly if you want to commission a transgender influencer regarding March Madness. What was the end goal here? To reposition its flagship brand, Bud Light, to make it more popular among a younger demographic? If so, there were dozens of superior ways to accomplish this. Thus, it seems like those in charge of the brand also wanted a more liberal clientele to add to their existing aging conservatives. As detailed in Chapter 1, this proved to be a bridge too far. They went in to kill (or let's say free) two birds with one stone (brand) and ended up sabotaging themselves. Did they not know their core customers at all? And if the goal was to serve the LGBTQ+

community, could not AB InBev reposition another brand in its vast port-folio or develop a new brand to serve them well? Please do not call this exclusion; market segmentation, positioning a brand, and market targeting are essentials of marketing. Unless your brand is failing so badly that a Hail Mary pass makes sense (which clearly was not the case for market leader Bud Light), we advise using sub-brands or even developing new brands from scratch. If you go after a massive fragmentation with your mainstream brand, be aware that it can cause a tectonic shift. More on this later.

CASE IN POINT: CHICK-FIL-A

Fast-food chicken sandwich chain Chick-fil-A's stance on social issues, particularly its donations to organizations with anti-LGBTQ+ stances, has been a subject of controversy and debate for many years.[36] CEO Dan Cathy has been quite open about where he stands, "We know that it might not be popular with everyone, but thank the Lord, we live in a country where we can share our values and operate on biblical principles."[37] While the company has enjoyed immense financial success, the back-lash has also been significant. Thus, it is fair to say the success has come despite its activism and not because of it.

The controversy surrounding Chick-fil-A's donations to organizations like the Fellowship of Christian Athletes and the Salvation Army, which have histories of opposing same-sex marriage and LGBTQ+ rights, came to a head in 2012 when then-CEO Dan Cathy publicly expressed his opposition to same-sex marriage. This sparked widespread protests, boycotts, and calls for the company to change its policies.[38]

While Chick-fil-A has not publicly disclosed the exact financial impact of the controversy, there have been some indications of both negative and positive effects:

Negatives:
Boycotts and protests: Many individuals and organizations have organized boycotts of Chick-fil-A, urging consumers to avoid the res-taurant due to its stance on LGBTQ+ issues. These boycotts have likely impacted sales, particularly in more liberal areas.

Loss of business opportunities: Some cities and universities have banned Chick-fil-A from opening locations on their premises due to the controversy, limiting the company's growth potential.[39]

Negative publicity: The ongoing controversy has generated negative publicity for Chick-fil-A, tarnishing its brand image and alienating potential customers who disagree with its values.[40]

Positives:
Increased sales among supporters: While some consumers have boycotted Chick-fil-A, others have rallied behind the company, viewing it as a champion of conservative values. This has led to increased sales among certain segments of the population.[41]

Brand loyalty: Chick-fil-A has cultivated a loyal customer base who appreciates its quality food and customer service. Many of these customers remained loyal despite the controversy.

Continued growth: Despite the backlash, Chick-fil-A has continued to expand rapidly, opening new locations across the US and achieving impressive sales figures. This suggests that the negative impact of the controversy may be limited to certain regions or demographics.[42]

Quantifying the exact financial impact of Chick-fil-A's brand of activism is difficult, as the company is privately held and does not disclose detailed financial information. However, it's clear that the controversy has had both positive and negative effects on the company's bottom line. While the boycotts and negative publicity may have impacted sales in some areas, the increased support from loyal customers and continued expansion suggest that the overall impact may be relatively small.

Ultimately, the Chick-fil-A case demonstrates the complexities and potential risks of brand activism on highly divisive issues. While taking a stand can resonate with certain consumers and strengthen brand loyalty, it can also alienate others and lead to negative consequences. Brands must carefully weigh the potential benefits and risks before engaging in such activism and ensure that their actions align with their core values and the expectations of their target audience. By the way, it appears that even Chick-fil-A has received the message. In 2019, the company announced it would no longer support charities with anti-LGBTQ+ stances.[43] Ironically, when the company hired a VP for Diversity Equity, and Inclusion in 2023, it then faced boycotts from conservatives who claimed Chick-fil-A had gone "woke."[44]

Besides the activism resonance tolerance of the business, brand activism is also informed by Abraham Maslow's hierarchy of needs, which we discuss in the next chapter.

References

1   Sheth, Jagdish N., Can Uslay, and Rajendra S. Sisodia (2020), *The Global Rule of Three: Competing with Conscious Strategy*, Palgrave MacMillan. Uslay, Can, Ekaterina Karniouchina, Ayca Altintig, and Martin Reeves (2017), "Do Businesses Get Stuck in the Middle? The Peril of Intermediate Market Share," Social Sciences Research Network, https://papers.ssrn.com/sol3/papers.cfm?abstract_id=3043330. Uslay, Can, Z. Ayca Altintig, and Robert D. Winsor (2010), "An Empirical Examination of the "Rule of Three": Strategy Implications for Top Management, Marketers, and Investors," *Journal of Marketing*, 74(2), 20–39.
    The former was finalist for the American Marketing Association's Berry Best Book Award in 2022, and the latter was finalist for Harold H. Maynard Award for most significant contribution to marketing theory and thought, and the MSI/H. Paul Root Award for most significant contribution to the advancement of the practice of marketing, 2010.
2   For example, the total enrollment of an Ivy school, Princeton University, which is around 9,000 students is dwarfed by its neighbor Rutgers University's 70,000 students. Rutgers Business School alone enrolls more students than the entirety of Princeton University.
3   De Rossi, Fabio, "Ferrari: Record Sales in 2023, 13,663 Cars Delivered," Motor1.com, February, 3, 2024 (accessed October 26, 2024). https://uk.motor1.com/news/707244/ferrari-2023-record-sales-profit-figures/.
4   "Market Capitalization of Ferrari," *CompaniesMarketCap.com*, October 26, 2024 (accessed October 26, 2024).. https://companiesmarketcap.com/ferrari/marketcap/. "Market Capitalization of General Motors (GM)," *CompaniesMarketCap.com*, October 26, 2024 (accessed October 26, 2024). https://companiesmarketcap.com/general-motors/marketcap/. "Market Capitalization of Ford," *CompaniesMarketCap.com*, October 26, 2024 (accessed October 26, 2024). https://companiesmarketcap.com/ford/marketcap/.
5   We have substantially augmented the original list from Kotler and Sarkar to develop our list. Also see: https://www.marketingjournal.org/finally%ADbrand-activism-philip-kotler-and-christian-sarkar/ (accessed October 30, 2024).
6   Shatter, Alan (2021), "Unilever's Ben & Jerry's Crisis is Escalating," *The Jerusalem Post*, October 20 (accessed October 30, 2024). https://www.jpost.com/opinion/unilevers-ben-and-jerrys-crisis-is-escalating-682640.
7   Zilber, Ariel, "Unilever Stock Loses $2B Amin Calls to Boycott Ben & Jerry's Over Tweet," *New York Post*, July 6, 2023 (accessed October 30, 2024). https://nypost.com/2023/07/06/ben-jerrys-boycott-calls-unilever-stock-falls/.
8   Horst, Peter, "Gillette's Controversial 'Toxic Masculinity' Ad And the Opportunity It Missed," Forbes, January 19, 2019 (accessed October 29, 2024). https://www.forbes.com/sites/peterhorst/2019/01/18/gillettes-controversial-toxic-masculinity-ad-and-the-opportunity-it-missed/?sh=ed30ac155066.
9   Koning, Rembrand, M., "Innovating in the Feminine Care Market," *Harvard Business School Working Knowledge*, (accessed October 30, 2024). https://hbswk.hbs.edu/item/cold-call-innovating-in-the-feminine-care-market.
10 Mohan, Pavithra, "Thinx's First National Ad Campaign Imagines a World Where Men Get Periods, Too," *Fast Company*, October 3, 2019 (accessed October 30, 2024).

https://www.fastcompany.com/90412779/thinx-menstruation-ad-campaign-imagines-men-getting-periods.

11 Coughlin, Sara, "Are These Ads Too Controversial for the NYC Subway?" *Refinery 29*, October 27, 2015 (accessed October 30, 2024). https://www.refinery29.com/en-us/2015/10/96159/thinx-subway-ads-controversy.

12 Mohan, Pavithra, "Thinx's First National Ad Campaign Imagines a World Where Men Get Periods, Too," *Fast Company*, October 3, 2019 (accessed October 30, 2024). https://www.fastcompany.com/90412779/thinx-menstruation-ad-campaign-imagines-men-getting-periods.

13 Molland, Maria, "Thinx Breaks Another Barrier as Kimberly-Clark Completes Its Acquisition of a Majority Stake in the Company," *Thinx.com*, February 24, 2024 (accessed October 30, 2024). https://www.thinx.com/thinx/blogs/periodical/voices/thinx-breaks-another-barrier-as-kimberly-clark-completes-its-acquisition-of-a-majority-stake-in-the-company.

14 McIntyre, Karen, "Not Sure What to Thinx," *Nonwovens Industry*, March 1, 2024 (accessed October 30, 2024). https://www.nonwovens-industry.com/issues/2024-03-01/view_editorials/not-sure-what-to-thinx/.

15 MacLellan, Lila, "How Thinx, the Buzzy Underwear Company Once Worth $230M, Lost its Way," *Aol.com*, May 28, 2024. (accessed October 30, 2024). https://www.aol.com/finance/thinx-buzzy-underwear-company-once-110000565.html.

16 "Kimberly-Clark Acquires Majority Interest in Thinx," *Kimberly-Clark News*, February 24, 2022 (accessed October 30, 2024). https://www.news.kimberly-clark.com/2022-02-24-Kimberly-Clark-Acquires-Majority-Interest-in-Thinx.   "Kimberly-Clark Invests in Thinx." *Nonwovens Industry*, September 17, 2019 (accessed October 30, 2024).   https://www.nonwovens-industry.com/contents/view_breaking-news/2019-09-17/kimberly-clark-invests-in-thinx/.   "Kimberly-Clark   Corporation acquired an additional majority stake in Thinx, Inc.," *MarketScreener*, March 4, 2024 (accessed October 30, 2024). https://www.marketscreener.com/quote/stock/KIMBERLY-CLARK-CORPORATIO-13266/news/Kimberly-Clark-Corporation-acquired-an-additional-majority-stake-in-Thinx-Inc-39595452/.

17 "Tushy Campaign Has Many Butts About it," Campaign Canada, June 2, 2023 (accessed October 30, 2024). https://www.campaigncanada.ca/article/1855776/tushy-campaign-butts.

18 Hessekiel, David, "The Rise and Fall of the Buy-One-Give-One Model at TOMS," *Forbes*, April 28, 2021 (accessed October 26, 2024). https://www.forbes.com/sites/davidhessekiel/2021/04/28/the-rise-and-fall-of-the-buy-one-give-one-model-at-toms/.

19 "WRBY Market Cap," *YCharts*, [October 26, 2024]? (accessed October 26, 2024). https://ycharts.com/companies/WRBY/market_cap.

20 "Warby Parker's Dave Gilboa and Neil Blumenthal: A Vision for Business," CNBC (accessed October 26, 2024). https://www.cnbc.com/warby-parkers-dave-gilboa-and-neil-blumenthal-a-vision-for-business/.

21 Miller, Hannah. "Warby Parker," *Leaders*, October 12, 2022 (accessed October 26, 2024) https://leaders.com/articles/leaders-stories/warby-parker/.

22 "Pupils Project," *Warby Parker* (accessed October 26, 2024). https://www.warbyparker.com/pupils-project.

23 "Warby Parker Foundation," *Warby Parker* (accessed October 26, 2024). https://www.warbyparkerfoundation.org/.

24 "Warby Parker's Dave Gilboa and Neil Blumenthal: A Vision for Business," CNBC (accessed October 26, 2024)https://www.cnbc.com/warby-parkers-dave-gilboa-and-neil-blumenthal-a-vision-for-business/.

25 "Tobacco-Free for Five Years," *CVS Health*, September 3, 2019 (accessed October 30, 2024).https://www.cvshealth.com/news/community/tobacco-free-for-five-years.html. Statistics from an August 2019 Morning Consult poll of 2,200 adults.

26 "Current Cigarette Smoking Among Adults — United States, 2005–2014." Centers for Disease Control and Prevention (CDC) (2015), *Morbidity and Mortality Weekly Report* (*MMWR*), 64 (44): 1233–40. https://www.cdc.gov/mmwr/preview/mmwrhtml/mm6444a2.htm "US Cigarette Smoking Rate Steady Near Historical Low," *Gallup News*, December 21, 2023 (accessed October 26, 2024). https://news.gallup.com/poll/509720/cigarette-smoking-rate-steady-near-historical-low.aspx.

27 Jacobo, Julia, "Walgreens Raises Minimum Age to Buy Tobacco to 21," *ABC News*, May 8, 2019 (accessed October 26, 2024). https://abcnews.go.com/US/walgreens-raises-minimum-age-buy-tobacco-21/story?id=62577762.

28 Amelang, Soren, "Volkswagen Places Massive EV Bet to Master Green Mobility Shift," *Clean Energy Wire*. June 18, 2021 (accessed October 26, 2024). https://www.cleanenergywire.org/factsheets/dieselgate-forces-vw-embrace-green-mobility.

29 Baraniuk, Chris, "Lego Is Haunted by Its Own Plastic," *Wired*, November 21, 2023 (accessed October 26, 2024). https://www.wired.com/story/lego-haunted-by-its-own-plastic/.

30 "Making LEGO Bricks More Sustainable," *Lego*, March 12, 2024 (accessed October 26, 2024). https://www.lego.com/en-us/aboutus/news/2024/march/making-lego-bricks-more-sustainable-.

31 "Our Credo," *Johnson & Johnson* (accessed October 26, 2024). https://www.jnj.com/our-credo.

32 "This Award-Winning Technology Is Improving Disaster Relief Efforts Across the Globe," *Johnson & Johnson*, November 30, 2022 (accessed October 26, 2024). https://www.jnj.com/global-community-impact/this-award-winning-technology-is-improving-disaster-relief-efforts-across-the-globe.

33 "Johnson & Johnson Impact Ventures Invests in Clinify Health to Support Financial Sustainability of Community Health Centers in the U.S. and to Improve Patient Health Outcomes," *Johnson & Johnson Impact Ventures*, September 12, 2023 (accessed October 26, 2024). https://impactventures.jnj.com/news/johnson-johnson-impact-ventures-invests-in-clinify-health-to-support-financial-sustainability-of-community-health-centers-in-the-u-s-and-improve-patient-health-outcomes.

34 "3 Unique Ways Johnson & Johnson Is Making a Difference in the Lives of Mothers and Babies in China," *Johnson & Johnson*, January 12, 2021 (accessed October 26, 2024). https://www.jnj.com/gph/3-unique-ways-johnson-johnson-is-making-a-difference-in-the-lives-of-mothers-and-babies-in-china.

35 "Reaching the Last Mile Welcomes Collective Commitment to Boost Support to Community Health Workers," *Reaching the Last Mile*, November 14, 2023 (accessed October 26, 2024). https://www.reachingthelastmile.com/news/reaching-the-last-mile-welcomes-collective-commitment-to-boost-support-to-community-health-workers/.

36   "Chick-fil-A Donated Nearly $2 Million to Anti-Gay Groups in 2009," *Pride Source*, October 27, 2011 (accessed October 26, 2024). https://pridesource.com/article/49938.

37   Greenfield, Beth, "Why Are People Mad at Chick-fil-A? A History of Anti-LGBTQ Controversies," *Yahoo! Life*, July 20, 2023 (accessed October 26, 2024). https://www.yahoo.com/lifestyle/why-are-people-mad-chick-fil-a-anti-lgbtq-controversies-205302238.html.

38   Greenfield, Beth, "Why Are People Mad at Chick-fil-A? A History of Anti-LGBTQ Controversies," *Yahoo! Life*, July 20, 2023 (accessed October 26, 2024). https://www.yahoo.com/lifestyle/why-are-people-mad-chick-fil-a-anti-lgbtq-controversies-205302238.html.

39   Fernandez, Madison, "Plans for New Chick-Fil-A Cause Controversy at University of Notre Dame," *Forbes*, July 15, 2021 (accessed October 26, 2024). https://www.forbes.com/sites/madisonfernandez/2021/07/15/plans-for-new-chick-fil-a-cause-controversy-at-university-of-notre-dame/.

40   Tice, Carol, "How Chick-fil-A's Social Media Bungle Fueled a Gay-Rights Backlash," *Forbes*, August 14, 2012 (accessed October 26, 2024). https://www.forbes.com/sites/caroltice/2012/07/20/how-chick-fil-a-social-media-bungle-fueled-gay-rights-backlash/. Maze, Jonathan, "Chick-fil-A's Unit Volumes at Stand-Alone Restaurants Hit $9M Last Year," *Restaurant Business*, April 4, 2014 (accessed October 26, 2024). https://www.restaurantbusinessonline.com/financing/chick-fil-unit-volumes-stand-alone-restaurants-hit-9m-last-year.

41   "Tea Party Urges Chick-fil-A 'Buycott,'" *NBC10 Philadelphia*, August 1, 2012 (accessed March 4, 2025). https://www.nbcphiladelphia.com/news/local/tea-party-urges-chick-fil-a-buycott/1936049/.

42   Lucas, Amelia, "Every Restaurant Chain Wants to Beat Chick-fil-A, But It's Stronger Than Ever," *CNBC*, December 21, 2023 (accessed March 4, 2025). https://www.cnbc.com/2023/12/21/chick-fil-a-stronger-than-ever-amid-more-competition.html.

43   Del Valle, Gaby, "Chick-fil-A's Many Controversies, Explained," *Vox*, November 19, 2019 (accessed March 4, 2025). https://www.vox.com/the-goods/2019/5/29/18644354/chick-fil-a-anti-gay-donations-homophobia-dan-cathy.

44   Harling, Danielle, "Chick-fil-A is Facing a Boycott With Customers Claiming They've Gone 'Woke'," *Yahoo! Life*, June 9, 2023 (accessed March 4, 2025). https://www.yahoo.com/lifestyle/chick-fil-facing-boycott-customers-203000306.html. Valinsky, Jordan, "How Chick-fil-A Became a Target for Going 'Woke'," *CNN Business*, June 2, 2023 (accessed March 4, 2024). https://edition.cnn.com/2023/06/02/business/chick-fil-a-fake-controversy/index.html.

9

THE HIERARCHY OF NEEDS
AND THE S-CURVE OF ACTIVISM

Our Brand Activism Alignment framework is complemented by Abraham Maslow's Hierarchy of Needs Model, with each need superseded by another. Maslow summed up his highly prominent work aptly: "It is quite true that man lives by bread alone—when there is no bread. But what happens to man's desires when there is plenty of bread and when his belly is chronically filled? At once other (and 'higher') needs emerge and these, rather than physiological hungers, dominate the organism. And when these in turn are satisfied, again new (and still 'higher') needs emerge and so on. This is what we mean by saying that the basic human needs are organized into a hierarchy of relative prepotency."[1]

According to the theory, one must first take care of physiological needs for survival (e.g., food, water) and then focus on safety (e.g., security, stability, order). Once those needs are satisfied, the priority becomes love and belonging (e.g., friends, intimacy). After that level is satisfied, the primary need becomes esteem (e.g., prestige and feeling of accomplishment), and finally self-actualization (achieving full potential), in that order.[2] But that model is for individuals, you say? It has been long established in academia and practice that brands can also have personas.[3]

DOI: 10.4324/9781003593690-9

To be clear, brands aren't just names or logos, but living, breathing entities with personalities all their own. Each brand has its unique voice, values, and quirks, just like the people we interact with every day.

Take Apple, for example. It's the sleek, minimalist artist, always pushing boundaries and seeking perfection. Its products are elegant, intuitive, and designed to inspire creativity. Its marketing campaigns are bold and often challenge the status quo.

Then there's Nike, the energetic athlete, always striving for greatness and pushing its limits. Its products are designed for performance, built to endure the toughest challenges. Its marketing messages are inspiring and celebrate the power of human potential.

Or consider Patagonia, the rugged environmentalist, always advocating for the planet and sustainable practices. Its products are durable, eco-friendly, and built to last. Its marketing campaigns often highlight environmental issues and encourage consumers to make conscious choices.

Even the humble Dove soap has a personality. It's the gentle caregiver, always nurturing and embracing diversity. Its products are gentle, moisturizing, and designed to enhance natural beauty. Its marketing campaigns celebrate real women and challenge unrealistic beauty standards.

These are just a few examples, but the point is clear: brands are more than just products or services. They're characters in the story of our lives, each with its unique personality and role to play. As consumers, we're drawn to brands whose personalities resonate with our own. We want to connect with brands that share our values, inspire us, and make us feel good about ourselves.

For brands, self-reflection is essential for building a strong brand identity and connecting with the target audience. Crafting a consistent message, voice, and visual identity that reflects the brand's values and resonates with its customers is essential. Given this context, brand activism that is consistent with a brand's personality enables authentic differentiation in the minds of consumers.

Hopefully, by now you are convinced that brands have (winning or losing) personalities that interact with their conduct and help or hurt them in the marketplace. However, you may still not be clear about what we mean by it, so let's get to it.

Stanford Professor Jennifer Aaker, a pioneer in the field of brand personality, defines it as "the set of human characteristics associated with a brand." Just as we perceive and describe people's personalities, we can similarly attribute traits like sincerity, excitement, competence, sophistication, and ruggedness to brands. In fact, these five traits were found to explain over 90% of all variation across brands! (More specifically, sincerity explains 27%, excitement 25%, competence 18%, sophistication 12%, and ruggedness explains 9% of the variation).[4] These five traits are akin to building blocks for a brand's DNA. Thus, it is important to know where you stand. (To illustrate, please see hypothetical brand ratings for each dimension in Figure 9.1.) Naturally, just like we can overlook certain personality excesses or lack thereof based on the context, a brand need not rank high on each dimension. For example, there is not much need for TikTok to be rugged or Pepsi to be sophisticated. In fact, investing to build the excitement trait for a security brand like ADT may not even be considered a positive.

Note: In case you have lost your 20-20 vision like we have, the logos below are Facebook, Nike, Apple, Tesla, Coca-Cola, and The Honest Company in their order for the sincerity dimension.

Once a brand understands where they are and identifies where they want to be, the corresponding personality traits are then conveyed through various brand elements, including advertising, product design, packaging,

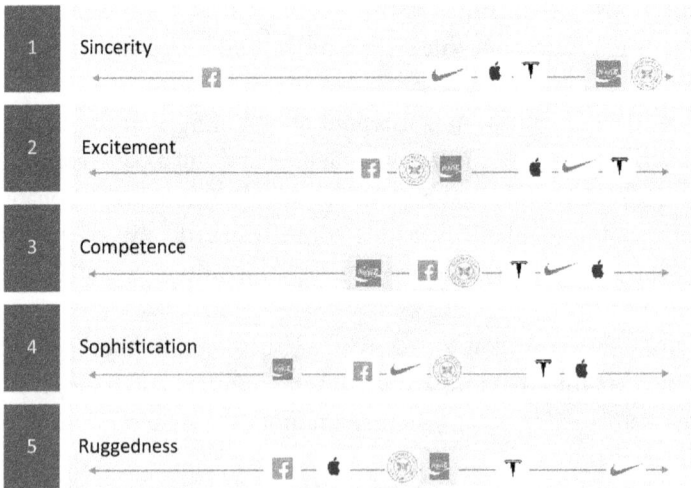

Figure 9.1 Hypothetical Brand Personality Ratings

customer service, and overall brand communication. Before we digress further, let us iterate why this is important. Brand personality is, by and large, a proxy to a brand's DNA and enables differentiation, relationship building, and consumer self-expression. Authenticity is essential for share of heart, mind, and performance, and effective brand activism can shape a brand's personality in a cost-effective manner and enable *authentic differentiation* in the minds of consumers, which is *absolutely fundamental* for marketing impact as previously discussed.

So now that we have established that brands have personalities (and what that means) and that Maslow's Hierarchy of Needs could also be applicable to brands, let's end our detour and get back to how the same hierarchy of needs can also be used to understand brand activism.

Maslow's theory is intended to explain stages of motivation and human behavior. Just as individuals prioritize different needs at different stages of their development, brands also prioritize different goals based on their level of maturity and established presence in the market. We examine each stage next.

Physiological Needs (Survival)

Food and water for brands means viability and cash flow. In the survival stage, fledgling brands are akin to newborns, focused primarily on meeting their basic needs for existence in the competitive market. Their primary goals revolve around generating awareness, attracting customers, and establishing a foothold in their industry. However, even during this vulnerable and nascent phase, some brands recognize the potential of brand activism to gain visibility and appeal to consumer segments. This is where we see the emergence of *survival activism*, where fledgling brands can deliberately take on causes, even highly divisive ones, to carve a viable niche for themselves in crowded markets.

Examples of survival activism include:

Cause-related marketing partnerships: new brands may partner with established charities or nonprofits for cause-related marketing campaigns. This allows them to leverage the reputation and reach of the organization while contributing to a good cause. For example, a new clothing brand might donate a portion of their profits to an environmental organization, aligning themselves with a popular cause and attracting eco-conscious consumers.

Take, for instance, the sustainable sneaker brand Allbirds. From its inception, Allbirds wove environmental consciousness into its DNA, using eco-friendly materials and promoting sustainable practices. While their primary focus was on creating comfortable, stylish shoes, their commitment to sustainability attracted eco-conscious consumers, helping them gain a loyal following and differentiate themselves from traditional footwear brands.[5]

A variant of this approach is the aforementioned "buy one, give one" model, where brands donate a product or service to someone in need for every purchase made. This model appeals to consumers' desire to give back and can generate positive publicity for the brand. We already discussed how Warby Parker utilized this approach successfully and became a unicorn (currently valued over two unicorns with a $2.05 billion market cap, actually).

Social media activism: social media platforms provide an accessible and cost-effective way for new brands to engage in activism. They can share content related to social issues, participate in relevant hashtags, and voice their support for various causes. This can help them build a following and connect with potential customers who share their values.

For example, the organic skincare brand Cocokind leveraged Instagram to build a community around their brand. They shared educational content about skincare, sustainability, and social justice issues, fostering a loyal following that resonated with their values. This approach allowed them to grow organically and authentically, without relying on expensive traditional advertising.[6]

Divisive activism: A promising third option for fledgling brands to distinguish themselves in a cluttered market is to engage in activism on decidedly divisive issues, as early as launch. While this strategy can be risky and potentially alienate some consumers, it can also quickly create a strong brand identity and attract loyal customers who share their values to generate significant media attention and word-of-mouth.

Here is a hypothetical case for Y'R BRAND (brought to you by Gemini AI):

[Enter your future brand name here aka Y'R BRAND], an activewear brand founded in ... [enter your year of establishment], quickly gained recognition for its stylish and comfortable athletic apparel designed for "doing more"—a mantra that resonated with its target audience of recreational exercisers. However, the brand also chose to incorporate a strong stance on inclusivity and LGBTQ+ rights into its brand identity early on as follows:

Diverse Representation: Y'R BRAND consistently features diverse models in their marketing campaigns, including people of different races, body types, genders, and sexual orientations. This approach reflects their belief that everyone should feel comfortable and empowered to engage in physical activity, regardless of their background.

Inclusive Language: The brand utilizes inclusive language in marketing materials, avoiding gendered terms and focusing on the joy of movement and community. This resonates with a broad audience and creates a welcoming atmosphere for LGBTQ+ individuals.

Partnerships with LGBTQ+ Organizations: Y'R BRAND partners with organizations like the Human Rights Campaign and the Trevor Project, donating a portion of their proceeds to support LGBTQ+ advocacy and mental health resources.

Social Media Activism: The brand actively uses social media platforms to express support for LGBTQ+ rights, celebrating Pride Month, sharing stories of LGBTQ+ athletes, and raising awareness about relevant issues.

Employee Engagement: Y'R BRAND fosters an inclusive workplace culture that celebrates diversity and provides a safe space for LGBTQ+ employees. They also encourage employee participation in Pride events and other activism initiatives.

While this inclusive approach resonates with many consumers and helps Y'R BRAND build a loyal following, you also face a backlash from conservative groups who disagree with your stance on social issues. Some customers boycott the brand or criticize you for being too political.

Despite the criticism, Y'R BRAND continues to champion inclusivity and LGBTQ+ rights, demonstrating the courage and conviction of a young brand willing to take a stand. This approach ultimately strengthens your brand identity and attracts a passionate community of consumers who value diversity and social responsibility.

Y'R BRAND's experience demonstrates that even fledgling brands can successfully incorporate activism on potentially divisive issues into their brand strategy.

Does this hypothetical example sound too far-fetched to work? Take a look at the case of Penzeys Spices for a real-world example of decidedly divisive brand activism for a fledgling brand in Chapter 11.

It's important to note that survival activism can be a double-edged sword. While it can generate positive attention and attract customers, it can also backfire if it appears inauthentic or opportunistic. Consumers are increasingly savvy and can easily detect when brands are simply jumping on the bandwagon to boost their image.

Therefore, brands in the survival stage should approach activism with caution and ensure that their actions are genuine and aligned with their core values. They should focus on building trust and credibility with their audience rather than trying to capitalize on popular trends. By doing so, they can lay a solid foundation for future activism efforts as they move up Maslow's hierarchy and their brand matures.

Bottom line: Fledgling brands focused on survival are primarily concerned with establishing their presence in the market, generating sales, and ensuring—you guessed it—survival. Activism at this stage can help define a brand's identity and differentiate it in a cluttered market and may involve deliberately aligning with divisive causes to gain visibility and attract loyal customers even as they repel others.

Safety Needs (Security)

In the safety stage of a brand's development, the focus shifts from mere survival to building a foundation of trust, reliability, and legitimacy. From cash flow to retained earnings and financial stability. From start-up mode to job security for employees. Having established a foothold in the market, the brand now seeks to solidify its position. Hence, the brand may become more risk-averse, where the brand reassures consumers about the brand's trustworthiness and responsible practices through *security activism* as follows:

Transparency and Accountability: Brands may prioritize transparency in their supply chains, disclosing information about their manufacturing processes, labor practices, and environmental impact. They can also demonstrate their commitment to ethical business practices by treating their employees fairly, supporting their communities, and avoiding harmful environmental practices. This openness can build trust with consumers who are increasingly concerned about ethical production and sustainability.

For example, Everlane, a clothing brand, built its reputation on "radical transparency," revealing the true cost breakdown of their products and the factories where they are made.[7] This approach appeals to consumers seeking ethical and sustainable fashion options.

Data Security and Privacy: In an era of increasing data breaches and privacy concerns, brands can demonstrate their commitment to security by implementing robust data protection measures and communicating transparently about their data practices. This can reassure consumers that their personal information is safe and secure.

For example, encrypted email service ProtonMail prioritizes user privacy and security by offering end-to-end encryption and zero-access encryption, ensuring that even they cannot access their users' emails. They have also been vocal about the need for stronger privacy protections online and have challenged government surveillance practices.[8]

Product Safety and Quality: Brands can prioritize product safety and quality by adhering to rigorous standards, conducting thorough testing, and ensuring that their products meet or exceed industry regulations. This can help build trust with consumers who rely on the brand to provide safe and reliable products.

For example, naturally extending from the sustainability focus of Patagonia are quality products built to last. They also offer a lifetime "iron-clad" warranty on their products, demonstrating their confidence in the quality of their craftsmanship.[9]

By prioritizing security activism, brands can cultivate trust, loyalty, and a positive reputation among consumers. This can lead to increased sales, stronger brand equity, and a more sustainable business model in the long run.

Bottom line: Brands that have survived and crossed the chasm may focus on building trust and loyalty with their customers, job security for their employees, and acceptable returns for their investors. Activism at this stage may involve initiatives that demonstrate corporate social responsibility and ethical practices, aiming to reassure consumers about the brand's reliability and commitment to quality.

Love and Belonging Needs (Connection)

The "Love and Belonging" stage in Maslow's hierarchy reflects a brand's desire to foster a sense of community, connection, and belonging among its consumers. This goes beyond mere transactions or cyclical relationships and aims to create a shared identity and emotional bond between the brand and its audience.

Thus, the focus is on creating spaces and experiences that foster social bonding and, consequently, brand love. If brand liking and consideration are the two most powerful drivers of sales, imagine what brand love can do! It predicts loyalty and the propensity to generate positive word-of-mouth. In fact, there is a whole stream of academic literature on brand love and how to bring it about.[10] (Hint: authenticity works wonders for brand love as well).[11]

Connection activism can manifest in various ways:

Building Community: Brands can create online and offline communities where customers can connect, share experiences, and support each other. This fosters a sense of belonging and loyalty toward the brand.

For example, Sephora's Beauty Insider Community is a vibrant online platform where beauty enthusiasts can exchange tips, reviews, and connect with fellow makeup lovers.[12] This creates a sense of community and belonging for Sephora customers.

Celebrating Diversity: Brands can celebrate diversity in their marketing campaigns, showcasing people from different backgrounds, cultures, and identities. This sends a message of inclusivity and connects a wider range of consumers.

Fenty Beauty, founded by Rihanna, launched with a wide range of foundation shades catering to diverse skin tones. This inclusive approach disrupted the beauty industry and resonated with consumers who felt previously underserved.[13]

Creating Shared Experiences: Brands can create events, campaigns, or initiatives that bring people together and foster a sense of shared experience. This can be anything from organizing community events to launching social media challenges that encourage participation and interaction.

Energy drink brand Red Bull is known for its extreme sports events and sponsorships, creating thrilling experiences for athletes and spectators alike. Their events, like the Red Bull Air Race and Red Bull Cliff Diving, bring people together to witness extraordinary feats of human skill and athleticism, fostering a sense of excitement and shared passion.[14]

The classic case of connection activism that embodies community building and shared experiences among users is Harley Davidson. This iconic motorcycle brand has cultivated a passionate community of riders who share a love for the open road and the freedom of riding. Their events, like the Sturgis Motorcycle Rally, bring together thousands of riders from around the world to celebrate their shared passion and create lifelong memories.[15]

By tapping into their customers' passions, interests, and aspirations, these brands create a sense of belonging and community, fostering loyalty and brand advocacy.

Bottom line: Brands seeking to foster brand love among their customers may engage in activism that promotes social connections, diversity, or shared experiences. By prioritizing connection activism, brands can create a loyal and engaged community of customers who feel a sense of belonging and identification with the brand. This can lead to increased brand advocacy, positive word-of-mouth, and lifelong customers.

Esteem Needs (Recognition)

Having achieved financial success and garnered devoted customers, actions during the Esteem Needs stage in Maslow's hierarchy reflect a brand's desire for broader recognition, respect, and status within its industry and society at large. Brands at this stage have established themselves in the market but they seek to further enhance their reputation and leave a legacy that stands the test of time.

Thus, recognition activism focuses on highlighting the maturing brand's contributions to society and positioning it as a leader and innovator in its field:

Championing Social Causes: Brands may take stances on social issues, aligning themselves with movements that resonate with their target audience and values. This can generate media attention and position the brand as a thought leader and advocate for change.

For example, Unilever, under CEO Paul Polman, set ambitious sustainability goals, aiming to reduce their environmental impact and improve the social and economic well-being of the communities where they operate. Their Sustainable Living Plan focused on reducing waste, conserving water, and sourcing sustainable ingredients. This commitment to sustainability resonated with consumers who are increasingly concerned about the environmental impact of their purchases. Consequently, Unilever's 28 sustainable brands (including US-centric brands such as Dove, Vaseline, Seventh Generation, and others such as Brooke Bond, Lifebuoy, and Rin) outperformed peers, "growing 69% faster than the rest of the business and delivering 75% of the company's growth,"[16] in 2018, enabling it to get a leg up on its perennial competitor, P&G.[17]

Philanthropy and Corporate Social Responsibility: Brands may engage in philanthropic activities, donating to charitable causes or establishing foundations to support social initiatives. This demonstrates their commitment to giving back to society and making a positive impact beyond their business operations.

For example, Microsoft's "AI for Good" Lab initiative uses artificial intelligence to address global challenges.[18] It provides access to AI technology, expertise, and financial support to non-profit organizations and researchers working on solving societal challenges like environmental sustainability, accessibility, and humanitarian crises with the primary goal of creating a positive social impact rather than direct commercial gain, essentially donating their AI capabilities to tackle global issues. The lab showcases Microsoft's technological expertise and commitment to using it for social good.

Awards and Recognition: Brands may actively seek awards and recognition for their products, services, or corporate practices. This can enhance their reputation and credibility, reinforcing their position as leaders in their industry.

For example, Tesla has received numerous awards for its innovative technology and sustainable practices.[19] These accolades have helped solidify Tesla's reputation as a leader in the automotive industry and a pioneer in sustainable transportation. Consequently, Tesla's advertising spending remains negligible to this day.

As an alternative route, brands can also seek recognition and accolades through campaigns to build their esteem. "The Fearless Girl" featuring the bronze statue of a girl facing down the charging bull on Wall Street won numerous awards for its creativity and impact. Notably, the campaign won three Grand Prix awards at the prestigious Cannes Lions International Festival of Creativity in 2017, including in the categories of PR, outdoor, and glass (which recognizes work that positively impacts gender inequality).[20] The campaign also won awards at other prestigious advertising and marketing competitions, such as the Clio Awards, the One Show, and the D&AD Awards.

"The reaction appears to have been greater than anyone involved expected. On Twitter, 'Fearless Girl' generated more than 1 billion impressions in its first 12 hours and broke 4.6 billion impressions within 12 weeks. On Instagram, 'Fearless Girl' sparked almost a quarter-million unique posts featuring the statue in three months. The statue cost an estimated $250,000, but generated free marketing worth at least $7.4 million, according to Adweek."[21] It was commissioned by State Street Global Advisors (SSGA), a large asset management company, to promote their SHE fund, which invests in companies with a high percentage of women in senior leadership. The advertising agency McCann New York proudly developed the campaign and executed the installation of the statue. Both SSGA and McCann benefited tangibly from the critical success of the campaign. Overall, the "Fearless Girl" campaign's success in garnering awards reflects its widespread recognition as a powerful piece of brand activism.

Interestingly, upon receiving the spotlight, SSGA was also criticized for not employing many women or investing in enough women-owned businesses. It also settled a lawsuit about salary gaps and agreed to pay $5 million to 305 female employees and 15 African American employees "deemed to have been discriminated against." Another caution that undertaking a full brand audit that survives our five rings of brand activism is critical before engaging your brand or you risk snatching 'defeat from the jaws of victory' like SSGA.[22]

Thought Leadership: Brands may publish thought leadership content, such as research reports, white papers, or blog articles, to share their expertise and insights on relevant topics. This positions them as experts in their field and contributes to the broader discourse on important issues.

Google regularly publishes research on various topics, including artificial intelligence, climate change, and public health.[23] This demonstrates their thought leadership and commitment to using their resources to address global challenges.

Blackrock Chairman and CEO Larry Fink, who annually sends a letter to fellow CEOs focusing on the need for purpose, sustainability, and stakeholder orientation, is also an example of such thought leadership even as he is seeking self-actualization for his brand.[24]

Bottom line: By engaging in recognition activism, brands can enhance their reputation, strengthen their brand image, and attract a larger following of consumers who admire their values and contributions to society. Activism at this stage may involve taking stances on issues, championing social causes, and positioning themselves as leaders in their industry through awards or thought leadership. The result is increased sales, brand equity, and long-term business success.

Self-Actualization Needs (Purpose)

The Self-actualization stage is the pinnacle of Maslow's hierarchy, representing a brand's desire to fulfill its highest potential and make a meaningful contribution to the world. Brands at this stage have often achieved significant success, stability, brand love, and recognition. They seek to go beyond profit and create a positive impact on society and the environment.

Activism in this stage, often referred to as *purpose-driven activism* (aka conscious capitalism), reflects a deep integration of social and environmental responsibility into the brand's core values and mission.[25] Striving high and being all you can be can manifest in various ways:

Mission-Driven Business Models: Brands may adopt business models that prioritize social and environmental impact alongside financial performance. This can involve using sustainable materials, reducing waste, promoting fair trade, or investing in renewable energy.

For example, cleaning products company Seventh Generation is built on the mission of creating a healthier planet for future generations. They prioritize using plant-based ingredients, reducing waste, and advocating for policies that protect the environment. Their mission drives every aspect of their business, from product development to packaging to marketing.[26]

Advocacy for Systemic Change: Brands may use their influence and resources to advocate for policy changes and systemic solutions to social and environmental problems. This can involve lobbying governments, supporting grassroots movements, or raising awareness about critical issues.

Ben & Jerry's is renowned for its commitment to social justice and environmental sustainability. Their mission goes beyond making delicious ice cream; they actively campaign for climate action, racial equity, and LGBTQ+ rights. They also source fair trade ingredients and use eco-friendly packaging.[27]

Philanthropy and Impact Investing: Brands may invest in philanthropic initiatives or impact investments that support social and environmental causes. This can involve funding research, supporting community projects, or investing in businesses that create positive social or environmental impacts.

Google invests in projects that address global challenges like climate change, poverty, and access to education through its philanthropic arm, Google.org.[28] They also support innovative solutions to social problems through their Impact Challenge program, which provides funding and resources to nonprofits and social enterprises.[29]

Employee Engagement and Empowerment: Brands may empower their employees to participate in social and environmental initiatives, encouraging them to volunteer their time and skills to support causes they care about. This can foster a sense of purpose and engagement among employees and create a positive workplace culture.

Whole Foods Market is known for its commitment to employee well-being and community engagement. They offer competitive wages and benefits, including health insurance and employee discounts. They also encourage employee involvement in local community projects and support initiatives that promote health and wellness.[30]

By embracing purpose-driven activism, brands can achieve self-actualization by fulfilling their highest potential and making a meaningful contribution to the world. This not only benefits society and the environment but also strengthens the brand's reputation, grows its base of loyal customers, and inspires employees. And if there is any doubt as to what big hairy audacious goals a brand may seek in its quest for self-actualization, the United Nations offers guidance through 17 goals for responsible businesses:

(1.) No poverty, (2.) Zero hunger, (3.) Good Health and Well-Being, (4.) Quality Education, (5.) Gender Equality, (6.) Clean Water and Sanitation, (7.) Affordable and Clean Energy, (8.) Decent Work and Economic Growth, (9.) Industry, Innovation and Infrastructure, (10.) Reduced Inequalities, (11.) Sustainable Cities and Communities, (12.) Responsible Consumption and Production, (13.) Climate Action, (14.) Life Below Water, (15.) Life on Land, (16.) Peace, Justice and Strong Institutions, and (17.) Partnerships for the Goals.[31]

There is something for every brand that dares.

Bottomline: Brands that have reached the pinnacle of success may strive to fulfill a higher purpose beyond profit maximization. Activism at this stage may be deeply integrated into the brand's core values, driving initiatives that address global challenges, promote sustainability, and create a positive impact on the world.

Overall, Maslow's Theory of Hierarchy of Needs doubles as a framework for understanding why brands engage in different types of activism at different stages of their development. It complements our own framework and helps marketers tailor their activism strategies to align with their brand's current needs and priorities. It can also help consumers better understand the motivations behind brand activism and evaluate the authenticity of their commitments. As with all theories, it is stylistic of the real world. In practice, other factors, such as industry norms, competitive pressures, and leadership values, also influence brand activism decisions.

Importantly, no brand is ever really confined to one need only. Maslow himself clarified "the false impression that a need must be satisfied 100% before the next need emerges"[32] and that "any behavior tends to be determined by several or all of the basic needs simultaneously rather than by only one of them."[33] Thus, even though their engagement may be primarily focused on one level, brands can pursue activism at multiple levels. For example, Johnson & Johnson may seek brand love with localized campaigns and self-actualization by pursuing several UN Sustainable Development Goals simultaneously. Meanwhile, advertising agencies faced with increasing pressure from Google, Meta, and various competitors from the Martech space can seek security and esteem concurrently.[34] Finally, even though there is empirical support for the universality of the needs, the hierarchy among them is still debatable. A hungry person can still find friendship and love just like a struggling brand may nevertheless have devout followers. Importantly, activism at different levels requires different levels of effort and offers different payoff potential. We focus on these next.

The S-Curve of Brand Activism Elasticity

The concept of elasticity is important for quantifying the potential outcomes of marketing actions. For example, the price elasticity of demand concerns how demand might be impacted given a price change. If the elasticity is bigger than (negative) one, then price cuts are likely to result in higher revenues, whereas if the elasticity is less than one, price increases may be more beneficial for the bottom line. Similarly, an average advertising elasticity of 0.12 (which happens to be the aggregate average for the elasticity of short-term advertising impact)[35] implies that doubling the ad budget might result in a 12% lift in sales.[36] In the context of brand activism, the elasticity would correspond to the sales impact of brand activism when the brand activism budget is enhanced. Admittedly, the use of average elasticity to allocate one's budget is somewhat simplistic—coming up with better ad copy may be more effective than doubling the ad budget. Nevertheless, it is still a useful pedagogical tool.

While we are not aware of any efforts to calculate actual brand activism elasticities to date, we posit that the relationship between Maslow's Hierarchy of Needs and the brand activism elasticity is S-shaped, which is very common in business literature such as in the case of diffusion of innovations.[37] This relationship is depicted in Figure 9.2.

This figure may be interpreted as follows.

Survival: Most brands struggling for survival have little time, energy or resources for brand activism. Thus, the returns on brand activism during this stage are likely to be minimal. As mentioned, the major exception to this is the case of a new brand deliberately designed with brand activism in mind.

Security: Brands engaging in brand activism may be able to solidify their core customers and start seeing positive returns on their activism at this stage.

Love: This is the stage where brands can untangle the love-hate formula between issues and consumer segments. For brands that can nurture a

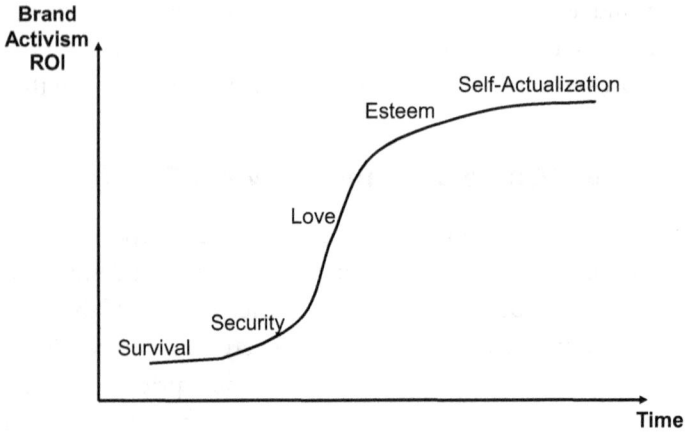

Figure 9.2 The S-Curve of Brand Activism Elasticity

growing community of brand lovers the potential returns are highly significant.

Esteem: While critical acclaim may boost the egos of executives, these do not always reflect in sales. Thus, the returns begin to taper off during this stage.

Self-Actualization: Individuals achieving self-actualization are quite rare. Maslow reportedly believed only about 1% of the population may reach this stage.[38] And even then, one may not be able to stay at the summit permanently. Thus, while a very worthy goal, results may often be fleeting when it comes to brand activism and transcending to a brand's full potential. Realizing any one of the UN's 17 goals will likely prove elusive for any given brand. Hence, we suggest paying attention to the last of the 17 goals: Partnerships for the Goals. We had mentioned the vast potential of coalitions for brand activism back in Chapter 4. We now explore this highly promising concept further.

When Brands Have Friends

If brands can have personalities as scores of academic studies suggest, why can't they have friends like people do? Conventional wisdom suggests that multiple brands clutter the consumer's mind and diminish brand recall for each. Thus, almost all ad spots feature one brand at a time.

But we'd like to push back on that notion. We live in an era where the majority of consumers are frustrated with out-of-context ads. We don't like to watch ads but, when we do, a vast majority of us prefer ads related to content being viewed. Given this backdrop, we posit that brands that can establish their friendship can observe several positive outcomes:

1. Brands with friends should increase the perceived authenticity of the message.
2. Recall for brands with friends in the same spot should not necessarily decrease as one will aid the recall of another (say Horizon Milk and Oreo Cookie).
3. And recall can even increase for BFFs! (e.g., Coca-Cola and Jack Daniel's aka Coke and Jack; Harley Davidson and Marlboro [Man]).

If our hunch is accurate:

1. Advertisers can unlock inter-brand activation collaborations and increase revenue.
2. Marketers can save money per spot or increase exposure by pooling their activism budgets.
3. The media may be able to charge a bit more for the same spot.

The typical ad agency motto goes as follows: "We focus on serving each client individually; we dedicate expert teams and provide superior value to each of them to the best of our abilities."

But what if brands bundled and activated together can create even more value? What if superior value meant going beyond a focus on one brand/ client at a time?

Welcome to a world where activist brands have activist friends!

Identifying an activist brand's friends can happen at different levels, much like the hierarchy of needs.

1. *Within Brand Portfolio:* An ad agency can start with the existing brand portfolio of their client's roster. For example, P&G used to own both Gillette (Fusion) and Duracell. They could've been brought together for activism.

2. *Within Agency Portfolio:* An ad agency can assess its own roster for typically non-competing brands. For example, chip-maker AMD and computer-maker Dell or Ball Park hot dogs and Goldfish crackers could be brought together by their ad agency VML.
3. *Within Group Portfolio:* Even large ad agencies like VML typically belong to large conglomerates like WPP. Brands served by different agencies owned by the same group could be brought together. For example, Port Authority and IBM.
4. *New Business:* An agency could also identify a best friend for an existing client and pitch a potential activism collaboration to a non-client brand to gain new business. Alternatively, an agency could research a brand-new brand and reverse engineer friends from within its portfolio to pair it with. In the extreme, both brands could be non-clients. For example, MTV and Red Bull could be brought together for activism.

In the old days of baron kings, financiers like JP Morgan played the role of market-makers. Nowadays, as marketers prepare to play the role of royal brand matchmakers, consumer perspectives can be used not only to identify but also verify the perceived authenticity of friendships. For example, co-mentions in social media posts and online chatter can be used to extract potential friends and focus groups or A/B experiments can be used to validate them. Retaining tried and tested influencers by either brand can also enhance impact. While brand friends focusing on the same customer segments may be most viable, other approaches can also reveal market development opportunities for both friends. For example, Coca-Cola and Oreo cookies recently became "besties" for limited-edition drinks and cookies featuring each other's flavors.[39] Why could they not stay besties for activism too? For example, wouldn't they gain major authenticity points if they asked you to moderate your daily sugar intake?

A final but tremendous opportunity in matchmaking comes in the form of innovative tri-sector coalitions. As alluded to and exemplified in Chapter 4, the tri-sector approach brings the under-utilized assets and capabilities of not only private and public but also government together for impact. While private-public partnerships are commonplace and top-of-mind, governments also have tremendous and often underutilized assets and human resources. A tri-sector approach can be very impactful as

Coinstar founder Jens Molbak has discovered (see case in point). And while there are exceptions to this, being a friend of the government is usually a plus and boon for business in the long run.[40]

CASE IN POINT: COINSTAR, A CASE STUDY IN TRI-SECTOR COLLABORATION[41]

The idea for Coinstar originated when Jens Molbak, then an MBA student at Stanford, was faced with the common problem of having a jar full of coins and no convenient way to convert them into paper money. Unable to find an existing solution, he founded Coinstar in 1991. The company installed its first coin exchange kiosk in San Francisco in 1992, and experienced rapid growth, reaching 1,000 kiosks in just four years and 10,000 kiosks within a decade.

Initially, Molbak focused on the business opportunity presented by the large volume of idle coins in the US economy (estimated at $7 billion out of $15 billion in circulation), but he soon realized that Coinstar's services also provided significant benefits to the US government. By enabling the frictionless recirculation of coins, Coinstar helped the US Mint save over $2 billion in manufacturing and distribution costs, a fact that initially surprised even the Federal Reserve.

Coinstar's success was not limited to its financial gains; it also prioritized social impact from its early days. The company partnered with leading non-profit organizations, enabling customers to make charitable donations directly at the kiosks, generating over $100 million in donations. This feature not only provided convenience for customers but also enhanced accountability for individually collected donations. Charities actively encouraged their volunteers to use Coinstar.

The company's unique model, combining business success with public purpose, earned it recognition and made the business a bona fide unicorn. The Federal Reserve's endorsement even paved the way for Coinstar's expansion into the UK market. Coinstar's story serves as an example of how tri-sector collaborations, involving the business, government, and social sectors, can create sustainable value and positive societal impact.

In the next three chapters, we focus on lessons for mainstream, niche, and person(al) brands, respectively.

References

1   Maslow, A. H. (1943), "A theory of human motivation," *Psychological Review*, 50(4), p. 375.

2   Maslow, A. H. (1943), "A theory of human motivation," *Psychological Review*, 50(4), 370–96.
    Maslow, A. H. (1954), *Motivation and personality*. Harper and Row.

3   Aaker, Jennifer (1997), "Dimensions of Brand Personality," *Journal of Marketing Research*, 34 (August), 347–356.
    Calderon-Fajardo, Victor, Sebastian Molinillo, Rafael Anaya-Sanchez, and Yuksel Ekinci (2023), "Brand Personality: Current Insights and Future Research Directions," *Journal of Business Research*, 166 (November). https://www.sciencedirect.com/science/article/pii/S0148296323004204?via%3Dihub.

4   Aaker, Jennifer (1997), "Dimensions of Brand Personality," *Journal of Marketing Research*, 34 (August), 347–356.

5   Allbirds, Accessed October 26, 2024. https://www.allbirds.com/. "Allbirds and Voice for Nature," Sugi Project (accessed October 26, 2024). https://www.sugiproject.com/partners/allbirds-and-voice-for-nature. Allbirds, *Allbirds Sustainability Report 2020*, last updated September 10, 2021 (accessed October 26, 2024). https://cdn.allbirds.com/image/upload/v1625161698/marketing-pages/Allbirds_Sustainability_Report_2020.pdf.

6   "CEO Monthly Letter - February 2021." Cocokind, February 16, 2021 (accessed October 26, 2024). https://www.cocokind.com/blogs/news/ceo-monthly-letter-february-2021. Cocokind Instagram Page. Accessed October 26, 2024. https://www.instagram.com/cocokind/?hl=en.

7   "About," *Everlane* (accessed October 26, 2024). https://www.everlane.com/about.

8   Jancis, Mindaugas, "ProtonMail Review: Have We Found the Most Secure Email Provider in 2024?" *Cybernews*. January 24, 2024 (accessed March 4, 2025). https://cybernews.com/secure-email-providers/protonmail-review/.

9   "Returns," Patagonia (accessed October 26, 2024). https://www.patagonia.com/returns.html.

10 For those interested, Brand Love was found to have "seven core elements: self-brand integration, passion-driven behaviors, positive emotional connection, long-term relationship, positive overall attitude valence, attitude certainty and confidence (strength), and anticipated separation distress." Batra, Rajeev, Aaron Chaim Ahuvia, and Richard P. Bagozzi (2012), "Brand Love," *Journal of Marketing*, 76(2), 1–16. Tran, Trang P., Seung Hyun Lee, and Nazmus Sakib (2024), "The Effect of Customer Brand Engagement on Brand Love in Sharing Economy," *Journal of Marketing Theory & Practice*. (May). [IS THIS COMPELTE?it has been accepted and published online with no issue/page numbers yet].

11 Ahmad, Fayez, Francisco Guzman, and Blair Kidwell (2022), "Effective Messaging Strategies to Increase Brand Love for Sociopolitical Activist Brands," *Journal of Business Research*, 151, 609–622.

12 "Sephora," *Sephora Community*, (accessed October 26, 2024). https://community.sephora.com/.

13 Saputo, Sandy, "How Rihanna's Fenty Beauty Delivered 'Beauty for All' – And a Wake-up Call to the Industry," *Think with Google*, June 2019 (accessed October 26,

2024). https://www.thinkwithgoogle.com/future-of-marketing/management-and-culture/diversity-and-inclusion/-fenty-beauty-inclusive-advertising/.

14 "Best Red Bull Events to Visit," Red Bull, July, 29, 2023 (accessed October 26, 2024). https://www.redbull.com/us-en/best-red-bull-events-to-visit.

15 "Sturgis Motorcycle Rally," Harley-Davidson, August 2, 2024 (accessed October 26, 2024). https://www.harley-davidson.com/us/en/content/event-calendar/sturgis-rally.html?srsltid=AfmBOorfmkU61lW6Bp6zh0XsAIdxSs6OotdV2PlSTyUSVUkiZAjizPLc.

16 Sarkar, Christian and Philip Kotler, "The ROI of Brand Activism: Unilever's Latest Findings," November 27, 2019 (accessed October 26, 2024). https://www.activistbrands.com/the-roi-of-brand-activism-unilevers-latest-findings/.

17 Geller, Martinne, "Unilever Says Socially Responsible Brands Outperform the Rest." *Yahoo! Finance.* February 1, 2017 (accessed March 4, 2025). https://ca.finance.yahoo.com/news/unilever-says-socially-responsible-brands-outperform-rest-011916082--finance.html.

18 "AI for Good Research Lab," Microsoft, (accessed October 26, 2024). https://www.microsoft.com/en-us/research/group/ai-for-good-research-lab/.

19 Armstrong, Kevin, "Tesla Dominates Award Show, Clinches Top Honors in Innovation, Efficiency, and Three Additional Categories," November 27, 2023 (accessed October 26, 2024). https://www.notateslaapp.com/news/1716/tesla-dominates-award-show-clinches-top-honors-in-innovation-efficiency-and-three-additional-categories. "Tesla Wins Multiple 2023 Brand Image Awards from Kelley Blue Book," *Tesmanian,* April 6, 2023 (accessed October 26, 2024). https://www.tesmanian.com/blogs/tesmanian-blog/tesla-wins-multiple-2023-brand-image-awards-from-kelley-blue-book.

20 Beer, Jeff, "Fearless Girl Wins Glass Lion Grand Prix at Cannes Lions Festival," *Fast Company.* June 19, 2017 (accessed March 4, 2025). https://www.fastcompany.com/40432883/fearless-girl-wins-glass-lion-grand-prix-at-cannes-lions-festival.

21 Reeves, Benjamin, "Did *Fearless Girl* Change Anything for Women on Wall Street?" *Worth,* April 17, 2019 (accessed March 8, 2023). https://worth.com/did-fearless-girl-change-anything-for-women-on-wall-street/.

22 Campbell, Lily, "Did Fearless Girl Change Anything for Women on Wall Street?" *Worth,* April 17, 2019 (accessed March 8, 2023). https://worth.com/did-fearless-girl-change-anything-for-women-on-wall-street/.

23 Google Research, accessed October 26, 2024. https://research.google/.

24 "Larry Fink's 2022 Letter to CEOs: The Power of Capitalism," BlackRock (accessed October 26, 2024). https://www.blackrock.com/corporate/investor-relations/larry-fink-ceo-letter?cid=ppc%3ABlackRock_USWA%3Agoogle%3Alarryfinkletter&gclid=Cj0KCQiAj4biBRC-ARIsAA4WaFgVuZHgIsbSVVBCPX8f1hdprlBH5unUZiAnWQSJTlHO2W88fFJFHhUaAqbUEALw_wcB&gclsrc=aw.ds.

25 Mackey, John and Raj Sisodia (2013), *Conscious Capitalism: Liberating the Heroic Spirit of Business.* Harvard Business Review Press.

26 "Our Company," *Seventh Generation,* (accessed October 26, 2024). https://www.seventhgeneration.com/company.

27 "Our Values, Activism, and Mission," Ben & Jerry's, (accessed October 26, 2024). https://www.benjerry.com/values#:~:text=Our%20Product%20Mission%20drives%20us,the%20Earth%20and%20the%20Environment.

28 Google.org, Accessed October 26, 2024. https://www.google.org/.

29 "Google Impact Challenge for Tech for Social Good," *Google*, (accessed October 26, 2024). https://impactchallenge.withgoogle.com/techforsocialgood/.

30 "Our Commitment to Worker Welfare," *Whole Foods Market*, (accessed October 26, 2024). https://www.wholefoodsmarket.com/mission-in-action/responsible-sourcing/worker-welfare.

31 "The 17 Goals," *United Nations*, (accessed October 26, 2024). https://sdgs.un.org/goals.

32 Maslow, A. H. (1987), *Motivation and personality* (3rd ed.). Pearson Education, p. 69.

33 Maslow, A. H. (1987), *Motivation and personality* (3rd ed.). Pearson Education, p. 71.

34 Uslay, Can (2018), "Is Advertising Stuck in the Middle? A Commentary," *Journal of Advertising Education*, 22(2), 147–151.

35 Sethuraman, Raj, Gerard J. Tellis, and Richard Briesch (2011), "How Well Does Advertising Work? Generalizations from Meta-Analysis of Brand Advertising Elasticities," *Journal of Marketing Research*, 48(3), 457–471.

36 The averages mentioned are for illustration purposes only. The actual elasticities should be calculated based on the applicable range and context for the business. For example, advertising elasticity is higher for new products than established ones, for Europe than the US, for durables than nondurables, and for print than TV. Tellis, Gerald J. (2010), "Generalizations About Advertising Effectiveness in Markets," *Journal of Advertising Research*, 49(2) [PAGES?].

37 Nieto, Mariano, Francisco Lopez, and Fernando Cruz (1998), "Performance Analysis of Technolofy Using the S Curve Model: The Case of Digital Signal Processing (DSP) Technologies," *Technovation*, 18 (6/7), 439–457, (accessed October 26, 2024). https://gide.unileon.es/admin/UploadFolder/73.pdf.

38 Robinson-Kiss, Shella, "Self-Actualization: The Milestone You Missed," *Psychology Today*. May 15, 2024 (Accessed March 4, 2025). https://www.psychologytoday.com/us/blog/theyre-not-coming/202405/self-actualization-the-milestone-you-missed.

39 "Coca-Cola and the Oreo Brand are Teaming Up," *The Coca-Cola Company*, August 13, 2024 (accessed October 26, 2024). https://www.coca-colacompany.com/media-center/coca-cola-and-the-oreo-brand-are-teaming-up.

40 Uslay, Can (2023), "Scaling Collaboration and Innovation through Tri-Sector Partnerships," *METU Studies in Development*, Ahmet Acar SI, 50 (December), 539–558. http://www2.feas.metu.edu.tr/metusd/ojs/index.php/metusd.
    Amin, Anjali, John Impellizzeri, and Can Uslay, "Unlocking Macro-Value Through the Tri-Sector Mindset: The Case of the NJ CEO Council," *Rutgers Business Review*, forthcoming.

41 "About Us," Coinstar, (accessed October 26, 2024). https://coinstar.com/aboutus/#:~:text=The%20Coinstar%20Story,no%20way%20to%20do%20it.
    Sheth, Jagdish N., Can Uslay, and Rajendra S. Sisodia (2020), *The Global Rule of Three: Competing with Conscious Strategy*, Palgrave MacMillan, 238–239.

10

LESSONS FOR MAINSTREAM BRANDS

Advertising, by definition, is public. Typically, marketing managers dream that the campaign they are about to embark on goes viral and creates a buzz. However, the dream is not so straightforward when it comes to brand activism. Thus, a litmus test for any activism campaign is this: would you have engaged in the campaign even if you knew it would transcend your target market, become very public, and attract mainstream media attention? For the case of Bud Light/Mulvaney, the answer is clearly no, based on the reactions of AB InBev management once caught in the spotlight.

Hopefully, we have made a compelling case by now that it would also be wise to go through the Five Rings analysis, determine where you are on the Hierarchy of Needs S-curve, and identify the right cause and strategy for successful brand activation. Beyond these common steps, there are significant differences in lessons for mainstream generalists who serve the mass market versus niche/specialist brands that do not. In fact, this empirical reality holds true for brand activism as much as it holds marketing strategy in general.[1]

DOI: 10.4324/9781003593690-10

For example, stakeholder pressure (consumer pressure, employee pressure, and other galvanizing events) and brand resources (dedicated budget and inclusion-committed staff and partners) have been identified as antecedents for the development of an inclusive brand marketing strategy in extant literature. Meanwhile, the business case, willful ignorance, and fear of alienating the majority or marginalized consumers have been identified as moderators.[2] However, different stakeholders will not be equally influential for mainstream versus niche brands. Mainstream brands serving a mass audience should care more about public sentiment, whereas it is more critical for specialist or niche brands to distinguish between consumers in general and paying customers. On the other hand, niche brands typically employ smaller numbers whom the executives may even know personally, and they may be compelled to pay more attention to the opinion of their employees than mainstream brands do.

People of color will become the majority in the US by 2045.[3] This demographic shift presents a massive opportunity for businesses that are willing to embrace inclusivity and understand the unique needs and preferences of these consumers. Historically, companies have overlooked this vast market. But ignore them at your own peril. "How big is this blind spot? Over $6 trillion domestically, and $16 trillion globally. It is estimated that Black Americans' spending power sits between $1.4 trillion and $1.8 trillion annually,[4] a powerful economic bloc that's comparable to the gross domestic product of Mexico, Canada, and Italy. Latinos' purchasing power in the US reached $3.4 trillion in 2021[5] and grew over 2× faster than non-Latino counterparts, and Asian Americans, with $1.3 trillion in buying power and median household incomes of $104,646 is well above average income for the US Having grown 314% over the past two decades, becoming the fastest growing among all ethnicity groups."[6] Ignoring these consumers is not only a missed business opportunity but also a detriment to the overall US economy. Companies that proactively build bridges and cultivate relationships with these communities will be best positioned for success in the decades to come. And this obviously is not merely a US-specific phenomenon. According to a global study of more than 23,000 consumers across 18 countries, "three quarters (75%) of people decide what to buy based on a brand's diversity and inclusion record."[7]

Without further ado, we list our lessons for mainstream brands.

1. *Think twice if you are a generalist serving the mass market* Yes, consumers consume, and research clearly shows they do so based on their self-identity. Negativity bias is also among the most strongly evidenced research topics in psychology. If you are happy, you carry on. If you are pissed off, you seek retribution.

   Fanatics are not convinced by rationality. It is very hard to change emotions since most resist conversion. Thus, everything else being equal, large brands will be worse off by engaging in activism on an issue that divides the public evenly.[8] The math is not complicated here: assume that customers' negative reaction is twice the strength of those that support your activism and that you lead a dominant brand with a 60% share of your market. By taking a divisive stand, you risk losing 15% of your customers while adding only 5% more. The asymmetric impact of a negative stance is well established by research and robustly applies to consumers, employees, as well as shareholders[9] regardless of media used.[10] To further exacerbate matters, large is near-synonymous with inauthentic in consumer-speak, especially when it comes to sustainability efforts.[11] Thus, everything else being equal, you will have to put in more effort than your smaller competitors.

2. *Find causes that unite not divide* Again, public opinion matters significantly more for mainstream brands than they do for niche brands. And public opinion is typically highly heterogeneous. Issues are called divisive for a reason; they tend to be complex. Interviews with marketing executives suggest that market inclusion should really be the motto for mainstream brands due to associated financial benefits.[12] By extension then, mainstream brands cannot reap financial benefits by being divisive. Demonstrating exemplarity means presenting an alternative moral construct and is inherently provocative, since it can construe existing customer behavior as unacceptable.[13] Howard Becker, in his seminal book, noted that "social groups create deviance by making the rules whose infraction constitutes deviance and by applying those rules to particular people and labeling them as outsiders."[14] He noted that such labels are also used to delineate moral and immoral. Are you really qualified to be a moral judge for all of your customers in your chosen cause? There is a world of activism beyond going woke, woke-washing, or broke. Expressing hope is much more effective than expressing frustration, unless you merely mean to be rhetorical.[15] Identify causes that different

sides can reason with. Recall that misalignment creates stronger immediate reactions than alignment.[16] Furthermore, research suggests that even "a woke brand can be seen as more authentic if it communicates a neutral and inclusive message when taking a social stand."[17]

3. *Do not let employee sentiment drive your strategy*   As a generalist brand, you have the responsibility to serve the public at large. Taking a stand and dismissing those who disagree with your position is relatively easy. Leading to unite is hard. The notion of employee sentiment also extends to those of the founder(s) or other key executives (Elon Musk, we hope you are reading this). Also, gauge the sentiment right; a significant number of employees are known to support or protest their employer's activism to influence peer or executive action. Nevertheless, those who act are often in the minority, and their voice may not speak for the majority.[18] Evaluate the position of all stakeholders carefully before weighing in. Some employees may quit if they disagree with your choice. You have to be okay with that. On the other hand, you should also be okay with embracing diversity of thought much like other aspects of it. Scores of employees at Microsoft and Google have signed letters to detach their companies from working on certain government projects with ICE or the Pentagon.[19] Yet, Google fired 28 employees because they protested Project Nimbus (cloud services to the Israeli military) by way of organizing sit-ins at Google offices.[20] Google said they violated company policy by disrupting work. However, a demonstration disrupts by definition, or it is a parade. Why did the reaction to an alternative point of view have to be so extreme? Was dialogue with supposedly valued employees so impossible that Google had to get rid of them? That also says something about your authenticity and values as a company. Do not let your strategy drive employees of different sentiments out either. Diversity (of thought) matters.

4. *Do not let peer sentiment drive your strategy either*   Monitor (the social media of) your peers but do not necessarily follow their lead. A recent study found that while more tweets by other brands across industries, Twitter mentions of a brand, (no one calls it X, sorry Elon Musk), and positive user sentiment all increase the likelihood of engagement by a focal brand; it found no such effect among industry peers.[21] You also do not need to match others necessarily in post quantity to be a great improviser and play off of them.

5. *Improvisation can pay off* The speedier your response to a sociopolitical event, the higher your perceived authenticity, consumer sentiment, and purchase intentions. However, such benefits taper off when it comes to divisive issues (regardless of political orientation)[22] so niche/specialist brands have more leeway when it comes to improvisation.

6. *Location, location, location of your HQ matters* If your key executives, main suppliers, and even main competitors are all clustered in the same area (say, Silicon Valley), it can also cloud the diversity of your judgment and lead to groupthink. While a liberal stance from a company whose HQ is in a blue state may be perceived as more authentic than if it was in a red one, you will nevertheless alienate many customers in more conservative areas if you activate your brand without examining the issue at length.[23]

7. *Unless your business is politics, keep politics out of your business* Research shows that not only does the market value of brands that are perceptually similar to the winning political party increase following an election, but those perceptually similar to the losing side lose sales following the election. These results are even more pronounced for consumer-facing brands.[24] Billions of dollars are at stake.[25] But let's leave the challenges of creating genuine perceptual political similarity aside for a moment. The real question is, do you want to be in the political guessing game as a corporate leader? And even if you manage what most pundits fail to do and correctly figure out the winning side for the duration of your tenure, what happens when the tides turn? It is a tough sell to convert a historically Democrat-affiliated brand to a Republican one and vice versa. (The fact that Trump has done it does not make the feat any easier).[26] Even as the average lifespan of companies listed in the S&P 500 has shrunk from six decades to two over the past century, one would still hope a company survives more than a couple of election cycles. Finally, consider that a growing number of citizens vote independently rather than based on party lines. For example, a whopping 62% of registered voters in the very blue state of Massachusetts are independent.[27] Thus, the Switzerland option of focusing on business rather than politics sure sounds like good business sense in the long run. Not that corporate America necessarily heeds this advice.[28] (Meanwhile, if you are a fledgling brand, one successful election cycle may be all you need to come out and become legitimate. More on that in the next chapter).

8. *Strategic flexibility is an asset, except when it comes to brand activism* Do your homework to learn the lay of the land well so you can avoid changing or reversing course later. No matter how agile you (think you) are, (social) media never sleeps… or forgets. Also, make sure you have garnered a sufficient supply of assets (financial, relational, or otherwise) to push through when the roads get rocky. Marketing (like military) involves campaigns that require going the distance. Conflicts come with the terrain and should be anticipated, come headwinds, tailwinds, rain, or blizzards.

9. *Avoid acquiring divisive brands if you are a mainstream brand operator* It does not work out in the long run. There is a good chance it will lose its buzz in the market as it clashes with and conforms to corporate policy, becomes generic, and loses its value. Like the illustrative case of Thinx underwear and Kimberly Clark.[29] And that is the better outcome. Things get even worse when the renegade child brand does not get in line and its actions reflect badly on the typically more conservative parent company. For example, even the sustainability leader Unilever seems to have finally had it with Ben & Jerry's after the former faced public protests and lost business due to the latter's aggressive brand activism campaigns. Ben & Jerry's mission statement reads: "We love making ice cream—but using our business to make the world a better place gives our work its meaning. In other words: we use ice cream to change the world." The brand is clearly authentic about brand activism. Unilever knew this going in and even agreed to special concessions to run it quasi-independently. However, it is currently planning a demerger of its ice cream business[30] which may be followed by a sale.

10. *B2B brands can learn from B2C brands when it comes to activism* While much of the brand activism activity and focus has revolved around B2C brands, B2B brands can also activate to achieve differentiation and signal suitability as a vendor/partner.[31] In fact, their B2B activism is even more noticeable in a typically less crowded arena. Moreover, B2B brands have fewer customers and stakeholders than B2C brands, which makes value alignment among them more feasible.[32]

11. *Focus on purpose, but don't jump on the bandwagon of higher purpose* Unless there are deliberate reasons to do so. The number of CEOs who prioritized purpose as the top factor for creating long-term value almost doubled from 34% to 64% in the span of a year from 2021 to 2022.[33] Marketing

without purpose will amplify mistrust of your marketing. Following the herd without contemplation leads to inauthentic differentiation. While it may be okay to champion a UN grand challenge as part of a portfolio (assuming you have resources to spare), do not make the moonshot your only shot. And we stress that going beyond profits necessarily requires having performed well financially in the first place. Faking till you make it will not do. Your brand can facilitate purpose by being a profit ally, an image builder, a change agent, or a value facilitator.[34] But not all at the same time. Be clear as to what you are trying to do and act consistently. Henry Ford's purpose was to "democratize the automobile" and Sam Walton's was to "give ordinary folk the chance to buy the same things as rich people." They were both able to achieve their purpose in their lifetimes via the companies they founded. By the way, one does not need to be a founder to have a purpose. Can you identify a worthwhile purpose that your brand can help fulfill under your tenure during your lifetime? Let the marketing function be the trustee and your brand be the steward of that purpose. Let mindful marketing, where you promote mindful consumption practices as opposed to maximizing short-term sales, be your guide.[35] Choose wisely (i.e., abide by the lessons) and the customers and other outcomes will follow.

12. *Results regarding ESG are a mixed bag of marbles, so do your homework when allocating resources* While consumers reward companies for strong environmental performance (E), institutional investors are less enthusiastic due to the perceived costs. Conversely, consumers may not prioritize good governance (G), but institutional investors favor it. Social performance (S) is less of a priority for investors, potentially due to cost concerns. Over 80% of global investors said they would "accept only a one percentage point or smaller reduction in returns to advance ESG objectives."[36] About half of those would not accept any amount of reduction. However, all three ESG factors play a crucial role for companies, as they influence financial risk perception among both consumers and institutional investors, impacting a company's overall financial health.[37]

13. *Think again, and consider alliances* The issue is perceived as more legitimate, and any backlash can be mitigated, when a group of firms act in unison.[38] We suggest industry-based coalitions focusing on unification; cross-brand activism can mean strength in numbers. For example, former

Unilever CEO Paul Polman has created IMAGINE to "take bold stands on climate, plastics, and human rights… to tip an entire industry."[39]

14. *Determine where you are on the curve of brand activism elasticity* Review the previous chapter. What kind of reaction(s) should you expect from the market-place if you doubled your brand activism efforts? Consumers are being bombarded with activism. Many consumers have become skeptical, and they actively label extant brand activism tactics as woke- or green-washing. Will you be justifiably authentic and effective? Or, as per financial lingo, are you allocating your resources inefficiently by needlessly increasing the risk of your cash flows, and should you rather invest differently?[40] Then, go back one more chapter and review it to reassess and make sure that the activism you have chosen is the right one for your context.

15. *Whether you are a mainstream generalist or a specialist can make all the difference* Your brand may have the heritage or high brand recognition to be considered a mainstream generalist (e.g., Toyota, Amazon, or Samsung) or a mainstream specialist (e.g., Tesla, Red Bull, or Gucci). The lessons above apply to mainstream generalists. They also typically apply to mainstream *product specialists* such as Lego, WD-40, and Dunkin' Donuts, since their customers tend to be representative of the market. However, if you are a *market specialist*, say with a geographic (e.g., In-N-Out Burger) or high-end market dominance (e.g., Bang & Olufsen), you'd better also review the activism playbook of niche brands. You may be able to find common ground among those in your target market. For example, those in your geography or intended income bracket may be more sensitive to climate change, income inequity, immigration policy, animal rights, and so on than others. Finally, if your brand is main-stream *and* specializes in both product and market (e.g., Aston Martin, Dyson, or Peloton), there may be unique opportunities for genuinely effective activism since both product and market heterogeneity will arguably be lower than all other categories.

References

1   Sheth, Jagdish N., Can Uslay, and Rajendra S. Sisodia (2020), *The Global Rule of Three: Competing with Conscious Strategy*, Palgrave MacMillan.

2   Nickerson, Dionne, Sundar Bharadwaj, and Omar Rodriguez-Vila (2023), "Antecedents and Consequences of an Inclusive Brand Marketing," *Marketing Science Institute Working Paper Series*, 23–138.

3   Morrison, Cassidy. "Majority of Americans Will Be Minorities by 2045," *Daily Mail*, August 7, 2023 (accessed March 4, 2025). https://www.dailymail.co.uk/health/article-12382253/Majority-Americans-minorities-2045-White-population-dip-50-time-history-according-to-analysis-of-census-data.html.

4   "Black Buying Power," Blavity Inc., May 17, 2023 (accessed October 26, 2024). https://blavityinc.com/black-buying-power/.

5   "U.S. Latino Economic Output Grows to $3.2 Trillion, New Study Says," CNBC, September 27, 2023 (accessed March 4, 2025). https://www.cnbc.com/amp/2023/09/27/us-latino-economic-output-grows-to-3point2-trillion-new-study-says.html.

6   "Consumers," Asian American Advertising Federation (accessed October 26, 2024). https://asianamericanadvertising.com/consumers. Melville, Doug, "DEI Is a Trillion-Dollar Blind Spot. Sephora Gets It—You Should Too," *Forbes*, July 22, 2024 (accessed March 4, 2025). https://www.forbes.com/sites/dougmelville/2024/07/22/dei-is-a-trillion-dollar-blind-spot-sephora-gets-ityou-should-too/.

7   Bowler, Hannah, "Why the 'Get Woke, Go Broke' Narrative is All Wrong," *The Drum*, July 17, 2024 (accessed October 15, 2024). https://www.thedrum.com/news/2024/07/17/why-the-get-woke-go-broke-narrative-all-wrong

8   Hydock, Chris, Neeru Paharia, and Sean Blair (2020), "Should Your Brand Pick a Side? How Market Share Determines the Impact of Corporate Political Advocacy," *Journal of Marketing Research*, 57(6), 1135–1151.

9   Bhagwat, Yashoda, Nooshin L. Warren, Joshua T. Beck, George F. Watson IV (2020), "Corporate Sociopolitical Activism and Firm Value," *Journal of Marketing*, 84(5), 1–21. Burbano, Vanessa (2020), "The Demotivating Effects of Communicating a Social Political Stance: Field Experimental Evidence from an Online Labor Market Platform," *Management Science*, 67(2), 1004–1025. Mukherjee, Sourjo and Niek Althuizen (2020), "Brand Activism: Does Courting Controversy Help or Hurt a Brand?" *International Journal of Research in Marketing*, 37(4), 772–788

10 Divisive issues examined have included refugee rights, transgender bathrooms, abortion, gun control, LGBTQ rights and Brexit (for a UK sample). Social media, and press releases have led to the same results. Also see Jongblut, Marc and Marius Johnen (2022), "When Brands (Don't) Take My Stance: The Ambiguous Effectiveness of Political Brand Communication," *Communication Research*, 49(8), 1092–1117.

11 Wallach, Karen Anne and Deidre Popovich (2023), "When Big is Less Than Small: Why Dominant Brands Lack Authenticity in Their Sustainability Initiatives," *Journal of Business Research*, 158, March.

12 Nickerson, Dionne, Sundar Bharadwaj, and Omar Rodriguez-Vila (2023), "Antecedents and Consequences of an Inclusive Brand Marketing," *Marketing Science Institute Working Paper Series*, 23–138.

13 Sibai, Olivier, Laetitia Mimoun, Achilleas Boukis (2021), "Authenticating Brand Activism: Negotiating the Boundaries of Free Speech to Make a Change," *Psychology & Marketing*, 38, 1651–1669.

14 Becker H. S. (1963). *Outsiders: Studies in the sociology of deviance*. The Free Press, p. 9.

15 Ahmad, Fayez, Francisco Guzman, and Blair Kidwell (2022), "Effective Messaging Strategies to Increase Brand Love for Sociopolitical Activist Brands," *Journal of Business Research*, 151, 609–622.

16 Hydrock, Chris, Neeru Paharia, and Sean Blair (2021), "Should Your Brand Pick a Side? How Market Share Determines Corporate Political Stances," NIM Marketing Intelligence Review, 13(2), 26–31.

17 Mirzaei, Abas, Dean C. Wilkie, and Helen Siuki (2022), "Woke Brand Activism Authenticity or Lack the of It," Journal of Business Research, 139 (February), 1–22.

18 "Employee Activism in the Age of Purpose: Employees (Up)rising," Weber Shandwick, May 29, 2019 (accessed October 26, 2024). https://webershandwick.com/news/employee-activism-in-the-age-of-purpose-employees-uprising.

19 Frenkel, Sheera, "Microsoft Employees Protest Work with ICE, as Tech Industry Mobilizes Over Immigration." The New York Times. June 19, 2018 (accessed March 4, 2025).   https://www.nytimes.com/2018/06/19/technology/tech-companies-immigration-border.html

20 Wakeman, Nick, "Google Fires Employees Who Protested Israel Cloud Contract." Washington Technology. April 19, 2024 (accessed March 4, 2025). https://www.washingtontechnology.com/opinion/2024/04/google-fires-employees-who-protested-israel-cloud-contract/395902/

21 Guha, Mithila and Daniel Korschun (2024), "Peer Effects on Brand Activism: Evidence from Brand and User Chatter on Twitter," Journal of Brand Management, 31, 153–167.

22 Nam, Jimin, Maya Balakrishnan, Julian De Freitas, Alison Wood Brooks (2022), "Speedy Activists: How Firm Response Time to Sociopolitical Events Influences Consumer Behavior," Journal of Consumer Psychology, 33, 632–644.

23 Warren, Nooshin "Boycott vs. Buycott: The aftermath of corporate activism," YouTube, TEDxUufA, August 22, 2019 (accessed March 4, 2025) https://www.youtube.com/watch?v=zpsWAsIfl1c.

24 Pavlov, Eugene and Natalie Mizik (2021), "Brand Political Positioning: Implications of the 2016 US Presidential Election," MSI Report 21–122, (accessed March 4, 2025). https://www.msi.org/working-paper/brand-political-positioning-implications-of-the-2016-us-presidential-election/.

25 Knight, Brian (2006), "Are Policy Platforms Capitalized into Equity Prices? Evidence from the Bush/Gore 2000 Presidential Election," Journal of Public Economics, 90(4), 751–773.

26 Smith, David (2024), "Donald Trump was Once a Registered Democrat and Party Donor. So Why Did He Jump Ship?" United States Studies Centre. July 24, 2024 (accessed March 4, 2025). https://www.ussc.edu.au/donald-trump-was-once-a-registered-democrat-and-party-donor-so-why-did-he-jump-ship.

27 Rosciglione, Annabella, "Massachusetts Has Highest Percentage of Independents Despite Heavy Democratic Lean." Washington Examiner. May 20, 2024 (accessed March 4, 2024).   https://www.washingtonexaminer.com/news/campaigns/state/3008338/massachusetts-has-highest-percentage-independents-despite-democratic-lean/. Griffiths, Shawn, "Top 10 States for Independent Voter Registration," Independent Voter Network, January 24, 2024 (accessed October 26, 2024). https://ivn.us/posts/top-10-states-where-independent-voter-numbers-dominate.

28 The following were identified as the top companies that were perceived to be most politically aligned during 2016 Q3:

Republican: IDT, Flagstar Bank, BP, EarthLink, Sun Trust, Tiffany, Xplore, Prudential Insurance, Duke Energy, Belmond. *Democratic:* Google, Apple, Tesla, Microsoft, Facebook, Amazon, Lockheed Martin, Sony, Western Digital, State Street.

Pavlov, Eugene and Natalie Mizik (2021), "Brand Political Positioning: Implications of the 2016 US Presidential Election," *MSI Report* 21–122, May 14, 2021 (accessed March 4, 2025). https://www.msi.org/working-paper/brand-political-position ing-implications-of-the-2016-us-presidential-election/.

29   MacLellan, Lila, "How Thinx, the Buzzy Underwear Company Once Worth $230 Million, Lost Its Way," *AOL.* May 28, 2024 (accessed March 4, 2025). https://www. aol.com/finance/thinx-buzzy-underwear-company-once-110000565.html.

30   Meddings, Sabah and Deirdre Hipwell, "Unilever CEO Steps Up With Plan to Shed Ben & Jerry's, Jobs," *Bloomberg*, March 19, 2024 (accessed March 4, 2025). https://www.bloomberg.com/news/articles/2024-03-19/unilever-to-separate-ice-cream-unit-as-new-ceo-cuts-7-500-jobs?fbclid=IwY2xjawFdTCJleHRuA2Flb QIxMAABHXDUQifFnmmjC085P8BNwrGzfNWyP8d6tXrrCa0Iw3jHFnVXshsLn_ pRPw_aem_HJ3zceFDLSSC3iK5CAYpzQ&embedded-checkout=true.

31   Kapitan, Sommer, Joya A. Kemper, Jessica Vredenburg, Amanda Spry (2022), "Strategic B2B Brand Activism: Building Conscientious Purpose for Social Impact," *Industrial Marketing Management*, 107(5), 14–28.

32   Guenther, Miriam, and Peter Guenther (2019), "The Value of Branding for B2B Service Firms—The Shareholders' Perspective," *Industrial Marketing Management*, 78 (April), 88–101.

33   Allen, Dave, *Brandpie CEO Purpose Report 2022* (accessed March 4, 2025). https:// www.brandpie.com/insights/ceo-purpose-report/2022.

34   Blocker, Christopher P., Joseph P. Cannon, and Jonathan Z. Zhang (2024), "Purpose Orientation: An Emerging Theory Transforming Business for a Better World," *Journal of the Academy of Marketing Science*. https://doi.org/10.1007/s11747-023-00989-5.

35   Uslay, Can and Emine Erdogan (2014), "The Mediating Role of Mindful Entrepreneurial Marketing (MEM) Between Production and Consumption," *Journal of Research in Marketing & Entrepreneurship*, 16(1), 47–62.

      Malhotra, Naresh K., Olivia F. Lee, and Can Uslay (2012), "Mind the Gap: The Mediating Role of Mindful Marketing Between Market and Quality Orientations, Their Interaction, and Consequences," *International Journal of Quality & Reliability Management*, 29(6), 607–625.

      Bayraktar, Ahmet, Emine Erdogan, Can Uslay, Olivia F. Lee (2020), "Mindful Entrepreneurial Marketing for Small and Medium Enterprises," in *Handbook of Entrepreneurship and Marketing*, I.R. Fillis and N. J. M. Telford Eds., Edward Elgar, 262–274.

36   Gassmann, Peter and Will Jackson-Moore, "The CEO's ESG Dilemma," *Harvard Law School Forum on Corporate Governance*, January 23, 2023 (accessed March 4, 2025). https://corpgov.law.harvard.edu/2023/01/23/the-ceos-esg-dilemma/.

37   Malshe, Ashwin, Yi Yin, Anatoli Colicev, Yakov Bart, and Koen Pauwels (2023), "How ESG Reduces Risk: The Role of Consumers and Institutional Investors," *MSI Report* 23–129, April 7, 2023 (accessed March 4, 2025). https://www.msi.org/ working-paper/how-esg-reduces-risk-the-role-of-consumers-and-institutional-investors/

38   Warren, Nooshin, "Boycott vs. Buycott: The Aftermath of Corporate Activism," *YouTube. TEDxUufA*, August 22, 2019 (accessed March 4, 2025). https://www.yout ube.com/watch?v=zpsWAsIfl1c.

39   Sarkar, Christian and Philip Kotler, "Cross-Brand Activism: The Way Forward," November 17, 2020 (accessed October 30, 2024). https://www.activistbrands. com/cross-brand-activism-the-way-forward/.

40   Bhagwat, Yashoda, Nooshin Warren, Joshua T. Beck, George F. Watson IV (2020), "Corporate Sociopolitical Activism and Firm Value," *Journal of Marketing*, 84(5), 1–21.

11

LESSONS FOR NICHE BRANDS

Unlike mainstream brands that serve the mass market, brand activism offers a significant upside for niche brands. They can find kindred spirits among the consumers and have galvanized support and loyalty toward the beloved activist brand.

Consider the push activism case of Oatly. The Swedish oat milk company became a shining example of effective brand activism by a niche brand. It boldly challenged industry norms and sparked conversations, not just about their product, but about sustainability and ethical consumption. Their "It's Like Milk, But Made for Humans" campaign, with its playful yet provocative messaging, directly confronted the dairy industry while promoting plant-based alternatives.[1] Oatly's activism extends beyond marketing and they've launched petitions to increase transparency around the environmental impact of food production and even funded grassroots initiatives through their "*Je ne sais quoi*" (I don't know what) fund.[2] The company also touts its carbon footprint or lack thereof: "replacing one liter of cow milk with a liter of Oatly *saves* 1,160 CO2e, which is the equivalent to the CO2 produced driving the average gas-powered car about six miles."[3] Their approach, combining humor, transparency, and a genuine commitment to

DOI: 10.4324/9781003593690-11

change, has resonated with consumers seeking brands that align with their values. Oatly demonstrates that brand activism, when done authentically and strategically, can build brand loyalty, drive market disruption, and contribute to a larger societal shift. Oprah Winfrey, Natalie Portman, Jay Z, and Howard Schultz of Starbucks have been named among early investors. They likely had a good payday when Oatly had a successful IPO in 2023 that saw the shares rise by 30% and valued the company at $10 billion.[4] Though such success brings challenges. Oatly now has to deal with its newfound status as a mainstream specialist, currently sold in 60,000 retailers and 32,000 coffee shops in 20 countries around the world.[5]

Then consider the case of Penzeys Spices, whose activist CEO has embraced divisiveness. The Wisconsin-based purveyor of seasonings, clearly a product specialist, has become a fiery example of how a company can take a bold political stance and thrive. Founder and CEO Bill Penzey, unafraid to infuse his progressive values into the brand, has repeatedly called out racism, social injustice, and political extremism, directly criticizing Republican politicians and policies in his newsletters and public statements.[6] The website also prominently features an "About Republicans" section that criticizes them not so gently.[7] The unapologetic approach, while alienating some customers, has galvanized a loyal following who appreciates the company's commitment to social justice. Remarkably, Penzey's divisive push activism has fueled financial success. Many were drawn to the brand's outspokenness. Following the election of Trump in 2016, an email about the "open embrace of racism by the Republican party" resulted in double the gift box orders and increased online sales by 60%.[8] This pattern continued with subsequent political statements, demonstrating that taking a stand can attract customers who align with those values. Penzeys proves that, in a polarized world, authenticity and a willingness to engage in political discourse can be a powerful recipe for business growth, even if it means adding a little spice to the controversy. Though apparently, it is also possible to add too much spice to a commercial conversation. When subscribers received an email promotion named "Republicans are Racists Weekend" during Martin Luther King Jr. Weekend in 2022, 40,000 customers—or 3% of those on the list—unsubscribed.[9]

As you can imagine, political activism is not purely the domain of Democrats. There are those who support Republicans through brand activism too. In July 2020, Robert Unanue, the CEO of Goya, one of the largest Hispanic-owned food businesses in the US, praised President Donald Trump, simultaneously triggering a boycott and a buycott of the brand. On the surface, the push for a boycott was stronger: Twitter posts seeking a boycott were 75% more than those urging to buy more.[10] However, a rigorous study found that "boycott-related social media posts and media coverage dominated buycott ones, but the sales impact was the opposite: Goya sales temporarily increased by 22%" dissipating within three weeks.[11] The study also reported "large sales increases (56.4%) in heavily Republican counties" but did "not find a strong countervailing boycott effect in heavily Democratic counties or among Goya's core customer base—Latino consumers" possibly due to brand loyalty and switching costs.[12] Moreover, since the initial level of market penetration for the product specialist Goya was relatively low, the potential from vetting the appetite and gaining business from *non-customer Republicans* was higher than the potential loss from *pre-existing Democrat customers* which is merely a fraction of the overall customer base.

Below are our lessons for fledgling and niche brands:

1. *It is okay for niche brands to delve into politics and other divisive issues* But you need to be strategic as well as authentic about it. As a small brand, you have a lot more to gain than you have to lose. Thus, everything else being equal, niche brands will be better off by engaging in activism on an issue that divides the public evenly. Again, the math is not complicated: assume that customers' negative reaction is twice the strength of those that support your activism and that you lead a niche brand with a 5% share of the market. By taking a divisive stand, you risk losing about 25% of your existing customers (1.25% overall share) while you could potentially more than double your market share from new customers. And this assumes your existing customers are evenly divided on the issue. More likely is the scenario where they will have already self-selected into your brand due to its congruity with their self-identity, hence, the actual defection rate will likely be much smaller. For mainstream brands, the perceived importance of the issue may be average even as some feel the issue is very important where others do not. For niche brands with heritage, the customer sentiment is also likely to be more uniformly distributed. In fact, the potential gains from growing the segment are likely to surpass potential losses even when the divisive issue is supported by a minority of non-users.

2. *It is not just about holding party lines. The choice of the political issue is also important* Research suggests that Americans' views of political parties have evolved around gender implicitly as well as explicitly. Republicans, and by extension, the Republican party, have been viewed as experienced, strong, independent, realistic, cocky, selfish, taking undeserved credit, and hence, masculine. Democrats have been viewed as caring, generous, compassionate, weak, impractical, inexperienced, and hence feminine![13] (So easy to get into crossfire here. Don't shoot the messenger, not our research, nor our conclusions; also note, this research was published in 2010 so a replication may be overdue). Yet another study examined candidate appearance and advertising strategies and found Democrats were perceived to be more intelligent, whereas Republicans were more competent.[14] Book-smarts versus street-smarts? So much to chew here for the fledgling brand that is willing. Other party associations that could be relevant include endorsement by a younger person, small size, warmth, and concern for others (Democrats); endorsement by older/professional person, expensive, white-collar (Republicans).[15] In any case, make sure your category is not already taken. Once someone has established itself as the Democrat/Republican "spice" in your category, the value to be extracted will be subject to diminishing returns for every brand thereafter. Whether you are going after inclusion, tolerance, exceptionalism, freedom or strength, it is clear getting political is a real option for niche brands if you can be authentic.

3. *The narrative of a niche brand can be deliberately critical, ideological, and transformative to enhance the perceived authenticity and ultimate impact of its activism*[16] Critical because it does not necessarily seek or need a common ground to attract the mainstream. Ideological and transformative because it seeks and sometimes demands improvement and social change from its followers, aka customers.[17] It asks them to be and do better. We emphasize, challenging the status quo and establishment is a viable option for fledgling brands. This can be profitable even when the majority of consumers oppose your activism.[18] Divisiveness has another upside: divisive issues have the power to be more identity-relevant and carry greater signaling power. In other words, the more people disagree on a stance, the better it distinguishes between a desirable ingroup (customers) and an undesirable outgroup (others).[19]

4. *Going woke (or anti-woke) does not need to mean going broke* With fewer customers to lose and many more to gain, it can mean the opposite for small brands. However, again authenticity is key.[20] The majority of consumers do not trust the sincerity of brands' commitment to social causes.[21]

5. *Fledgling brand CEO activism can be very powerful if perceived as authentic* And everything else being equal, is especially appreciated by Republicans. Meanwhile, employee activism has a higher bar to clear when it comes to perceived authenticity. Does the sentiment really represent the vast majority of your employees? If so, was your workforce really as diverse as your ads suggest when the nation is divided on the issue? In general, employee activism resonates more with Democrats.

6. *Game Theory says go on the offensive when everyone else is focused on defense* In poker lingo, when others play tight, it pays off to play loose. Fear of recession and boycotts have put many mainstream brands on the defensive.[22] Many have caved in to pressure and revised their DEI policies.[23] In such a climate, a niche brand can find more issues to activate, and less competition to differentiate from. Even better if you can identify a small but fast-growing segment and ride the wave.

7. *For a brand that has nothing to lose, brand activism may also come from shock value (combined with humor)*[24] For example, Liquid Death with its aluminum cans and "murder your thirst" tagline mocks the traditional plastic-bottled water brands. It donates a portion of profits to environmental causes. The brand has a cult following among younger audiences, and successfully differentiates itself in a crowded market.[25] Meatless Farm (plant-based meats) has used provocative and attention-grabbing ad campaigns such as "M*** F***",[26] generating buzz and sparking debate about sustainable food and environmental impact. Thinx (period underwear) featured suggestive imagery (e.g., grapefruit halves, runny eggs) in its early ads to challenge period stigma, pushing boundaries of what is considered acceptable in advertising.[27]

8. *Seek organic endorsements from celebrities/influencers by proactively offering your brand/ cause for their alignment* Personal brands need authentic activism too! (More on this in the next chapter). This can be a win-win for both brands.

9. *Act your age* Is your brand still young at heart or should your causes also mature with your customers? Abercrombie & Fitch recently found success through targeting a more mature audience[28] whereas Jaguar

was criticized heavily for acting like a brand that has nothing to lose and getting its heritage wrong with its "celebration of modernism" brand repositioning toward a younger, "woke" audience.[29]

10. *Brand activism implemented well will often look like entrepreneurial marketing* Much like entrepreneurial marketing, brand activism is an equalizer for small brands with small resources. Large brands will have fewer causes they can rationally engage in without alienating a large portion of their customers. Meanwhile, niche brands can carve subsegments and fortify them with strong positions.

11. *Determine if you are a fledgling brand, mainstream specialist, or stuck in the middle* Mainstream specialists need to examine their current and potential customer base carefully to identify the issue(s) to activate. Entrepreneurial marketing uniquely boosts the performance of mid-sized businesses,[30] and we suspect the same is true for brand activism too.

12. *Do not bite off more than you can chew* Unless you are a mainstream specialist with resources, small brands are better off focusing on lower-level needs on the hierarchy since engaging with higher levels can get very resource intensive. Yes, Gen Z appreciates brand activism more than others. However, despite what you may have heard, they are not more focused on social values than those who came before them.[31] Meanwhile, evidence that they care more about local issues than global is piling.[32] Sustainability, despite being a higher-level issue, may be an exception to this because its impact is also felt at the local level. For example, can you source locally and encourage your customers to do so too, by buying your (local) brand?

References

1   Croagh, Liv, "Oatly Make "Milk, Only Made For Humans." June 29, 2022 (accessed October 30, 2024). https://www.marketingmag.com.au/news/oatly-make-milk-but-only-for-humans/.

2   "Things We Do," Oatly, (accessed October 30, 2024). https://www.oatly.com/sv-se/things-we-do.

3   "No Dairy, No Problem: How Oatly Is Crushing the Competition," Talkroute (accessed October 30, 2024). https://talkroute.com/how-oatly-is-crushing-the-competition/.

4   Lauren Hisrch and Jack Ewing, "Oatly Shares Soar 30% in Their Public Debut," *The New York Times*. May 20, 2021 (accessed March 6, 2025). https://www.nytimes.com/2021/05/20/business/oatly-stock-price-IPO.html.

5 "Oatly Raised $1.4 Billion in Stock Market Debut," Vegan Kind, October 5, 2023 (accessed October 30, 2024). https://vegankind.com/mag/oatly-raised-1-4-billion-in-stock-market-debut.

6 Bruce, Tammy, "Penzeys Spices and the Business of Hate," *The Washington Times.* February 2, 2022. https://www.washingtontimes.com/news/2022/feb/2/penzeys-spices-and-the-business-of-hate/.

7 "About Republicans," Penzeys Spices (accessed October 30, 2024). https://www.penzeys.com/shop/about-republicans/.

8 "Your Brand Doesn't Have to Be Political to be Authentic," MarketSmiths (accessed October 30, 2024). https://www.marketsmiths.com/2022/politics-in-content-marketing/.

9 "Your Brand Doesn't Have to Be Political to be Authentic," MarketSmiths (accessed October 30, 2024). https://www.marketsmiths.com/2022/politics-in-content-marketing/.

10 Oller, Samantha, "Goya Boycott After CEO's Praise of Trump Resulted in Higher Sales: Study." Food Dive. August 30, 2022 (accessed March 6, 2025). https://www.fooddive.com/news/goya-sales-rise-after-boycott-trump/630737/.

11 Liaukonyte, Jura, Anna Tuchman, and Xinrong Zhu (2022), "Frontiers: Spilling the Beans on Political Consumerism: Do Social Media Boycotts and Buycotts Translate to Real Sales Impact?" *Marketing Science* 42(1), 11–25.

12 Liaukonyte, Jura, Anna Tuchman, and Xinrong Zhu (2022), "Frontiers: Spilling the Beans on Political Consumerism: Do Social Media Boycotts and Buycotts Translate to Real Sales Impact?" *Marketing Science* 42(1), 11–25.

13 Winter, Nicholas J. G. (2010), "Masculine Republicans and Feminine Democrats: Gender and Americans' Explicit and Implicit Images of the Political Parties," *Political Behavior*, 32(4), 587–618.

14 Hoegg, JoAndrea, and Michael V. Lewis (2011), "The Impact of Candidate Appearance and Advertising Strategies on Election Results," *Journal of Marketing Research*, 48(5), 895–909.

15 Gelb, Betsy D. and Alina B. Sorescu (2000), "Republican Brands, Democrat Brands," *Journal of Advertising Research*, 40(1), 95–102.

16 Andersen, S.E., and T.S. Johansen (2021), "Corporate Citizenship: Challenging the Corporate Centricity in Corporate Marketing," *Journal of Business Research* 131, 686–699.

17 Andersen, S.E., and T.S. Johansen (2021), "Corporate Citizenship: Challenging the Corporate Centricity in Corporate Marketing," *Journal of Business Research* 131, 686–699.

18 Hydrock, Chris, Neeru Paharia, and Sean Blair (2021), "Should Your Brand Pick a Side? How Market Share Determines Corporate Political Stances," *NIM Marketing Intelligence Review*, 13(2), 26–31.

19 Verlegh, Peeter W. J. (2024), "Perspectives: A Research-Based Guide for Brand Activism," *International Journal of Advertising*, 43(2). https://www.tandfonline.com/doi/full/10.1080/02650487.2023.2228117

20 Mirzaei, Abas, Dean C. Wilkie, and Helen Siuki (2022), "Woke Brand Activism Authenticity or Lack the of It," *Journal of Business Research*, 139 (February), 1–22. Hydrock, Chris, Neeru Paharia, and Sean Blair (2021), "Should Your Brand Pick

a Side? How Market Share Determines Corporate Political Stances," NIM *Marketing Intelligence Review*, 13(2), 26–31.

21 "The Dangers of 'Woke-Washing'," *WARC*, September 9, 2019 (accessed October 30, 2024). https://www.warc.com/newsandopinion/news/the-dangers-of-woke-washing/en-gb/42604.

22 Graham, Megan, Katie Deighton, and Patrick Coffee, "Super Bowl Ads Launch Celebrity Blitz with Goal of Playing It Safe." February 11, 2024 (accessed March 6, 2025). https://www.wsj.com/articles/super-bowl-commercials-ads-roundup-e86f561c?mod=djem10point.

23 For example, when conservative activist Robby Starbuck called out Harley Davidson and a number of other businesses for their "woke" DEI initiatives, Harley Davidson announced that it no longer has a DEI function and that it would cease participating in an index about LGBTQ+ inclusion produced by Human Rights Campaign (HRC). Tractor Supply and John Deere also changed their DEI policies after being targeted by Starbuck. As of Summer 2024, Lowe's, Brown-Forman (producer of Jack Daniel's), and AB InBev rival Molson Coors were also "dialing down diversity initiatives … and said they would distance themselves from HRC." In all, DEI-related job postings declined 44% in 2023. Even perceived DEI leaders like Meta and Google slashed such jobs.
Pisani, Joseph, "Harley-Davidson Changes DEI Policy Following Activist Pressure," *The Wall Street Journal*, August 19, 2024. https://www.wsj.com/business/harley-davidson-changes-dei-policy-following-activist-pressure-b544ba26. "The Harley Davidson Boss Caught in an 'Anti-Woke' Squall," *Financial Times*, August 23, 2024 (accessed March 6, 2025). https://www.ft.com/content/bf37e875-32ac-4b2c-926e-54226e104cdd?segmentId=b0d7e653-3467-12ab-c0f0-77e4424cdb4c. Francis, Theo and Lauren Weber, "Ford, Coors Light, and Other Brands Retreat from a Gay-Rights Index." *The Wall Street Journal*. September 5, 2024 (accessed March 6, 2025). https://www.wsj.com/business/ford-coors-gay-rights-index-dei-04c4ff94?mod=djemCMOToday. "Big Tech Companies Made Cuts to DEI-Related Jobs in 2023 Despite Their Prior Commitments," *Business & Human Rights Resource Centre*, December 27, 2023 (accessed March 6, 2025). https://www.business-humanrights.org/en/latest-news/big-tech-companies-made-cuts-to-dei-related-jobs-in-2023-despite-their-prior-commitments/.

24 Sibai, Olivier, Laetitia Mimoun, Achilleas Boukis (2021), Authenticating Brand Activism: Negotiating the Boundaries of Free Speech to Make a Change," *Psychology & Marketing*, 38, 1651–1669.

25 Liquid Death (accessed October 30, 2024). https://liquiddeath.com/?srsltid=AfmBOoo1rDKL0RuL2h3XFiI5ZAUj15MvzpgRyH3-u0C1SHay0N2exBKp.

26 Smithers, Rebecca, "Vegan Food Company Provokes with M*** F*** Advertising Campaign," *The Guardian*, August 3, 2020 (accessed March 6, 2025). https://www.theguardian.com/lifeandstyle/2020/aug/03/vegan-food-company-provokes-advertising-campaign-meatless-farm-coronavirus.

27 Mohan, Pavithra, "Thinx's First National Ad Campaign Imagines a Worlds Where Men Get Periods., Too," *Fast Company*, October 3, 2019 (accessed March 6, 2025). https://www.fastcompany.com/90412779/thinx-menstruation-ad-campaign-imagines-men-getting-periods.

28 Kerr, Tom, "Abercrombie & Fitch: Rich History and Solid Turnaround," *Yahoo! Finance*. June 14, 2023 (accessed March 6, 2025). https://finance.yahoo.com/news/abercrombie-fitch-rich-history-solid-152030050.html.

29 Schultz, E.J., "Jaguar's Polarizing Rebrand—Marketing and Design Pros Weigh In," *AdAge*, November 20, 2024 (accessed December 9, 2024). https://adage.com/article/marketing-news-strategy/jaguar-rebrand-criticized/2592666

30 Alqahtani, Nasser, Can Uslay, and Sengun Yeniyurt, "Entrepreneurial Marketing and Firm Performance: Scale Development, Validation, and Empirical Test," *Journal of Strategic Marketing, forthcoming. .*
Alqahtani, Nasser, Can Uslay, and Sengun Yeniyurt, "Comparing the Moderated Impact of Entrepreneurial Orientation, Market Orientation, and Entrepreneurial Marketing on Firm Performance," *Journal of Small Business Management, forthcoming.*
Alqahtani, Nasser, Can Uslay, and Sengun Yeniyurt (2024), "Strategic Performance Blueprint: Optimizing Business Performance Through Tailoring Strategic Postures to Environmental and Institutional Contexts," *Journal of the International Council for Small Business*, 5(3), 216–231.

31 Lebow, Sara, "Gen Z No More Focused on Brand's Social Values Than Older Generations." eMarketer. January 12, 2023 (accessed October 30, 2024). https://www.emarketer.com/content/gen-z-no-more-focused-on-brand-s-social-values-than-older-generations.

32 Frisbie, Sonnet, "For Gen Z, The Future of Corporate Activism Is Local First, Global Second," *Morning Consult*, January 9, 2023 (accessed October 30, 2024). https://pro.morningconsult.com/analysis/gen-z-corporate-activism-is-local-first.

12

LESSONS FOR PERSON(AL) BRANDS

In a world where consumer attention span is continuously decreasing, the quest to overcome consumer skepticism of advertising messages started with product placements in movies well over a century ago.[1] These placements made advertising an integral part of the original content and enhanced perceived authenticity. Patrick Quinn, CEO and CCO of PQ Media famously argued that, "There is no advertising, marketing or consumer-driven media tactic that can match the durability, consistency or growth trajectory of product placement."[2]

However, movies remain costly to produce and are released infrequently. Hence the strategies to gain authentic influence have evolved with social media. Today, influencers and marketers co-produce movies (in the form of short clips) and reach millions of consumers cost-effectively, daily. Influencers, like Zach King (80 million TikTok followers), Virginia Fonseca Costa (46 million Instagram followers), Huda (Beauty) Kattan (54 million Instagram followers), have become celebrities in their own right. These influencers can help marketers achieve brand authenticity (demonstrating the unique values of the brand) as well as content authenticity (demonstrating a credible and believable message). Dismayed by advertising,

DOI: 10.4324/9781003593690-12

consumers look to influencers for more genuine guidance. Marketers have taken notice and spent over \$34B on influencer marketing in 2023,[3] a figure projected to exceed \$56 billion by 2029.[4]

Enter influencer 3.0. Forget corporations or influencers, you are the ultimate brand. In today's world, personal branding isn't just for celebrities and influencers—it's for everyone. Every tweet, every LinkedIn post, and every interaction builds your unique identity in the marketplace. Think of yourself as a walking, talking advertisement, constantly shaping how others perceive your skills, values, and personality. Coke sells refreshment, Apple sells innovation, and you're vending your own unique blend of talents and experiences. Whether you're aiming for a promotion, seeking new clients, or simply building a strong network, cultivating a compelling personal brand is no longer optional—it's essential for success in the human marketplace.

In a world saturated with information and choices, standing out is paramount. This is where personal branding becomes your secret weapon. Just as Nike evokes athletic prowess, you too possess a unique set of qualities and experiences that define your value proposition. Are you the creative problem-solver, the reliable team player, or the passionate advocate? Consciously crafting your personal brand allows you to showcase these strengths, shaping how others perceive you and opening doors to opportunities you might otherwise miss.

Personal branding goes beyond self-promotion to aligning your actions with your values. This is where brand activism enters the equation. As Patagonia champions environmental sustainability and Ben & Jerry's fights for social justice, you can leverage your personal brand to advocate for causes you believe in. By publicly supporting issues that resonate with you, you not only attract like-minded individuals but also inspire others to act. Whether it's volunteering your time, donating to charities, or speaking out against injustice, brand activism amplifies your impact and strengthens your personal brand by showcasing your authentic commitment to making a difference.

In the age of social media, where everyone has a platform, personal brand activism becomes even more potent. Every post, every share, every comment contributes to the narrative you're creating around yourself. By thoughtfully curating your online presence and engaging in meaningful conversations, you can build a community of support around your values and amplify your message. Remember, your personal brand is a reflection of your character, passions, and contributions to the world. So, embrace your unique voice, stand up for what you believe in, and let your brand activism illuminate the change you want to see. From raw content to deepfake AI bots (yes, even your own) delivering niche messages at scale and at bargain prices, the future of (not so) authentic influence is here. Below are our lessons for person(al) brands.

1. It is crucial for person(al) brand activists to practice what they preach, lest their message ring hollow Take, for instance, a sustainability advocate who constantly jets around the world or a vegan influencer caught wearing leather. Such inconsistencies erode trust and credibility, undermining the very cause they champion. Conversely, when actions align with words, the impact is amplified. Consider Jane Goodall, whose lifelong dedication to chimpanzees speaks volumes about her commitment to conservation, or Greta Thunberg, whose unwavering stance on climate action inspires millions. Their authenticity strengthens their message, transforming them into powerful catalysts for change. Ultimately, practicing what you preach is not just about personal integrity, it's about demonstrating a genuine commitment to the cause, building a loyal following, and maximizing your influence for a positive impact. As we have underlined several times already, a lack of authenticity is a deal-breaker. While the use of influencers can be very effective, "influencer vetting is now an arduous process and often legal teams are at the center of planning, which has never been the case previously."[5]

2. Celebrity brands can engage in activism too, and it is more effective when organic When the Duchess of Sussex, Meghan Markle, was spotted wearing Outland Denim twice in the same week in October 2018, the jeans she wore sold out within a week, and the company that was started on the promise of profit-for-purpose saw a 640% uptick in sales. The influx enabled the company to employ more victims of sex trafficking and forced labor. Leonardo DiCaprio also wore and endorsed their jeans. Consequently, Outland Denim "was able to upgrade its Cambodian plants, land accounts with Bloomingdale's and Nordstrom in the United States, collaborate with Global Fashion Agenda, Karen Walker and Nudie Jeans, and plot an entry into ready-to-wear."[6] By choosing a lesser-known brand known for its ethical practices and commitment

to social impact and validating it, Meghan Markle further solidified her public image as someone who cares about responsible fashion. This aligned with her existing philanthropic efforts and values and amplified her voice for ethical fashion.

3. *Celebrity brands can engage in activism too, and it is most effective with personal sacrifice*   Muhammad Ali's journey from Cassius Clay to conscientious objector was a masterclass in brand activism, long before the term even existed. He understood that his athletic prowess was a platform to amplify his beliefs, transforming himself into a symbol of resistance against racial injustice and the Vietnam War. His refusal to be drafted, famously declaring, "I ain't got no quarrel with them Viet Cong," cost him his heavyweight title, and risked imprisonment, but solidified his commitment to his principles.[7] This bold act of defiance resonated with a generation disillusioned by war and inequality, cementing his status as not just a boxing champion, but a champion of civil rights. Ali's unwavering stance transcended sports, demonstrating the power of aligning personal brand with social activism to ignite change and leave an indelible mark on history. No wonder he is considered among the greatest athletes of all time.

4. *(Financial) sacrifice is a significantly more important driver of authenticity for person brands/influencers than corporations*   While corporations are viewed as merely spending other people's money, consider the entrepreneur who invests their life savings in their startup, the artist who works multiple jobs to fund their passion project, or the activist who takes a pay cut to work for a non-profit. These actions speak louder than a marketing campaign, demonstrating a level of dedication that goes beyond mere profit-seeking. This authenticity builds trust and loyalty, attracting investors, customers, and collaborators who admire their dedication. While the immediate financial hit might be painful, the long-term rewards in terms of reputation, influence, and ultimately, financial success can be substantial. In a world saturated with superficiality, genuine sacrifice cuts through the noise and establishes a personal brand as truly authentic and purpose-driven. While the short-term sacrifices can pay off in the long or even medium run, signaling a genuine commitment matters, and resonates deeply with audiences.

5. *Person brands can stand to benefit from their activism financially, and that is okay*   Consider *Playboy* editor-in-chief, Hugh Hefner, whose legacy extended beyond the realm of adult entertainment, encompassing a surprising

history of social activism. While controversial for his role in sexualizing women, Hefner also challenged societal norms and advocated for civil rights. Through *Playboy* magazine, he provided a platform for Black artists and writers during the civil rights era, and openly supported LGBTQ+ rights long before it was mainstream. He financially backed organizations like the ACLU and fought against censorship laws. While his activism is complex and intertwined with his business ventures, it's undeniable that Hefner used his influence to push for greater sexual and social freedom, leaving a progressive yet mixed legacy on the fight for equality.[8]

6. *Advice-taking can uniquely engage the customers of a person-brand while improving activism outcomes* There is experimental evidence that when brands seek consumers' opinions and advice regarding which cause(s) to support, they achieve higher brand activism support. Moreover, brands do not suffer from negative behavioral or attitudinal outcomes even when they do not follow the advice received.[9] This suggests influencers can uniquely engage their followers to guide their activism, even when they know their tendency toward an issue.

7. *Humor is the official lubricant of the influencer wheel* It can be incredibly disarming and effective. Influencers like Celeste Barber, Lilly Singh, and Seth "Dude With Sign" Phillips have been successfully using humor to address social issues for positive change. So can you and your influencers. And your brand can also use humor to attenuate negative sentiments on social media.[10] However, look to partner with influencers that entertain, educate, or curate to create value as opposed to those that just look pretty and/or crack jokes with no purpose.

8. *Don't trivialize a serious issue* Remember how Pepsi and Kendall Jenner fell flat on MLK Day? Blake Lively's It Ends With Us movie promotion serves as another, more recent, stark reminder. Her initial focus on fashion and aesthetics urging audiences to "grab your friends and wear your florals," trivialized the film's serious themes of domestic violence. The backlash underscored the importance of authenticity, sensitivity, and understanding the nuances of social issues when leveraging a platform for change, especially in the age of social media where missteps can quickly amplify into a crisis. While course correction may save the day, it's best to get it right from the start to avoid reputational damage.[11] And

while death is no trivial matter, Indian model/actress Poonam Pandey was also criticized when she faked her own death to raise awareness of cervical cancer.[12]

9. *There may be U-shaped relationship between the number of followers of an influencer and perceived authenticity* Micro-influencers are unlikely to be compensated to push a social issue and mega-influencers, like Cristiano Ronaldo, do not need compensation for doing so. Make sure that there is alignment between their causes and your brand's. Similarly, you can identify up-and-coming influencers without deliberate activism and make your brand's activism their long-term cause as well. Long term or even life-long partnerships are naturally perceived as much more authentic.

10. *For influencers, authentic alignment with a sustainability cause can be sustainable activism* According to a recent study by McKinsey, customers are finally willing to pay for sustainable brands. However, the product category makes a difference. They found the biggest growth potential for ESG claims came from paper and plastics household brands, whereas baby food and beer categories carried the lowest potential.[13]

11. *Brand activism is for everyone who wants to make an impact* "I am the master of my fate, I am the captain of my soul," (from the poem "Invictus" by William Ernest Henley) for Oprah Winfrey; "Success isn't always about greatness. It's about consistency. Consistent hard work gains success. Greatness will come," for Dwayne "The Rock" Johnson; and "Don't you ever let a soul in the world tell you that you can't be exactly who you are," by Lady Gaga all make sense as mantras for their respective celebrities.[14] What is your personal brand manifesto or mantra in a few words? Brand activism is for everyone. Recently, UCLA Professor Lucina Qazi Uddin sued six academic publishers alleging that not paying for peer reviews of academic articles, for which they collectively reap billions of dollars in revenues, constitutes a price-fixing scheme.[15] This issue has been something academics around the world have been complaining about by the side of their water coolers for decades. Yet Professor Uddin is the first academic to do something about it. If Professor Uddin's personal brand mantra is "Know Your Worth" or "My Value, My Pay," her activism on this topic would be very fitting indeed.

References

1   Karniouchina, Ekaterina V., Can Uslay, and Grigori Erenburg (2011), "Do Marketing Media Have Life Cycles? The Case of Product Placement in Movies," *Journal of Marketing*, 75(3), 27–48.

2   "Product Placement Grows," *WARC*, June 17, 2015 (accessed October 30, 2024). https://www.warc.com/newsandopinion/news/product-placement-grows/en-gb/34937

3   "Influencer Marketing Spending Worldwide and in the United States in 2022 and 2023," *Statista*, November 30, 2023 (accessed October 30, 2024). https://www.statista.com/statistics/1414663/influencer-marketing-spending-global-us/.

4   "Influencer Advertising – Worldwide," *Statista* (accessed October 30, 2024). https://www.statista.com/outlook/amo/advertising/influencer-advertising/worldwide.

5   Bowler, Hannah, "Brand Marketers Confess Why They Chose to Hide Pride This Year," *The Drum*, July 2, 2024 (accessed March 6, 2025). https://www.thedrum.com/news/2024/07/02/brand-marketers-confess-why-they-chose-hide-pride-year.

6   Malik, Jasmin C., "Outland Denim Is Ready for Its Post-Covid CloseUp," *Sourcing Journal*, May 13, 2024 (accessed March 25, 2025). https://sourcingjournal.com/denim/denim-brands/outland-denim-covid-finances-us-relaunch-510344/.

7   Wolfson, Andrew, "Muhammad Ali Lost Everything in Opposing the Vietnam War. But in 1968, He Triumphed," *USA Today*. March 2, 2018 (accessed March 6, 2025). https://www.usatoday.com/story/news/2018/02/19/1968-project-muhammad-ali-vietnam-war/334759002/.

8   "Hugh Hefner's Little-Known History as Civil Rights Activist," *Ebony*, September 28, 2017 (accessed October 30, 2024). https://www.ebony.com/hugh-hefner-civil-rights/. Leah, Rachel, "Hugh Hefner's Real Progressive Legacy Isn't Sexual, It's Racial," September 28, 2017 (accessed March 6, 2025). https://www.salon.com/2017/09/28/hugh-hefners-real-progressive-legacy-isnt-sexual-its-racial/.

9   Thurridl, Carina and Frauke Mattison Thompson (2023), "Making Brand Activism Successful: How Advice-Giving Can Boost Support Behavior and Reap Benefits for the Brand," *Marketing Letters*, 34, 685–696.

10 Batista, Juliana Moreira, Lucia Salmonson Guimarães. Barros, Fabricia Volotao Peixoto, and Delane Botelho (2022), "Sarcastic or Assertive: How Should Brands Reply to Consumers' Uncivil Comments on Social Media in the Context of Brand Activism?" *Journal of Interactive Marketing* 57(1), 141–158.

11 Murray, Conor, "'It Ends With Us' Actor Brandson Sklenar Addresses Alleged Cast Drama—Here's Why Fans Think Blake Lively, Justin Baldoni Are Feuding." *Forbes*. August 14, 2024. https://www.forbes.com/sites/conormurray/2024/08/14/why-fans-think-it-ends-with-us-stars-blake-lively-justin-baldoni-are-feuding-as-baldoni-reportedly-hires-crisis-pr/.

12 "Indian Model Poonam Pandey Fakes Death in Cervical Cancer Publicity Stunt to Raise Awareness of Disease," *Sky News*, February 3, 2024 (accessed March 6, 2025). https://news-sky-com.cdn.ampproject.org/c/s/news.sky.com/story/amp/indian-model-poonam-pandey-fakes-death-in-cervical-cancer-publicity-stunt-to-raise-awareness-of-cancer-13063230

13 Am, Jordan Bar, Vinit Doshi, Steve Noble, Anandi Malik, and Sherry Frey, "Consumers care about sustainability-and back it up with their wallets."McKinsey & Co, February 6, 2023 (accessed March 6, 2025). https://www.mckinsey.com/industries/consumer-packaged-goods/our-insights/consumers-care-about-sus tainability-and-back-it-up-with-their-wallets

14 Pursell, Stacy, "Veterinary Jobs: What Dwayne Johnson Can Teach You About Career Success," *The Vet Recruiter* (accessed October 30, 2024). https://thevetrecruiter. com/veterinary-jobs-what-dwayne-johnson-can-teach-you-about-career-succ ess/. Lady Gaga, "Don't you ever let a soul in the world tell you that you can't be exactly who you are," *Goodreads* (accessed October 30, 2024). https://www. goodreads.com/quotes/288926-don-t-you-ever-let-a-soul-in-the-world-tell. Oprah has referenced this quote throughout her career. A notable instance is in her 2013 OWN Network special, "Oprah's Lifeclass: The Power of Words," where she discusses the poem and its significance to her. You can find clips of this episode on YouTube and the OWN website.

15 "Class Action Complaint," Lieff Cabraser Heimann & Bernstein, LLP, September 12, 2024 (accessed October 30, 2024). https://www.lieffcabraser.com/pdf/Academi cPublicationsComplaintFinal.pdf.

13

THE AUGMENTED ACTIVISM
ALIGNMENT MATRIX

Given the additional nuances introduced since chapter 8, we augment the basic Sheth-Uslay Brand Activism Alignment Matrix as follows in Figure 13.1.

The augmented matrix captures additional brand characteristics to be taken into account when choosing an appropriate action. That is to say, if the focal brand is a niche brand (low mind and market share serving a niche market), is it a fledgling or heritage brand? Fledgling brands can authentically take on more divisive issues than heritage brands, which must take their history and legacy into account. Fledgling brands like Thinx or heritage brands like Dr. Bronner's Soap thrive here.

Similarly, if the focal brand is a mainstream brand (high mind share), is it a specialist (low share of the overall market) or generalist (high share overall)? It is not advisable for generalists to pick divisive issues. Instead, they should strive to unite instead like Coke did with "America the Beautiful" back in 2014 or Microsoft's AI for Good Lab initiative.

On the other hand, mainstream specialists (like niche brands) may be able to find relatively homogenous pockets of customers based on the appropriate issue even if it is divisive for the mass market. Chick-fil-A

DOI: 10.4324/9781003593690-13

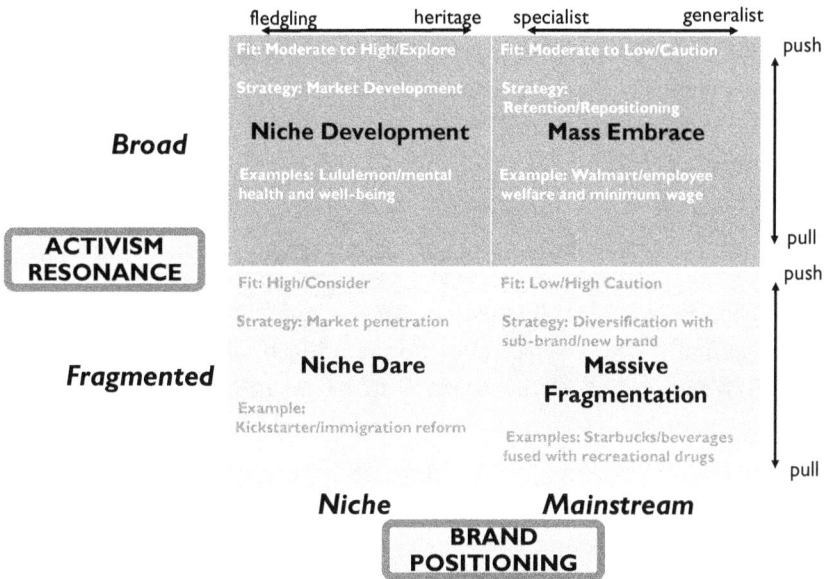

Figure 13.1 Augmented Sheth-Uslay Activism Alignment Matrix

(traditional family values), Dove (beauty standards), Etsy (fair trade and small business support), Harley Davidson (personal freedoms), and Lego (inclusivity and diversity) are all examples of mainstream specialists.

Issues like LGBTQ+ rights, gun control, and immigration will garner strong support or opposition based on how you segment the market. Values-based segmentation, grouping consumers based on their beliefs and values, such as environmentalism or social justice), demographic segmentation, considering factors like age, gender, and ethnicity (e.g., Gen Z, LGBTQ+ community), and behavioral segmentation, analyzing consumer actions and purchasing habits, say to focus on those buying sustainable products could all serve as starting points.

The augmented matrix also captures the nature of the activism in question. Is it pull(ed) or push activism? Disney's involvement regarding "Don't Say Gay" legislation in Florida is in the former category, whereas Dove, and hopefully your brand, belong in the latter.

Subsequently, the augmented matrix also includes assessments of commensurate strategy and risk for Niche Dare (market penetration), Niche Development (market development), Mass Embrace (retention/

repositioning), and Massive Fragmentation (diversification/new brand). The same order also applies based on perceived fit and risk. That is, Niche Dare by a fledgling brand is considered the highest fit/least risky option, whereas Massive Fragmentation by a mainstream generalist offers the lowest fit and is the riskiest.

Example of Niche Dare

Kickstarter, as a platform for creative projects and entrepreneurial ventures, aligns naturally with the values of immigration reform. A disproportionately high number of immigrants are driven by an entrepreneurial spirit, seeking opportunities to build a better future for themselves and their families. By supporting immigration reform, Kickstarter advocates for policies that empower these individuals to pursue their dreams and contribute to the economy. This stance would resonate with their user base of creators, innovators, and entrepreneurs who value diversity and inclusivity. Furthermore, it positions Kickstarter as a company that champions opportunity and supports a more just and equitable society. The authentic alignment with their business model could strengthen their brand image and attract more users who share those belief

Example of Niche Development

As a brand rooted in promoting physical health and well-being through yoga and athletic apparel, lululemon has a natural connection to the realm of mental health. Their focus on mindfulness, self-care, and personal growth aligns seamlessly with advocating for mental well-being. By supporting initiatives that address mental health challenges, lululemon can deepen its relationship not only with its customer base, who are often drawn to activities and practices that promote both physical and mental wellness but also attract new customers who are not physically active. The authentic alignment with their brand values can foster a stronger sense of community and purpose. Furthermore, by taking a stand on an issue that often carries stigma, lululemon can position itself as a brand that cares about the whole person, not just their physical fitness. In the process, it can also compel more consumers to exercise regularly.[1]

Example of Mass Embrace

For Walmart, the retail behemoth employing millions and serving a vast, diverse customer base, taking a stand on employee welfare and minimum wage makes sense on multiple levels. Firstly, it aligns with the growing consumer sentiment that demands fair treatment and living wages for workers, especially from large corporations with substantial resources. By championing employee well-being, Walmart can enhance its brand image and attract customers who prioritize ethical and socially responsible businesses. Secondly, improving employee welfare can lead to increased productivity, reduced staff turnover, and a more motivated workforce, ultimately benefiting the company's bottom line. Surely it would also increase costs and decrease profitability, you say? Maybe, and that is why the usual fit is assessed as moderate to low. However, as a major employer, Walmart has the potential to influence industry standards, even Congress, and spark a broader conversation about fair wages and worker rights in America, positioning itself as a leader in creating a more equitable and sustainable economy.[2]

Hypothetical Example of Massive Fragmentation

Starbucks, the ubiquitous coffeehouse chain, already walks a tightrope with its highly caffeinated beverages. Venturing into the realm of recreational (yet legal) drug-infused drinks could be a daring leap forward or a disastrous fall from grace. On one hand, it aligns with their image as an innovator and trendsetter. Imagine a "Cannabis Cold Brew" or a "Magic Mushroom Mocha" attracting a new generation of consumers seeking enhanced experiences. This could position Starbucks as a pioneer in a burgeoning market, capturing a loyal following and generating significant buzz. However, the risks are substantial. Negative associations with drug use, even if legal, could alienate a significant portion of their customer base. Regulatory hurdles and potential backlash from conservative groups could create a PR nightmare. Furthermore, it could clash with their family-friendly image and their efforts to promote responsible consumption. Ultimately, the success of such a venture would depend on careful consideration of the legal and social landscape, meticulous product development, and targeted marketing that emphasizes responsible use and avoids sensationalism. It would be a high-stakes gamble that could redefine Starbucks' brand identity or backfire spectacularly.

References

1   "lululemon Announces the Formation of Mental Wellbeing Global Advisory Board," lululemon, August 3, 2023 (accessed March 6, 2025). https://corporate.lululemon.com/media/press-releases/2023/08-03-2023-113020778.
2   "Walmart CEO: America's Minimum Wage is 'Too Low'," CNN Business, June 5, 2019 (accessed March 6, 2025). https://www.cnn.com/2019/06/05/business/walmart-shareholders-meeting-minimum-wage/index.html.

14

AROUND THE WORLD
IN 80 CASES

We readily admit that most of the brand activism examples we used had a Western slant. They were primarily from the US, England, or the EU. In this chapter, we aim to demonstrate that brand activism is truly a global phenomenon by going around the world in 80 cases. Indeed, brand activism may be more welcome outside of the US. A non-US location for the HQ or a non-US CMO was found to enhance the digital impact of CSR communications and attenuate any negative impact from sociopolitical activism.[1] While some of the brands we cover are native to the associated geographies, others you may recognize due to their continental or global stature. In any case, we bypass the US and the UK (with the exception of one example from Scotland) and focus on the rest of the world for our examples, primarily from emerging markets.

We begin our journey with Asia, destined to be the world's growth engine for the next half of the 21st century.[2] Dear reader, please make sure your seat backs and tray tables are in their full upright position and that

DOI: 10.4324/9781003593690-14

your seat belt is securely fastened. No carry-on luggage is allowed on this journey. Thank you.

Asia

Brand activism across Asia is a complex and multifaceted landscape. Unlike a singular approach seen in some regions, activism here has to factor in a mind-boggling array of cultural, political, and economic differences from nation to nation and region to region. Many brands focus their efforts on tackling urgent issues within their own countries, whether that's combating poverty, improving healthcare, or championing education. This focus on local needs means you can find initiatives specifically tailored to the challenges faced by people in that locale.

Some of the largest Asian companies are rising to global prominence. Their activism often mirrors national aspirations, highlighting technological breakthroughs, infrastructure development, and a desire to be seen as forces of progress. Simultaneously, brands with deep roots in Asian societies must delicately balance honoring centuries-old traditions while embracing modernity. This can lead to activism on issues like women's empowerment that delicately navigate social norms in ways distinct from Western equivalents.

The role of government also shapes brand activism in Asia. In some countries, you might see initiatives closely aligned with official policy, while others provide space for brands to take the lead on social issues the government might lag in. Environmental concerns often become central to activism, not just out of idealism, but sheer necessity. The consequences of pollution and climate change are starkly visible in many Asian nations, compelling more brands to confront these issues head-on.

China

1. Alibaba

Jack Ma's Alibaba, China's e-commerce giant, is weaving a complex narrative with its brand activism efforts focusing on education and rural development. On the surface, initiatives like the "Alibaba Rural Taobao Partnership" paint a heartwarming picture. By training villagers in e-commerce, Alibaba appears to be empowering rural communities and bridging the digital divide.[3] This aligns perfectly with China's stated goals of rural development and poverty alleviation, potentially boosting Alibaba's image with both consumers and the government.[4] However, beneath the feel-good headlines lies a strategic calculation. China's business environment is tightly controlled and Alibaba faces constant scrutiny. Its activism can be seen as a form of risk management, a way to curry favor with regulators and deflect potential criticism. The "One Hundred Thousand Villages" initiative, aiming to connect remote areas to online commerce, must translate into tangible improvements for rural residents.[5] If it simply ends up funneling villagers into Alibaba's ecosystem without boosting their livelihoods, questions will abound about the initiative's true purpose. Ultimately, Alibaba's brand activism will be judged by its bottom line—both the financial kind, and the impact it has on the communities it claims to be helping.[6]

2. BYD

BYD, the Chinese electric vehicle (EV) powerhouse, isn't just pushing clean cars—it's pushing boundaries through brand activism which goes beyond the typical green marketing, focusing on building a sustainable future through technological innovation.[7] Take BYD's battery technology, a core strength. They're not just churning out lithium-ion batteries like everyone else. Their "Blade Battery" boasts superior safety and longevity, addressing a major concern for EV adoption. This innovation not only benefits BYD's own cars but potentially paves the way for a safer future for the entire EV industry.[8] Additionally, BYD has heavily invested in renewable energy solutions, developing solar power plants and energy storage systems. This holistic approach positions BYD as a leader, creating a truly sustainable transportation ecosystem.[9] The true test of BYD's brand activism lies in its execution. Can BYD scale up its renewable energy projects to make a real dent in China's carbon footprint? BYD is not only selling cars, it is also selling a vision for a cleaner future, a vision that could propel the company to the forefront of the global EV market.

3. Haier

Haier, the Chinese appliance giant, has embarked on an interesting journey of brand activism focused on fostering a culture of silent yet impactful achievement. Their "Silent Performers" campaign celebrates individuals, particularly women, who excel in diverse fields like sports and entrepreneurship. This campaign recognizes those who let their work speak for itself, aligning with Haier's own commitment to reliable, high-quality products that quietly improve consumers' lives. The campaign resonates strongly with consumers seeking brands that align with the values of dedication and making a difference beyond flashy gestures.[10]

4. Huawei

Huawei's brand activism is a high-wire balancing act. The Chinese tech giant finds itself caught between its aspirations for global tech leadership and the geopolitical realities of increased scrutiny and suspicion. Huawei's activism isn't about tree-planting and charitable donations—it's about shaping the global narrative around technology infrastructure by promoting technological innovation and bridging the digital divide, particularly in developing nations. The company invests heavily in R&D, touting 5G innovations and patents as proof of a commitment to technological advancement. This feeds into a narrative of national pride, with Huawei seen as a symbol of China's tech prowess. Initiatives like their "Seeds for the Future" program, which trains young engineers from developing countries, paint Huawei as a force for global tech education.[11] This counteracts accusations of intellectual property theft and security risks that dog the company, especially in Western markets. However, Huawei's brand activism remains deeply intertwined with the Chinese state. Their emphasis on secure and stable networks is both a technological claim and a thinly veiled political reassurance amid spying fears.[12] The success of Huawei's activism will hinge on whether it can convince the world that technological innovation and geopolitical influence are separate entities. Their ability to decouple their products from the controversies surrounding the Chinese government will determine if they can truly achieve the global tech dominance they strive for.[13]

5. Pinduoduo

The Chinese e-commerce disruptor has built its brand activism on redefining value for money. Its team purchase model, where users can unlock lower prices by buying in groups, has shaken up China's online retail landscape, particularly appealing to lower-income and rural consumers.[14] This focus on affordability and accessibility aligns with the Chinese government's poverty alleviation goals, positioning Pinduoduo as a force for social good. Furthermore, Pinduoduo's direct connection to agricultural producers aims to eliminate intermediaries and reduce costs.[15] This initiative has the potential to revitalize rural economies and improve the livelihoods of farmers.[16] However, questions remain about the long-term sustainability of this model. Can Pinduoduo ensure product quality and fair prices for farmers while maintaining its own profitability even as it diversifies to other markets?

6. Xiaomi

Xiaomi, the Chinese tech company known for its budget-friendly smartphones, has built its brand activism on the twin pillars of affordability and tech accessibility. Their focus on delivering high-spec phones at accessible price points has been a disruptive force in the industry, especially in developing markets.[17] This strategy aligns with the growing demand from tech-savvy but budget-conscious consumers, positioning Xiaomi as the people's champion against premium brands like Apple and Samsung. Beyond smartphones, Xiaomi has expanded into a range of smart home products, aiming to democratize the internet of things experience. This feeds into a narrative of tech empowerment, bringing the conveniences of a connected home to the masses. However, Xiaomi's brand activism rests on maintaining this delicate balance between affordability and innovation. Its long-term success and reputation will depend on delivering on the promise of accessible tech without compromising performance or user experience. It has also entered the EV market successfully in 2024.[18]

India

7. Amul

India's beloved dairy cooperative embodies a unique form of brand activism deeply rooted in the country's social and economic fabric. Founded on the principles of empowering farmers, Amul's activism extends beyond catchy advertising and clever slogans. Its success is built on a model that transformed India's dairy industry by giving small-scale farmers control over the supply chain, ensuring fair prices and a steady income stream. This has had a profound impact on rural communities, lifting countless families out of poverty.[19] Beyond its business model, Amul's iconic 'Amul girl' mascot and its satirical ads have become a cultural phenomenon in India. These ads tackle everything from political scandals to social issues with wit and humor, holding a mirror to society and sparking discussion.[20] Though these ads might not directly address Amul's business, they solidify the brand's connection to India's identity and position it as a company with a social conscience.

8. Dettol

Dettol, the ubiquitous hygiene brand in India, has made its brand activism synonymous with public health and sanitation. Its "Handwashing Heroes" campaign, targeting school children, aims to educate and instill healthy habits from a young age.[21] This initiative aligns with India's national sanitation goals, making Dettol not just a product, but a partner in improving health outcomes for millions.[22] Dettol's activism also extends to rural areas, with programs focused on hygiene awareness and access to clean water. This emphasis on addressing the basic needs of sanitation disproportionally affecting these regions boosts the brand image and positions Dettol as a socially responsible brand committed to the well-being of all Indians.[23]

9. Fabindia

Fabindia's brand activism is woven into the very fabric of its existence. Its mission, to create sustainable livelihoods for traditional artisans across India, transcends profit motives and becomes a powerful form of social and economic change. By showcasing handloom textiles, natural dyes, and time-honored techniques, Fabindia not only creates beautiful products but preserves India's rich craft heritage and empowers entire communities.[24] This commitment to sustainability extends beyond the products themselves. Fabindia promotes ethical sourcing, fair trade practices, and organic farming, demonstrating a holistic approach that aligns with the growing consumer demand for conscious consumption.[25]

10. Lifebuoy Soap

Lifebuoy Soap's brand activism is to promote hand hygiene, particularly among children, which has evolved into a global public health crusade. The "Help a Child Reach 5" campaign, with its simple yet powerful message, has spread awareness about the life-saving power of handwashing to prevent childhood mortality from preventable diseases in underserved communities.[26] Beyond educational messages, Lifebuoy partners with NGOs and governments to implement scalable hand hygiene programs, often tailoring its efforts to fit the cultural and logistical needs of each region.[27] The company's commitment to measurable outcomes sets them apart. Lifebuoy has made a tangible difference by significantly improving hand hygiene practices and reducing illness. This activism not only positions Lifebuoy as a champion of global health but also reinforces its core brand as a germ-fighting protector of families worldwide.[28]

11. Tata Group

Tata Group, the Indian conglomerate with a legacy spanning over a century, stands out for its commitment to responsible and sustainable business practices. Its brand activism isn't just about a single cause or campaign, but a philosophy embedded throughout its various companies.[29] This commitment manifests in initiatives ranging from education and healthcare programs by Tata Trusts to employee welfare practices and environmental conservation efforts across its diverse portfolio of brands. Notable examples include Tata Steel's community development programs fostering self-sufficiency in tribal areas,[30] or Tata Motors' efforts to reduce emissions in their manufacturing processes. This comprehensive approach underscores a belief that businesses have a duty to create value for all stakeholders, including society and the environment. Though individual initiatives vary, Tata Group's activism embodies a long-term vision where ethical practices, community development, and business success go hand in hand.[31]

12. Titan Watches

Titan Watches, India's leading watchmaker, has woven brand activism into its quest to challenge traditional gender roles. Its campaigns don't just sell watches; they advocate for a world where women's ambitions are embraced, and their potential is unleashed. From ads featuring women in non-traditional careers to celebrating diverse representations of womanhood, Titan positions itself as a champion of gender equality.[32] A notable example is their "Break the Bias" initiative featuring trailblazers like a female pilot, boxer, and firefighter.[33] These powerful portrayals challenge stereotypes and redefine societal expectations for women. Additionally, Titan's support for women's entrepreneurship programs puts action behind their words, demonstrating a commitment to creating opportunities for women.

13. Swiggy/Zomato

India's food delivery giants, Swiggy and Zomato, are carving out their brand activism in the realm of labor rights and sustainable practices. Faced with growing scrutiny and backlash about the working conditions of delivery/gig workers, both platforms have been forced to reevaluate their business models.[34] Initiatives like Swiggy's revamped pay structure, accident insurance, and rest stops for delivery partners all signal an awareness that their long-term success is tied to the well-being of their workers.[35] Moreover, these companies are beginning to address environmental concerns. Swiggy's plans for a nationwide electric vehicle fleet and Zomato's commitment to reduce waste in food packaging demonstrate a shift toward greener logistics.[36] However, the true impact of these actions remains to be seen. Their sustainability initiatives need to move beyond token gestures and address the deep-rooted environmental challenges of the food delivery industry.

Japan

14. Muji

Muji's brand activism is rooted in its minimalist aesthetic and emphasis on sustainability. The Japanese retailer's focus on simple, functional products made from natural materials aligns with the growing consumer demand for environmentally conscious and ethically sourced goods.[37] Muji's partnerships with local communities to preserve traditional crafts and its commitment to reducing waste throughout its supply chain further reinforces this ethical positioning.[38] While their efforts aren't as flashy as attention-grabbing campaigns, Muji's activism lies in offering consumers a way to buy better, where a pared-down lifestyle contributes to a greater good. This resonates with shoppers seeking to minimize their environmental footprint and support responsible businesses.

15. Rakuten

Japan's e-commerce and fintech giant positions its brand activism around diversity and inclusion.[39] Its sponsorship of the FC Barcelona football team, with its jersey prominently featuring the Rakuten name, strategically promotes inclusion on a global stage given the sport's diverse and passionate fanbase.[40] Additionally, Rakuten's internal diversity initiatives and support for multiculturalism within its workforce solidify its commitment to creating a more inclusive business environment. This activism aligns with growing expectations for global companies to embrace diversity and use their visibility to champion inclusivity.[41]

16. Uniqlo

Uniqlo initially struggled with a reputation for selling cheaply made clothing targeted at suburban markets. However, its 2004 Global Quality Declaration completely flipped this perception. The pledge to focus on quality rather than low prices, along with the success of their fleece jackets, transformed Uniqlo's brand image. They successfully moved from being seen as cheap to being known for affordable yet well-made clothing. Uniqlo's brand activism also centers on promoting sustainability and social responsibility within the fashion industry. Its focus on simple basics aligns with efforts to reduce waste from fast fashion trends.[42] Furthermore, Uniqlo's recycling initiatives, such as collecting old clothing for reuse and repurposing, demonstrate a commitment to circular fashion.[43] The company has also partnered with NGOs to improve working conditions in its supply chain and support refugee communities.[44] Though challenges remain in ensuring ethical labor practices across the board, Uniqlo's actions signal a growing awareness within the industry of the need for sustainable production and responsible sourcing.

Indonesia

17. Indomie

Indomie, the ubiquitous instant noodle brand in Indonesia, leverages its cultural significance for brand activism focused on national pride and supporting local communities.[45] Campaigns often celebrate Indonesian flavors, heroes, or sporting events, tapping into a sense of shared identity and fostering brand loyalty. Additionally, Indomie's disaster relief efforts, providing food and assistance during natural disasters, demonstrate a commitment to being there for the Indonesian people during difficult times.[46] These actions strengthen Indomie's position as not just a beloved food product, but a symbol of Indonesian resilience and community spirit.

Malaysia/Southeast Asia

18. AirAsia

AirAsia, the budget airline pioneer, built its brand activism on the democratization of travel within Southeast Asia.[47] Its focus on affordability and accessibility revolutionized air travel in the region, connecting people, businesses, and cultures. AirAsia's "Now Everyone Can Fly" slogan embodies this mission, demonstrating that low-cost carriers can significantly expand access to travel opportunities.[48] The carrier's support for regional tourism initiatives further reinforces its commitment to driving economic connectivity and development in Southeast Asia.

19. Grab

The Southeast Asia ride-hailing and delivery app centers its brand activism on financial inclusion and empowering the "unbanked."[49] Its platform offers a range of financial services, including microloans and insurance, to individuals and small businesses traditionally excluded from the formal banking sector. Grab's "Grow with Grab" initiative provides training and resources to help entrepreneurs in underserved communities thrive in the digital economy.[50] This focus on expanding access to opportunity aligns with a broader mission of improving livelihoods and promoting economic development within the region.[51]

20. Maybank

Maybank, a leading financial institution in Malaysia, positions its brand activism around financial inclusion and promoting sustainable business practices. Its focus on providing financial services to underserved communities, including micro-enterprises and women-led businesses, supports economic development and reduces inequalities within the region. Additionally, Maybank's commitment to ESG principles demonstrates a responsibility toward a sustainable future.[52] Initiatives like its "Reach Independence & Sustainable Entrepreneurship" program provide training and mentorship for small businesses, contributing to creating a more resilient and equitable economy.[53]

Singapore

21. Sea Limited

The Singapore-based tech conglomerate behind Shopee (e-commerce), Garena (gaming), and SeaMoney (fintech) focuses its brand activism on fostering digital inclusion and entrepreneurship across Southeast Asia. Its Shopee platform empowers small businesses to access online markets, particularly in less developed regions. Additionally, initiatives like Shopee University provide training in e-commerce and digital marketing skills to help these businesses succeed. Through Garena, Sea Limited also invests in developing the region's e-sports ecosystem, creating new entrepreneurial opportunities related to gaming. This commitment to upskilling and providing digital infrastructure aligns with efforts to bridge economic divides and drive digital literacy across Southeast Asia.[54]

South Korea

22. Amorepacific

The South Korean beauty giant blends brand activism with a commitment to environmental sustainability and women's empowerment.[55] The company's focus on using natural ingredients and reducing its environmental footprint aligns with the growing consumer demand for responsible beauty products. Their "2030 A More Beautiful Promise" initiative sets ambitious goals for sustainable production and waste reduction.[56] Additionally, Amorepacific supports female entrepreneurship programs, establishing a dedicated fund to help women start their own businesses.[57]

23. Hyundai/Kia

Hyundai and Kia, South Korea's automotive powerhouses, are increasingly focusing their brand activism on sustainability and technological innovation in the automotive industry.[58] Their significant investments in EVs, hydrogen fuel cell technology, and autonomous driving solutions demonstrate a commitment to building a greener future for transportation. Hyundai and Kia are positioning themselves at the forefront of technological innovation while attempting to address the pressing environmental concerns facing the automotive sector.[59]

24. LG

Similarly, LG, the South Korean electronics giant, positions its brand activism around sustainability and technology that improves lives. Its "Life's Good When It's Green" initiative demonstrates a commitment to reducing the company's environmental footprint, with ambitious goals for energy efficiency, waste reduction, and responsible sourcing.[60] Additionally, LG invests in developing smart home technologies and appliances that promote convenience and energy conservation. This focus resonates with increasingly eco-conscious consumers and highlights the potential of technology to create a more sustainable future.[61]

The Philippines

25. Jollibee

The Filipino fast-food giant anchors its brand activism in promoting Filipino pride and family values.[62] Its iconic mascot and cheerful marketing campaigns emphasize the joy of shared meals and togetherness, resonating deeply with Filipino culture. Jollibee's "Farmer Entrepreneurship Program" demonstrates a commitment to supporting local farmers and sourcing ingredients domestically, contributing to the country's agricultural development. Additionally, the Jollibee Foundation invests in education and disaster relief efforts, positioning the brand as a socially responsible company dedicated to improving its home market.[63]

Africa

We now move on to Africa, which is destined to take over economic development from Asia in the second half of the 21st century. Across Africa, a fascinating trend of brand activism is emerging, shaped by the continent's unique challenges and opportunities. Unlike activism often seen in the West, brands here aren't just reacting to social trends; they're directly addressing the core issues hindering progress. A strong emphasis lies on economic empowerment, with initiatives focused on financial inclusion, supporting small businesses, and bridging the digital divide. Brands also prioritize pressing social needs like food security, healthcare access, and education—demonstrating an understanding that true development goes beyond profits.

Technology plays a transformative role. Recognizing Africa's reliance on mobile phones, platforms like M-Pesa revolutionized banking while countless startups continue to leverage tech for education, agriculture, and overcoming logistical hurdles. Notably, there's a strong pan-African focus. Brands aren't limiting themselves to national borders but aim for continent-wide impact, reflecting a growing desire for economic connectivity within Africa. Importantly, brand activism in Africa often tackles systemic issues, the very problems that hold back the continent's potential, head-on. This isn't just about feel-good campaigns, but about developing innovative and localized solutions designed to create lasting change.

Ethiopia

26. Ethiopian Airlines

Ethiopian Airlines, Africa's largest and most successful airline, positions its brand activism around connecting Africa to the world and driving economic progress within the continent. Its extensive network of routes provides crucial air connectivity between African nations and fosters trade and economic development. Additionally, Ethiopian Airlines invests heavily in its aviation academy, training pilots and engineers from across the continent, contributing vital human capital to Africa's growing aviation industry.[64] This activism showcases the airline as an engine for progress, a proud symbol of African achievement, and a key player in enabling intra-African connectivity and development.[65]

Kenya

27. Safaricom/M-Pesa

Safaricom's M-Pesa, the pioneering mobile money platform that originated in Kenya, leverages brand activism to promote financial inclusion and economic empowerment at the grassroots level. By enabling secure and easy financial transactions through even basic mobile phones, M-Pesa has revolutionized access to banking services in previously unbanked and underbanked communities.[66] This has had transformative effects, enabling individuals to save, send remittances, and start businesses.[67] Their success spurred additional mobile-driven solutions for healthcare, education, and agriculture. Additionally, Safaricom's investments in renewable energy and sustainability initiatives demonstrate a commitment to responsible growth.[68] M-Pesa's success highlights the potential for technology to address systemic inequality and drive economic development in emerging markets, contributing to their wider narrative as not just a payment platform, but a catalyst for social change.

28. Twiga Foods

Twiga Foods, a Kenyan B2B platform, tackles inefficiencies within the agricultural supply chain through its brand activism focused on farmer empowerment and improved food distribution.[69] By connecting rural farmers directly with urban retailers, Twiga cuts out exploitative middlemen and ensures better prices for producers. They leverage technology-driven logistics to streamline the movement of produce, reducing wastage and guaranteeing fresher goods for consumers. This activism not only creates efficiencies but also impacts the lives of farmers by providing a more reliable and profitable market for their crops. Additionally, it combats food insecurity within urban areas by increasing the availability of affordable, fresh produce.[70]

Nigeria

29. *Andela*

Andela, the global talent network connecting African software developers with remote opportunities, embodies a powerful form of brand activism focused on bridging the digital divide and fostering inclusive economic growth. Their mission to unlock Africa's untapped tech potential not only disrupts traditional outsourcing models but also challenges stereotypes about African innovation. Andela's commitment to rigorous training programs, ensuring developers meet global standards, is reflected in their high placement rates with top companies worldwide.[71] This model directly benefits African tech talent, boosts local economies, and provides clients with access to a diverse pool of skilled developers. Andela's "Power of X" campaign spotlights the transformative impact of these individual opportunities, amplifying success stories to inspire others.[72] By demonstrating the tangible benefits of investing in African tech talent, Andela is reshaping perceptions and creating a pathway for a more inclusive, equitable global tech sector.[73]

30. *Globacom*

Globacom, a major Nigerian telecom company, focuses its brand activism on empowering Nigerians through technology and supporting educational initiatives.[74] Its investments in expanding telecom infrastructure to underserved areas demonstrates a commitment to bridging the digital divide within the country. Additionally, Globacom sponsors educational programs, scholarships, and STEM initiatives, signaling investment in Nigeria's future workforce.[75] This brand activism positions Globacom as a force for development and progress, aligning with a desire for improved opportunities among its customer base.

31. *Jumia*

Jumia, the pan-African e-commerce platform dubbed the "Amazon of Africa," centers its brand activism on expanding access to goods and services across the continent. By connecting sellers and consumers in previously underserved markets, Jumia helps create new economic opportunities for small businesses and entrepreneurs.[76] Additionally, its focus on developing its own logistics network addresses infrastructure challenges and increasing market accessibility. This activism resonates with the growing middle class in Africa and aligns with their desire for greater convenience and broader product selection. Their activism also involves consumer education and promoting digital literacy, fostering broader inclusion in the e-commerce space.[77] This positions Jumia as a catalyst for economic growth across the continent by bridging access gaps and empowering African entrepreneurs.

South Africa

32. Amarula

Amarula Cream Liqueur, the iconic South African brand, has a focused activism attitude and built its brand activism around elephant conservation.[78] Their Amarula Trust supports a wide range of initiatives to protect African elephants from poaching and habitat loss.[79] This partnership aligns the brand's luxurious image with the majesty and vulnerability of a beloved African symbol. Their "Name Them, Save Them" campaign, inviting consumers to name elephants being tracked by the Trust, creates an emotional connection to the cause.[80] This activism positions Amarula as not just a delicious liqueur, but a brand deeply invested in the preservation of Africa's natural heritage.

33. Castle Lager

Castle Lager, a dominant South African beer brand, leverages its widespread popularity by confronting gender-based violence, a critical social issue in the country.[81] Their "#SmashTheLabel" campaign uses its platform to raise awareness, challenge harmful social norms, and encourage bystander intervention. This activism demonstrates a willingness to address difficult topics head-on and use its influence to advocate for positive change.[82] While measuring the direct impact on reducing gender-based violence is challenging, the campaign succeeds in keeping the conversation alive and positioning Castle Lager as a brand that stands against this pervasive social problem.[83]

34. Investec

Investec, the South African financial institution, has made a significant commitment to combat rhino poaching, a critical conservation issue in the country. Their support for anti-poaching units, technology development, and public awareness campaigns directly contributes to the efforts to protect rhinos. The "Investec Rhino Lifeline" initiative brings tangible results by funding equipment, training, and operations that make a difference on the frontline. This activism positions Investec as a responsible corporate citizen actively protecting South Africa's endangered wildlife and aligning its brand with the preservation of a vital part of the country's natural heritage.[84]

35. Mr Price

Mr Price, the South African value fashion retailer, positions its brand activism around the democratization of fashion and providing affordable on-trend style to a wide market. Its focus on fast fashion cycles and accessible price points aligns with the demands of trend-conscious but budget-minded shoppers.[85] Moreover, Mr Price's efforts to incorporate sustainable materials and reduce waste in its supply chain demonstrate an awareness of the fashion industry's environmental impact.[86] While the extent of its sustainability commitment remains debated, Mr Price's activism aims to show that consumers shouldn't have to sacrifice style or affordability to make conscious choices.

36. MTN

MTN, a leading South African telecom provider with a pan-African presence, positions its brand activism on bridging the digital divide and empowering communities through technology. Its investments in expanding network coverage to underserved areas demonstrate their commitment to increasing connectivity across the continent. The MTN Foundation focuses on education, healthcare, and arts and culture, which further reinforces its mission to improve lives and promote development. MTN's activism highlights the potential of telecommunications to drive economic growth, foster innovation, and address social disparities in Africa.[87]

37. MultiChoice/DStv

MultiChoice/DStv, the dominant satellite TV provider in South Africa, positions its brand activism around supporting local content creation and showcasing African stories. Initiatives like the "MultiChoice Talent Factory" invest in training filmmakers and developing original African programming. This focus on promoting African talent and narratives aligns with a growing demand for diverse and authentic content. Additionally, investments in broadcasting infrastructure expand access to information and entertainment, particularly across rural areas.[88] While MultiChoice faces criticism over costs and occasional programming controversies,[89] its efforts position the company as a champion of the African creative industry and a force for connecting viewers with culturally resonant content.

38. Nando's

Nando's, the South African restaurant chain famous for its flame-grilled chicken, infuses its brand activism with a playful and satirical approach to tackling social and political issues. Its often provocative advertising campaigns use humor and bold visuals to spark conversations on diversity, inequality, and current events.[90] This approach reinforces Nando's cheeky image, appealing to a younger, socially conscious demographic. While individual campaigns might stir debate, Nando's positions itself as a progressive brand with a strong voice, not afraid to challenge the status quo.[91]

39. Woolworths

Woolworths, the South African retailer, positions its brand activism around sustainability and ethical sourcing. Its "Good Business Journey" initiative sets ambitious targets for reducing its environmental footprint.[92] Woolworths' focus on sustainable farming practices and local sourcing demonstrates a commitment to responsible production and supporting South African agriculture. Moreover, its "Farming for the Future" program trains farmers in sustainable techniques, ensuring long-term benefits for the environment and the agricultural economy. This activism aligns with the growing consumer demand for responsible consumption and resonates with shoppers seeking retailers that share their values.[93]

Zimbabwe

40. Econet Wireless

Econet (enhanced communications network) Wireless, founded by Strive Masiyiwa, intertwines its brand activism with economic empowerment and technological progress in a country facing significant challenges.[94] Its pioneering mobile money platform, EcoCash, drove financial inclusion for previously unbanked citizens.[95] Additionally, Econet invests heavily in education.[96] This aligns with a longstanding commitment to leverage technology and innovation to improve lives and promote national development within Zimbabwe.

Australia

Next, we hop on to the continent of Australia with its own distinct flavor of brand activism. A deep-seated focus on sustainability runs through many initiatives, with companies embracing eco-friendly practices and championing conservation causes. This reflects the strong environmental consciousness woven into the fabric of these societies. Additionally, brands often incorporate themes of social equality, inclusivity, and respect for Indigenous cultures into their activism. This arises from a history of progressive movements and a growing demand for businesses to reflect the values of the communities they serve.

While Aussie and Kiwi brands might approach activism with a laid-back attitude, that doesn't mean they're any less committed to doing the right thing. There's an expectation that businesses operate with integrity and stand for positive values. The proximity to Asia and its growing influence is subtly shaping activism as well, with some brands becoming more vocal on human rights and responsible sourcing issues.

However, a unique cultural trait called "tall poppy syndrome," discourages boastfulness.[97] This means brand activism here often favors concrete actions over flashy campaigns. Companies might let their positive impact speak for itself, knowing the public will be skeptical of those who oversell their good deeds. Finally, with smaller domestic markets compared to global giants, brands in Australia and New Zealand have to carefully consider if their activism will resonate with enough people at home or if a broader global stance might be a better option.

Australia

41. Atlassian

Atlassian, the Australian software company, anchors its brand activism on fostering teamwork and collaboration and driving positive impact through technology. Their emphasis on open communication and knowledge-sharing within their own workforce sets a standard for healthy company culture. The Atlassian Foundation supports education initiatives, particularly in STEM fields, empowering the next generation of innovators.[98] Additionally, Atlassian's strong stance on climate action, including its pledge to reach net-zero emissions, demonstrates its commitment to responsible growth. This multi-pronged activism approach positions Atlassian as not just a tech leader, but a force for good, championing both internal values and external impact.[99]

42. Blackmores

Blackmores, a leading Australian vitamin and natural health brand, positions its brand activism around empowering people to take charge of their well-being through natural solutions. Their "Be a Well Being" campaign served as a wake-up call, encouraging Australians to understand their individual health needs and make conscious choices. This initiative, coupled with their focus on evidence-based products and transparent ingredient sourcing, aligns with a growing consumer desire for proactive wellness and control over their health journey. Blackmores' activism positions them not just as a supplement provider but as a partner in self-care, fostering a more informed and empowered approach to personal well-being.[100] However, controversies surrounding a major shareholder's (in this case, the son of the founder) views on social issues highlight the potential challenges of navigating brand activism when ownership and corporate values don't fully align.[101]

43. Canva

Canva, the graphic design platform known for its user-friendliness, focuses its brand activism on democratizing design and empowering individuals and organizations to communicate their ideas effectively.[102] Their commitment to accessibility includes a vast library of free templates, design elements, and educational resources. Additionally, Canva for Nonprofits provides free access to their premium services, empowering NGOs and other purpose-driven groups with limited resources to create impactful communication materials. This positions Canva as a design tool and champion of visual expression for everyone, regardless of skill level or budget, and highlights the power of design to drive social change.[103]

44. Thankyou

Thankyou, the Australian consumer goods brand, has built its entire business model around brand activism. Every product sold contributes to the Thankyou charitable foundation, funding projects that address global poverty, such as clean water access, sanitation programs, and maternal healthcare. Their radical transparency model displays exactly how much of each product's price goes toward these social causes. Thankyou's success challenges conventional businesses by demonstrating that profit and purpose can be intrinsically linked. Their activism positions them as disruptive innovators, empowering consumers to make everyday purchases that directly create positive changes in the world.[104]

New Zealand

45. Kathmandu

Kathmandu, the outdoor gear and apparel company from New Zealand, puts sustainability and ethical production at the heart of its brand activism. The company champions the use of recycled and responsibly sourced materials, like organic cotton, and emphasizes transparency throughout its supply chain. Kathmandu's longstanding support for conservation projects and its commitment to minimizing its environmental footprint demonstrate a deep respect for nature. Their Certified B Corporation status further reinforces this mission-driven approach.[105] This activism positions Kathmandu not just as a provider of outdoor gear but as a partner to environmentally conscious adventurers who value mindful consumption.[106]

46. Xero

Xero, an accounting software company, focuses its brand activism on championing small businesses and entrepreneurs. Its cloud-based platform aims to streamline accounting processes, freeing small business owners from tedious tasks and allowing them to focus on core operations. Xero's emphasis on user-friendly interfaces and educational resources combats the intimidation factor many entrepreneurs experience when dealing with finances. Additionally, the company partners with organizations and initiatives supporting small business development. This activism positions Xero as an enabling force for small businesses, contributing to greater entrepreneurial success and economic empowerment.[107]

Middle East

Activism in the Middle East exists within a unique context where religion, societal norms, and political systems intertwine with business in ways that shape what kind of activism is possible and how brands approach it. Companies must delicately navigate complex cultural sensitivities alongside the region's often volatile geopolitical landscape.

Some activism focuses on causes like female empowerment, addressing the evolving role of women in the workforce, and challenging traditional gender norms. Others emphasize pan-regionalism, fostering a unified Middle Eastern identity and greater regional cooperation. However, activism directly challenging governments or entrenched power structures remains less common, as many countries in the region have limitations on public critique and dissent.

Additionally, several large companies in the Middle East are government-backed or closely tied to state power. Their activism often amplifies narratives of national progress, highlighting infrastructure projects or technological advancements as symbols of pride. This reflects the unique interplay of business and state power within the region.

It's important to remember the Middle East is not a monolith. Brand activism in a liberalized Gulf state will differ vastly from that in a more conservative nation. Furthermore, what might be seen as brand activism in Western cultures could be perceived as paternalistic in parts of the Middle East. This is because Western-style activism often focuses on companies taking a stand on behalf of people, while Middle Eastern cultures may place more value on grassroots movements and consumer-led initiatives. There is no denying that the Middle East is flush with resources and ambitions to make global brands, and making global headlines will increasingly involve their activism.

Israel

47. Netafim

While Israeli companies often face scrutiny for their actions within the complex political landscape of the region, one prominent example of positive brand activism is Netafim. This global leader in smart irrigation solutions has been a pioneer in sustainable agriculture and water conservation. Netafim's drip irrigation technology helps farmers increase yields while significantly reducing water consumption, a crucial contribution in arid regions facing water scarcity. They actively promote sustainable farming practices and partner with organizations to provide access to water-efficient technologies in developing countries. This commitment to environmental sustainability and social impact positions Netafim as a positive force for change, demonstrating how Israeli innovation can contribute to addressing global challenges.[108]

Kuwait

48. Talabat

Talabat, the Middle Eastern food delivery giant, focuses its brand activism on improving working conditions for riders and addressing wider labor issues within the gig economy.[109] Facing strikes, it revised its payment structures, providing accident insurance, and establishing rest stops for riders. Additionally, their support for rider-led initiatives and dialogue with worker representation seeks to empower those fulfilling deliveries.[110] This positions Talabat as a company grappling with the complexities of the gig economy and striving for a more ethical and sustainable model. While long-term success remains to be seen, their actions signal a willingness to address the vulnerabilities of delivery workers, differentiating themselves in a competitive market.

Qatar

49. Qatar Airways

Qatar Airways positions its brand activism around connecting the world and building global relationships through travel. Their extensive network of routes promotes international exchange and cultural understanding, fostering connectivity, particularly between underrepresented regions. Additionally, their support for sports and cultural events with global sponsorships showcases the power of bringing people together through shared experiences. While their carbon footprint as an airline is substantial, initiatives to invest in sustainable aviation fuels and operations demonstrate an awareness of their environmental responsibility.[111] This activism positions Qatar Airways as a facilitator of global interconnectedness, championing a world where travel unlocks new opportunities and shared understanding.[112]

United Arab Emirates

50. Careem (owned by Uber since 2020)

Careem, the Middle Eastern ride-hailing app, centers its brand activism on expanding economic opportunities for women and promoting mobility in the region.[113] Their initiative to recruit female captains (drivers) challenges traditional gender roles and provides a safe and empowering income source for women in a society where their participation in the workforce is often restricted.[114] Additionally, Careem's expansion into markets with limited transport infrastructure contributes to increased mobility for all. This activism positions Careem as a force for modernization and progress, disrupting the status quo by empowering women and improving access to transportation.[115]

51. Souq.com

Souq.com (now Amazon.ae after being acquired for $580 million in 2017), the e-commerce leader in the Middle East, focused its brand activism on boosting regional development and expanding opportunities for local sellers. Its initiatives emphasized providing SMEs access to the online marketplace, particularly in underserved areas. Souq.com's training programs and dedicated support aimed to empower these businesses to thrive in the digital economy. This activism aligned with broader goals of economic diversification and reducing reliance on traditional retail models. While currently integrated into Amazon, Souq.com's initial focus on fostering regional e-commerce and empowering local entrepreneurs played a role in the Middle East's growing digital marketplace.[116]

52. Etisalat (UAE)

Etisalat, a major telecom provider in the UAE, focuses its brand activism on bridging the digital divide in the Middle East and supporting education initiatives. Their investments in expanding network infrastructure to underserved areas seek to ensure greater internet connectivity across the region. Additionally, Etisalat supports programs centered on digital literacy and STEM education, particularly initiatives geared toward empowering women in tech. This activism demonstrates a commitment to leveraging technology for progress and positions Etisalat as a driving force for economic development and inclusion within the region.[117]

Saudi Arabia

53. Almarai

One of the largest dairy companies in the Middle East, Almarai focuses on environmental initiatives related to responsible water use and resource conservation in an arid region. It promotes sustainable practices and raises awareness about water scarcity. This demonstrates how brands can align activism with pressing local issues, making a tangible impact.[118]

54. Aramco

As the world's largest oil and gas company, Aramco's approach to brand activism is complex and faces inherent challenges due to its industry. Its activism centers on technological innovation and sustainability within the energy sector. Initiatives like their Namaat partnership program, focused on carbon capture, utilization, and storage, and their investment in low-carbon hydrogen technologies showcase a desire to mitigate the industry's environmental impact.[119] Aramco's focus on cleaner energy fuels a narrative of transitioning toward a more sustainable future, though critics often argue these efforts fall short given the core business remains fossil fuel extraction.[120] The activism aims to position Aramco as a responsible player within a sector undergoing major shifts, balancing the need for energy security with the urgent demand for climate action.[121]

55. Savola Group

The Savola Group, a major Saudi Arabian food conglomerate, aligns its brand activism with addressing food insecurity and promoting responsible consumption. Its focus on reducing food waste throughout its production and distribution processes demonstrates an awareness of inefficiencies within the food supply chain. Additionally, the Savola Group supports local farmers and sustainable agricultural practices, contributing to strengthening the regional food system. This activism positions the Savola Group as a responsible player within the food industry, committed to both minimizing its environmental footprint and ensuring access to affordable and nutritious food for the Saudi population and beyond.[122]

Central and South America

Brand activism in Central and Latin America is fueled by a deep-seated desire for social justice and a resolve to address the historical inequalities that continue to shape the region. Many brands take bold stances on poverty reduction, empowering marginalized groups, and demanding access to necessities, like education and healthcare. This reflects an understanding that businesses have a responsibility to contribute to building a more equitable future.

The influence of the past lingers, particularly when large corporations have historically held significant sway. Brand activism becomes a way for these companies to reposition themselves, shedding past negative associations by demonstrating a commitment to the betterment of society and fostering trust within the communities they operate in. Protecting the region's precious natural resources is another vital front for activism. Brands engage in conservation efforts, promote sustainable practices, and empower communities who are stewards of these irreplaceable ecosystems.

Technology plays a transformative role in South America. Brand activism leverages mobile phones and digital platforms to drive initiatives around financial inclusion, spread education programs far and wide, and raise awareness of environmental threats. Multinational companies operating within the region face intense scrutiny, with consumers demanding transparency and ethical practices. Activism, in this case, becomes a means to assure communities that their needs and concerns are being taken seriously. Importantly, there's a shift underway from simply charitable donations toward initiatives that actively empower communities. Rather than temporary aid, brands are seeking to create long-term solutions that build resilience and self-sufficiency within societies.

Mexico

56. Cemex

Cemex, the Mexican construction materials giant, focuses its brand activism on providing affordable housing solutions and contributing to sustainable development.[123] Its "Patrimonio Hoy: A Home for Everyone" program offers micro-financing, building material packages, and technical assistance to help low-income families in Mexico construct or improve their homes.[124] Additionally, Cemex invests heavily in research and development to create low-carbon concrete and other sustainable building materials. This activism positions Cemex as a company dedicated to addressing both social needs and responsible construction practices, contributing to a more accessible and sustainable built environment.[125]

57. Cinépolis

The Mexican cinema chain with a global footprint, centers its brand activism on expanding access to entertainment and enriching lives through the power of film. Beyond commercial operations, its foundation runs extensive social responsibility programs, bringing the moviegoing experience to underserved populations in rural areas or hospitals. Additionally, Cinépolis supports film festivals and initiatives promoting diversity in cinema. This activism positions the company as a force for democratizing access to the arts and using film as a tool for positive social impact.[126]

58. Grupo Bimbo

Bimbo, one of the world's largest baked goods companies, focuses its brand activism on promoting healthy lifestyles and environmental sustainability. Its Bimbo Global Race encourages employees and communities to engage in physical activity, fighting childhood obesity and sedentary lifestyles.[127] Additionally, Bimbo commits to using renewable energy sources, reducing waste, and sustainable packaging to lessen its environmental footprint. This activism positions Bimbo not merely in the business of selling baked goods but as a company invested in the well-being of its consumers and the planet.[128]

59. Grupo Lala

Grupo Lala, a major Mexican dairy company, centers its brand activism on food insecurity and sustainable agriculture. Their emphasis on providing affordable, nutritious dairy products aligns with the goal of reducing hunger and malnutrition within Mexico. Additionally, initiatives supporting Mexican dairy farmers, such as training programs and investment in technology, aim to strengthen the domestic dairy industry and promote responsible, sustainable practices. Grupo Lala's focus on community development through education and social welfare projects further reinforces their commitment to improving lives. This activism positions Grupo Lala as not just a provider of dairy products but a force for combating food insecurity, supporting Mexican farmers, and investing in the well-being of rural communities.[129]

Panama

60. Copa Airlines

Copa Airlines, the Panamanian flag carrier, anchors its brand activism on connectivity and economic development within Latin America. Its extensive network of routes throughout Central and South America fosters increased regional travel, tourism, and business opportunities. By connecting destinations often underserved by major airlines, Copa Airlines positions itself as a vital link between countries and communities. Additionally, their support for tourism initiatives and infrastructure development projects amplifies economic benefits for the region. This activism highlights Copa

Airlines' role as a driving force behind regional integration and economic progress—making it easier for people and businesses to connect within South America and beyond.[130]

Argentina

61. Mercado Libre

Mercado Libre, the Latin American e-commerce giant often dubbed the "Amazon of the region," centers its brand activism on democratizing access to markets and expanding economic opportunities.[131] Its platform gives small businesses and entrepreneurs a chance to reach a vast customer base across Latin America, particularly in underserved areas. Mercado Libre's integrated logistics and payment solutions (Mercado Pago) address common barriers faced by smaller sellers. Additionally, their financial inclusion initiatives, including microloans, further empower those traditionally excluded from formal banking systems. This activism positions Mercado Libre as a catalyst for economic growth throughout Latin America, leveling the playing field for entrepreneurs and businesses of all sizes.[132]

Brazil

62. Havaianas

The iconic Brazilian flip-flop brand leverages its global popularity for brand activism, focusing on conservation and cultural preservation. The company partners with organizations like Conservation International to support efforts to protect Brazil's unique biodiversity.[133] Limited-edition flip-flop designs featuring endangered species raise both awareness and funds for conservation efforts. Additionally, Havaianas' support for traditional craft communities reinforces its connection to Brazilian heritage. This activism positions the brand not just as synonymous with a fun and relaxed lifestyle, but as a defender of Brazil's environmental and cultural treasures.[134]

63. Magazine Luiza

Magazine Luiza, a major Brazilian retailer, centers its brand activism on diversity, inclusion, and social progress.[135] Its pioneering trainee program prioritizing Black Brazilians has significantly increased representation within the company's leadership. Additionally, Magazine Luiza's vocal support for LGBTQ+ rights and its use of inclusive advertising campaigns challenge traditional norms in Brazilian society. The company's focus on fostering a diverse workplace extends to initiatives for empowering female entrepreneurs and supporting small businesses owned by underrepresented groups. This activism positions Magazine Luiza as not just a retail giant, but a force for promoting greater equity within Brazilian society.[136]

64. Natura

Natura, the Brazilian cosmetics giant (that you may also recognize as the former owner of The Body Shop), has made environmental sustainability and ethical sourcing core pillars of its brand activism. The company's longstanding commitment to utilizing Amazonian biodiversity in its products is coupled with initiatives supporting Indigenous communities and regenerative practices. The "Ekos" product line showcases ingredients sourced responsibly from the rainforest, fostering a direct link between consumers and conservation efforts.[137] Furthermore, Natura's pioneering work on refillable packaging and carbon neutrality demonstrates a holistic approach to reducing the company's environmental footprint. This activism positions Natura as a champion of the Amazon, aligning its success with the preservation of a vital global resource.[138]

65. Nubank

Nubank, the Brazilian digital banking disruptor, has built its brand activism around challenging Brazil's traditional banking system and fighting for financial inclusion. Its emphasis on providing fee-free banking services and transparent user experiences targets those under-served or exploited by conventional banks. Nubank's mobile-first approach expands access to financial services, including those outside major urban centers. Furthermore, its focus on creating user-friendly, jargon-free financial products aims to demystify banking and increase financial literacy. This activism positions Nubank as a champion for the average Brazilian consumer, empowering them to take greater control of their financial lives.[139]

66. O Boticário

O Boticário, the beloved Brazilian beauty brand, focuses its brand activism on sustainability and social responsibility. The company's emphasis on natural ingredients, refillable packaging, and environmentally conscious production processes demonstrates a commitment to reducing its ecological footprint. Additionally, O Boticário supports the Fundação Grupo Boticário, a non-profit dedicated to nature conservation.[140] The campaigns to raise awareness about endangered species and protect Brazilian biodiversity further reinforce their connection to the country's natural heritage. This activism positions O Boticário not simply as a cosmetics company but as a protector of the environment, aligning its success with the preservation of Brazil's unique ecosystems. While competitor Natura is more deeply intertwined with specific conservation ethos and relies on direct connections with the Amazon rainforest, O Boticário takes a broader, sustainability-focused approach with a wider appeal to eco-conscious consumers.[141]

Colombia

67. Juan Valdez Café

Juan Valdez Café, the iconic Colombian coffee brand, has woven brand activism into its identity through its focus on the well-being of coffee farmers and sustainable coffee production. For decades, their symbol of Juan Valdez, the fictional yet emblematic Colombian coffee farmer, has emphasized the human aspect of coffee production. Juan Valdez directly invests in coffee-growing communities, ensuring fair prices, training, and support for long-term sustainability. The "Rainforest Alliance" certification on many of their products reinforces a commitment to responsible farming practices.[142] This shows Juan Valdez is a provider of quality coffee and a champion for the thousands of Colombian families whose livelihoods depend on the crop, successfully linking their success to that of the coffee communities.[143]

68. Rappi

Rappi, the Colombian super-app offering delivery of everything from groceries to medicine, positions its brand activism around fostering economic opportunity and empowerment within Latin America. Its core business model offers flexible work opportunities for delivery drivers, expanding income-earning possibilities in a region where formal employment can be scarce. Additionally, Rappi partners with small businesses, giving them access to a vast delivery network and online marketplace essential for competing in a digital world. Their activism casts Rappi as a force for inclusion and entrepreneurship, aligning brand growth with the creation of economic opportunities for its workers and business partners throughout the region.[144]

Europe

Belgium

69. Ecover

Ecover, the Belgian pioneer in ecological cleaning products, has exemplified brand activism since its inception. Their unwavering commitment to plant-based, biodegradable ingredients and fully recyclable packaging challenged industry norms decades ago. Ecover's activism extends beyond product innovation, venturing into collaborations like utilizing waste from brewing alcohol-free beer to creating new cleaning solutions. This forward-thinking shows tackling environmental challenges demands continuous innovation and a willingness to reimagine traditional processes. Ecover's legacy is one of proving that sustainability and business success can coexist, forcing competitors to follow suit and ultimately raising the bar for the entire cleaning product industry.[145]

Denmark

70. Too Good To Go

The Danish-born company has revolutionized the fight against food waste with its innovative approach to brand activism. Their core concept centers on a user-friendly app that connects consumers with businesses selling surplus food at discounted prices, preventing perfectly good food from ending up in landfills. This win-win-win model empowers consumers to make sustainable choices, helps businesses reduce waste, and lessens the environmental impact of the global food system. Too Good To Go has expanded rapidly across Europe and beyond, boasting impressive figures in meals saved and carbon emissions prevented, demonstrating the power of purpose-driven business models that create both social and economic value.[146]

France

71. Veja

The French sneaker brand has disrupted the footwear industry with its unwavering commitment to ethical and sustainable production. Their brand activism centers on transparency, tracing every step of their sneakers' creation—from fair trade organic cotton and wild Amazonian rubber to recycled materials and socially conscious manufacturing. Veja avoids traditional advertising campaigns, instead letting their dedication to ethical practices speak for themselves. This authenticity has resonated with a growing consumer base seeking conscious alternatives, proving that sustainable fashion can be both stylish and impactful. Veja sets a bold example, demonstrating that brand activism can redefine industry norms and inspire a more responsible approach to consumption.[147]

Germany

72. REWE

REWE Group, a major German food retailer with almost 4,000 locations, known for its healthy products, zooms in on the issue of sugar consumption. By 2019, they had already reduced sugar in over 100 of their own-brand products and launched a campaign to educate customers about healthy eating. This activism aligned perfectly with their "Your Market" positioning and their commitment to providing high-quality products for everyday needs. As a leading retailer, REWE's influence extends beyond mere advocacy; their control over product assortment allows them to drive tangible changes in consumer behavior and promote healthier lifestyles.[148]

Greece

73. Apivita

This natural cosmetics company emphasizes its Greek roots, sourcing ingredients like honey and herbs from local producers. It highlights the importance of bee conservation and supports sustainable agriculture. Apivita's focus on protecting biodiversity and promoting ethical sourcing resonates with consumers seeking products aligned with environmental responsibility.[149]

Hungary

74. Pick Szeged

Pick Szeged is a prominent Hungarian meat processing company. It has focused its activism on preserving Hungarian culinary traditions and supporting local farmers. Their "Pick Your Tradition" campaign highlights the importance of authentic Hungarian ingredients and recipes, fostering a sense of national pride and heritage. This campaign taps into consumer sentiment around supporting local producers and traditional food culture. By aligning itself with these values, Pick Szeged strengthens its brand identity and reinforces its connection to Hungarian consumers.[150]

Norway

75. Norwegian Seafood Council

The 2021 Netflix documentary *Seaspiracy* led to a campaign from the Norwegian Seafood Council to promote seafood as a sustainable and healthy protein source. The campaign highlighted the environmental benefits of consuming seafood compared to other animal proteins and aimed to educate consumers on its nutritional value. While successful in raising awareness and boosting demand for Norwegian seafood, the campaign faced criticism from some environmental groups who questioned the sustainability of certain fishing practices.[151]

Scotland

76. Brewdog

Brewdog, the Scottish craft brewery, embodies a rebellious spirit that permeates both its products and brand activism. They've consistently championed causes like clean water initiatives, mental health support, and fighting inequality, often using bold, disruptive campaigns to generate attention.[152] Their controversial "anti-sponsorship" of the 2022 Qatar

World Cup because of human rights concerns was a defining moment, showcasing a willingness to challenge the status quo even at potential commercial risk.[153] Brewdog's approach is polarizing, but effective in building a fiercely loyal customer base attracted to their authenticity and willingness to stand (and sometimes stumble) for their values.

Sweden

77. IKEA

IKEA, the Swedish furniture giant, is undertaking a bold transformation to embrace sustainability and circular economy principles. Their commitment to using renewable and recycled materials, shift toward designing for longevity, and offering repair and buy back programs exemplifies this shift.[154] IKEA's "Buy Back Friday" initiative, a direct counterpoint to the consumer frenzy of Black Friday, encourages customers to return used IKEA furniture for resale or recycling. This innovative campaign underscores a fundamental shift in IKEA's brand activism, fostering responsible consumption and demonstrating that sustainability and profitability can go hand in hand.[155]

The Netherlands

78. Heineken

In 2019, Dutch beer brand Heineken launched a campaign called "Worlds Apart" that aimed to promote dialogue and understanding between people with opposing views. The campaign featured pairs of strangers with conflicting beliefs participating in social experiments where they worked together on a task and then discussed their differences. The campaign video went viral, generating millions of views and sparking conversations about the importance of open dialogue and tolerance. While the campaign received praise for its message of unity, it also faced criticism for oversimplifying complex issues and potentially profiting from social divisions.[156]

Turkiye

79. Eczacıbaşı

A leading industrial group with diverse holdings, Eczacıbaşı supports women's empowerment and gender equality. The company combats violence against women by providing resources and support.[157] This demonstrates Eczacıbaşı's commitment to driving positive social change and aligns with its position as a trusted household name in the Turkish market.[158]

80. Vestel

Vestel, the Turkish electronics giant, made a bold move into brand activism with its "Wedding Gold" campaign aimed at combating the socially harmful practice of requiring a dowry in certain cultures. By transforming appliances into promotional gold pins with codes on the back, Vestel offered a practical, modern alternative to traditional dowry gifts. Couples could redeem these pins for the corresponding appliance after their wedding. The campaign's messaging not only aligned with the brand but also challenged deeply ingrained customs, promoting financial independence for women. This innovative approach struck a chord, resulting in a year-long campaign, increased market share for Vestel, and a shift in public discourse around a sensitive issue.[159]

This concludes our global journey of brand activism. Obviously, there are many more such examples from countries we covered, as well as others we did not have space to include. Please let us know of any outstanding examples from your countries. We are very much looking forward to hearing about them!

References

1   Ozturan, Peren and Amir Grinstein (2022), "Impact of Global Chief Marketing Officers' Corporare Social Responsibility and Sociopolitical Activism Communication on Twitter," *Journal of International Marketing*, 30(3), 72–82.

2   Sheth, Jagdish N., Can Uslay, and Rajendra S. Sisodia (2020), *The Global Rule of Three: Competing with Conscious Strategy*, Palgrave MacMillan.

3   Luo, Xubei "E-Commerce and Poverty Alleviation in Rural China," The World Bank, *East Asia & Pacific on the Rise.* March 19, 2019 (accessed March 6, 2025). https://blogs.worldbank.org/en/eastasiapacific/e-commerce-poverty-alleviation-rural-china-grassroots-development-public-private-partnerships

4   Khanna, Tarun, Ryan Allen, and Wesley Koo, "Rural Taobao: Alibaba's Expansion into Rural E-Commerce," *Harvard Business School Case* 719–433, January 2019. https://www.hbs.edu/faculty/Pages/item.aspx?num=55441.

5   Liu, Lizhi and Barry R. Weingast (2018), "Taobao, Federalism, and the Emergence of Law, Chinese Style," *Minnesota Law Review.* 111: 1563–1590. https://scholarship.law.umn.edu/cgi/viewcontent.cgi?article=1110&context=mlr.

6   "Overview," The World Bank, *E-Commerce Development: Experience from China* (accessed October 30, 2024). https://documents1.worldbank.org/curated/en/8237715 74361853775/pdf/Overview.pdf.

7   "Our Future," BYD (accessed October 30, 2024). https://www.bydglobal.com/cn/ en/BYD_ENOurFuture_mob.html;jsessionid=CHOJgd5JXohfkV2h6m9NBLYYw K8bDE3zKSdP6uNWYB_DQBAhR8yo!900745659!1381741582.

8   "New Generation Blade Battery by BYD Close to Launch," Sustainable Bus, April 10, 2024 (accessed October 30, 2024). https://www.sustainable-bus.com/com ponents/byd-blade-battery-new-generation-2024/.

9   "Chuanfu Wang, Chairman of BYD, on Why Cities Are Key to a Sustainable Future," *C40 Cities*, November 29, 2016 (accessed October 30, 2024). https://www.c40.org/news/ chuanfu-wang-chairman-of-byd-on-why-cities-are-key-to-a-sustainable-future/.

10 "Haier India Salutes the 'Silent Performers; of India with Its Latest TV Commercial," *Haier*, October 18, 2019 (accessed March 6, 2025). https://www.haier.com/in/ about-haier/news/20191126_111272.shtml.

11 "Seeds for the Future 2023," Huawei (accessed October 30, 2024). https://www. huawei.com/minisite/seeds-for-the-future/index.html.

12 Berman, Noah, Lindsay Maizland, Andrew Chatzky, "Is China's Huawei A Threat to U.S. National Security?" *Council on Foreign Relations*. February 8, 2023 (accessed October 30, 2024). https://www.cfr.org/backgrounder/chinas-huawei-threat- us-national-security.

13 Kelly, Makena "Congress Called Huawai a National Security Risk—It's Still in US Networks," *The Verge*, May 15, 2023 (accessed March 6, 2025). https://www.theve rge.com/23721573/huawei-zte-rip-and-replace-china-telecom-carriers-fcc.

14 "'More Affordability+Good Service' Continues to Drive Platform Consumption Growth," *Webull*, March 20, 2024 (accessed October 30, 2024). https://www.web ull.com/news/10434948870759424.

15 Sentence, Rebecca, "The Rise of Pinduoduo: How a Group Buying App Grew to Rival Alibaba," March 2024 (accessed October 30, 2024). https://econsultancy. com/pinduoduo-growth-story-china-ecommerce/.

16 van Wyk, Barry, "Pinduoduo, the E-Commerce Platform for Chinese Farmers, Had a Profitable Quarter Despite the Slowing Economy," *The China Project*. May 31, 2022 (accessed March 6, 2025). https://thechinaproject.com/2022/05/31/pinduo duo-the-ecommerce-platform-for-chinese-farmers-had-a-profitable-quarter-desp ite-the-slowing-economy-2/.

17 "How Xiaomi Is Dominating the Global Smartphone Market?" *The Marco Avenue*, December 10, 2023 (accessed October 30, 2024). https://www.themarcomave nue.com/blog/how-xiaomi-is-dominating-the-global-smartphone-market.

18 Wei, Ruyi and Qiong Long (2021), "Research on Xiaomi's Internationalized Business Model," *Open Journal of Business and Management*, 9(3), 1050–1063. https:// www.scirp.org/journal/paperinformation?paperid=108939

19 Deshpandé, Rohit, Tarun Khanna, Namrata Arora, and Tanya Bijlani, "India's Amul: Keeping Up with the Times," *Harvard Business School Case* 516–116, May 2016 (Revised June 2017).

20 Benu, Parvathi (2023), "How Sylvester daCunha Picked the First-Ever Amul Baby," *Hindu Businessline*, June 22, 2023 (accessed March 6, 2025). https://www.thehi ndubusinessline.com/news/variety/how-sylvester-dacunha-picked-the-first- ever-amul-baby/article66997878.ece

21   NDTV-Dettol Banega Swasth India (2022), "Dettol Banega Swasth India Celebrates Global Handwashing Day 2022," October 15, 2022 (accessed March 6, 2025). https://swachhindia.ndtv.com/dettol-banega-swasth-india-celebrates-global-handwashing-day-2022-72069/

22   "Swachh Bharat Mission: Driving India's Sanitation Rennaisance" Ministry of Jal Shakti Department of Drinking Water & Sanitation. Accessed October 30, 2024. https://swachhbharatmission.gov.in/sbmcms/index.htm

23   "Dettol Hygiene Quest," *Preloaded* (accessed October 30, 2024). https://preloaded.com/work/dettol-hygiene-quest/.

24   "Philosophy," Fabindia, [DATE?] (accessed October 30, 2024). https://www.fabindia.com/philosophy.

25   Mahajan, Sahana P., Prena Prasad, Neha S. Shivapujimath, Rajesh Varma, Richa Gupta, Shaichith Rai B., "Fabindia: Navigating the Crossroads of Tradition and Enterprise," February 2024 (accessed October 30, 2024). https://www.researchgate.net/publication/378499165_FabIndia_Navigating_the_crossroads_of_Tradition_and_Enterprise.

26   "Help a Child Reach 5," *Lifebuoy* (accessed October 30, 2024). https://www.lifebuoy.com/global/mission/help-a-child-reach-5.html.

27   "Lifebuoy and Education Ministry Launch a Unique Children's Book," *Adgully*, October 16, 2021 (accessed March 6, 2025). https://www.adgully.com/lifebuoy-and-education-ministry-launch-a-unique-children-s-book-110036.html.

28   "Lifebuoy," Unilever (accessed October 30, 2024). https://www.unilever.com/brands/personal-care/lifebuoy.html.

29   "Tata Group Makes Compliance to ESG Standards Top Priority," *The Economic Times*, March 1, 2021 (accessed March 6, 2025). https://economictimes.indiatimes.com/news/company/corporate-trends/tata-group-makes-compliance-to-esg-standards-top-priority/articleshow/81259822.cms?from=mdr.

30   "Tata Steel Sustainability Report 2020-21," Tata Steel (accessed October 30, 2024). https://www.tatasteel.com/media/10772/tcs-report-tata-steel-digital-version.pdf.

31   "Tata Power Hits Record High After Near-Term Sustainability Targets Gets Validated by SBTi," Business Standard, March 7, 2024 (accessed March 6, 2024). https://www.business-standard.com/markets/capital-market-news/tata-power-hits-record-high-after-near-term-sustainability-targets-gets-validated-by-sbti-124030700829_1.html.

32   "Titan to Turn Its Focus on Women," *The Economic Times*, February 14, 2007 (accessed March 6, 2025). https://economictimes.indiatimes.com/industry/cons-products/durables/titan-to-turn-its-focus-on-women/articleshow/1613624.cms?from=mdr.

33   Shah, Gouri, "Break the Bias, Says Titan Raga's New Ad," Livemint, March 8, 2016 (accessed March 6, 2025). https://www.livemint.com/Consumer/lVXBOR8iUZLHx2VHWNesIN/Break-the-bias-says-Titan-Ragas-new-ad.html.

34   "Rights of the Delivery Partners of Zomato and Swiggy in Light of the Social Security Code 2020," Jus Corpus, February 17, 2023 (accessed October 30, 2024). https://www.juscorpus.com/rights-of-the-delivery-partners-of-zomato-and-swiggy-in-light-of-the-social-security-code-2020/.

35   Iqubbal, Ashreef, "Food Delivery Workers in India: Emerging Entrepreneurs or
     Informal Labor?" April 2021 (accessed October 30, 2024). https://defindia.org/
     wp-content/uploads/2021/04/swiggy-zomato-delivery-workers-india-entrep
     reneurs-labour.pdf.

36   "Gogoro and Swiggy Announce Electric Vehicle Partnership in India," *Swiggy*,
     August 17, 2023 (accessed March 6, 2025). https://blog.swiggy.com/
     2023/08/17/gogoro-and-swiggy-announce-electric-vehicle-partnership-in-
     india/.

37   "Muji: The Global Strategy Behind the Japanese No-Brand Brand," *Martin Roll*.
     November 2020 (accessed October 30, 2024). https://martinroll.com/resour
     ces/articles/strategy/muji-the-global-strategy-behind-the-japanese-no-brand-
     brand/.

38   "Case Study: MUJI: Building Capacity of Artisans," The Business Call to Action
     (accessed October 30, 2024). https://static1.squarespace.com/static/6049e33a3
     512a120620cfe14/t/604c5cfb46b621178f1ecfb0/1615617277800/BCtA_+
     Case+Study_MUJI_web.pdf.

39   "Rakuten Launches 'Service Inclusion' Initiative to Develop Services Embracing
     Diversity, Equity, and Inclusion," *Rakuten*, March 28, 2024 (accessed March 6,
     2025). https://global.rakuten.com/corp/news/press/2024/0328_06.html.

40   "Rakuten to Become FC Barcelona Main Global Partner form 2017-2018 Season,"
     Rakuten. November 16, 2016 (accessed October 30, 2024). https://global.rakuten.
     com/corp/news/press/2016/1116_02.html.

41   "Diversity and Inclusion Is in Rakuten's DNA," *Rakuten Today*, October 4, 2023
     (accessed October 30, 2024). https://rakuten.today/blog/diversity-and-inclus
     ion-is-in-rakutens-dna.html.

42   "Uniqlo: The Strategy Behind the Global Japanese Fast Fashion Retail Brand," *Martin
     Roll*, January 2021 (accessed October 30, 2024). https://martinroll.com/resour
     ces/articles/strategy/uniqlo-the-strategy-behind-the-global-japanese-fast-fash
     ion-retail-brand/.

43   "Sustainability Report 2022: Giving Back to the World," Uniqlo, August 2021
     (accessed October 30, 2024). https://www.uniqlo.com/jp/en/contents/sustain
     ability/report/2022/community/#:~:text=UNIQLO%20has%20provided%20
     support%20to,meals%20to%20socially%20vulnerable%20people.

44   "Sustainability Report 2022: Giving Back to the World," Uniqlo, August 2021
     (accessed October 30, 2024). https://www.uniqlo.com/jp/en/contents/sustain
     ability/report/2022/community/#:~:text=UNIQLO%20has%20provided%20
     support%20to,meals%20to%20socially%20vulnerable%20people.

45   "About Us," Indomie (accessed November 1, 2024). https://indomie.ng/
     about-us/.

46   "Power Oil and Indomie Noodles Team Up to Provide Essential Products to
     Displaced victims of the Lokoja Flood," *BellaNaija*, November 8, 2022 (accessed
     March 6, 2025). https://www.bellanaija.com/2022/11/power-oil-x-indomie-
     outreach/.

47   "One Million Reasons to Travel with AirAsia Philippines: 1 Million AirAsia Points
     Up for Grabs," *AirAsia Newsroom*, August 8, 2022 (accessed March 6, 2025). https://
     newsroom.airasia.com/news/2022/8/8/one-million-reasons-to-travel-with-aira
     sia-philippines-1m-airasia-points-up-for-grabs#gsc.tab=0.

48 "Why We Fly: AirAsia's New Campaign Tells Why," *AirAsia Newsroom*, July 29, 2020 (accessed March 6, 2025). https://newsroom.airasia.com/stories/2020/7/29/why-we-fly-airasias-new-campaign-tells-why#gsc.tab=0.

49 "Grab Targets ASEAN's Unbanked in 'Once-in-a-Lifetime Opportunity'," *Nikkei Asia*, November 26, 2021 (accessed November 1, 2024). https://asia.nikkei.com/Editor-s-Picks/Interview/Grab-targets-ASEAN-s-unbanked-in-once-in-a-lifetime-opportunity.

50 "Grab Financial Group Expands 'Grow with Grab' Initiative to Empower SMBs to Ride the E-Commerce Wave in Southeast Asia," *Grab*, October 21, 2021 (accessed November 1, 2024). https://www.grab.com/sg/press/others/grab-financial-group-expands-grow-with-grab-initiative-to-empower-smbs-to-ride-the-e-commerce-wave-in-southeast-asia/.

51 Campbell, Charlie, "Grab Was Already the Uber of Southeast Aisa. Now the 'Super-App' Wants to Deliver Financial Equality, Too," *Time*, June 1, 2023 (accessed March 6, 2025)https://time.com/6283751/grab-superapp-anthony-tan/.

52 "Maybank ESG Commitment," Maybank (accessed November 1, 2024). chrome-extension://efaidnbmnnnibpcajpcglclefindmkaj/ https://www.maybank.com/iwov-resources/corporate_new/document/my/en/pdf/Maybank-ESG-Commitment.pdf

53 "Maybank's R.I.S.E. Uplifts Lives of Over 19,000 PWDs Across ASEAN," *Maybank*, October 5, 2022 (accessed March 6, 2025). https://www.maybank.com/en/news/2022/10/05.page.

54 "Sea Sustainability Report 2022," *Sea Limited* (accessed November 1, 2024). chrome-extension://efaidnbmnnnibpcajpcglclefindmkaj/ https://cdn.sea.com/webmain/static/resource/seagroup/Sustainability/Social%20Impact%20reports/Sea%20Sustainability%20Report%202022_1.pdf

55 "Amorepacific Declares Support for UN WEPs," AP Group, July 20, 2020 (accessed March 6, 2025). https://www.apgroup.com/int/en/news/2020-07-20.html.

56 Tan, Hannah, "2030, A MORE Beautiful Promise: Amorepacific Reveals Ambitious Sustainability Roadmap," *Moodie Davitt Report*, June 18, 2021 (accessed November 1, 2024). https://moodiedavittreport.com/2030-a-more-beautiful-promise-amorepacific-reveals-ambitious-sustainability-roadmap/.

57 "Amorepacific Supports Female Entrepreneurs," *Korea JoongAng Daily*, June 26, 2017 (accessed March 6, 2025). https://koreajoongangdaily.joins.com/2017/06/26/nationalGuestReports/Sponsored-Report-AmorePacific-supports-female-entrepreneurs/3035113.html

58 "Sustainability," *Hyundai Motor Company* (accessed November 1, 2024). https://www.hyundai.com/worldwide/en/company/sustainability. "Sustainability," Kia Corporation (accessed November 1, 2024). https://worldwide.kia.com/int/sustainability.

59 "Hyundai and Motor Kia to Introduce Blockchain-based Carbon Emission Monitoring System to Foster a Sustainable Value Chain," *Hyundai Newsroom*, July 27, 2023 (accessed March 6, 2025). https://www.hyundainews.com/en-us/releases/3895.

60 Andrew, Ian, "LG Launches 'Life's Good When It's Green' Global Initiative," *Greener Ideal.* February 20, 2017 (accessed March 6, 2025). https://greenerideal.com/news/business/6129-lg-launches-lifes-good-when-its-green-global-initiative/.

61 Back, Adrian, "Enabling Consumers to Be More Eco-Conscious," *LG* (accessed November 1, 2024). https://www.lg.com/uk/lg-experience/inspiration/enabling-consumers-to-be-more-eco-conscious/.

62 "Inspiring, Leading, and Making a Difference: Jollibee Honors Exemplary Families in 9th Jollibee Family Values Awards," *Business Inquirer*, October 11, 2019 (accessed March 6, 2025). https://business.inquirer.net/280789/inspiring-leading-and-making-a-difference-jollibee-honors-exemplary-families-in-9th-jollibee-family-values-awards.

63 "Farmer Entrepreneurship Program," *Jollibee Group Foundation* (accessed November 1, 2024). https://annualreport.jollibeefoundation.org/farmer-entrepreneurship-program.

64 "Pilot Training School," *Ethiopian Airlines* (accessed November 1, 2024). https://corporate.ethiopianairlines.com/eaa/training-schools/pilot-training.

65 "Ethiopian Airlines Group Launches Sustainability Initiative," Ethiopian Airlines, October 23, 2019 (accessed November 1, 2024). https://corporate.ethiopianairlines.com/Press-release-open-page/ethiopian-airlines-group-launches-sustainability-initiative.

66 "M-Pesa Revolution: How Mobile Money Is Transforming Finance in Africa," *Medium*, February 12, 2024 (accessed November 1, 2024). https://medium.com/@everythingza/m-pesa-revolution-how-mobile-money-is-transforming-finance-in-africa-6d1e4c673b12.

67 Murray, Sab, "How Mobile Money Fosters Financial Inclusion," *Wharton University of Pennsylvania*, December 15, 2023 (accessed November 1, 2024). https://knowledge.wharton.upenn.edu/article/how-mobile-money-fosters-financial-inclusion/.

68 "Kenya's Safaricom Secures $103 Million Loan for Sustainable Projects," *ESG News*, September 5, 2023 (accessed March 6, 2025). https://esgnews.com/kenyas-safaricom-secures-103m-loan-for-sustainable-projects/.

69 "Twiga Foods Works with Micro, Small and Medium Enterprises (MSMEs) to Transform the Kenyan Food System," *CGIAR*, June 27, 2023 (accessed November 1, 2024). https://www.cgiar.org/news-events/news/twiga-foods-works-with-micro-small-and-medium-enterprises-msmes-to-transform-the-kenyan-food-system/.

70 Schoeman, Stephan and Niral Patel, "Reducing Food Insecurity and Transforming the Grow-to-Grocery Cycle in Africa with Cloud Technology," *Google Cloud Blog*, May 23, 2023 (accessed March 6, 2025). https://cloud.google.com/blog/topics/partners/twiga-foods-uses-tech-to-reduce-food-insecurity/.

71 "Learning Community," *Andela* (accessed June 15, 2024). https://andela.com/learning-community.

72 "Press: Andela Launches 'The Power of X' Campaign as It Scales Engineering Teams Across the Continent," *Andela* (accessed June 15, 2024). https://andela.com/blog-posts/press-andela-launches-the-power-of-x-campaign-as-it-scales-engineering-teams-across-the-continent.

73 "From Startups to Studies: African Developers Are Inspiring Innovation Across the World," *Andela* (accessed June 15, 2024). https://andela.com/blog-posts/from-startups-to-studies-african-developers-are-inspiring-innovation-across-the-world.

74   "Administrator Lauds Glo Over Education Initiative," PM News Nigeria November 13, 2014 (accessed March 6, 2025). https://pmnewsnigeria.com/2014/11/13/administrator-lauds-glo-over-education-initiative/.

75   "Focus on STEM Subjects, Glo Charges Female Students," Vanguard, May 18, 2022 (accessed March 6, 2025). https://www.vanguardngr.com/2022/05/focus-on-stem-subjects-glo-charges-female-students/.

76   "Rural Areas and the Future of E-commerce in Africa," Jumia Group, June 5, 2023 (accessed November 1, 2024). https://group.jumia.com/news/rural-areas-and-the-future-of-e-commerce-in-africa.

77   "UNICEF and Jumia Launch Partnership to Help Giga Connect Schools in Africa to the Internet," UNICEF, [November 21, 2021] (accessed November 1, 2024). https://www.unicef.org/innovation/press-releases/unicef-and-jumia-launch-partnership-help-giga-connect-schools-africa-internet.

78   Ranahan, Jared, "Amarula: The Spirits Brand Dedicated to Protecting Native Elephants," Cool Hunting, March 23, 2023 (accessed November 1, 2024). https://coolhunting.com/food-drink/amarula-the-spirits-brand-dedicated-to-protecting-native-elephants/.

79   "Amarula Trust," Amarula (accessed November 1, 2024). https://amarula.com/amarula-trust/.

80   "Amarula Launches Phase Two of the 'Name Them Save Them' Campaign," Save the Elephants, April 17, 2017 (accessed November 1, 2024). https://www.saveelephants.org/news/amarula-launches-phase-two-of-the-name-them-save-them-campaign/.

81   De Barros, Luiz, "Castle Lager Shows Its Support for the LGBTQ Community," MambaOnline, October 26, 2018 (accessed March 6, 2025). https://www.mambaonline.com/2018/10/26/castle-lager-gives-it-support-to-the-lgbtq-community/.

82   Bratt, Michael, "Behind the Brand: Castle Lager Smashes Labels with New Advertising Campaign," The Media Online, July 25, 2018 (accessed March 6, 2025). https://themediaonline.co.za/2018/07/behind-the-brand-castle-lager-smashes-labels-with-new-advertising-campaign/.

83   "#NoExcuse: Bold New Movement Against Gender-Based Violence," Stadium Management, July 2, 2018 (accessed March 6, 2025. https://www.stadiummanagement.co.za/2018/07/noexcuse-bold-new-movement-against-gender-based-violence/.

84   "Investec Rhino Lifeline," Investec (accessed June 1, 2024). https://www.investec.com/en_za/welcome-to-investec/sustainability/our-environment/rhino-lifeline.html.

85   "About Us," Mr Price Group (accessed June 1, 2024). https://www.mrp.com/en_za/features/about-us.

86   "Our Commitment to Change," Mr Price Group (accessed November 1, 2024). https://www.mrp.com/en_za/inspiration/sustainability-journey/our-commitment-to-change.

87   "Bridging the Digital Divide: Empowering Rural Communities in Zambia," MTN, April 24, 2024 (accessed June 1, 2024). https://www.mtn.com/case-study/extending-mobile-network-coverage-deep-into-rural-africa/.

88 "MultiChoice Training Investment a Massive Boost for African TV," MultiChoice (accessed June 1, 2024). https://www.multichoice.com/media/news/multichoice-training-investment-a-massive-boost-for-african-tv.

89 Onyekachi, Nnaemeka, "MultiChoice Nigeria Challenges Tribunal's Jurisdiction to Restrain DStv/GOtv Price Hike, Others," Nairametrics, May 7, 2024 (accessed March 6, 2025). https://nairametrics.com/2024/05/07/multichoice-nigeria-challenges-tribunals-jurisdiction-to-restrain-dstvgotv-price-hike-others/.

90 "Nando's Advertising, Marketing Campaigns and Videos," Campaign Live (accessed November 1, 2024). https://www.campaignlive.co.uk/the-work/advertiser/nandos/10143.

91 Faull, Jennifer, "'If You Can't Back Words with Action, Stay Away': Nando's Brand Boss on When to Get Political," The Drum. March 7, 2022 (accessed March 6, 2025). https://www.thedrum.com/news/2022/03/07/if-you-can-t-back-words-with-action-stay-away-nando-s-brand-boss-when-get-political.

92 "Woolworths Drives Good Business Journey," Enterprise Africa (accessed November 1, 2024). https://enterprise-africa.net/woolworths-drives-good-business-journey/.

93 King, Lucy and Susan Thobela (2014), "Woolworths Farming for the Future." International Food and Agribusiness Management Review. 17(B): 161–166. https://www.ifama.org/resources/Documents/v17ib/King-Thobela.pdf.

94 Orla, Ryan, "Econet's EcoSure Solution: Driving Women's Financial Inclusion in Zimbabwe," GSMA, December 23, 2019 (accessed November 1, 2024). https://www.gsma.com/solutions-and-impact/connectivity-for-good/mobile-for-development/blog/econet-driving-womens-financial-inclusion-in-zimbabwe/.

95 Muzanechita, Rindai S., "The significance of The Ecocash mobile money Service in Fostering Financial Inclusion in the Zimbabwean Informal Sector," University of Pretoria, July 2022 (accessed November 1, 2024). chrome- extension://efaidnbmnnnibpcajpcglclefindmkaj/ https://repository.up.ac.za/bitstream/handle/2263/86221/Muzanechita_MobileMoney_2022.pdf?sequence=3

96 "Econet Wireless Pledges Support for Girls' Education Awareness Program," Global Partnership for Education, June 2, 2021 (accessed November 1, 2024). https://www.globalpartnership.org/news/econet-wireless-pledges-support-girls-education-awareness-program. "Econet Life Launches US$30 000 'Smart Schools' Promotion," The Herald, February 4, 2024 (accessed November 1, 2024). https://www.herald.co.zw/econet-life-launches-us30-000-smart-schools-promotion/.

97 O'Brien, Vanna, "Unpacking Tall Poppy Syndrome," Refinery29, August 2, 2023 (accessed November 1, 2024). https://www.refinery29.com/en-au/what-is-tall-poppy-syndrome.

98 "Atlassian's Commitment to Education: The Future," Atlassian (accessed June 1, 2024). https://www.atlassian.com/blog/archives/atlassians-commitment-education-future.

99 "Atlassian Sustainability Report," Atlassian (accessed June 1, 2024). https://www.atlassian.com/company/corporate-social-responsibility/report.

100 "Be a Well Being," Blackmores (accessed November 1, 2024). https://www.blackmores.com.au/be-a-well-being.

101 Lackey, Brett, "Why Thousands of Furious Aussies are Planning on Throwing Their Blackmores Vitamins in the Bin," *The Daily Mail*, February 25, 2023 (accessed March 6, 2025). https://www.dailymail.co.uk/news/article-11793 549/Blackmores-boycott-Indigenous-Voice-Parliament-referendum-Marcus-supports-Jacinta-Price.html.

102 "The Affinity and Canva Pledge," Canva, March 27, 2024 (accessed November 1, 2024). https://www.canva.com/newsroom/news/affinity-canva-pledge/.

103 "Canva for Nonprofits," Canva (accessed November 1, 2024). https://www.canva.com/canva-for-nonprofits/.

104 Kuehlwein, JP, "Thankyou: Admirable Activism or Brand-Based Bullying?" *Ueberbrands*. November 30, 2020 (accessed March 6, 2025). https://ueberbrands.com/2020/11/30/thankyou-admirable-activism-or-brand-based-bullying/. "Our Story," *Thankyou*, (accessed November 1, 2024). https://thankyou.co/pages/our-story.

105 "B Corp," Kathmandu, (accessed November 1, 2024). https://www.kathmandu.com.au/kathmandu-b-corp.

106 Stefanoff, Nikki, "For Kathmandu, Sustainability Is a whole company affair," *Pro Bono Australia*, January 24, 2022 (accessed March 6, 2025). https://probonoaustralia.com.au/news/2022/01/for-kathmandu-sustainability-is-a-whole-company-affair/.

107 "Small Businesses: The Support They Need," Xero Blog (accessed June 1, 2024). https://blog.xero.com/accountants-bookkeepers/small-businesses-support-they-need/.

108 "Sustainable Business," *Netafim* (accessed November 1, 2024). https://www.netafim.com/en/sustainable_agriculture/sustainable-business/ "Sustainable Agriculture," *Netafim* (accessed November 1, 2024). https://www.netafim.com/en/sustainable-agriculture/.

109 "Talabat Jordan: Transforming from a Profit-Led Business to a Purpose-Led Powerhouse," *Talabat*, April 26, 2021 (accessed November 1, 2024). https://blog.talabat.com/ar/talabat-jordan-transforming-from-a-profit-led-business-to-a-purpose-led-powerhouse/.

110 Abdulla, Nasreen, "Pay Hikes, Lounge Areas: UAE Delivery Companies Improve Riders' Working Conditions," *Khaleej Times*. July 24, 2022 (accessed November 1, 2024). https://www.khaleejtimes.com/uae/pay-hikes-lounge-areas-uae-delivery-companies-improve-riders-working-conditions.

111 "Qatar Airways Signs Deal with Shell for Sustainable Aviation Fuel Supply at Amsterdam Schiphol Airport," *Qatar Airways*, May 31, 2023 (accessed March 6, 2025). https://www.qatarairways.com/press-releases/en-WW/226578-qatar-airways-signs-deal-with-shell-for-sustainable-aviation-fuel-supply-at-amsterdam-schiphol-airport.

112 "Climate & Energy," Qatar Airways, [DATE?N/A] (accessed June 1, 2024). https://www.qatarairways.com/en/about-qatar-airways/environmental-awareness/climate-energy.html.

113 "Cab-Hailing Company Careem Launches Women Drivers in Conservative Pakistan," *Yahoo! Finance*, December 7, 2016(accessed March 6, 2025). https://sg.news.yahoo.com/finance/news/cab-hailing-company-careem-launches-090458273.html.

114 Hassan, Sarah, "Uber and Careem Recruit First Female Drivers in Saudi Arabia," *CNN*, January 11, 2018 (accessed March 6, 2025). https://www.cnn.com/2018/01/10/asia/saudi-uber-women-drivers-ime/index.html.

115 Rana, Amit, "The Careem Business Model," *Code Brew*, June 8, 2023 (accessed November 1, 2024). https://www.code-brew.com/careem-business-model/.

116 "Ahlibank Launches 'Souq' Initiative Aiming to Support SMEs," *Ahlibank*, April 25, 2023 (accessed November 1, 2024). https://ahlibank.om/news/ahlibank-launches-souq-initiative-aiming-to-support-smes/. "Funding Souq & SHAMS Join Forces to Support SMEs!" *Funding Souq*, July 20, 2022 (accessed November 1, 2024). https://fundingsouq.com/ae/en/blog/funding-souq-and-sharjah-media-city-shams-join-forces-to-support-the-small-and-medium-sized-enterprise/.

117 "EdTech Middle East: Etisalat and Alef Education Sign MoU," *Global EdTech*, March 4, 2020 (accessed November 1, 2024). https://global-edtech.com/etisalat-and-alef-education-sign-mou-to-develop-edtech-in-the-middle-east/. "Etisalat Empowers 1 Million Students to Support E-Learning," *Etisalat*, April 4, 2020 (accessed March 6, 2025). https://www.eand.com/en/news/04-apr-2020-etisalat-empowers-1-million-students.html.

118 "KSA Sustainability Champions Initiative," *Almarai*, May 6, 2024 (accessed November 1, 2024). https://www.almarai.com/en/corporate/media-center/almarai-news/ksa-sustainability-champions-initiative. "Climate Change," *Almarai* (accessed November 1, 2024). https://sustainability.almarai.com/climate-change.html.

119 "Namaat," *Aramco* (accessed November 1, 2024). https://www.aramco.com/en/what-we-do/commercial-ecosystems/namaat.

120 "UN Experts Challenge Saudi Aramco over Climate Change," *Phys.org*, August 27, 2023 (accessed March 6, 2025). https://phys.org/news/2023-08-experts-saudi-aramco-climate.html.

121 "Sustainability," *Aramco* (accessed November 1, 2024). https://www.aramco.com/en/sustainability.

122 "CSR," *Savola Group* (accessed November 1, 2024). https://www.savola.com/en/csr.

123 "CEMEX Announces Progress on Its Affordable Housing Initiative," CEMEX, October 13, 2011 (accessed November 1, 2024). https://www.cemex.com/w/cemex-announces-progress-on-its-affordable-housing-initiative.

124 "Patrimonio Hoy: A Home for Everyone," CEMEX, October 7, 2015 (accessed November 1, 2024). https://www.cemex.com/w/patrimonio-hoy-a-home-for-everyone.

125 "Sustainable Construction," CEMEX, . https://www.cemexusa.com/sustainability/sustainable-construction.

126 "Communication of Progress," *Cinepolis*, March 15, 2008 (accessed November 1, 2024). https://ungc-production.s3.us-west-2.amazonaws.com/attachments/261/original/COP.pdf?1262614178.

127 "Bimbo Global Race," Grupo Bimbo (accessed November 1, 2024). https://bimboglobalrace.com/region/us/index.html.

128 "We Launch Our New Sustainability Strategy with More Ambitious Goals for the Future," *Grupo Bimbo*, May 18, 2022 (accessed November 1, 2024). https://www.grupobimbo.com/en/press/releases/business/we-launch-our-new-sustainability-strategy-more-ambitious-goals-future.

129 "Sustainability Report 2022," *Grupo Lala*, (accessed November 1, 2024). chrome-extension://efaidnbmnnnibpcajpcglclefindmkaj/ https://www.lala.com.mx/storage/app/media/Reportes%20de%20sustentabilidad/2022%20SUSTAINABILITY%20REPORT_LALA.pdf

130 "Sustainability Report 2021," Copa Airlines (accessed November 1, 2024). https://www.copaair.com/assets/COPA_Design_Memoria_2021_ENG_HQ-.pdf

131 Brandom, Rusell, "Why Amazon Isn't the Amazon of Latin America," *Rest of World*, August 31, 2023 (accessed November 1, 2024). https://restofworld.org/2023/exporter-amazon-mercadolibre/.

132 "Transforming Latin America," *MercadoLibre* (accessed November 1, 2024). https://investor.mercadolibre.com/transforming-latin-america/. "Sustainability," *MercadoLibre* (accessed November 1, 2024). https://investor.mercadolibre.com/sustainability/.

133 "Havaianas Tacking Biodiversity Crisis Head-On," *Alter* (accessed November 1, 2024). https://alter-agency.com/havaianas-biodiversity-crisis-conservation-collaboration-2/.

134 "Havaianas," *Conservation International* (accessed November 1, 2024). https://www.conservation.org/corporate-engagements/havaianas.

135 "Luiza Trajano Speaks on Inclusivity, Prosperity, and Success in Business in Brazil," *Georgetown Americas Institute*, December 15, 2022 (accessed November 1, 2024). https://americas.georgetown.edu/features/luiza-trajano-speaks-on-inclusivity-prosperity-and-success-in-business-in-brazil.

136 Wierson, Arick, "A Company in Brazil Made a Controversial Move to Fight Racism. Other CEOs Should Try It," CNN, November 17, 2020 (accessed March 6, 2025). https://www.cnn.com/2020/11/17/perspectives/magazine-luiza-racial-diversity/index.html.

137 "Ekos," *Natura* (accessed November 1, 2024). https://www.naturabrasil.fr/en-us/about-natura/our-range-of-products/ekos.

138 "Our Commitments," *Natura* (accessed November 1, 2024). https://www.naturabrasil.com/pages/our-commitments.

139 Torres, Marcela, "Financial Inclusion and Digital Transformation: The Future of Banking in Our Region," *Nubank*, December 7, 2023 (accessed November 1, 2024). https://international.nubank.com.br/company/financial-inclusion-and-digital-transformation-the-future-of-banking-in-our-region/.

140 "How We Work," *Fundação Grupo Boticário* (accessed November 1, 2024). https://www.fundacaogrupoboticario.org.br/en/Pages/Home.aspx.

141 "Sustainability," *Grupo Boticário* (accessed November 1, 2024). https://www.boticario.com/pages/sustainability.

142 "Sustainable Line Coffees," *JuanValdez* (accessed November 1, 2024). https://www.juanvaldezcafestore.com/sustainable-line-coffees/.

143 "Sustainability Report 2022," *JuanValdez* (accessed November 1, 2024). https://juanvaldez.com/wp-content/uploads/2023/06/Sustainability-Report-2022-Juan-Valdez.pdf.

144 "Our Impact," *Rappi* (accessed November 1, 2024). https://about.rappi.com/our-impact.

145 "Commitments," Ecover (accessed November 1, 2024). https://www.ecover.com/commitments/.

146 "Save Good Food From Going to Waste," *Too Good To Go* (accessed November 1, 2024). https://www.toogoodtogo.com/en-us

147 "Transparency," *Veja* (accessed November 1, 2024). https://project.veja-store.com/en/single/transparency.

148 "We See Ourselves as a Partner to Our Customers Seeking a Well-Balanced Diet," *REWE Group*, February 1, 2023 (accessed November 1, 2024). https://www.rewe-group.com/en/press-and-media/newsroom/opinions/we-see-ourselves-as-a-partner-to-our-customers-seeking-a-well-balanced-diet/.

149 "Apivita for Saving Bees," *Saving Bees* (accessed November 1, 2024). https://www.savingbees.org/en/partners/apivita/.

150 "About Us," *Pick* (accessed November 1, 2024). https://pick.hu/en/the-pick-brand/about-us/.

151 "NSC Launches Unique Seafood Sustainability Campaign in UK," *Norwegian Seafood Council*, June 1, 2022 (accessed November 1, 2024). https://en.seafood.no/news-and-media/news-archive/nsc-launches-unique-seafood-sustainability-campaign-in-uk/. Williams, Gary. W and Oral Capps Jr. (2022), "The Apparent Conflict of Norwegian Pelagic Fisheries Management and Norwegian Seafood Council Export Promotion," *International Food and Agribusiness Management Review*, 25(3): 427–440. https://www.wageningenacademic.com/doi/10.22434/IFAMR2021.0059. Holmyard, Nikki, "Norwegian Seafood Council Implementing 'Think Global, Act Local' Strategy," *SeafoodSource*, May 1, 2023 (accessed November 1, 2024). https://www.seafoodsource.com/news/premium/supply-trade/norwegian-seafood-council-implementing-think-global-act-local-strategy.

152 Ormesher, Ellen, "Brewdog: Timeline of a Controversial Brand," *The Drum*, May 8, 2024 (accessed March 6, 2025). https://www.thedrum.com/news/2022/01/24/brewdog-timeline-controversial-brand.

153 "The World F*Cup," Brewdog (accessed November 1, 2024). https://www.brewdog.com/uk/anti-sponsor-qatar.

154 "A Circular Ikea –Making the Things We Love Last Longer," *Ikea* (accessed November 1, 2024). https://www.ikea.com/us/en/this-is-ikea/sustainable-everyday/a-circular-ikea-making-the-things-we-love-last-longer-pub9750dd90.

155 "Buy Back Friday," *Shorty Awards* (accessed November 1, 2024). https://shortyawards.com/2021-impact/buy-back-friday.

156 "Heineken Worlds Apart," *Edelman* (accessed November 1, 2024). https://www.edelman.com/work/heineken-worlds-apart. McGrath, AbiGail, "Social Marketing Example #5: Heineken, Worlds Apart," *Brogan & Partners*, August 21, 2019 (accessed November 1, 2024). https://brogan.com/blog/social-marketing-example-5-heineken-worlds-apart/. "Some People Hated the Depolarizing Heineken Beer Ad. Why?" *Starts With Us*, March 6, 2024 (accessed March 6, 2025). https://startswith.us/2024/03/06/some-people-hated-the-depolarizing-heineken-beer-ad-why/.

157 "TUR W: Eczacibasi VitrA Joins 'One Billion Rising' Campaign to Stop Violence on Women," *WorldofVolley*, February 17, 2013 (accessed March 6, 2025). https://worldofvolley.com/latest_news/turkey/11529/tur-w-eczacibasi-joins-one-billion-rising-campaign-to-stop-violence-on-women.html.

158 "Gender Equality & Equal Opportunities Policy," *Eczacıbqsı Group*, December 29, 2021 (accessed November 1, 2024). https://www.gensenta.com.tr/_assets/pdf/en/policies/eczacibasi_group_gender_equality_equal_opportunities_policy.pdf.
159 "Turkish White-Goods Retailer Strikes Gold with Wedding Gift Promo," *Contagious*, May 4, 2021 (accessed November 1, 2024). https://www.contagious.com/news-and-views/campaign-of-the-week-vestel-wedding-gold-promotion.

15

CONCLUSION: A DOCTRINE FOR BRAND ACTIVISM

Over half a century has gone by since Milton Friedman made the singular profit maximization objective popular. We have come a long way since then. Times have changed and many of those paying ESG objectives mere lip service have come around. Admittedly, replacing the comfortable simplicity of profit maximization with the uncomfortable complexity of stakeholder satisfaction takes work. Making everyone happy is often a fool's errand. Corporate hypocrisy abounds.

Yet brands must strive to create value beyond that for shareholders to stand the test of time. That increasingly means engaging in some form of brand activism. At times, you will need the courage to persist, even when short-term investors vote otherwise with their wallets, or when your own employees threaten to hijack, weaponize, or sabotage your brand—thanks to social media, your deepest secrets are merely confined to someone's fingertips. But what if your core customers would rather you created value elsewhere? As marketers, this is where we must draw the line. Your buyers, payers, users; current and potential customers matter.[1] Changing your

DOI: 10.4324/9781003593690-15

narrative through creative storytelling is often not enough. We don't blame you for losing sleep; it is the stuff of C-suite nightmares.

Are you going to be a conformist (bare minimum, pull(ed) activism only), a pragmatist (engaging only when it suits your bottom line), a strategist (investing and engaging for long-term merits), or an idealist (true north, no matter what) when it comes to brand activism?[2] Hopefully, one of the latter two, but most importantly, decide and act consistently.

We hope reading this book has shown you the tremendous value brand activism can offer for achieving the all-elusive brand of authenticity and differentiation in the marketplace. Indeed, there are cases where a response to an issue is appropriate and, dare we say, profitable for a brand. In fact, given that we live in capital-driven societies, no brand should have to apologize for finding a cause to move the needle and doing so successfully.

With no profit motive, corporate action is akin to charity, and investors, as well as consumers, know their favorite cause much better than you or your CEO. Do not play charity with stakeholder money. Who is to decide you have chosen wisely? As long as your brand is under the umbrella of a for-profit organization, consumers will not perceive you as less authentic when you also have a profit motive.[3] And if you disclose your joint social/profit motives, you can even build credibility via the route of perceived trustworthiness and expertise.[4] However, charity is best conducted with your own money rather than an investor's. Consider that the Bill and Melinda Gates Foundation Trust invested $95 million in AB InBev stock during the collapse following the Mulvaney controversy.[5] Given the Foundation's mission and grant record, this may not have been a purely financial decision.

With the multitude of challenges, from environmental to social to cultural to business ethics that their predecessors did not have to contend with, brand managers have often resorted to purpose as one encompassing solution. What the mission, vision, doctrine, or manifesto has not captured has been rolled into purpose. Brand and marketing consultancies love the P-word buzz and promote it as the holy grail to their clients. But it isn't. Running a corporate retreat where you "repurpose" your brand will not, by default, make you trustworthy, nor will it motivate your staff or lead to higher profitability. There is no quick fix for authenticity.

Walking a fine line for genuine impact will become the new gold standard of brand management. Yes, creating shareholder value is too simplistic, and creating stakeholder value is too complex. Yet being stuck in the middle, focusing on the squeakiest wheel of the day, is the worst position of all. How can any management be expected to create the future of a business if they manage stakeholders in this fashion when there are already so many challenges to deal with? What will be your north star?

Hence, here is our brand activism doctrine:

Every brand activism effort must come with a justification of the business case, like any other campaign. If a strategic approach to CSR is prescribed as the most rational,[6] the same logic should also apply to brand activism. Similarly, if "the acid test of good corporate philanthropy is whether the desired social change is so beneficial to the company that the organization would pursue the change even if no one ever knew about it"[7] then the same standard should be applied to brand activism.

Brand Purpose is more than a buzzword. It is hard work. Importantly, it is "not a mere tagline or marketing campaign; it is a company's fundamental reason for being" and not something to be managed like the marketing mix.[8] You need to get your house in order first. When a brand's internal actions reflect its external social advocacy, it's less likely to face accusations of hypocrisy.[9] Essentially, walking the walk alongside talking the talk protects a brand's authenticity and prevents consumer backlash. For example, you will have no business talking about equal anything if you have not achieved equality at home. How can you expect to pass moral judgments to customers even as your employees are blowing whistles on the same issue?[10] Instead, announcements about internal changes you are making are generally much more convincing.[11]

In the wake of the overturn of Roe v. Wade, Amazon, instead of tweeting about what is right or wrong, announced that it would cover up to $4,000 in travel expenses for employees seeking medical treatments, including abortions. The new internal policy on this contested topic received nation wide news coverage. Amazon North America's 2022 segment sales increased 13% year-over-year. Variants of the same policy were also embraced by dozens of other companies, such as Bank of America, BuzzFeed, Cigna, Citigroup, Comcast, Dick's Sporting Goods, Estee Lauder, Idea US, Kroger, Lyft, MasterCard, Patagonia, Starbucks, and Target.[12,13]

Fuse purpose and profit by changing policy and practice. Balance goals such as cash flow, quarterly earnings, and long-term viability. Invest in marketing skills for employees and community branding. Focus on the long-term development of purpose-driven brands and redefine raison d'être of marketing as a trustee and steward for the brand and its stakeholders.[14,15]

Balance timeliness with timelessness. Use evolving narratives to your advantage by acting spontaneously when possible, but also put effort into social context-independent activism. You will be perceived as much more authentic if you are the locomotive on an issue rather than the stranger who likes to jump on bandwagons.[16]

A fledgling brand shall pay attention to very few—ideally one and no more than three—stakeholders to create value and be very clear about it. These stakeholders should always include customers (as buyers, payers, and users)[17] but can also include others, such as investors. For example, VCs often have an outsized impact on the operations of tech start-ups through formal board memberships or otherwise. Meanwhile, be aware that institutional investors generally care more about governance than your social or environmental initiatives, and your brand activism efforts may actually decrease their ownership of your stock.[18]

A viable consumer sub-segment can be a focal stakeholder. For example, a medical or medical-adjacent firm, or even a coffee shop that is not directly related to the issue, can choose autism relief as its brand activism purpose. In the process, these firms can find loyal customers from families dealing with autism and their ally supporters without necessarily losing business from others. Such a differentiated position may be sufficient to be a viable business if it survives the Five Rings (if it is authentic, etc.).

The focal cause may even be deliberately chosen to be divisive for niche and specialist brands. Those who agree with you are likely to become very dedicated to your brand. Truth be told many esoteric cults were sprung like this. For every attack on (social) media, others who sympathize with your cause will be galvanized and become even more staunch supporters and may cast multiple votes with their wallets to keep you afloat or make you soar. Why should the same principle not apply to start-ups and their fledgling brands? And the choice is not to go either MyPillow-level radical or hopelessly woke.[19]

Later, as a thriving organization is garnering more resources, *brand activism can be diversified to develop programs and campaigns to make more stakeholders happy,* just like brands can choose to serve multiple customer segments. *There may also* be a business case to use sub-brands or launch new brands for specific causes instead. Even so, astute managers should find ways to do so profitably and not out of personal agendas.

Finally, like Apple, Meta, Amazon, Nike, or Google, when an organization reaches apex predator status in its domain, it is then expected of this corporation to have a strategic imperative to satisfice all stakeholders. This has become the norm because the society perceives the collateral damage of these giants to be so high. In some sense, these corporations are even expected to mend some of the government's failings, such as those caused by tax policy. That the economic growth in the US has been terribly uneven is a major problem.[20] Unfortunately, the rest of the world is not too far behind either. "At the current rate, it will take an estimated 300 years to end child marriage, 286 years to close gaps in legal protection and remove discriminatory laws..., and 47 years to achieve equal representation in national parliaments" globally.[21] These are not corporate problems.

Thus, while the expectation from apex predator brands is to "satisfice"[22] every stakeholder with thoughtful programs and campaigns, and they should do better with respect to that expectation, we humbly suggest the real onus is on the politicians who shirk their responsibility to serve their main stakeholders, aka citizens. Maslow's Hierarchy of Needs prevails, and social progress without matching economic outcomes is inconsistent with the raison d'être of a capitalist system. Political parties and the government need brand activism too! Let us take care of the economic problems and that will leave fewer social ones to deal with by default.

Nevertheless, please do not forget to go through the appendix, where we review over a hundred cases of brand activism and score them using the Five Rings introduced in this book. We take you through a fascinating journey from 1787 to 2024 with examples of pull and push activism, flagship as well as local brands, products and services, retail and experience, pure play e-commerce brands, and more. While you will remember some of these cases from previous chapters, most you will discover for the first time.

In Conclusion

Brand activism is like physical activity for your brand's soul. Just as exercise strengthens your body, meaningful activism builds your brand's reputation and relevance. And like mindless busywork keeps you glued to your desk, ineffective activism leads to stagnation. And just as war wreaks havoc, ill-conceived activism can inflict serious damage on your brand's image and relationships. Brand activism is not merely CSR or philanthropy. When implemented with the principles laid out in this book, it is truly impactful and mindful marketing. The World Advertising Research Center defines it as the "reason for a brand to exist beyond making profit."[23] We hope we have given you the reasons why in this book. May your efforts of brand activism slide from the peak of inflated expectations and disillusionment onto the slope of enlightenment and productivity.

Brands. Can. Be. A. Catalyst. For. Social. Change.[24]
In a stable world, your success relied on building your brand.
In our turbulent world, your success relies on evolving your brand.
Brand coalitions can amplify impact.
But *authenticity* is key and *alignment* matters.[25]
Find ways for your customers to express their identity through your brand.
Strive for transformative brand activism.

Epilogue

This book is not a love letter for activism nor is it a bash of it. We wanted to offer objective evaluation and guidance on this topic which some initially considered to be "a bit too niche."[26] As we go to press, we are delighted to see activism receive more of the attention it richly deserves. An article in *Harvard Business Review*'s latest issue, "Reducing the Risks of Corporate Activism" draws from academic research and offers four lessons: (1.) Your organization's position on issues shouldn't be one person's decision, (2.) don't allow activism to distract you from your purpose, (3.) don't attack your base, and (4.) team up with others.[27] Obviously, we agree with these excellent starting points.

Given the inherent complexity of brand activism, our hope is that you have found our perspectives, dozens of additional lessons, and hundreds of examples of value, based on the local, global, applied, empirical as well as theoretical backdrop we have provided. We urge businesses of all sizes and sectors to follow our lead and develop their own doctrines of brand activism.

References

1   Sheth, Jagdish N. (2002), "A Generic Concept of Customer Behavior," *Journal of Customer Behavior*, 1(1), 7–18.
    Sheth, Jagdish N. and Can Uslay (2022), "Creating Enduring Customer Value," *Journal of Creating Value*, 8(2), 241–252.
    Malhotra, Naresh K., Can Uslay, and Nelson Oly Ndubisi (2008), "Commentary on "The Essence of Business Marketing Theory, Research and Tactics: Contributions by the Journal of Business-to-Business Marketing," by Lichtenthal, Mummalaneni, and Wilson: A Paradigm Shift and Prospection Through Expanded Roles of Buyers and Sellers," *Journal of Business-to-Business Marketing*, 15(2), 204–217.
2   Gassmann, Peter and Will Jackson-Moore "The CEO's ESG Dilemma," *Harvard Law School Forum on Corporate Governance*, January 23, 2023. https://corpgov.law.harvard.edu/2023/01/23/the-ceos-esg-dilemma/.
3   Chu, Shu-Chuan, Hyejin Kim, and Yoojung Kim (2023), "When Brand Get Real: The Role of Authenticity and Electronic Word of Mouth in Shaping Consumer Response to Brands Taking a Stand," *International Journal of Advertising*, 42(6), 1037–1064.
4   Wallach, Karen Anne and Deidre Popovich (2022), "Cause Beneficial or Cause Exploitative? Using Motives to Increase Credibility of Sustainability Efforts," *Journal of Public Policy & Marketing*, 42(2), 187–202.
5   Myers, Owen, "Panic and Rash Decision-Making: Ex-Bud-Light Staff on One of the Biggest Boycotts in US History," *The Guardian*, September 19, 2023 (accessed September 8, 2024). https://www.theguardian.com/world/2023/sep/19/dylan-mulvaney-bud-light-boycott.
6   Kotler, P., & Lee, N. (2005), *Corporate Social Responsibility: Doing the Most Good for Company and Your Cause*. Wiley.
7   Porter, M., and M. Kramer. 2002. "The Competitive Advantage of Corporate Philanthropy," *Harvard Business Review* (December), 57–68.
8   Blocker, Christopher P., Joseph P. Cannon, and Jonathan Z. Zhang (2024), "Purpose Orientation: An Emerging Theory Transforming Business for a Better World," *Journal of the Academy of Marketing Science*. https://doi.org/10.1007/s11747-023-00989-5.
9   Nickerson, Dionne, Sundar Bharadwaj, and Omar Rodriguez-Vila (2023), "Antecedents and Consequences of an Inclusive Brand Marketing," *Marketing Science Institute Working Paper Series*, 23–138.
10 Ahmad, Fayez, Francisco Guzman, and Md Al-Emran (2024), "Brand Activism and The Consequence of Woke Washing," *Journal of Business Research*, 170, 1–16.
11 Ahmad, Fayez, Francisco Guzman, and Md Al-Emran (2024), "Brand Activism and The Consequence of Woke Washing," *Journal of Business Research*, 170, 1–16.
12 Whitler, Kimberly, and Thomas Barta (2024), "The Enterprise Activism Risk Model: How Good Intentions Can Jeopardize Business Success," *Journal of Retailing*, 100(2), 330–340.
13 On the other hand, Starbucks' "Race Together" campaign did not reflect the company's own internal reality. All but one of the directors on its board of 20 were white. For brand activism to be perceived as authentic, your company should demonstrate genuine commitment through tangible actions and policies that reflect its values.
    Morrison, K., "What went wrong with the Starbucks #RaceTogether campaign?" *Adweek*, March 25, 2015 (accessed October 31, 2024). https://www.adweek.com/digital/starbucks-race-togethercampaign/

14   Sheth, Jagdish N. (2011), "Impact of Emerging Markets on Marketing: Rethinking Existing Perspectives and Practices," *Journal of Marketing*, 75(4), 166–182.

15   As an example of a change of practice, since "Race Together," Starbucks can boast that almost half of its board is now composed of people of color (albeit having downsized its board to 11). In fact, its Chairwoman even started calling out others, stating that failure to add people of color to leadership is akin to "committing corporate suicide." It will be interesting to see how the board compositions will evolve during the second Trump administration. The times they are a-changin'.
Brooks, Khristopher J., "Starbucks Chair Says Lack of Boardroom Diversity is 'Corporate Suicide'," *CBS News*, April 22, 2021 (accessed October 31, 2024). https://www.cbsnews.com/news/starbucks-hobson-diversity-suicide-bowdoin-boardroom/.

16   Mirzaei, Abas, Dean C. Wilkie, and Helen Siuki (2022), "Woke Brand Activism Authenticity or Lack the of It," *Journal of Business Research*, 139 (February), 1–22.

17   Sheth, Jagdish N. and Can Uslay (2022), "Creating Enduring Customer Value," *Journal of Creating Value*, 8(2), 241–252.

18   Malshe, Ashwin, Yi Yin, Anatoli Colicev, Yakov Bart, and Koen Pauwels (2023), "How ESG Reduces Risk: The Role of Consumers and Institutional Investors," *MSI Report*, 23–129. https://www.msi.org/working-paper/how-esg-reduces-risk-the-role-of-consumers-and-institutional-investors/

19   We thank an editor of a publishing group other than our publisher, Routledge, for bringing the perception "everything is either MyPillow or hopelessly woke," to our attention.

20   Unlike white families, underrepresented minorities in the US do not have $150,000 to invest in the stock market. (The average stock holdings is $80,000 for Black families and $97,000 for Hispanics, in contrast with $568,000 for White families). Furthermore, 61% of Black and 72% of Hispanic families do not participate at all in the stock market (as opposed to 34% of White families); 14% of Blacks and 11% of Hispanics in the US do not even have any bank accounts! Significant gaps also exist for retirement accounts in that 60% of White families have them versus 35% of Black and 28% of Hispanic families. The disparities do not end there. For example, Scott Galloway has been whistle-blowing that the elderly have been stealing the future of the young by hoarding wealth. The top 1% owns over 30% of the wealth in the US. Even the billionaires who pledged to give the most of their wealth away in their lifetime have seen their collective wealth triple over the past decade.
Desilver, Drew, "A Booming U.S. Stock Market Doesn't Benefit All Racial and Ethnic Groups Equally," *Pew Research Center*, March 6, 2024 (accessed March 8, 2025). https://www.pewresearch.org/short-reads/2024/03/06/a-booming-us-stock-market-doesnt-benefit-all-racial-and-ethnic-groups-equally/. ABA Banking Journal, "Fed Survey: Unbanked Status Continues to Vary Among Income, Ethnic Groups," May 21, 2024 (accessed March 8, 2025). https://bankingjournal.aba.com/2024/05/fed-survey-unbanked-status-continues-to-vary-among-income-ethnic-groups/. Galloway, Scott "Hoarders," *Medium*. June 7, 2024 (accessed March 8, 2025). https://medium.com/@profgalloway/hoarders-e52abf6c4e0a

21 "Achieve Gender Equality and Empower All Women and Girls," *United Nations* (accessed November 1, 2024). https://www.un.org/sustainabledevelopment/gender-equality/.

22 Coined by Nobel Laureate Herbert Simon in 1956, "satisficing" (satisfy + suffice) refers to decision-making where acceptable solutions are chosen over the best option due to complexity or cognitive limitations.

23 Aitken, Lucy, "What Brand Purpose Is… and What It Isn't," *WARC*, June 13, 2017 (accessed November 1, 2024). https://www.warc.com/newsandopinion/opinion/what-brand-purpose-is-and-what-it-isnt/en-gb/2447.

24 Moorman, Christine (2020), "Commentary: Brand Activism in a Political World," *Journal of Public Policy & Marketing*, 39(4), 388–392.

25 Verlegh, Peter (2024), "Perspectives: A Research-Based Guide for Brand Activism," *International Journal of Advertising*, 43(2), 388-402. https://www.tandfonline.com/doi/full/10.1080/02650487.2023.2228117.

26 As per the editor of a leading business press.

27 Meyer, Alex Eben, "Reducing the Risks of Corporate Activism," *Harvard Business Review*, November-December 2024 (accessed October 24, 2024). https://hbr.org/2024/11/reducing-the-risks-of-corporate-activism.

APPENDIX

In this appendix, we summarize and evaluate over 100 examples of brand activism. These include pull and push activism examples of global companies as well as local brands, products and services, retail and experience, e-commerce brands, and more. Before you jump in, please recall the Five Rings that constitute the basis for our scoring from Chapter 2:

Ring One: Mission, Vision, Cause
Ring Two: Passion and Brand Purpose
Ring Three: Business and Cause
Ring Four: A Legacy of Commitment
Ring Five: Authenticity

Table 1 100+ Cases of Brand Activism Scored

Focal company	Year	Activism	Aftermath	Score (5/5)
Wedgwood[1]	1787	The pottery firm produced medallions titled "Am I Not a Man and a Brother?" depicting a slave in chains. This medallion was released in the UK to support the abolishment of slavery.	Became a popular accessory for abolitionists in the UK who prominently displayed them on their clothes and in their homes.	5/5
Cadbury[2]	1879	Built a village called Bournville to improve work conditions. Each house came with a garden. The village also had many recreational facilities.	Increased employee morale and productivity, and became a role model for other companies due to its success.	5/5
Lever Brothers (now Unilever)[3]	1888	Like Cadbury, they built a village called Port Sunlight for their employees. The objective was to cultivate a "familial atmosphere."	Increased employee productivity and mood.	5/5
YMCA[4]	1914	Provided British Dominion, Chinese, and Portuguese troops with centers to unwind during WWI. After the Armistice in 1918, they provided free meals and facilities for 70,000 prisoners of war.	It is estimated that the YMCA spent $265.5 million (or $5.57 billion in today's money) during the war. The move further established their mission and helped establish them as patriotic.	4/5

(Continued)

Table 1 (Continued)

Focal company	Year	Activism	Aftermath	Score (5/5)
Coca-Cola[5]	1941	President of the company declared "that every man in uniform gets a bottle of Coca-Cola for 5 cents, wherever he is and whatever it costs the Company."	Established the brand as patriotic. Over 5 billion bottles of Coca-Cola were consumed during the war.	5/5
Levi Strauss & Co.[6]	1942	Hired Black sewing machine operators and laborers in factories.	Many existing employees resisted and some even quit, but this move likely helped Levi's reach younger, more socially active audiences.	4/5
Levi Strauss & Co.[7]	1960	When the city of Blackstone, VA, required Levi's to have their facility segregated, they fought to open one of the first desegregated facilities four years before the Civil Rights Act was passed.	Further strengthened Levi's brand around their main customer base.	4.5/5
Mary Quant[8]	1965	Sold miniskirts to the public as a symbol of women's liberation movement.	Miniskirts became extremely popular. Estimated that 7 million consumers owned an item with her logo by 1969. Quant also received an OBE[9] from the British Government for her contributions.[10]	5/5

Benetton[11]	1965	Used "shockvertising" for awareness and to challenge the public on social issues.	Sparked major controversies, but also boosted sales leading to Benetton opening 7,000 stores worldwide by the 1990s.	4/5
The Body Shop[12]	1976	Launched the company using ethically sourced and naturally based ingredients.	Helped The Body Shop reach socially active audiences, which later became their main customer base and led to international expansion.	4.5/5
Levi Strauss & Co.[13]	1982	Funded efforts to end HIV/AIDS and the discrimination faced by people living with it.	Companies and organizations in over 40 countries also stood up against the issue, contributing to a steady decline of HIV/AIDS.	4/5
Virgin[14]	1985	Virgin, fueled by Richard Branson's audacious spirit, has a long history of entwining business with social activism. One prominent example is an ongoing fight against HIV/ AIDS. When the disease was shrouded in fear and stigma in the 1980s, Virgin launched the non-profit, low-cost "Mates condoms."	Beyond awareness, Virgin actively supported research and treatment initiatives through the Virgin Unite Foundation. The sustained efforts to combat HIV/AIDS have undoubtedly contributed to raising awareness, reducing stigma, and promoting global health initiatives.	4/5

(Continued)

Table 1 (Continued)

Focal company	Year	Activism	Aftermath	Score (5/5)
Ben & Jerry's[15]	1988	Released "Rainforest Crunch" flavor, which was marketed as a means to support indigenous communities in the Amazon and help stop deforestation.	The campaign failed when the Orlando Sentinel reported that only 5% of the nuts were sourced from the Amazon, causing backlash.	2/5
New Belgium Brewing Company[16]	1991	Fort Collins, CO, based company gave equal benefits to LGBTQ+ spouses in 1991. Offered additional benefits in 2016 such as a wellness clinic, an all-expenses free trip to Belgium, and anniversary bike rides.[17]	The company grew revenues successfully while receiving a perfect 100 score from the HRC as one of the best places to work for LGBTQ+ community.	4/5
Disney[18]	1995	Offered health benefits to LGBTQ+ partners.	Disney did not back down despite the conservative boycott and gradually gained support from other businesses.	4/5
Etsy[19]	2005	The online marketplace for handmade and vintage goods empowers independent artisans and small businesses around the world. Its mission is to "keep commerce human," and prioritizes supporting creative entrepreneurs.	Its fight for fair competition and net neutrality has found support among the public.	3/5

TOMS[20]	2006	Advertised themselves as charitable with their "One for One" model, where they would donate one pair of shoes for each shoe sold.	Gained a lot of free press, which helped them sell 10,000 shoes in their first year.[21] A year later, the company was worth $625 million.[22]	5/5
Dr. Bronner's Magic Soaps[23]	2007	Adopted fair trade and gave employee benefits. Advocated regenerative organic agriculture, animal welfare, and drug policy reform. A certified B Corporation, it received the second-highest score (178) on the B Impact Assessment.	Gave jobs to hundreds of people in developing countries. Their fair trade practices helped them stay afloat during the pandemic and even grow by 46%.	4.5/5
Eileen Fisher[24]	2009	Dedicated to sustainability and social responsibility, the fashion brand prioritizes using organic and recycled materials, reducing waste, and supporting fair labor. With its "Renew" program, customers can return used items for resale or recycling.	"Renew" has diverted over 2.3 million garments from landfills since 2009, reselling, donating, or remaking them into new designs. This initiative has not only reduced waste, but also fostered customer loyalty and positioned Eileen Fisher as a leader in sustainable fashion.	4/5

(Continued)

Table 1 (Continued)

Focal company	Year	Activism	Aftermath	Score (5/5)
The Body Shop[25]	2009	Partnered with anti-trafficking organization ECPAT International to launch the "Stop Trafficking of Children and Young People Campaign" to bring an end to sex trafficking worldwide.	Their largest campaign ever, it gathered over 7 million signatures globally and 24 countries adopted new legislation. The petition was presented to the UN three years later.	4/5
Dawn[26]	2010	Released an ad expressing support for wildlife amid the BP oil spill. Raised up to $500,000 for wildlife groups.	The campaign generated a lot of positive buzz in the media while establishing Dawn's soap as an environmentally friendly "bird cleaner of choice."	3.5/5
Everlane[27]	2010	The founding mission of the direct-to-consumer clothing brand focused on pricing transparency in its supply chain, revealing the true cost of each item and the factories where they are made.	The unique business model has helped the company flourish. It had its most profitable year in 2023, with about $200 million in revenues.[28]	4/5
Chipotle[29]	2011	Partnered with farmers and started using pasture-raised animals in their food.	Helped to further position Chipotle offerings as high quality, fresh, and cruelty-free.	4/5
Warby Parker[30]	2011	Started the "Buy a Pair, Give a Pair" campaign, promising to give a pair of glasses to someone in need for every pair sold.	The campaign was a success, Warby Parker sold and donated 10 million glasses by 2022.	4/5

	Year			Rating
Chick-Fil-A[31]	2012	Donated large amounts of money to conservative anti-gay organizations. CEO Dan Cathy made anti-gay marriage statements.	#ChickFilGay became popular on social media with chicken recipes as an alternative in order to boycott the company. Chick-Fil-A later stopped donating money to these organizations.[32] Amid protests, CEO Dan Cathy admitted his statements made "the company a symbol in the marriage debate" and it would've been wiser "to stay focused on customer service."[33]	2/5
IKEA[34]	2012	Released the "People and Planet Positive" strategy to help IKEA be more energy independent and help millions live sustainably.	Made their stores more cost-effective. For example: IKEA used 85% less on lighting by relying on solar energy more.	4.5/5
Love Your Melon[35]	2012	The start-up that started with an entrepreneurship class sells beanies and mittens and donates $1 per item to organizations fighting pediatric cancer.	The company has given away over 270,000 beanies and over $9.8 million to date.	4/5

(Continued)

Table 1 (Continued)

Focal company	Year	Activism	Aftermath	Score (5/5)
LSTN	2012	This headphone company donates a portion of its profits to hearing restoration programs and promotes employee volunteerism.	Through a partnership with the Starkey Hearing Foundation, it has provided hearing aids to over 50,000 people in need.	4/5
Lush[36]	2012	To protest animal testing, they staged a performance lasting ten hours outside their flagship store in London to bring awareness to the horrors of the practice. The performance was also meant to symbolize the systemic abuse of women.	Received criticism due to the peculiar nature of this performance. Many were grossed out by their unorthodox approach to combat animal testing.	2.5/5
Tentree Apparel[37]	2012	Promised to plant ten trees for every piece of apparel sold.	Became popular with consumers; Planted 6 million trees by 2015 and 30 million by 2019. Their Instagram page has more than 2.7 million followers and one of their posts became the third most liked post on Instagram at the time.[38]	4.5/5
The Honest Company[39]	2012	The consumer goods company founded by Jessica Alba focuses on safe and natural products has a commitment to social responsibility. Staff are encouraged to volunteer for various causes.	The non-toxic product company became a unicorn in 2015 and went public in 2021.	4/5

Bombas[40]	2013	Donated a pair of socks to the homeless for every pair purchased. This closely followed the "One for One" model of TOMS.	They have sold and donated 8 million pairs of socks at an average retail price of $12/pair.	4/5
Coca-Cola[41]	2013	Released an advertising campaign to bring attention to obesity.	Received mixed reactions, some praising the message while others seeing it as an ironic and desperate act to help with the company's declining sales.	2/5
Unilever[42]	2013	Released "Project Sunlight," a campaign dedicated to promoting sustainable living practices.	Received 2.5 million likes on Facebook and 4 million views in just a few days.	4/5
Who Gives a Crap[43]	2013	The toilet paper start-up began donating 50% of their profits to non-profits improving sanitation infrastructure.	Helped build a strong customer base and spread their influence through word of mouth. This helped them experience exponential growth in 2020 when customers were panic buying toilet paper due to the outbreak.[44]	4/5

(Continued)

Table 1 (Continued)

Focal company	Year	Activism	Aftermath	Score (5/5)
Always[45]	2014	Began the "Like a Girl" campaign, bringing awareness to gender stereotypes and norms.	The ad got 76 million views with 4.5 billion impressions worldwide. #LikeAGirl trended on Twitter with around 600,000 mentions, including from singers, actors, and athletes. Always double its number of Twitter followers.	4.5/5
Bill and Melinda Gates Foundation[46]	2014	Divested tens of millions of dollars from private security firm G4S after the non-profit War on Want accused them of inhumanely treating Palestinian prisoners.	Prompted many others to divest. G4S pledged to not renew their 3-year contract after it expires.[47]	3.5/5
Cotopaxi Outdoor Clothing[48]	2014	Held the "Questival", an adventure race where teams of friends would complete tasks such as running miles to volunteering. Used this as an opportunity to expose consumers to the brand.	The competition had 5,000 participants and the Questival got 30,000 social media hits. Within five years they held another hundred more Questivals around the country.	4.5/5
Greenpeace[49]	2014	Greenpeace activists unfurled a massive banner proclaiming "Time for Change! The Future Is Renewable" next to a hummingbird	The demonstration backfired, generating outrage in Peru for disrespecting a sacred cultural site. This "ecofundamentalist" act, intended to promote	1.5/5

		Geoglyph/Nazca Lines, a UNESCO World Heritage site. This audacious act was intended to spur action at a UN climate conference in Lima.	renewable energy, was condemned as a violation of cultural heritage and a transgression of free speech. Greenpeace was forced to apologize.	
Hobby Lobby[50]	2014	The Supreme Court ruled in favor of Hobby Lobby, a craft store chain owned by a Christian family, exempting it from providing contraception coverage to employees under the Affordable Care Act due to religious objections.	The ruling put the company on the map and sparked a national debate about religious freedom and women's healthcare rights. A poll indicated that Americans were divided roughly evenly on the issue (49% disapprove; 47% approve).[51]	3.5/5
Lego[52]	2014	Ended their 50-year-old partnership with Shell due to their involvement in oil drilling in the Alaskan Arctic. This decision was made after much campaigning from Greenpeace, which released a YouTube video titled "Everything is not awesome" portraying a Lego recreation of the Arctic being covered in oil, which got 6 million views.	Shell ultimately ended their plans for drilling in the Arctic. Many Greenpeace activists and others praised Lego for their decision to end the partnership valued at £68M ($72.8M).	2.5/5

(Continued)

Table 1 (Continued)

Focal company	Year	Activism	Aftermath	Score (5/5)
Lemonade[53]	2015	This insurance company donates leftover premiums to charities chosen by its customers; also encourages employee volunteerism.	While Lemonade is not yet profitable, it has achieved over $120 million in revenues in 2023 and growing fast in a highly competitive sector with entrenched incumbents.	4/5
PGGM[54]	2014	Divested from Israeli banks that were involved in financing settlements in occupied Palestinian territories.	Faced major backlash from Israeli politicians after banks reported losses of millions of dollars. Meanwhile, the decision was welcomed by Palestinians.	3/5
Stella Artois[55]	2014	Partnered with Water.org and launched the "Buy a Lady a Drink" campaign, giving water to women in developing countries.	This campaign, lasting for three years, successfully brought awareness to the water crisis while also enabling Stella Artois to reach a more socially aware audience.	4/5
Adidas[56]	2015	Partnered with the non-profit "Parley for the Oceans" to create a limited edition drop of 7,000 pairs of sneakers. The equivalent of 11 plastic bottles was used for each sneaker.	The shoes sold out instantly. Three years later, Adidas announced it would sell 5 million more sneakers and was expected to make $1	4.5/5

	Year			Rating
REI[57]	2015	Began the #OptOutside movement, encouraging consumers to spend Black Friday outside instead of shopping. They also closed all their stores for Black Friday.	billion in revenue. They also announced that they would use 100% recycled polyester in all of their products. The campaign netted a 7,000% increase in social impressions due to the free press it received and got 2.7 billion media impressions in the first 24 hours.[58] REI's PR agency also won nine Cannes Lions.	4.5/5
Rothy's[59]	2015	Presented itself as an eco-friendly footwear option with its flat shoes made of recycled water bottles.	Became popular among Generation Z consumers and got many fans, including celebrities like Meghan Markle. This helped Rothy's make $140 million in 2018.	4/5
Walmart[60]	2015	CEO Doug McMillon got involved after Walmart's home state passed legislation that enabled discrimination against LGBTQ+ people for religious reasons.	Arkansas Governor vetoed the legislation.	4/5

(Continued)

Table 1 (Continued)

Focal company	Year	Activism	Aftermath	Score (5/5)
Chobani[61]	2016	Supported immigrants and refugees by hiring them. CEO Hamdi Ulukaya also started a non-profit called the Tent Partnership for refugees.	Got dozens of brands such as Microsoft, Hilton, and Uniqlo to pledge to help refugees.	4/5
Cora[62]	2016	Feminine hygiene company partnered with non-profits to provide menstrual products and education to girls in developing countries.	With over 24 million products given to date, this "buy one, give one" model not only appealed to consumers' desire to give back but also helped Cora establish a strong brand identity centered around social impact. The products are available through Target.	4/5
Dove[63]	2016	Started the Real Beauty campaign, aiming to build self-confidence among women.	Brand awareness increased with free marketing coverage valued at $150 million.	4/5
Girlfriend Collective[64]	2016	Used unedited pictures and diverse models to advertise their leisurewear. This was to give realistic body expectations and encourage body positivity.	Became popular among many consumers and sparked the attention of celebrities such as Arianna Grande and Kendall Jenner. This later earned them the People's 2022 Style Awards.[65]	4/5

Grubhub[66]	2016	CEO Matt Maloney sent an email to all employees citing "nationalist, anti-immigrant, and hateful politics of Donald Trump," and asked employees to resign if they disagreed.	When media reported, the hashtag #boycottgrubhub gained popularity. Maloney removed himself from Twitter amid backlash. Stock dropped 9% but recovered after a month.	1.5/5
New Balance[67]	2016	VP of Public Affairs Matt LeBretton told The Wall Street Journal that "The Obama administration turned a deaf ear to us and, frankly, with President-elect Trump, we feel things are going to move in the right direction" as a comment on trade policies.	A white supremacist blogger called New Balance shoes the "the official shoes of White [sic] people." Many videos of customers burning their New Balance shoes in protest began circulating. New Balance responded by dismissing this claim and started to hire more minority employees.	2/5
Patagonia[68]	2016	Donated 100% of Black Friday sales to environmental organizations to "ensure the US remains fully committed to … Paris Climate Agreement."	Campaign was very well received. Black Friday sales broke company records and exceeded $10 million instead of the projected $2 million.	4.5/5
Penzeys Spices[69]	2016	CEO Bill Penzey made multiple pro-impeachment statements about Trump.	Sales of spice spiked by 60% and orders for gift boxes grew by 135%.	4/5

(Continued)

Table 1 (Continued)

Focal company	Year	Activism	Aftermath	Score (5/5)
Ben & Jerry's[70]	2017	Banned selling two scoops of ice cream of the same flavor to protest Australia's laws on gay marriage.	72% of Australians supported same-sex marriage at the time.[71] After much controversy, the Australian government legalized gay marriage. Ben and Jerry's received strong praise from the LGBTQ+ community.	4/5
Cartier[72]	2017	Stopped the import of gems from Myanmar whose exports fund the Burmese military. This boycott was due to Myanmar's role in the genocide of Rohingya Muslims.	The boycott contributed to Myanmar's gemstone exports falling by 65% causing a significant decrease in military spending.[73]	3.5/5
Dove[74]	2017	In a follow-up campaign, Dove released body wash in six differently shaped bottles (e.g., tall and lean vs. heavily proportioned to the bottom).	The campaign was called offensive and reductive. Some bottles offered functional advantages, which was counterproductive to the intent of the campaign.	1.5/5

L.L. Bean, Amazon, Miller Coors, Walmart[75]	2017	Donated large amounts of money to the Trump Administration along with around 46 other companies.	Trump broke US Office of Government Ethics policy against endorsing brands when he said "Buy L.L. Bean."[76] #GrabYourWallet campaign took off, causing massive boycotts against these companies.	2/5
Lyft[77]	2017	President Joe Zimmer called the company and its community woke to position Lyft as the "woke alternative" to Uber.	The statement was criticized as Lyft's model was not that different from Uber. Uber also started to let customers tip drivers months later.	3/5
Papa John's[78]	2017	Brand was hijacked and became symbol of neo-Nazis after founder Joe Schnatter tied financial performance to NFL protests during an earnings call.	Sales declined 7.3%, Schnatter was forced out, and Papa John's spent $5.8 million on rebranding. It also made an endorsement deal with Shaquille O'Neal.	2/5
Starbucks[79]	2017	Promised to hire 10,000 refugees amid the four-month refugee moratorium under Trump.	Republicans boycotted the brand with #BoycottStarbucks trending on Facebook. However, many supported the move. Stock price impact was minimal.	4/5

(Continued)

Table 1 (Continued)

Focal company	Year	Activism	Aftermath	Score (5/5)
The Body Shop[80]	2017	Called for a worldwide ban on animal testing in cosmetic products by 2020 and released a petition for the public to sign. Launched #ForeverAgainstAnimalTesting to raise awareness.	The petition gained 8 million signatures and the hashtag went viral. The campaign reached a total of 26 million people. The Body Shop received 54,000 followers and over 5,000 comments related to the campaign.	4/5
Uber[81]	2017	Undermining NYC Taxi Driver Strike against Trump's travel ban.	#deleteuber became a movement and Uber's lead over Lyft in app downloads deteriorated from three digits to two.[82] Lyft donated $1 million to ACLU instead.	2/5
Brewdog[83]	2018	Launched the "Beer for Girls" campaign and sold beer to individuals identifying as women for a lower price (20% less). This was meant to address gender stereotypes and the pay gap.	Received positive reactions from Twitter. However, many criticized them for poor execution.	2.5/5
Dick's Sporting Goods[84]	2018	The company stopped selling all assault-style rifles and instituted 21-years age requirement for all gun sales following a school shooting in Florida.	The company chose to destroy $5 million in inventory rather than returning them to the manufacturers. Stock	4/5

Company	Year	Action	Outcome	Rating
			was unaffected.[85] The age requirement was also adopted by Walmart, Kroger, L.L. Bean.	
Delta Air Lines[86]	2018	Delta stopped offering discounts for NRA members following a school shooting in Florida.	CEO Ed Bastion stated they did not want to be seen as an advocate of NRA and maintained the decision was not political.	4/5
Levi Strauss & Co.[87]	2018	CEO Charles Bergh took a stance on gun control and the company set aside $1 million for non-profits and activists supporting gun control.	Faced backlash from gun-rights activists, including boycotts and threats. 2018 revenue increased by $600 million, however.[88]	3.5/5
Lush	2018	Had a whistleblowing campaign against unethical undercover detective actions. Decorated storefronts with fake police tape.	While criticized by the home secretary, the campaign brought to light uncomfortable truths and was appreciated by the public.	3.5/5
Lyft[89]	2018	Announced that it will become 100% carbon neutral through investing in offset projects with a goal of removing 1 million metric tons of carbon.	Appealed to environmentally conscious customers and contributed to their overall brand identity as the "Woke alternative to Uber."	4/5

(Continued)

Table 1 (Continued)

Focal company	Year	Activism	Aftermath	Score (5/5)
Nike[90]	2018	Released an ad titled "Dream Crazy" featuring Colin Kaepernick, an NFL athlete who had begun kneeling for the national anthem as a protest against racial injustice.	The advertisement won an Emmy award and the company had a spike in sales with a jump in income to $847 million.[91]	4.5/5
Starbucks[92]	2018	Two Black men were arrested in a Starbucks store in Philadelphia when employees called local authorities.	Starbucks put social justice over profit and closed 8,000 stores for a day to teach employees about unconscious bias. It is estimated it lost $16.7 million that day and another $16 million due to negative press.[93]	2.5/5
Yoplait[94]	2018	Released an ad supporting mothers and brought awareness to the criticism and judgment they face.	Was very well received by the audience and brand interest increased by 1,461%.	3/5
Gillette[95]	2019	Released an ad campaign addressing toxic masculinity and promised to donate $1 million to non-profits that promote boys and men being good role models.	#GilletteAd became trending on Twitter and the advertisement gained 12 million views on YouTube in a few days. The sentiment was mostly negative.	2/5

Gucci	2019	Gucci released a $890 black sweater that featured thick red lips when pulled up across the face; resembling blackface.	Gucci CEO admitted to a big mistake due to cultural ignorance and apologized.[96]	1/5
Nike	2019	Nike pulled the Betsy Ross flag (with 13 stars) from stores after Colin Kaepernick criticized the decision.	While the flag was not necessarily considered a symbol of hate or racism, Nike opted to be consistent and not to risk controversy with an Independence Day launch.[97]	3/5
The North Face[98]	2019	The outdoor wear company launched a campaign called "Walls Are Meant for Climbing," featuring images of climbers scaling walls and advocating for unity and inclusivity.	The campaign sparked controversy due to its timing, coinciding with heated debates about border walls and immigration policies. While some praised the brand for its bold stance, others criticized it for exploiting a political issue for marketing purposes.	4/5
Unilever India[99]	2019	Released an ad promoting peace between Hindus and Muslims. The ad depicted a young Hindu girl protecting a Muslim boy from ruining his thawb as he was on his way to a mosque to pray.	The ad was appreciated by both communities and many found it heartwarming and wholesome.	4/5

(Continued)

Table 1 (Continued)

Focal company	Year	Activism	Aftermath	Score (5/5)
Zomato[100]	2019	When a customer requested a different delivery person because of their religion, CEO Deepinder Goyal took a stand: "the company as well as food does not discriminate on the basis of caste, creed, and religion."	A lot of people supported the stand, but a few supported the customer and #BoycottZomato trended on Twitter.	3.5/5
Ben & Jerry's[101]	2020	Released multiple statements about promoting Black Lives Matter, defunding the police, and the roots of white supremacy after the BLM movement gained traction.	The company was praised by many social activists online applauding their dedication to combating these issues.	3.5/5
CrossFit[102]	2020	CEO Greg Glassman responded to a tweet by the Institute of Health Metrics and Evaluation, which declared racism and discrimination a critical public health issue with "It's FLOYD-19."	Faced a lot of backlash. Reebok and its affiliated gyms dropped their partnerships. Glassman apologized and stepped down.	2.5/5
Goya Foods[103]	2020	CEO Robert Unanue praised Trump for signing the executive order to launch the Hispanic Prosperity Initiative.	Faced instant backlash from Twitter. Despite this, the company had a 22% increase in sales.	3.5/5

L'Oreal[104]	2020	Expressed support for BLM and had many of their brands, such as Urban Decay, Maybelline, and NYX, donate money to BLM and the Minnesota Freedom Fund (an organization that helps bail arrested people).	Former L'Oreal ambassador and transgender model Munroe Bergdorf[105] spoke out against the hypocrisy of this support, revealing how she was fired by them after speaking out about white supremacy in 2017. The company immediately asked her to rejoin.[106]	2/5
Maple Leaf	2020	After one of his employees lost his family, CEO Michael McCain tweeted his anger at Trump and the US administration for escalating tensions with Iran.	The heartfelt message received attention and media coverage with 63,000 likes as opposed to the dozens the company's official tweets get. Even though McCain tweeted from his personal account, calls for a boycott sprung up in the US.[107]	4/5
Nike[108]	2020	Responded to unrest in America after the George Floyd incident with an ad and multiple Twitter statements. Nike revamped their famous motto in an ad: "For once, don't do it. Don't pretend there's not a problem in America. Don't turn your back on racism."	According to a study, consumers aged 16–48 perceived it as more empowering than 98% of other ads. Even long-time rival Adidas retweeted the statement. The campaign was widely regarded as one of the most authentic brand responses.	5/5

(Continued)

Table 1 (Continued)

Focal company	Year	Activism	Aftermath	Score (5/5)
Pernod Ricard[109]	2020	Launched the "#EngageResponsibly" campaign investing in solutions for marketers to collaborate with platforms to stop the spread of hate speech.	Garnered significant media attention, benefiting the company's visibility and reputation.	3.5/5
Tanishq[110]	2020	The Indian jewelry brand released an ad as part of their "Ektavam" (oneness) campaign, depicting an interfaith couple and their in-laws observing a baby shower.	Many consumers called for boycotts complaining that the advertisement glorified "Love Jihad"[111] and #BoycottTanishq trended. Tanishq had to apologize and withdrew the ad. Titan, who Tanishq is a subsidiary of, faced a 2.6% drop in shares on the Bombay Stock Exchange.	2/5
Uber[112]	2020	Uber tried to turn the tables around with a campaign "If you tolerate racism, delete Uber" using Wieden+Kennedy as its advertising agency.	It was criticized as being opportunistic, especially when Uber was found to employ price discrimination in non-white neighborhoods and was critiqued for unfair labor practices.	3/5

Company	Year	Action	Rating
Unilever, North Face, Microsoft and others[113]	2020	Halted all paid advertising activity on Facebook in support of the #StopHateForProfit campaign. The campaign was launched due to the lack of moderation on Facebook, allowing violent or racist content to spread.	Facebook shares dropped 8.3%, losing $55.6 billion from the total market value of $615.8 billion. The company hired more moderators rebranded itself as Meta in 2021.	4/5
Airbnb[114]	2021	Housed 20,000 Afghan refugees and asylum seekers partnering with non-profits and charities to help with hosting.	Earned praise among young and multicultural consumers. A study found, "supporting immigrants and refugees" was one of the top five main social issues Americans were passionate about.[115]	4/5
Boots[116]	2021	Boots, the largest health and beauty retailer in the UK, launched "Ani" (Action Needed Immediately) initiative, which allowed discreet victims of domestic abuse to seek assistance from Boots pharmacists using the code word "Ani."[117]	Thousands of pharmacists received training on domestic violence. Despite implementation challenges, the activism was considered to be on the mark and received acclaim.	4.5/5
Lyft[118]	2021	Covered all legal fees for employees after a new Texas law punishing drivers for driving customers to abortion centers was passed. Also pledged to donate $1 million to Planned Parenthood.	Gained traction and was widely supported. Uber followed, stating it would do the same. Helped further establish their brand image as the "Woke alternative to Uber."	4.5/5

(Continued)

Table 1 (Continued)

Focal company	Year	Activism	Aftermath	Score (5/5)
MyPillow[119]	2021	CEO and Founder Mike Lindell provided data suggesting that the 2020 elections were rigged. He displayed them at a Cyber Symposium in Sioux Falls and offered $5 million for anyone who can disprove the claim calling it the "Prove Mike Wrong Challenge."	Faced over $1.3 billion in lawsuits from voting machine companies for his acts of defamation. Software engineer Robert Zeidman disproved the claim and, after an arbitration case, won the $5 million.	3/5
Olay[120]	2021	Partnered with activist Joy Buolamwini and launched the "#DecodetheBias" campaign against discriminatory algorithm bias and help send more than 1,000 girls to a code camp with the non-profit Black Girls Code.	Well received by the media and generated a lot of free press. Buolamwini's partnership made the campaign look more authentic.	4/5
Zillow[121]	2021	Zillow, the online real estate marketplace, has taken a proactive stance on fair housing and combating discrimination in the real estate industry. Launched an initiative to address housing discrimination by providing resources and education.	Zillow's efforts aim to create a more equitable and transparent housing market, ensuring that everyone has access to fair housing opportunities regardless of race, ethnicity, or other protected characteristics.	4/5

Google[122]	2022	Pledged to completely delete users' location history for sensitive locations such as abortion clinics and domestic violence shelters.	As of August 2024, they have yet to do this. Many have criticized the company for its unwillingness to keep the promise. Many US senators have also scrutinized the company.	1/5
Halifax Bank[123]	2022	Gave their employees preferred pronoun badges as a solution to accidental misgendering. Told customers to leave if they didn't agree with the bank's policies.	Stirred outrage among many netizens, calling it "virtue signaling." Lost hundreds of thousands of dollars and hundreds of customers.	1.5/5
Peta[124]	2018	Ran a boycott against Burberry for using exotic fur.	Burberry banned exotic skin products and shifted to animal-free materials after seven years.	3/5
Seventh Generation[125]	2022	Evolved its brand to convey the message of environmental sustainability through changes in logo and packaging, adding emphasis to their organic eco-friendly products.	Gave consumers an environmentally conscious choice, which led to a peak revenue of $200 million in 2023.[126]	3.5/5

(Continued)

Table 1 (Continued)

Focal company	Year	Activism	Aftermath	Score (5/5)
Allbirds[127]	2023	Created a net zero carbon shoe and spent $50 million on marketing itself as an eco-friendly brand.	Net revenue decreased 14.7%. However, this can also be attributed to low repurchase rates,[128] higher marketing expenses, and lower selling prices.[129]	3/5
Bud Light[130]	2023	Partnered with transgender celebrity Dylan Mulvaney to endorse the brand during March Madness.	Lost billions of dollars from boycotts.	1/5
Closeup[131]	2024	Filipino toothpaste company released a billboard titled "dare to close the gap" with two men facing each other in support of the Filipino LBGTQ+ community.	Online sentiment praised the campaign and Closeup's progressive stance.	4/5
Microsoft[132]	2024	In the largest single carbon removal deal ever made, Microsoft agreed to finance the removal of 500,000 metric tons of carbon dioxide.	This deal enhanced Microsoft's brand image, contributing to a steady rise in its stock.	4/5

References

1 Momoh, Lucia, "'Am I Not a Man and a Brother?': Antislavery Art in the PMA's Collection," PMA Stories, March 14, 2024 (accessed August 23, 2024). https://blog.philamuseum.org/am-i-not-a-man-and-a-brother-antislavery-art-in-the-pmas-collection.

2 Ella, Jill, "BBC - Cadbury: The Legacy in Birmingham," December 15, 2009 (accessed August 23, 2024). http://news.bbc.co.uk/local/birmingham/hi/people_and_places/history/newsid_8412000/8412655.stm.

3 Chick, Joe, "Discover | Stories | Domestos and Domestics: the Family Metaphor at Lever Brothers | Unilever Archives," (accessed August 24, 2024). https://archives-unilever.com/discover/stories/domestos-and-domestics-the-family-metaphor-at-lever-brothers

4 Hanna, Emma, "Young Men's Christian Association (YMCA)," 1914-1918-Online International Encyclopedia of the First World War, January 29, 2015 (accessed August 27, 2024). https://encyclopedia.1914-1918-online.net/article/young-mens-christian-association-ymca/

5 "The Chronicle of Coca-Cola: A Symbol of Friendship," (2017) The Coca-Cola Company (accessed August 27, 2024). https://www.coca-colacompany.com/media-center/the-chronicle-of-coca-cola-a-symbol-of-friendship.

6 Panek, Tracey, "A Proud Heritage of Civil Rights," Levi Strauss & Co., January 19, 2015 (accessed August 27, 2024). https://www.levistrauss.com/2015/01/19/a-proud-heritage-of-civil-rights.

7 Panek, Tracey, "A Proud Heritage of Civil Rights," Levi Strauss & Co., January 19, 2015 (accessed August 27, 2024). https://www.levistrauss.com/2015/01/19/a-proud-heritage-of-civil-rights.

8 Christman-Campbell, Kimberly, "The Not-So-Sexy Origins of the Miniskirt," The Atlantic. April 14, 2023 (accessed August 28, 2024). https://www.theatlantic.com/culture/archive/2023/04/mary-quant-british-fashion-designer-miniskirt-legacy/673731/.

9 Officer of the Order of the British Empire, or OBE, is an honorary title given to individuals who have made significant contributions to their field.

10 Jackson, Lottie (2021), "Mary Quant & the Mini Skirt Revolution," (accessed August 27, 2024). https://www.lottievjackson.com/mary-quant-mini-skirt-revolution.

11 Mortimer, Natalie, "How Benetton Moved from Shockvertising to Be 'Never Shocking'," The Drum, July 27, 2016 (accessed August 27, 2024). https://www.thedrum.com/news/2016/07/27/how-benetton-moved-shockvertising-be-never-shocking.

12 "Our Story," (2023) The Body Shop, (accessed August 27, 2024). https://www.thebodyshop.com/en-gb/about-us/our-story/a/a00002.

13 "HIV/AIDS Summary Report," Levi Strauss & Co., September 2023 (accessed August 27, 2024). https://www.levistrauss.com/wp-content/uploads/2023/09/HIVAIDS-Summary-Report_Final.pdf.

14 "Our Story," Virgin (accessed November 1, 2024). https://www.virgin.com/about-virgin/timeline.

15   "The Crucial Reason Ben & Jerry's Is Rebranding Its 'Change Is Brewing' Flavor," *Mashed*, September 21, 2022 (accessed August 27, 2024). https://www.mashed.com/1024902/the-crucial-reason-ben-jerrys-is-rebranding-its-change-is-brewing-flavor/.

16   Salecka, Liz, "New Belgium Brewing CFO: How to Balance Profits with a Strong ESG Agenda," *The CFO*, December 7, 2022 (accessed August 27, 2024). https://the-cfo.io/2022/12/07/new-belgium-brewing-cfo-how-to-balance-profits-with-a-strong-esg-agenda/.

17   "Careers," (2024) *New Belgium Brewing* (accessed August 27, 2024). https://www.newbelgium.com/company/careers/. "How New Belgium Became One of America's Most LGBTQ-Friendly Breweries," *Hop Culture*, May 18, 2021 (accessed November 1, 2024). https://www.hopculture.com/how-new-belgium-became-one-of-americas-most-lgbtq-friendly-breweries/

18   Gogoi, Pallavi. "How the Bud Light Boycott Shows Brands at a Crossroads: Use Their Voice, or Shut Up?" NPR, June 28, 2023 (accessed August 31, 2024). https://www.npr.org/2023/06/28/1184309434/bud-light-boycott-lgbtq-pride

19   Dickerson, Chad, "Etsy CEO: How Net Neutrality Shaped My Life," *Wired*, February 20, 2015 (accessed October 30, 2024). https://www.wired.com/2015/02/etsy-ceo-how-net-neutrality-shaped-my-life/.

20   Tobin, Amy (2018), "Social Justice & TOMS Shoes: Not the Story You Might Expect," *ARCompany*, (accessed August 27, 2024). https://arcompany.co/social-justice-toms-shoes-not-the-story-you-might-expect/.

21   Pereira, Daniel, "TOMS Shoes Business Model," *Business Model Analyst*, May 24, 2023 (accessed August 27, 2024). https://businessmodelanalyst.com/toms-shoes-business-model/.

22   Kim, Irene Anna, "The Rise and Fall of TOMS Shoes," *Business Insider*, March 2020 (accessed August 27, 2024). https://www.businessinsider.com/rise-and-fall-of-toms-shoes-blake-mycoskie-bain-capital-2020-3.

23   Marquis, Christopher, "From Soap to Chocolate: Dr. Bronner's Launches into Food as Extension of Supply Chain's Positive Impact," *Forbes*, July 2, 2021 (accessed August 27, 2024). https://www.forbes.com/sites/christophermarquis/2021/07/02/from-soap-to-chocolate-dr-bronners-launches-into-food-as-extension-of-supply-chains-positive-impact/.

24   Fisher, Eileen, "From First Life to Next Life: What It Takes to Run Renew," August 28, 2024. (accessed November 1, 2024). https://www.eileenfisher.com/a-sustainable-life/journal/community/what-it-takes-to-run-renew.html?srsltid=AfmBOooF_ZK3iAcdrlGov6n2N2WhSVpD4K_xwIN0uFqqyN3rxxLTNWak.

25   "Activism," (2023) *The Body Shop* (accessed August 27, 2024). https://www.thebodyshop.com/en-sg/about-us/activism/a/a00015.

26   Shogren, Elizabeth, "Why Dawn Is the Bird Cleaner of Choice in Oil Spills," NPR, June 22, 2010 (accessed August 27, 2024). https://www.npr.org/2010/06/22/127999735/why-dawn-is-the-bird-cleaner-of-choice-in-oil-spills.

27   Kath, Sabrina "Everlane: Focusing on an Ethical Supply Chain." The Momentum. Accessed November 1, 2024. https://www.themomentum.com/articles/everlane-focusing-on-an-ethical-supply-chain.

28   Morris, Malique, "Everlane Still Wants To Be a $1 Billion Brand. Is that Even Possible?" *Business of Fashion*, February 27, 2024. Accessed November 1, 2024.

https://www.businessoffashion.com/articles/direct-to-consumer/can-everlane-still-be-a-billion-dollar-brand/.

29 Gilliland, Nikki, "Purchase with Purpose: How Four Brands Use Social Good," *Econsultancy*, July 20, 2016 (accessed August 27, 2024). https://econsultancy.com/purchase-with-purpose-how-four-brands-use-social-good.

30 "Warby Parker: Buy a Pair, Give a Pair," (2024), *Venture Lab*, (accessed August 27, 2024). https://venturelab.upenn.edu/warby-parker-buy-a-pair-give-a-pair.

31 Tice, Carol, "How Chick-fil-A Social Media Bungle Fueled Gay Rights Backlash," *Forbes*, July 20, 2012 (accessed August 28, 2024). https://www.forbes.com/sites/caroltice/2012/07/20/how-chick-fil-a-social-media-bungle-fueled-gay-rights-backlash/?sh=6c02be9ba459.

32 Valinsky, Jordan, "Chick-fil-A to Stop Donations to Charities with Anti-LGBTQ Views," CNN, November 18, 2019 (accessed August 28, 2024). https://www.cnn.com/2019/11/18/business/chick-fil-a-lgbtq-donations/index.html.

33 O'Connor, Clare, "Chick-fil-A CEO Cathy: Gay Marriage Still Wrong, But I'll Shut Up About It and Sell Chicken," *Forbes*, March 19, 2014 (accessed October 26, 2024). https://www.forbes.com/sites/clareoconnor/2014/03/19/chick-fil-a-ceo-cathy-gay-marriage-still-wrong-but-ill-shut-up-about-it-and-sell-chicken/?sh=3ef269e32fcb.

34 "IKEA Group Unveils New Sustainability Strategy: People & Planet Positive," *Newswire*, October 23, 2012 (accessed August 28, 2024). https://www.newswire.ca/news-releases/ikea-group-unveils-new-sustainability-strategy-people--planet-positive-511010301.html.

35 "The Story," *Love Your Melon* (accessed November 1, 2024). https://loveyourmelon.com/pages/thestory.

36 Omond, Tamsin, "Lush Animal Cruelty Performance Art," *The Guardian*, April 27, 2012 (accessed August 28, 2024). https://www.theguardian.com/commentisfree/2012/apr/27/lush-animal-cruelty-performance-art.

37 "This Apparel Company Turned Planting Trees into Good Business Sense," *Globe and Mail*, September 15, 2015 (accessed August 28, 2024). https://www.theglobeandmail.com/partners/advcibcembracinginnovation0915/this-apparel-company-turned-planting-trees-into-good-business-sense/article26678015/.

38 Leighton, Mara, "Tentree Sustainable Clothing Review," *Business Insider*, May 16, 2019 (accessed August 28, 2024). https://www.businessinsider.com/guides/style/tentree-sustainable-clothing-review.

39 "Our Story," *Honest* (accessed November 1, 2024). https://www.honest.com/our-story.

40 Leighton, Mara, "Meet Bombas, the Cult-Favorite Sock Startup That Has Donated 8 Million Pairs to Homeless Shelters Since Launching in 2013," *Business Insider*, February 20, 2019 (accessed August 28, 2024). https://www.businessinsider.in/meet-bombas-the-cult-favorite-sock-startup-that-has-donated-8-million-pairs-to-homeless-shelters-since-launching-in-2013/articleshow/68083128.cms.

41 "Coca-Cola Anti-Obesity Ad Addressing," *HuffPost*, January 15, 2013 (accessed August 28, 2024). https://www.huffpost.com/entry/coca-cola-anti-obesity-ad-addressing_n_2489357.

42   "Social Media Campaign Review: Unilever's Project Sunlight," *Social Samosa*, December 12, 2013 (accessed August 28, 2024). https://www.socialsamosa.com/2013/12/social-media-campaign-review-unilevers-project-sunlight/.

43   "Toilet Paper Startup Who Gives a Crap Donates Millions to Global Sanitation Projects," *WaterAid*, July 10, 2020 (accessed March 3, 2025). https://www.wateraid.org/us/media/toilet-paper-startup-who-gives-a-crap-donates-millions-to-global-sanitation-projects.

44   Prikhodko, Anastasia, "Who Gives a Crap: Profit with Purpose," *CEO Magazine*, January 14, 2021 (accessed August 28, 2024). https://www.theceomagazine.com/business/start-ups-entrepreneurs/who-gives-a-crap-profit/.

45   "Always #LikeAGirl: Turning an Insult into a Confidence Movement," *Institute for Public Relations*, N/A (accessed August 28, 2024). https://instituteforpr.org/wp-content/uploads/Always-LikeAGirl-Turning-an-Insult-into-a-Confidence-Movement.pdf.

46   "Gates Foundation Sells Down Its Shares in G4S," *War on Want*, May 29, 2014 (accessed August 28, 2024). https://waronwant.org/news-analysis/gates-foundation-sells-down-its-shares-g4s.

47   "G4S To End Israeli Jail Contracts Within 3 Years," *Financial Times*, May 16, 2014 (accessed August 31, 2024). https://www.ft.com/content/06e06252-ecc9-11e3-8963-00144feabdc0.

48   Loannou, Lori, "How the Founder of Cotopaxi Built a Cult Following for His Outdoor Gear Brand That Fights Poverty," *NB Dispatch*, N/A (accessed August 28, 2024). https://nbdispatch.com/how-the-founder-of-cotopaxi-built-a-cult-following-for-his-outdoor-gear-brand-that-fights-poverty/.

49   Sanders, Sam, "Greenpeace Apologizes for Stunt at Peru's Sacred Nazca Lines," NPR, December 11, 2014 (accessed March 3, 2025). https://www.npr.org/sections/thetwo-way/2014/12/11/370125769/greenpeace-apologizes-for-stunt-at-perus-sacred-nazca-lines.

50   "Hobby Lobby Case," *Hobby Lobby Newsroom* (accessed November 1, 2024). https://newsroom.hobbylobby.com/hobby-lobby-case.

51   Lipka, Michael "Americans' Views of Hobby Lobby Ruling Are Evenly Divided," *Pew Research Center*, August 1, 2014 (accessed March 3, 2025). https://www.pewresearch.org/short-reads/2014/08/01/kaiser-americans-views-of-hobby-lobby-ruling-are-evenly-divided/.

52   Vaughan, Adam, "Lego Ends Shell Partnership Following Greenpeace Campaign," *The Guardian*, October 9, 2014 (accessed August 28, 2024). https://www.theguardian.com/environment/2014/oct/09/lego-ends-shell-partnership-following-greenpeace-campaign.

53   England, Joanna, "Timeline: The Story of Lemonade," *Insurtech Digital*, May 6, 2021 (accessed November 1, 2024). https://insurtechdigital.com/insurtech/timeline-story-lemonade. "Giveback," *Lemonade* (accessed November 1, 2024). https://www.lemonade.com/giveback.

54   Browning, Noah, "Major Dutch Pension Firm Divests from Israeli Banks over Settlements," *Reuters*, January 8, 2014 (accessed August 28, 2024). https://www.reuters.com/article/markets/major-dutch-pension-firm-divests-from-israeli-banks-over-settlements-idUSL6N0KI2NG.

55 Gilliland, Nikki, "10 Brand Campaigns That Took a Stand on Social Issues," *Econsultancy*, February 18, 2021 (ace ssed August 28, 2024). https://econsultancy. com/brand-campaigns-that-took-a-stand-on-social-issues/.

56 Aziz, Afdhel, "The Power of Purpose: How Adidas Will Make $1 Billion Helping Solve the Problem of Ocean Plastic," *Forbes*, October 29, 2018 (accessed August 28, 2024). https://www.forbes.com/sites/afdhelaziz/2018/10/29/the-power-of-purpose-how-adidas-will-make-1-billion-helping-solve-the-prob lem-of-ocean-plastic/.

57 Kannenberg, Lizz, "Social Spotlight: REI," *Sprout Social* (accessed August 28, 2024). https://sproutsocial.com/insights/social-spotlight-rei/.

58 "REI: An Outstanding Social Media Success," *Digital Marketing Institute*, June 28, 2018 (accessed March 3, 2025). https://digitalmarketinginstitute.com/resources/case-studies/standing-out-on-social-media-rei-a-case-study.

59 "How Two Shoe Outsiders Are Making Rothy's One of the Most Talked-About New Footwear Brands," *Footwear News*, March 25, 2019 (accessed March 3, 2025). https://footwearnews.com/business/executive-moves/rothys-shoes-interview-roth-martin-stephen-hawthornthwaite-1202763598/.

60 Gogoi, Pallavi, "How the Bud Light Boycott shows brands at a crossroads: Use their voice, or shut up?" *NPR*, June 28, 2023 (accessed August 28, 2024). https://www. npr.org/2023/06/28/1184309434/bud-light-boycott-lgbtq-pride.

61 Alesci, Cristina, "Chobani CEO on Immigration Solution," *CNN*, September 30, 2018 (accessed August 28, 2024). https://www.cnn.com/2018/09/30/politics/chobani-ceo-immigration-solution/index.html.

62 "Our Impact," *Cora* (accessed October 30, 2024). https://cora.life/pages/our-impact.

63 "Dove Real Beauty Campaign," *VAIA*, N/A (accessed August 28, 2024). https:// www.vaia.com/en-us/explanations/marketing/marketing-campaign-examples/dove-real-beauty-campaign/.

64 "About Girlfriend Collective," *Girlfriend Collective* (accessed August 28, 2024). https://girlfriend.com/pages/about-girlfriend.

65 Stein, Jenni, "Girlfriend Collective Review," *The Quality Edit*, October 13 2022, 2024 (accessed August 28, 2024). https://www.thequalityedit.com/articles/girlfriend-collective-review.

66 Bryan, Llenas, "Boss Says Employees Who Agree with Trump's Rhetoric Should Resign," *Fox News*, November 10, 2016 (accessed August 28, 2024). https://www. foxnews.com/us/boss-says-employees-who-agree-with-trumps-rhetoric-should-resign.

67 "From Controversy to Culture: New Balance Quietly Takes the Culture by Storm," *CNK Daily*, September 27, 2022 (accessed August 28, 2024). https://www.cnkda ily.com/featured/2022/9/27/from-controversy-to-culture-new-balance-quietly-takes-the-culture-by-storm.

68 "100 Percent Today, 1 Percent Every Day," *Patagonia*, November 21, 2016 (accessed August 28, 2024). https://www.patagonia.com/stories/100-percent-today-1-percent-every-day/story-31099.html.

69 Weissman, Cale, "Inside One Spice Retailer's Anti-Trump, Pro-Impeachment Facebook Ad Strategy," *Modern Retail*, October 11, 2019 (accessed August 28, 2024).

https://www.modernretail.co/retailers/inside-one-spice-retailers-anti-trump-pro-impeachment-facebook-ad-strategy/.

70   Johnson, Alex, "Ben & Jerry's Bans Same Flavor Scoops in Support of Australian Same-Sex Marriage," NBC News, May 29, 2017 (accessed August 28, 2024). https://www.nbcnews.com/feature/nbc-out/ben-jerry-s-bans-same-flavor-scoops-australian-same-sex-n764791.

71   Kocay, Lisa, "Ben & Jerry's Bans Same-Flavored Ice Cream Scoops to Support Marriage Equality," Forbes, May 29, 2017 (accessed August 28, 2024). https://www.forbes.com/sites/lisakocay/2017/05/29/ben-jerrys-bans-same-flavored-ice-cream-scoops-support-marriage-equality/.

72   Sherwell, Phillip and Ungoed-Thomas, Jon, "Myanmar: Cartier Stops Sourcing Gemstones from Country in Response to Campaign Against 'Genocide Gems'," Business & Human Rights Resource Centre, December 10, 2017 (accessed August 28, 2024). https://www.business-humanrights.org/en/latest-news/myanmar-cartier-stops-sourcing-gemstones-from-country-in-response-to-campaign-against-genocide-gems/.

73   "History of Successful Boycotts," Ethical Consumer, February 17, 2023 (accessed August 28, 2024). https://www.ethicalconsumer.org/ethicalcampaigns/boycotts/history-successful-boycotts.

74   Bogost, Ian, "How Dove Ruined Its Body Image," The Atlantic. May 9, 2017 (accessed March 3, 2025). https://www.theatlantic.com/technology/archive/2017/05/dove-body-image/525867/.

75   Westervelt, Eric, "#GrabYourWallet's Anti-Trump Boycott Looks to Expand Its Reach," NPR, April 16, 2017 (accessed August 28, 2024). https://www.npr.org/2017/04/16/523960521/-grabyourwallets-anti-trump-boycott-looks-to-expand-its-reach.

76   "Grab Your Wallet: Trump," WBUR, January 16, 2017 (accessed August 28, 2024). https://www.wbur.org/hereandnow/2017/01/16/grab-your-wallet-trump.

77   Solon, Olivia, "Is Lyft Really the Woke Alternative to Uber?" The Guardian, March 29, 2017 (accessed August 28, 2024). https://www.theguardian.com/technology/2017/mar/29/is-lyft-really-the-woke-alternative-to-uber.

78   Jan, Tracey, "Can Shaq Rehab Papa John's Image as the Preferred Pizza of Neo-Nazis?" The Washington Post, March 22, 2019 (accessed August 28, 2024). https://www.washingtonpost.com/business/2019/03/22/can-shaq-rehab-papa-johns-image-preferred-pizza-neo-nazis/.

79   Emery, David, "Starbucks to Hire 10,000 Refugees," Snopes, January 30, 2017 (accessed August 28, 2024). https://www.snopes.com/news/2017/01/30/starbucks-to-hire-10000-refugees/.

80   Adjchavanich, Charlotte, et al., "The Body Shop: Forever Against Animal Testing," Shorty Awards, (accessed August 28, 2024). https://shortyawards.com/2nd-socialgood/the-body-shop-forever-against-animal-testing.

81   "Uber Accused of Strikebreaking During NYC Airport Protests," CBS News, January 30, 2017 (accessed August 28, 2024). https://www.cbsnews.com/news/uber-accused-of-strikebreaking-during-nyc-airport-protests/.

82   Molla, Rani, "Uber and Lyft App Reviews and Downloads Declining," Vox, June 28, 2017 (accessed August 28, 2024). https://www.vox.com/2017/6/28/15886792/uber-lyft-app-reviews-downloads-declining.

83   "BrewDog's Mock Pink IPA 'Beer for Girls' Splits Opinion," *BBC Newsbeat*, March 6, 2018 (March 3, 2025). https://www.bbc.com/news/newsbeat-43300969.

84   Barca, Jerry, "Florida School Shooting Prompts Dick's Sporting Goods to End Sale of Assault Weapons," *Forbes*, February 28, 2018 (accessed August 28, 2024). https://www.forbes.com/sites/jerrybarca/2018/02/28/florida-school-shooting-prompts-dicks-sporting-goods-to-end-sale-of-assault-weapons/?sh=1e4ee0785cbb.

85   Feloni, Richard and Cain, Áine, "Dick's CEO on Destroying $5 Million Worth of Assault Weapons," *Business Insider*, October 8, 2019 (accessed August 28, 2024). https://www.businessinsider.com/dicks-ceo-on-destroying-5-million-dollars-of-assault-weapons-2019-10.

86   "Delta CEO Ed Bastian on NRA Discount After Parkland Shooting," *The Points Guy*, February 17, 2019 (accessed August 28, 2024). https://thepointsguy.com/news/delta-ceo-ed-bastian-on-nra-discount-after-parkland-shooting/.

87   Thomas, Lauren, "Levi Strauss 'Simply Cannot Stand By Silently' on Gun Violence," *CNBC*, September 5, 2018 (March 3, 2025). https://www.cnbc.com/2018/09/05/levi-strauss-takes-a-stand-on-gun-violence.html.

88   "Levi Strauss Revenue 2010-2024," *Macrotrends*, [DATE?N/A] (accessed March 3, 2025). https://www.macrotrends.net/stocks/charts/LEVI/levi-strauss/revenue.

89   Bliss, Laura, "Lyfy Delivers Carbon-Neutral Rides," *Wired*, April 24, 2019 (accessed). https://www.wired.com/story/lyft-delivers-carbon-neutral-rides/.

90   "Nike's 'Dream Crazy' Advert Starring Colin Kaepernick Wins Emmy," *The Guardian*, September 16, 2019 (accessed March 3, 2025). https://www.theguardian.com/sport/2019/sep/16/nikes-dream-crazy-advert-starring-colin-kaepernick-wins-emmy.

91   Youn, Soo, "Nike Sales Booming After Colin Kaepernick Ad, Invalidating Critics," *ABCNews*, December 21, 2018 (March 3, 2025). https://abcnews.go.com/Business/nike-sales-booming-kaepernick-ad-invalidating-critics/story?id=59957137.

92   Associated Press, "Starbucks: Black Men Feared for Their Lives in Philadelphia," *The Guardian*, April 19, 2018 (accessed August 28, 2024). https://www.theguardian.com/business/2018/apr/19/starbucks-black-men-feared-for-lives-philadelphia.

93   Pontefract, Dan, "Did the Starbucks Racial Bias Training Plan Work?" *Forbes*, June 1, 2018 (accessed March 3, 2025). https://www.forbes.com/sites/danpontefract/2018/06/01/did-the-starbucks-racial-bias-training-plan-work/.

94   Gilliland, Nikki, "10 Brand Campaigns That Took a Stand on Social Issues," *Econsultancy*, February 18, 2021 (accessed November 1, 2024). https://econsultancy.com/brand-campaigns-that-took-a-stand-on-social-issues/.

95   Dreyfuss, Emily, "Gillette's Ad Proves the Definition of a Good Man Has Changed," *Wired*, January 16, 2019 (accessed March 3, 2025). https://www.wired.com/story/gillette-we-believe-ad-men-backlash/.

96   Ong, Tasmin, "Gucci CEO Faces Blackface Backlash: 'We Made a Mistake. A Big One,'" *Queen Mary University of London*. February 8, 2019 (accessed March 3, 2025). https://www.qmul.ac.uk/lac/our-legal-blog/items/gucci-ceo-faces-blackface-backlash-we-made-a-mistake-a-big-one.html.

97   Olson, Alexandra "Why Nike Pulled Betsy Ross Flag Shoes After Kaepernick Criticism," *PBS NewsHour*, July 3, 2019 (accessed March 3, 2025). https://www.pbs.org/newshour/nation/why-nike-pulled-betsy-ross-flag-shoes-after-kaepernick-criticism.

98 Palmieri, Jeana, "The North Face's New Campaign Supports Building Walls," *WWD*, August 15, 2017 (accessed March 3, 2025). https://wwd.com/business-news/media/the-north-faces-new-campaign-supports-building-walls-10959779/.

99 Gupta, Shashi, "2019 in Review: When Brands Courted Controversy on Social Media," *BrandEquity.com*. December 26, 2019 (accessed March 3, 2025). https://brandequity.economictimes.indiatimes.com/news/digital/2019-in-review-when-brands-courted-controversy-on-social-media/72976619?redirect=1.

100 Gupta, Shashi, "2019 in Review: When Brands Courted Controversy on Social Media," *BrandEquity.com*, December 26, 2019 (accessed March 3, 2025). https://brandequity.economictimes.indiatimes.com/news/digital/2019-in-review-when-brands-courted-controversy-on-social-media/72976619?redirect=1.

101 Zlady, Hanna, "Why Ben & Jerry's Statement on White Supremacy is So Extraordinary," CNN *Business*, June 5, 2020 (accessed March 3, 2025). https://www.cnn.com/2020/06/03/business/ben--jerrys-george-floyd/index.html

102 Helsel, Phil, "CrossFit CEO Steps Down After Inflammatory George Floyd Comments," *NBCNews*, June 9, 2020 (accessed March 3, 2025). https://www.nbcnews.com/news/us-news/crossfit-ceo-steps-down-after-inflammatory-george-floyd-comments-n1228941.

103 Oller, Samantha "Goya Boycott After CEO's Praise of Trump Resulted in Higher Sales." Food Dive. August 30, 2022. https://www.fooddive.com/news/goya-sales-rise-after-boycott-trump/630737/.

104 McGonagle, Emmet, "L'Oreal Faces Backlash for Black Lives Matter Post," *Campaign Asia*, June 2, 2020 (accessed March 3, 2025. https://www.campaignasia.com/article/loreal-faces-backlash-for-black-lives-matter-post/461394.

105 Bergdorf had made insensitive comments about white people leading up to her termination, tweeting: "Your entire existence is drenched in racism" among other offensive comments.
Ibrahim, Nur, "Did L'Oréal Release a Statement Critiquing the 'Violent' White Race?" *Snopes*, June 16, 2020 (accessed March 3, 2025). https://www.snopes.com/fact-check/loreal-violent-white-race/.

106 Picheta, Rob, "L'Oréal Dropped This Model for Commenting on Systemic Racism. Now It Wants Her Back," CNN *Business*. June 10, 2020 (accessed March 3, 2025). https://www.cnn.com/2020/06/10/business/munroe-bergdorf-loreal-rehired-scli-gbr-intl/index.html.

107 Kirby, Jason, "Michael McCain Takes the Era of the Outspoken CEO to the Next Level," *Maclean's*, January 14, 2020 (accessed March 3, 2025). https://macleans.ca/economy/business/michael-mccain-takes-the-era-of-the-outspoken-ceo-to-the-next-level/.

108 Gilliland, Nikki, "10 Brand Campaigns That Took a Stand on Social Issues," *Econsultancy*, February 18, 2021 (accessed November 1, 2024). https://econsultancy.com/brand-campaigns-that-took-a-stand-on-social-issues/.

109 "Advertising Industry Doubles Down on Commitments to Combat Online Hate Speech," Pernod Ricard USA, September 20, 2021 (accessed March 3, 2025). https://www.pernod-ricard-usa.com/media-blog/2021/9/20/advertising-industry-doubles-down-on-commitments-to-combat-online-hate-speech.

110 "Tata Group's Tanishq Pulls Ad Featuring Hindu-Muslim Family After Social Media Criticism," *The Economic Times*, October 14, 2020 (accessed March 3, 2025). https://economictimes.indiatimes.com/industry/services/advertising/tata-groups-tanishq-pulls-ad-featuring-hindu-muslim-family-after-social-media-criticism/articleshow/78656783.cms?from=mdr.

111 Love Jihad is a term used by right-wing Hindutvas to describe the conversion of Hindu women to Islam through marriage.

112 Bain, Phoebe, "Why Uber's Recent AntiRacism Campaign Generated Criticism," *Marketing Brew*, August 31, 2020 (accessed March 3, 2025). https://www.marketingbrew.com/stories/2020/08/31/ubers-recent-antiracism-campaign-generated-criticism.

113 Villagra, Nuria, Abel Monfort, and Mariano Mendez-Suarez (2021), "Firm Value Impact of Corporate Activism: Facebook and the Stop Hate for Profit Campaign," *Journal of Business Research*, 137, 319–326. https://www.sciencedirect.com/science/article/abs/pii/S0148296321006135.

114 "Airbnb Provides Accommodations for Refugees," *Mintel*, February 13, 2024 (accessed November 1, 2024). https://www.mintel.com/insights/travel-and-tourism/thought-bubble-airbnb-provides-accommodations-for-refugees/.

115 "US Multicultural Young Adults and Social Activism Consumer Report 2021," *Mintel* (accessed November 1, 2024). https://store.mintel.com/report/us-multicultural-young-adults-and-social-activism-market-report.

116 "Boots to Offer Lifeline to Domestic Abuse Victims Through New Codeword Scheme," *Boots*, January 14, 2021 (accessed March 3, 2025). https://www.boots-uk.com/newsroom/news/boots-to-offer-lifeline-to-domestic-abuse-victims-through-new-codeword-scheme/.

117 Walker, Peter, "UK Abuse Victims Given 'Ani' Codeword to Ask Pharmacists for Help," *The Guardian*, January 14, 2021 (accessed March 3, 2025). https://www.theguardian.com/society/2021/jan/14/uk-abuse-victims-given-ani-code-word-ask-pharmacists-help.

118 Bursztynsky, Jessica, "Lyft, Uber Will Cover Legal Fees for Drivers Sued Under Texas Abortion Law," *CNBC*. September 3, 2021. https://www.cnbc.com/2021/09/03/lyft-will-cover-legal-fees-for-drivers-sued-under-texas-abortion-law.html.

119 "MyPillow Founder Mike Lindell Is Ordered to Pay $5 Million in Election Fraud Challenge," *NPR*. April 21, 2023 (accessed March 3, 2025). https://www.npr.org/2023/04/21/1171193932/mypillow-founder-mike-lindell-is-ordered-to-pay-5m-in-election-fraud-challenge.

120 Hiken, Asa, "Olay Takes on Computer Algorithms to Fight Biased Beauty Standards," *MarketingDive*, September 14, 2021 (accessed March 3, 2025). https://www.marketingdive.com/news/olay-takes-on-computer-algorithms-to-fight-biased-beauty-standards/606509/.

121 Daimler, Susan, "Zillow Group's Commitment to Fair Housing," April 6, 2022 (accessed November 1, 2024). https://www.zillowgroup.com/news/homeownership-gap-fair-housing/.

122 Davis, Jessica, "Senators Scrutinize Google's Claim to Delete Users' Sensitive Location Data," *SC Magazine*, May 25, 2023 (accessed March 3, 2025). https://www.scworld.com/news/senators-scrutinize-googles-claim-delete-users-sensitive-location-data.

123 "Halifax is Branded 'Old Fashioned Bullies' as MORE Customers Close Their Accounts After Social Media Manager Told Them to LEAVE if They Don't Like Staff Sharing Pronouns on Badges," *The Daily Mail*, July 1, 2022 (accessed March 3, 2025). https://www.dailymail.co.uk/news/article-10973289/Halifax-pronouns-scandal-customers-close-accounts-social-media-manager-told-to.html.

124 Douglass, Rachel, "Burberry Bands Exotic Skins Following Seven Year PETA Campaign," *Fashion United*, May 20, 2022 (accessed March 3, 2025). https://fashionunited.in/news/business/burberry-bans-exotic-skins-following-seven-year-peta-campaign/2022052034772.

125 "Seventh Generation Unveils Brand Evolution, Showcases Commitment to Sustainability," VermontBiz, April 7, 2022 (accessed March 3, 2025). https://vermontbiz.com/news/2022/april/07/seventh-generation-unveils-brand-evolution-showcases-commitment-sustainability.

126 "Seventh Generation's Revenue is $200.0 Million," Zippia (accessed November 1, 2024). https://www.zippia.com/seventh-generation-careers-125264/revenue/.

127 Verry, Peter, "Allbirds Makes Further Strides in Sustainable Footwear by Creating a Net Zero Carbon Shoe," *Footwear News*, May 21, 2023 (accessed March 3, 2025). https://footwearnews.com/business/business-news/allbirds-net-zero-carbon-shoe-moonshot-release-info-1203432780/.

128 Ciment, Shoshy, "Top Analyst on Why Allbirds Is Not Replicating the Success of Other Emerging Brands Like On and Hoka," March 6, 2023 (accessed March 3, 2025). https://footwearnews.com/business/retail/allbirds-growth-stalls-compared-on-hoka-1203424024/.

129 "Allbirds Reports Fourth Quarter and Full Year 2023 Financial Results," Allbirds, March 14, 2024 (accessed March 3, 2025). https://ir.allbirds.com/news-releases/news-release-details/allbirds-reports-fourth-quarter-and-full-year-2023-financial.

130 "Fact Check: Did Anheuser-Busch Lose $4 Billion in Value Amid Dylan Mulvaney Issue?" *Newsweek*, April 14, 2023 (accessed March 3, 2025). https://www.newsweek.com/fact-check-did-anheuser-busch-lose-4bn-value-amid-dylan-mulvaney-issue-1793996.

131 Villanueva, Angelica, "Toothpaste Brand Wants to 'Close the Gap' in New Pride Month Campaign," *Manila Standard*, June 3, 2024 (accessed March 3, 2025). https://manilastandard.net/lifestyle/314455012/toothpaste-brand-wants-to-close-the-gap-in-new-pride-month-campaign.html.

132 Swinhoe, Dan, "Microsoft Signs 500,000 Metric Ton Carbon Removal Deal With 1PointFive," *Data Center Dynamics*. July 9, 2024 (accessed March 3, 2025). https://www.datacenterdynamics.com/en/news/microsoft-signs-500000-metric-ton-carbon-removal-deal-with-1pointfive/.

INDEX

For Product Safety Concerns and Information please contact our EU
representative GPSR@taylorandfrancis.com
Taylor & Francis Verlag GmbH, Kaufingerstraße 24, 80331 München, Germany

www.ingramcontent.com/pod-product-compliance
Lightning Source LLC
Chambersburg PA
CBHW061236220326
41599CB00028B/5439

9 781032 974408